G.W. Griffin

New South Wales

Her commerce and resources

G.W. Griffin

New South Wales
Her commerce and resources

ISBN/EAN: 9783337324049

Printed in Europe, USA, Canada, Australia, Japan

Cover: Foto ©Andreas Hilbeck / pixelio.de

More available books at **www.hansebooks.com**

NEW SOUTH WALES:

HER COMMERCE AND RESOURCES.

BY

G. W. GRIFFIN,
United States Consul at Sydney.

AUTHOR OF "MY DANISH DAYS," "STUDIES IN LITERATURE," "MEMOIR OF C. S. TODD,"
"NEW ZEALAND, HER COMMERCE AND RESOURCES," ETC.

SYDNEY: CHARLES POTTER, GOVERNMENT PRINTER.
1888.

PREFACE.

The following pages consist of a series of papers prepared for the Department of State since my appointment as Consul at Sydney, and printed among the United States Consular Reports.

The papers are now republished, under direction of the Honorable J. F. Burns, Colonial Treasurer, to whom I am indebted for facilities for making such alterations and additions as were necessary to bring the information up to the latest date.

I desire to tender my thanks to the Premier, Sir Henry Parkes, G.C.M.G., and to Members of his and of preceding Administrations, for the uniform courtesy I have received when applying for information during my residence in the Colony.

To the Under Secretaries of Departments, and to Merchants and others, who have aided me in my researches I am placed under obligation; while without the ready and valuable assistance accorded me at all times by the Government Statist, the Collector of Customs, and the Curator of the Technological Museum, it would have been difficult for me to comply with requirements of my Government.

The rapid and satisfactory manner in which the papers have been published at the Government Printing Office, Sydney, deserves the highest commendation.

G. W. GRIFFIN.

United States Consulate,
    Sydney, March, 1888.

INDEX.

	PAGE
IMMIGRATION	1
IRRIGATION	13
FORESTS	22
COAL	50
KEROSENE	73
DIAMONDS	84
GOLD	100
SILVER	110
COPPER	124
TIN	132
AGRICULTURE	141
WOOL	155
SUGAR	170
TOBACCO	190
FRUIT	200
WINE	208
BEER	216
DAIRY FARMING	228
LEATHER	242
HARDWARE	255
CUSTOMS TARIFF	261
FISH	270
PEARL SHELL	284

Note.—Throughout these papers, British money is computed at the values as laid down by the United States Treasury Regulations.

TABLE for the Reduction of Sterling Money of Great Britain to United States Gold Coin, under Act approved 3rd March, 1873, fixing the value of the Pound Sterling at $4.8665.

	0	1	2	3	4	5	6	7	8	9
1 ..	4.8665	53.5315	58.398	63.2645	68.131	72.9975	77.864	82.7305	87.597	92.4635
2	9.733	102.1965	107.063	111.9295	116.796	121.6625	126.529	131.3955	136.262	141.1285
3	14.5995	150.8615	155.728	160.5945	165.461	170.3275	175.194	180.0605	184.927	189.7935
4	19.466	199.5265	204.393	209.2595	214.126	218.9925	223.859	228.7255	233.592	238.4585
5	24.3325	248.1915	253.058	257.9245	262.791	267.6575	272.524	277.3905	282.257	287.1235
6	29.199	296.8565	301.723	306.5895	311.456	316.3225	321.189	326.0555	330.922	335.7885
7	34.0655	345.5215	350.388	355.2545	360.121	364.9875	369.854	374.7205	379.587	384.4535
8	38.932	394.1865	399.053	403.9195	408.786	413.6525	418.519	423.3855	428.252	433.1185
9	43.7985	442.8515	447.718	452.5845	457.451	462.3175	467.184	472.0505	476.917	481.7835

NOTE.—To find the value of any number of pounds represented by one figure, find the figure in the left-hand margin of the table, and its value will appear in the column adjoining opposite that figure. To find the value when expressed by two figures, look for the *tens* in the left-hand column, and for the *units* in the top margin, and the value will be shown in the place where the two columns meet: thus, the value of £57 is $277.3905. To find the value of £576, look for 57 as before, and move the decimal point one place to the right, and it shows $2,773.905; then add £6 as already shown, $29.199, and it gives the sum of $2,803.104.

One shilling equals 24⅓ cents.   One penny equals 2 1/24 cents.

	0	1	2	3	4	5	6	7	8	9	10	11	12	13	14	15	16	17	18	19
0		.24	.48	.73	.97	1.21	1.46	1.70	1.94	2.19	2.43	2.67	2.92	3.16	3.40	3.65	3.89	4.13	4.38	4.62
1	.02	.26	.50	.75	.99	1.23	1.48	1.72	1.96	2.21	2.45	2.69	2.94	3.18	3.42	3.67	3.91	4.15	4.40	4.64
2	.04	.28	.52	.77	1.01	1.25	1.50	1.74	1.98	2.23	2.47	2.71	2.96	3.20	3.44	3.69	3.93	4.17	4.42	4.66
3	.06	.30	.54	.79	1.03	1.27	1.52	1.76	2.00	2.25	2.49	2.73	2.98	3.22	3.46	3.71	3.95	4.19	4.44	4.68
4	.08	.32	.56	.81	1.05	1.29	1.54	1.78	2.02	2.27	2.51	2.75	3.00	3.24	3.48	3.73	3.97	4.21	4.46	4.70
5	.10	.34	.58	.83	1.07	1.31	1.56	1.80	2.04	2.29	2.53	2.77	3.02	3.26	3.50	3.75	3.99	4.23	4.48	4.72
6	.12	.36	.60	.85	1.09	1.33	1.58	1.82	2.06	2.31	2.55	2.79	3.04	3.28	3.52	3.77	4.01	4.25	4.50	4.74
7	.14	.38	.62	.87	1.11	1.35	1.60	1.84	2.08	2.33	2.57	2.81	3.06	3.30	3.54	3.79	4.03	4.27	4.52	4.76
8	.16	.40	.64	.89	1.13	1.37	1.62	1.86	2.10	2.35	2.59	2.83	3.08	3.32	3.56	3.81	4.05	4.29	4.54	4.78
9	.18	.42	.66	.91	1.15	1.39	1.64	1.88	2.12	2.37	2.61	2.85	3.10	3.34	3.58	3.83	4.07	4.31	4.56	4.80
10	.20	.44	.68	.93	1.17	1.41	1.66	1.90	2.14	2.39	2.63	2.87	3.12	3.36	3.60	3.85	4.09	4.33	4.58	4.82
11	.22	.46	.70	.95	1.19	1.43	1.68	1.92	2.16	2.41	2.65	2.89	3.14	3.38	3.62	3.87	4.11	4.35	4.60	4.84

NOTE.—This table shows the value of every combination of shillings and pence less than £1; the upper margin representing the shillings, and the left-hand margin the pence. Thus, to find the value of 17s. 6d., follow column 17 downwards until it meets the left-hand column opposite 6, and it shows $4.25. By this method any number of pounds, shillings, and pence can be reduced to United States gold quickly and accurately.

NEW SOUTH WALES: HER COMMERCE AND RESOURCES.

IMMIGRATION.

THE history of immigration to Australia is a very interesting one. The growth of the various settlements on the great island continent has been so rapid and of such recent date that it is impossible not to think of it without feelings of astonishment, while that of some of the younger colonies, for instance Victoria or New Zealand, has, perhaps, been even more rapid than that of New South Wales. The sources of progress can be better illustrated in the elder Colony than in any others of the group.

It would be difficult to imagine a more gloomy prospect than the one which opened before the little band of colonists which landed in the harbour of Sydney under the command of Captain Arthur Phillip. The place chosen for settlement was never intended for the establishment of a colony in the common acceptance of the term colony. The immigrants numbered in the aggregate 1,030, of whom 192 were women, and 18 children. The death-rate amongst them was at first appalling, and it was feared very few would be left to tell the story of their sufferings. It is worthy of mention here that the first foreign vessel to arrive in New South Wales after the establishment of the Colony was the American brigantine "Philadelphia," commanded by Captain Patrickson. This vessel came into the harbour on the 1st November, 1792, with a full cargo of provisions, which were speedily absorbed by the half-famished colonists.

In 1793, the first immigrant ship arrived with free settlers. These immigrants were furnished with agricultural implements, provisions for two years, and grants of land to be selected by themselves.

In 1830, New South Wales, which included the colonies of Victoria and Queensland, had a population of 46,302. In 1831, the Government assisted immigration policy was inaugurated, and from that time to the present has been a popular measure with sections of the community.

In 1851, a separate Government was given to the Colony of Victoria, and in 1859, a like privilege was extended to Queensland. While the colonists from time to time encouraged the assisted immigration, the transportation of convicts here by Great Britain always met with the most determined opposition. In June, 1849, the opposition to this course grew so intense that when the ship "Hashemy," arrived at Port Jackson, with convicts on board, an attempt was made to prevent them from landing. Shortly after this occurrence the order for the transportation of convicts was rescinded by the British Government. The

A

evil effects, however, of the convict classes upon the population, it is believed, have long since disappeared under the reforming institutions of the various colonial Governments. The rapid progress of the Colonies is said to be largely due to the superior class of immigrants, selected by the authorities in London.

In 1873, the people of New South Wales began to weary of the assisted immigration policy, and only 110 arrived during that year. Voluntary immigration, however, showed no signs of falling off, for, during the same period, 23,712 immigrants arrived here at their own cost. The largest number of assisted immigrants who arrived during any one year was in 1883, when the number was 8,369. The number who paid their own expenses during the same period was 58,837. In 1885, the number of assisted immigrants declined to 5,554, and to 1,362 in 1887. The largest number of immigrants of all classes, arriving in one year, was in 1885, when they reached 78,138; of these 54,843 were males, and 23,295 females. The total number of immigrants who arrived in 1887, was 67,605.

No account is kept of the arrivals and departures by land, and, as large numbers are constantly arriving and departing in that way, the returns are necessarily incomplete.

The following table shows the number of emigrants who departed from New South Wales seaward, for each year, from 1876 to 1887, inclusive:

Year.	Adults.			Children.			Chinese.	Total Males.	Total Females.	General Total.
	Males.	Females.	Total.	Males.	Females.	Total.				
1876	14,689	4,945	19,634	1,162	787	1,949	340	16,191	5,732	21,923
1877	12,908	5,150	18,058	980	646	1,626	490	14,378	5,796	20,174
1878	13,691	5,393	19,084	1,409	860	2,269	1,560	16,660	6,243	22,913
1879	12,653	5,415	18,268	1,215	655	1,870	557	14,625	6,070	20,695
1880	16,270	7,054	23,324	1,612	747	2,359	876	18,758	7,801	26,559
1881	15,101	6,704	21,805	1,324	667	2,091	929	17,454	7,371	24,825
1882	17,683	7,080	24,763	1,547	778	2,325	884	20,114	7,858	27,972
1883	21,039	8,845	29,884	1,845	1,265	3,110	1,402	24,286	10,110	34,396
1884	25,903	10,580	35,483	2,173	1,560	3,733	1,038	28,364	11,890	40,254
1885	23,385	10,136	33,521	1,865	1,343	3,208	1,726	26,976	11,479	38,455
1886	27,411	9,805	37,246	1,670	1,097	2,767	1,883	30,994	10,902	41,896
1887	27,460	10,636	38,096	1,930	1,290	3,220	2,773	32,163	11,026	44,089

The largest number of departures occurred in 1887, when they were 44,089, of whom 2,773 were Chinese. The arrival of Chinese during the same period was 4,136. The immigration authorities do not note the exact ages of persons arriving and departing, but classify all those over 12 years of age as adults, and all under that age as children.

The number of persons introduced into New South Wales at the public expense since 1831, when the assisted immigration policy was inaugurated, to the close of 1887, was 212,487.

The table following shows the number of immigrants who arrived in New South Wales at the public expense and the number paying their own expense, for each year from 1876 to 1887 inclusive.

IMMIGRATION.

Year.	Immigrants at the Public Expense from the United Kingdom (under the Assisted Immigration Regulations).							Immigrants at their own Expense from all Countries.								
	Adults.			Children.				Adults.			Children.				Chinese.	Total.
	Male.	Female	Total.	Male.	Female	Total.	Total.	Male.	Female.	Total.	Male.	Female.	Total.		
1876	642	429	1,071	208	184	392	1,463	20,614	6,315	26,930	2,156	1,668	3,824	696	31,479
1877	2,892	1,627	4,519	743	756	1,499	*6,318	20,746	7,020	27,766	2,152	1,808	3,960	884	32,610
1878	2,091	1,754	3,845	699	646	1,345	†5,190	20,769	7,427	28,196	2,173	1,835	4,008	2,485	34,689
1879	1,906	2,141	4,047	840	844	1,684	5,731	23,832	8,528	32,360	2,297	2,134	4,431	1,979	38,770
1880	1,150	1,195	2,345	414	375	789	3,134	25,744	9,304	35,048	2,518	2,228	4,746	2,942	42,736
1881	929	1,029	1,958	227	392	619	2,577	25,783	9,741	35,524	2,689	2,468	5,157	4,465	45,146
1882	1,209	991	2,200	509	524	1,033	3,233	27,207	10,542	37,749	2,755	2,545	5,300	1,007	44,056
1883	3,370	2,718	6,088	1,154	1,127	2,281	8,369	36,576	13,412	49,988	3,507	3,406	6,913	1,936	58,837
1884	2,785	2,606	5,391	1,095	1,082	2,177	7,568	40,214	15,244	55,458	3,887	3,382	7,269	2,191	64,918
1885	1,871	2,211	4,082	736	736	1,472	5,554	45,047	16,618	61,665	4,260	3,730	7,990	2,929	72,584
1886	1,044	1,905	2,949	572	560	1,132	4,081	41,758	14,763	56,521	3,768	2,926	6,694	3,092	66,307
1887	131	687	818	286	258	544	1,362	41,259	14,405	55,664	3,391	2,752	6,143	4,436	66,243

Total Number of Immigrants arrived.

Year.	Adults.			Children.			Chinese.	Total Males.	Total Females.	General Total.
	Male.	Female.	Total.	Male.	Female.	Total.				
1876	21,256	6,774	28,030	2,364	1,852	4,216	696	24,316	8,626	32,942
1877	23,638	8,647	32,285	2,895	2,564	5,459	884	27,417	11,211	38,628
1878	22,860	9,181	32,041	2,872	2,481	5,353	2,485	28,217	11,662	39,879
1879	25,738	10,669	36,407	3,137	2,978	6,115	1,979	30,854	13,647	44,501
1880	26,894	10,499	37,393	2,932	2,603	5,535	2,942	32,768	13,102	45,870
1881	26,712	10,770	37,482	3,016	2,760	5,776	4,465	34,193	13,530	47,723
1882	28,416	11,533	39,949	3,264	3,069	6,333	1,007	32,687	14,602	47,289
1883	39,946	16,130	56,076	4,661	4,533	9,194	1,936	46,343	20,663	67,206
1884	42,999	17,850	60,849	4,782	4,664	9,446	2,191	49,972	22,514	72,486
1885	46,918	18,829	65,747	4,996	4,466	9,462	2,929	54,843	23,295	78,138
1886	42,802	16,668	59,470	4,340	3,486	7,826	3,092	50,234	20,154	70,388
1887	41,390	15,092	56,482	3,677	3,010	6,687	4,436	49,503	18,102	67,605

* Includes 761 assisted Immigrants who arrived from New York.   † Includes 173 assisted Immigrants who arrived from New York.
Note.—No account is kept of the number of persons who arrive overland from the adjacent colonies.

In the Government returns no mention is made of the nationalities of persons arriving in the Colony other than those assisted here at the public expense. A separate return, however, is kept of the Chinese arriving, partly because there is a poll tax of £10 ($48.66) per head up on every Chinaman arriving in the Colony. The estimated population of New South Wales at the close of the year 1887 was 1,042,919, of whom over 95 per cent. were of British and colonial origin.

The average cost of passage for an adult assisted immigrant during the last decade has been about £11 ($53.53) to the Colony. The comparatively isolated condition of Australia and its remote distance from Europe seems to have required special efforts on the part of the Government to obtain suitable immigrants for the Colonies. The long sea voyage lasting, by steamer, from forty-five to fifty days, and by sailing vessel, from seventy to one hundred and thirty days, and the attractions offered by the United States and Canada have deterred many from coming to these shores.

About one-half of the assisted immigrants were selected by the Agent-General in Europe, and the remainder were nominated in the Colony. The authorities have always paid a due regard to the question of the nationality of the immigrants, and have taken pains to see that each division of the United Kingdom is properly represented. After a fair proportion is accorded to the English, Welsh, Scotch, and Irish, about 10 per cent. of the remainder are taken from other than British subjects. It is a singular incident in connection with the history of immigration to Australia that in 1877 four vessels arrived at Sydney, bringing 831 immigrants from the United States. The first vessel, the "Anna Boyton," brought a number from New York city.

In the report of the Agent for Immigration of the 27th May, 1877, reference is made to these immigrants:—"The immigrants from New York thus introduced appear to be of a most useful description, and as far as information can be obtained, the greater portion have readily obtained employment in Sydney."

In 1873, the Colonial Government required all applicants for immigration to New South Wales to make a deposit of £5 ($24·33) each for adults, and £2 10s. ($12·16) for children. Under the regulations for 1876 these deposits were reduced to £2 ($9·73) for adults, and £1 ($4·86) for children between 3 and 12 years of age.

By far the greater portion of immigrants arriving here usually linger about Sydney or some of the towns, showing in the strongest possible manner a fondness for city life. The truth is, one-third of the whole population of the Colony reside in Sydney and its suburbs, at all events, considerably more than one-half of the population live in municipalities or incorporated towns. The proportion of those belonging to the agricultural or pastoral classes is not as large as many would expect from the vast pastoral interests of the Colony. The census for 1881 shows that only 54,486 persons belong to the pastoral and agricultural classes, and these include persons engaged in farming, freehold proprietors, leasehold proprietors, and tenant farmers, persons assisting, not being hired servants, and hired farm servants. The number of sheep-farmers is given at 17,110, of whom 16,725 were males, and 385 females. The number engaged in horticulture was 4,820, of these 4,798 were males, and 122 females. The wine-growers numbered 256, sugar-growers 120, making a total of 76,792 of all the farming classes.

The total number engaged in commercial pursuits was 22,901; distributors of drink and food, 12,882; law and other learned professions, 10,184; Government service, 5,787; mining, 17,709; skilled workmen and artificers, 50,580. These include master workmen, apprentices, photographers, printers, coachmakers, jewellers, cabinetmakers, bookbinders, boatbuilders, brickmakers, tailors, shoemakers, and hairdressers. Of the 50,580 belonging to the preceding classes, 7,630 were females. Those classified as unskilled labourers were 38,994. Seafaring persons, including seamen of the merchant marine, ballast men, divers, numbered 5,501, or about 0·73 per cent. of the total population of the Colony.

By far the most numerous class in the Colony is set down in the census under the head of domestic. This includes all persons engaged in household duties, infants and children not attending school, domestic servants, persons of independent means. This class comprises about one-half of the total population of the Colony.

The subjoined table shows the total population of New South Wales for each year, from 1874 to 1887 inclusive, together with the number of births, deaths, arrivals, and departures by sea:—

Year.	Persons.	Male.	Female.	Births.	Deaths.	Sea.	
						Arrivals.	Departures
1874	574,943	312,843	262,100	22,178	8,652	29,756	19,279
1875	594,297	323,080	271,217	22,528	10,771	30,967	20,350
1876	614,181	333,515	280,666	23,298	11,193	32,942	21,923
1877	643,707	350,329	293,378	23,851	9,869	38,628	20,174
1878	671,888	365,625	306,263	25,328	10,763	39,879	22,913
1879	709,459	386,926	322,533	26,933	10,200	44,501	20,695
1880	741,893	405,277	336,616	28,162	11,231	45,870	26,559
1881	778,690	426,944	351,746	28,993	11,536	47,723	24,825
1882	810,833	443,314	367,519	29,702	12,816	47,289	27,972
1883	857,744	470,009	387,735	31,281	12,249	67,206	34,396
1884	903,948	495,571	408,377	33,946	14,220	72,486	40,254
1885	957,914	527,533	430,381	35,043	15,282	78,138	38,453
1886	1,001,966	551,343	450,623	36,284	14,587	70,388	41,896
1887	1,042,919	574,012	468,907	37,236	13,448	67,605	44,089

It will be seen from the foregoing that the number of males in excess of females shows a heavy increase for each year, and that, at the close of 1887, the number of males exceeded that of the opposite sex by 105,105 or more than 10 per cent.

The following table shows the trades and callings of the male adult assisted immigrants for each year, from 1877 to 1887 inclusive:—

	1877.	1878.	1879.	1880.	1881.	1882.	1883.	1884.	1885.	1886.	1887.
Pastoral, farming and general labourers	1,205	1,218	1,320	892	606	592	1,508	1,324	1,047	627	42
Miners	337	114	33	20	19	35	48	99	112	46	19
Building trades	304	270	255	84	85	207	899	579	282	146	11
Iron trades	320	161	72	36	32	59	149	68	138	58	4
Clothing trades	116	58	37	23	20	50	109	93	44	20	3
Provision trades	66	38	15	9	9	33	106	64	23	23	1
Manufacturing trades	72	45	38	7	7	26	116	77	43	15	..
Miscellaneous trades	283	187	136	70	55	117	354	481	182	109	60
Male immigrants over 12 years	2,892	2,091	1,906	1,150	929	1,200	3,370	2,785	1,871	1,044	131

From the care taken by the immigration authorities in selecting immigrants, it may be inferred that the general moral character is good.

The following table shows the religious persuasions of the assisted immigrants who arrived in New South Wales during the year ended December 31st, 1886.

Nationality.	Classification of Religion.													Grand Total.
	Church of England.		Church of Scotland.		Wesleyan Methodists.		Other Protestants.		Roman Catholics.		Jews.		Other Persuasions.		Totals.	
	M.	F.	M.	F.	M.	F.	M.	F.	M.	F.	M.	F.	M.	F.	M.	F.	
English	674	884	31	29	134	224	78	112	7	23	17	13	3	5	944	1,291	2,235
Scotch	13	24	215	285	..	7	1	4	17	16	..	..	..	..	246	336	582
Irish	65	109	35	53	4	6	1	5	299	602	..	..	..	..	405	775	1,180
Other Countries	6	22	5	4	..	..	2	6	7	7	7	12	3	3	30	54	84
	759	1,039	286	371	138	237	82	128	330	648	24	25	6	8	1,625	2,456	4,081

The subjoined table shows in detail their educational attainments.

Nationality.	Classification of Education.						Totals.
	Under 12 years.			Over 12 years.			
	Cannot read.	Read only.	Read and write.	Cannot read.	Read only.	Read and write.	
England and Wales	599	3	201	26	15	1,391	2,235
Scotland	142	......	54	1	2	383	582
Ireland	58	2	30	31	7	1,052	1,180
Other Countries	21	......	5	10	......	48	84
	820	5	290	68	24	2,874	4,081

There is no reason to doubt that the greater portion of immigrants make good citizens. It is certain that after a time they become attached to the country and are self-reliant and self-supporting. Their opportunities for advancement are not as great as in the United States, but there can be no question about their condition being much better than that of similar classes in European countries. It should also be remembered that New South Wales, and indeed all the Australasian Colonies, have institutions in many respects like those of the United States. For instance, universal suffrage prevails, and the system of public education is practically the same; moreover there are no class distinctions in the colonies, no union of Church and State, and no laws of primogeniture and entail. They have also the right to regulate their institutions in their own way, very few Acts of the colonial legislatures have ever been disallowed by, or even require the sanction of, the Imperial Government.

In these circumstances it is only natural to expect a large increase of population in the near future.

Sydney, the capital of New South Wales, has made such rapid strides in wealth and population during late years that her claim to be called the metropolitan city of Australasia will no longer be questioned. Her population, including the suburbs, cannot be less than 350,000. In ten years, from 1876 to 1886, it increased from 170,514 to 332,709. During that period the city ratable property was more than quadrupled.

The capital value of ratable property in the city is £42,529,525 ($206,969,933), and the total annual assessed value is £1,936,253 ($9,422,775). The annual revenue of the City of Sydney for 1887 was £215,288 ($1,047,699).

The city has about 176 miles of streets and about 6 miles of wharves. The Circular Quay has a length of 3,100 feet, and there are about 25 miles of deep-water frontage suitable for wharves. The public buildings, parks, and gardens will compare favorably with those of the most celebrated cities of Europe. The University is the first in the southern hemisphere. The streets and thoroughfares are always crowded, and it is said that the principal business streets, such as George, Pitt, York, King, Sussex, and others, have as heavy a traffic per yard as any other streets in the world. The average number of vehicles passing George-street near the Town Hall every day of 12 hours is 10,960, and the estimated weight in tons daily passing over the road 20,470. There are about 21,000 houses, and no less than 65 miles of sewerage works in the city.

The water supply for Sydney cost over £2,000,000 ($9,733,000), and is practically inexhaustible. The water has been brought through aqueducts, tunnels, and immense iron pipes from the Nepean River. The average daily consumption is 30 gallons per head, or about 8,000,000 gallons, and the reticulations for the supply of the suburbs are being fast extended.

The system of paving the streets of Sydney with wood blocks, of which there are 216,483 square yards or about 44½ acres laid down, is becoming general. There are about 105 miles of streets and roads in the city to keep in repair and cleanse, and this work requires quite an army of labourers.

The Municipality of Sydney raised a loan of £200,000 ($973,300) on the English market to erect Town Hall buildings, and during 1888 the Town Hall will be completed. It will be the largest in the world and will contain a magnificent organ. The building will be a fitting memorial to commemorate the centennial of the foundation of British colonies in Australasia, in which Sydney is the empire city.

The harbour, which has often been described as the finest in the world, is more beautiful than that of Rio Janeiro, or of Lisbon, or the Gulf of Spezia. The bay of Naples cannot compare to it either in capacity for shipping or in color and variety of scenery. The Sydney harbour stretches 15 miles in one direction, and 9 miles in another, in an interminable labyrinth of lakes. It contains 12 square miles of deep water, and is so intersected and islanded that none of its innumerable bays and inlets is ever more than 2 miles in width from one jutting point of land to another. The entrance to the harbour is about a mile in width, the rocks rising on each side to a considerable height and forming a natural gateway. The distance from the ocean to Sydney is about 4 miles, and along the route the slopes of the hills and cliffs are ornamented with innumerable villa residences, the grounds of many being laid out in a unique style of landscape gardening.

The laws conferring upon emigrants to New South Wales grants of land have long since been repealed. At one time, large tracts of land were conferred upon certain officers and soldiers of the British army, who settled in the Colony. Every non-commissioned officer was entitled to 130 acres if single, and if married 150 acres. Privates if single 80 acres, and if married 100 acres, and for each child at the time of granting allotments, 10 acres. These grants were free of taxes, quit rents, and other payments for five years. All such privileges have been repealed, nor is there any exemption from taxation in New South Wales. The land laws of the Colony are voluminous and complicated, but perhaps throw no more obstacles in the way of purchasers than those of other British Colonies. The Crown Lands Act of 1884 now in force here, divides the Colony into three great divisions—the Eastern, the Central, and the Western.

The intending farmer can secure tracts of country suitable for agriculture from 40 to 640 acres along the coast, and for some distance within the Eastern Division, by paying a deposit of 2s. (49 cents) per acre at the date of application, and the balance of 18 shillings ($4·38) per acre, in yearly instalments of 1s. (24 cents.) per acre, with four per cent. interest until the whole debt is paid off. In addition to this, adjoining land if available, not to exceed in the aggregate 1,280 acres, may be taken up as a conditional lease, at a minimum yearly rent of 2d. (4 cents) per acre; and at the end of five years the selector may purchase from the Crown the leased part of his holding, and become a landowner to the extent of 1,280 acres as a maximum, or he may at the end of five years renew his lease without the right of purchase.

The conditions imposed on the selector are those of residence and fencing. The residence must be *bona fide*, and extend over the first five years. The fencing is to be of a special kind, and to be erected on the boundaries of the holding, within a period of two years. In the

Central Division a person may purchase land conditionally, from 640 acres to 2,560 acres upon the same conditions. In the Great Western Division, which is so well adapted to sheep farming and cattle raising, and which includes the famous Riverina district, the Crown lands are open to purchase, except in the neighbourhood of towns, and in areas especially proclaimed for the purpose of alienation, but large tracts are open to lease in blocks of from 5,760 acres to 10,240 acres, called homestead leases at a minimum rental of 1d. (2 cents) per acre. To renew a homestead lease an application must be lodged with the land agent of the district in which the land is situated. Care must be taken to see that the land has not already been taken up. The conditions prescribed are fencing round the boundaries within two years, and residence for at least six months of each year during the first five years of the lease. Should the intending purchaser fail to comply with the conditions, he will be liable to certain penalties. For instance, all classes of Crown lease will be liable to forfeiture for any breach of covenant or for non-payment of rent; but rentals may be paid within three months of due date with the addition of a fine of 5 per cent., or within six months with a fine of 10 per cent.

The only tax levied upon any class of immigrants is the poll tax of £10 ($48·66) per head on the Chinese. The wisdom of this class discrimination has been seriously questioned by colonial statesmen, but there can be little doubt that public opinion favours the measure, and that the prejudice against the Celestials is becoming stronger from year to year. Their want of a proper knowledge of the requirements of higher civilization and their ignorance of sanitary regulations have intensified the opposition to this class of immigrants. It is said that they are all of one sex and hold themselves apart from the community, and quit it altogether for their own country after they have secured a competency, and further, that they are never really free, but are bound to some unknown or mysterious authority, and consequently are a constant danger to the State.

The number of Chinese in New South Wales at the close of 1886 was estimated at 13,500, against 10,205 for the year 1881. The number in Victoria in 1881 was 12,128, it is now estimated at 15,160. The total number in the whole of Australasia at the last census (1881) was given at 43,730, of whom only 362 were women. The number of Chinese in Queensland was 11,253; South Australia, 4,151; Western Australia, 145; Tasmania, 844; New Zealand, 5,004. The total number in the whole of Australasia for 1886 is estimated at 56,113. The Chinese began to immigrate to Australia in 1853. At the census of 1854, there were 2,000 in Victoria, and 3,116 in New South Wales. Steps were taken in Victoria as early as 1855 to limit their immigration. An Act was passed by the legislature of that colony, imposing a tax of £10 ($48·66) per head upon them, and forbidding vessels to carry more than one Chinaman for every ten tons burden. Although the strongest measures were taken to enforce the Act, the law was evaded by large numbers pouring in from the neighbouring colonies. In 1857 there were over 42,000 Chinamen in Victoria alone. In the following year, 1858, there was a great influx of Chinamen into

New South Wales from Victoria, and Mr. Hayter, the Government Statist of Victoria, states that as many as 11,000 left that colony in one year for New South Wales, so that in 1861 the census showed that there were only 24,732 in Victoria.

In 1865, Victoria repealed her restrictions against the Chinese, but the law was revived again in 1881, and about the same time similar statutes were adopted in all the other colonies. The New South Wales law now in force, was passed on the 2nd August, 1881. It provides amongst other things, in addition to the tax of £10 ($48·66) per head, that no vessel shall bring more than one Chinaman for every hundred tons burden, under a penalty of £100 ($486·65). There is also a penalty of £50 ($243·32) for neglecting to pay the poll tax. A certificate is given to each Chinaman upon the payment of the tax, and there are no exemptions to the operations of the law, except those who are *bonâ fide* residents or British subjects.

The immigration policy of the Government has met with more or less opposition from the various trade and labour organisations in the Colony. One of the most prominent of the labour agitators went to London, for the purpose of warning intending immigrants from coming to Australia. In speeches and letters he denounced the policy of the Government, and said that there were over 40,000 unemployed in Australia, and 6,000 in the vicinity of Sydney.

The accusations were promptly refuted by the Agents-General in London, who stated that the colonies were in a fairly prosperous condition, and that those really in search of employment have no trouble in finding it. They also cited the fact that many thousand pounds are sent annually to Europe by the colonists to bring out their friends. There is no doubt that the depression existing in Australasia is only of a temporary character. Indeed, there is every prospect that in a few months there will be a very general renewal of trade throughout the colonies.

The copious rains over a vast area of country, which heretofore suffered from drought, the decided advance in the price of wool and other signs of progress, make the outlook for the future much brighter than the depression in the labour market would seem to indicate. Attention has already been directed to the heavy disproportion of males to females in the Colony. This surplus of single men is not confined to New South Wales but extends to every colony in the Australasian group. In Victoria the percentage of females was, at the last census, 90·05; in Queensland it was 70·28; South Australia, 88·00; Western Australia, 74·33; Tasmania, 88·07; New Zealand, 82·16. A large proportion of the single men of Australasia are of nomadic inclinations. They travel from colony to colony without a desire of securing permanent homes. These men invariably gravitate at certain periods to the large cities, and seriously disturb the labour market, which may also at that time be affected from other causes. In 1884, after a heavy increase of immigration, some disturbance arose in Sydney, which speedily attracted the attention of the Government. Relief works were established, principally around the capital, and a labour bureau was opened for the purpose of determining the amount of distress alleged to exist

and for ascertaining, if possible, the causes of the same, and for assisting those seeking work to find employment. Carefully prepared reports were made by the officer in charge of the bureau, who states that the number of single men who sought work was 365 against 228 married men, and that many of the former were unskilled labourers and had been in the Colony only a few months. On the relief works, the men received wages at the rate of 5s. ($1·22) per day, and were supplied with free fuel for cooking and tents to live in, together with free railway passes to and from their work from Saturday to Monday. Outside the bureau, labourers were being paid by employers from 6s. ($1·46) to 8s. ($1·95) per day. After a period of four months it was found very difficult to obtain workmen at 7s. 6d. ($1·82) per day. The following is an extract from the report of the officer in charge of the bureau :—
"Most of the present applicants on the Labour Exchange object to proceed into the country districts; the class of men who will take the current rate of wages in a country township, in which the cost of subsistance is less than in the Metropolis, and in which town their industrial progress would grow with the growth of the place, is not well represented at the present time."

The wages paid in the principal trades here will compare very favourably with the rates in the United States. A table has been printed with the approval of the New South Wales Government, in which the average rate of wages paid in some of the leading trades is as follows.

CURRENT WAGES.

Nominal rates of Wages of various Trades, &c., during 1887 :—

The rates are those accepted by the various Trade and Labour organisations.

Stonemasons .... 11/- ($2·68), per day of 8 hours.
Bricklayers .... 11/- ,, ,,
Plasterers .... 11/- ,, ,,
Quarrymen .... 7/- to 10/- ($1·70 to $2·43) ,,
Carpenters and joiners .... 9/- ($2·19) ,,
Painters .... 9/- ($2·19) ,,
Labourers (Builders) .... 8/- ($1·95) ,,
Plumbers, gasfitters, and galvanized-iron workers
                     10/- to 11/- ($2·43 to $2·68) ,,
Slaters .... 10/- to 12/- ($2·43 to $2·92) ,,
Iron-moulders........................... 8/- to 9/6 ($1·95 to $2·31) ,,
Boiler-makers and iron shipbuilders .... 10/- ($2·43) ,,
Engineers .... 9/- to 12/- ($2·19 to $2·92) ,,
Labourers working with engineers, boiler-makers, &c.
                     5/- to 7/- ($1·22 to $1·70) ,,
Shipwrights .... 11/- to 12/- ($2·68 to $2·92) ,,
Coachmakers, builders, wheelwrights, smiths,
     painters, and trimmers .... 6/- to 10/- ($1·46 to $2·43) ,,
Wheelwrights and blacksmiths ...... 36/- to 60/- ($8·76 to $14·60) per week of 9 hours per day.

Farriers ....35/- to 55/- ($8·51 to $13·38) per week, of 8 hours per day.
Pattern-makers ....8/- to 10/- ($1·95 to $2·43) per day of 8 hours.
Brass-founders and finishers ......8/- to 10/- ($1·95 to $2·43) ,,
Tinsmiths and sheet iron-workers...7/- to 9/- ($1·70 to $2·19) ,,
Ironworkers (Eskbank) ....8d. to 1/- (16c. to 24c.) per hour.
Saddle, collar, and harness-makers.................30/- to 50/- ($7·30 to $12·16) per week of 54 hours.
Sailmakers ....30/- to 50/- ($7·30 to $12·16) per week of 54 hours.
Tailors ....50/- to 60/- ($12·16 to $14·60) per week, piecework.
Pressers ....50/- to 60/- ($12·16 to $14·60) ,,
Silk-hatters ....50/- to 70/- ($12·16 to $17·03) ,,
Upholsterers ....10/- to 12/- ($2·43 to $2·92) per day.
Compositors ....25/- to 50/- ($6·08 to $12·16) per week of 48 hours; or piece-work, 1 1 per thousand day, and 1/2 per thousand night work.
Coopers..................40/- to 50/- ($9·73 to $12·16) per week, 1/- to 1/3 per hour.
Coal-miners...8d. to 1/3 (16c. to 30c.) per hour.
Coal-lumpers and trimmers ....1/3 per hour day, 1/6 per hour night work (30c. to 36c.)
Wharf labourers.. ....1/- (24c.) per hour.
Bootmakers, &c. (factory hands) ....25/- to 55/- ($6·08 to $13·38) per week.
Cooks and pastry-cooks ....30/- to 60/- ($7·30 to $14·60) ,,
Drapers .. ..30/- to 70/- ($7·30 to $17·03) ,,
Furniture-makers (cabinet-makers, French-polishers)............ 25/- to 50/- ($6·08 to $12·16) per week.
Tobacco operatives ....25/- to 50/- ($6·8 to $12·16) per week.
Gas-stokers ... .8d. to 1 - (16c. to 24c.) per hour, 8-hour shifts.
Brick and pipe makers .... 10½d to 1/- (22c. to 24c.) per hour.
Sawyers and mill-workers................. ....8d. to 1 3 (16c. to 30c.) ,,
Butchers......... ....8d. to 1/- (16c. to 24c.) ,,

IRRIGATION.

The recent publication of a series of elaborate reports by the Colonial Governments on the conservation of water, together with the arrival of American engineers and capitalists engaged in irrigation projects, has awakened very general interest in the subject. The art of irrigation, however, so far as the Colonies are concerned, is only in its theoretical stage. It is true private individuals have made a beginning, but as yet few important results have been attained.

None of the Australian Colonies have laws to regulate water conservancy, and nowhere in the world is the water supply of more importance. Australia possesses inexhaustible mineral treasures, vast tracts of the richest agricultural and pastoral lands, all lying unproductive, awaiting some well-considered scheme to ensure a certain and plentiful water supply.

The means adopted at present consist principally in raising the water out of the rivers on to the lands. American pumping appliances are usually employed, and are admitted to be superior to all others.

It should be remembered by those contemplating the inauguration of extensive irrigation works in Australia that the conditions of the country are altogether different from those in the United States. Unlike America, there are no large rivers and lofty mountains in Australia. Although the mountains in the latter country extend over a large area, their average elevation is only about 3,000 feet. The highest peak in Australia, Mount Kosciusko, 7,308 feet, is about 700 feet below perpetual snow.

The mountain system of Australia is described as a simple one. It can, perhaps, be very well understood by a brief reference to the various ranges in the Colony of New South Wales. The system is usually distinguished by four main ranges, viz. (1) the interior ranges, (2) the great dividing chain, (3) the coast ranges, (4) the isolated peaks and groups.

The interior ranges approach the western boundary of the Colony and form the western watershed of the Darling River. The greatest elevation of the interior ranges is 2,000 feet.

The great dividing chain contains the highest peaks in Australia and runs throughout the whole of the island continent. It is subdivided into seven main branches and separates the eastern and western watersheds.

The coast ranges are on the east side of the great dividing chain and form the edge of the high tableland. The highest peak of the coast ranges is Mount Coolungera, 3,712 feet.

The isolated peaks and groups contain a considerable number of mountains, but all of them are below 3,000 feet in height.

With the exception of a few small streams, all the rivers of New South Wales have their origin in the main dividing chain of mountains. The principal rivers of the eastern watershed are the Hawkesbury, the

Hunter, and Clarence. The Hawkesbury is 330 miles in length, the Hunter 300 miles, and the Clarence 240 miles. All the rivers of the eastern watershed flow into the Pacific Ocean, and are estimated to drain an area of about 50,000 square miles. The principal rivers of the western watershed are the Darling and its affluents, the Lachlan and its affluents, the Murrumbidgee and its affluents. These rivers all eventually unite with the Murray.

The Darling River is 1,160 miles in length. It drains, with its affluents, an area of 198,000 square miles. It is, however, a narrow stream and is navigable for only small steamers.

The Murray River is 1,120 miles in length. It flows westerly and north-westerly through the whole of New South Wales and Victoria, and falls into Lake Alexandria, which discharges into the Southern Ocean below Adelaide, South Australia. The average width of the Murray from Monara to Albury is about 240 feet, and the area drained by it and its affluents is 270,000 square miles.

There are no large fresh-water lakes in Australia, and indeed, with the exception of a few estuaries of the sea, they are all shallow and untrustworthy for water supply. In most cases they are mere depressions connected with the rivers, and receive their water only in times of flood.

It is maintained in the report of the Royal Commission of New South Wales for the conservation of water that there are three lakes in the course of the river Darling, each of which has an area of 60 square miles, and that their capacity is shown by the fact that when rapid falls occur in the Darling the overflow from them keeps the river navigable for nearly a fortnight longer than it would be otherwise. This, the report says, is an important feature, as the outlets from the Darling are in their natural state, and that with few exceptions no attempt has been made either to increase or regulate the supply of water.

In the lakes east of the Darling, in the county of Livingstone, an almost permanent supply of water is kept up through the construction of a dam across Tallawalka Creek. The cost of this, about £4,000 ($19,466), was incurred by the lessees of the land. It is said that this dam throw the water into a series of lakes extending north and south a distance of 80 miles.

The report of the Royal Commission states that the levels of the country between the Murray and Murrumbidgee show that it is well adapted for the construction of canals. The country between the Lachlan and Murrumbidgee is more irregular, but the vast area lying between the Lachlan and the Darling, which appears as a blank on the maps of the Colony, possesses some well-defined features. For instance, the waters of the Darling and Lachlan are ordinarily separated for about 200 miles, but in time of flood they spread out to within a distance of 25 or 30 miles of each other.

Mr. James Harold, of Sydney, who has had much experience in farming by irrigation in the United States, says that there is a great clamour throughout the Colony for a national scheme of irrigation by those who have no knowledge whatever of the cost of such an enterprise, or from what source the water is expected to be obtained. The truth is, Australia has no lofty snow-capped mountains from which to draw supplies, and therefore the rivers and streams very naturally become dry at a time when water is most needed for irrigation purposes. Indeed, during dry seasons the rivers amount to but little more than a chain of waterholes. The landowners on both sides of the Gwydir River, an affluent of the Darling, are clamouring for the right to dam the river without even a thought of the injury it may do to others. They do not seem to know that the lucky individual at the source of the river would get all the water and that the less fortunate one lower down the stream would not get any. It has been proposed by graziers to place weirs or obstructions in the rivers for the purpose of turning their flood-waters into the numerous blind creeks and depressions which are found in various places upon the plains. This scheme is objectionable, for the reason that the country through which these rivers run is for the most part so level that the fall is only about 1 foot to the mile, and consequently the current is sluggish at best, whereas if obstructions were placed in the rivers, the current would be more sluggish still, and the loss from evaporation, soakage, and capillary attraction would be enormous. At present, on account of the recent heavy rainfall, the blind creeks and depressions along the plains are filled with water, but such water cannot very well be impounded.

There are numerous depressions on the western plains, many from 8 to 10 feet deep. These are partly formed by their banks being raised above the level of the surrounding plains, and if they could be kept full of water, much of it, doubtless, could be drawn off by gravitation for irrigation purposes. These lakes or depressions, so long as they contain water, may be of great advantage to the farmer, but in time of drought they are dried up, and therefore cannot be depended upon. The evaporation from these lakes will amount to about 10 inches per month, and the thought of obtaining a permanent supply of water from them is altogether out of the question. In the report of the Royal Commission it is stated that various opinions exist among farmers and graziers as to the extent of the evaporation of these lakes; and some contend that it is as much as a foot for three or four months, while others say that it will not amount to more than 2 feet per year.

The Government Engineer, who is charged with the construction of tanks—works undertaken principally for the watering of travelling stock—says that, from a tank containing 18 feet of water, evaporation would not exceed 4 or 5 feet per year. In the Gwydir district, 2,000 sheep were watered for more than a year from a tank 10 feet deep, and there was water remaining in it then, although none had run into it the whole time.

One witness before the Commission stated, that the average depth in a swamp into which water flowed from the Bulla River was fully 4 feet, and that the water lasted fifteen months before it disappeared from evaporation and soakage.

The conditions upon which observations are made differ materially. For instance, the hot winds which are, comparatively, of rare occurrence in the coast district, and which range in temperature at Sydney from 80° to 106° Fahrenheit, are frequent on the western plains. There the temperature sometimes records 130°, and for days stands at 110° to 116°. It would be a mistake, however, to suppose that this condition of wind continues for long periods, for the wind records show that, as compared with the coast districts, the country beyond the main dividing range has a comparatively tranquil atmosphere.

The subjoined table was furnished to the Commission by Mr. Russell, the Government Astronomer.

Result of observations with the tank evaporation:—

Month.	Bourke.	Hay.	Hillston.
	Inches.	Inches.	Inches.
March	1·579	......	......
April	4·770	......	......
May	3·037	......	......
June	2·858	......	......
July	1·637	......	......
August	3·793	2·762	2·074
September	3·975	2·736	3·280
October	7·559	......	......

A series of experiments has recently been made by Mr. Russell for the purpose of testing the evaporation of some of the larger lakes. In 1885 he placed a self-registering evaporation gauge in Lake George. This lake is about 19 miles in length and 6 in width. It is situated on the eastern side of the great dividing chain, at an elevation of 2,200 feet above the level of the sea. Its waters, however, have no outlet, and consequently are strongly impregnated with salts. Lake George has never been known to overflow, and in dry weather it has failed entirely. The following table shows the results of Mr. Russell's experiments.

The water-gauge at Lake George.

Date.	Evaporation.		Rainfall.	Total loss by evaporation.	
	Reading of gauge.	Loss or gain.		Amount.	Months.
1885.	Inches.	Inches.	Inches.	Inches.	
1 March	2·8	......	......	......	
1 April	6·8	−4·0	0·44	4·44	March
1 May	7·7	−0·9	1·54	2·44	April
1 June	8·8	−1·1	1·92	5·03	May
1 July	6·7	+2·7	3·42	1·32	June
1 August	5·0	+1·7	1·82	0·12	July
1 September	5·4	−0·4	1·06	1·46	August
1 October	7·9	−2·5	1·15	3·65	September
31 October	10·7	−2·8	1·74	4·54	October
Total	......	−7·9	13·09	20·99	

NOTE.—Only the rain is added which fell on the lake, and not that which flowed into it. During the last fourteen years the lake has lost, by evaporation, 12 feet.

The Royal Commission in reporting upon wells were unable to express an opinion as to the theory of an underground flow of water in Australia to the ocean. They mention that water has been found at Tarkania, in South Australia, 150 miles from the western boundary of New South Wales, in latitude 29°, at a depth of 1,220 feet, or 1,040 feet below sea level. The water rose 20 feet above the surface. Water was struck at Hergott Springs, in the same colony, at 339 feet. The flow at Tarkania was only about 40 gallons per day, but the well at Hergott Springs yields 5,000 gallons per day. The diameter of the bore at Tarkania is 3 inches, and that at Hergott Springs is 6 inches.

At 75 miles from Bourke, on the road to Wanaaring, New South Wales, the deepest bore yet sunk by means of the water augur, has been lately completed, artesian water having been struck at a depth of 942 feet, and the bore having been continued to a depth of 960 feet, a supply of water equal to 33,000 gallons per twenty-four hours, rises to a height of 30 feet above the surface.

A supply of fresh water was also obtained on one sheep station in the Bourke district at a depth of 480 feet, and at another station in the same district at 550 feet.

Mr. W. H. J. Slee, Superintendent of Diamond Drills in New South Wales, reports : "The water supply has been tapped in one of the most arid parts of New South Wales, in the cretaceous formation, and is of immense value to the Colony at large. In my reports in 1885 and 1886, I stated that if artesian water was tapped along this road (Bourke to Wanaaring) boring operations could be successfully extended in the cretaceous basin to Milpakinka and Mount Brown Districts. In some parts the bores may have to be put down from 700 to 1,000 feet, in other parts 400 to 600 feet might be probable depths. The greatest drawback in these remote parts of New South Wales is the great scarcity of water, and if this was once overcome by artesian wells, stock and sheep would increase, and wool would be directed towards the Bourke railway station and thence to Sydney, and goods would be forwarded from the latter place."

The people in many districts have given up the practice of sinking for water from the fact that when found it is of a brackish nature, and they depend principally upon tanks for the conservation of water. Of course they have to wait for the wet season before their tanks can be filled. The tanks used are often too wide and shallow. In open tanks, from which the sheep take water freely, the loss is considerable through weak animals getting bogged. Tanks are less expensive than wells, but when the right kind of water cannot be found by ordinary sinking, the artesian well should be the farmers' main dependence. In some districts it has been noticed that in almost every case where water has been struck, salt water is invariably found at higher levels and not unfrequently near the surface. In these circumstances, the presence of salt water should not discourage those from undertaking deeper excavations.

The Colonial Geologist accounts for the prevalence of salt water in the alluvial districts from the fact of its fresh-water origin. The debris washed from the ranges has been deposited quickly, and the decomposition from the mineral constituents arising from the moisture has

B

converted the fresh water into salt. Sulphate of alumina, lime, and magnesia have been formed, and salts chemically produced. In the marine formations the soluble parts of the mineral have been washed out by the long-continued action of the sea-water. When the water flows underground it is fresh, but whenever it is stationary, as it may be in clay beds a few yards from the current, it will become salt. The saline nature of the soil has given rise to well-marked peculiarities in the herbage, such as the salt-bush.

Some good work in artesian boring has been done by private enterprise, but the great part of the work is left to the Government. The Australians need more than anything else a few good sets of the Pennsylvania oil-boring apparatus or appliances from 4 to 6 horse-power put into the hands of men experienced in that kind of work.

In that portion of New South Wales known as the Riverina district, and which is drained by the Murray, abundance of water can be found at a depth of 80 feet, but there is small prospect of striking artesian water in that district, as the country is of lacustrine formation, with a good clear soakage all along the course of the river. Artesian water, however, is found some distance back from the Murray on the plains where dykes of mineral-bearing rock occur. The most remarkable artesian belt in Australia occurs in the Liverpool Plains, in the north-eastern part of New South Wales, but very little has been done to develop it. In the early history of the country water was very scarce in that district. All the rivers and creeks in the summer were turned into sand tracks. Wells were sunk there, and the water has continued to flow from them ever since. The greater part of the district is what may be called good boring country, and trouble need not be apprehended from the swelling of the surfaces of the bores, as there is little soapstone.

In Queensland, great success seems to have attended operations in boring for water. At Barcaldine, 400 miles west of Rockhampton, on the Central Railway, in a district where thousands of sheep and cattle succumbed in the last drought, the Government of Queensland entered into a contract with Mr. J. Loughead, from America, of the Federal Boring Association, to bore for water. Government supplied the tubing, and fuel and water for the engine. Operations began on 18th of November. The bore was 12 inches in diameter. On 16th December, 1887, the drill suddenly dropped 7 feet, and water ascended the bore and rose 17 feet above the surface. The total depth was 691 feet 9 inches. The hydraulic engineer who inspected the well estimated the supply at 400 gallons per minute, or 576,000 gallons of water per day. It is said to be the biggest artesian well in the world. Other bores are to be put down in several places.

So much is said about the drought of Australia that very few persons are aware that the average rainfall in all the colonies will compare favourably with that of other countries. In New South Wales, a territory of 310,000 square miles, the average rainfall is 24 inches. At Sydney it is about 50 inches, at Eden it is 70 inches, but in the flat country it is only about 10 inches. The average rainfall in Queensland is about the same as that of New South Wales. The former colony, however, is more subject to tropical rains than the latter. The rainfall, therefore, in Queensland rises in some districts, as for instance Johnstone River, to 123 inches; in other places the average is as low as 8 inches.

At Adelaide, South Australia, where there are no high coast ranges to arrest the drift of the clouds, the rainfall is as low as 20 inches. At Port Augusta it falls to 8 inches. At Perth, Western Australia, the average is 31 inches, but at Carnarvon, in the same colony, it does not average more than 6 inches. At Eucla it is 10 inches. The rainfall in Victoria varies from 63 inches at Cape Schanck to 12 inches at Wycheproof. At Melbourne it is about 25 inches.

The trouble, however, in Australia is that whenever there is a diminished rainfall the effects are much more disastrous than in other places on account of the great heat and the absence of more general cultivation. A diminished rainfall of 50 per cent. has at times desolated whole tracts of country. The report of the New South Wales Royal Commission, however, states that while one part of the country suffers from a diminished rainfall other parts have an average supply and others again may be favoured with an abundant fall. In the basin of the Darling, excluding the hilly portion, the rainfall is 12·81 inches. In the plains between the Lachlan and the Murrumbidgee it is 16·33 inches, and in the corresponding district between the Murrumbidgee and the Murray it is 14·56. These rainfalls would be sufficient for ordinary crops of cereals if they came at proper periods, but the report of the commission admits that they do not. It says that as a rule in these districts when rain is most needed it comes in such small quantities as to be of little or no benefit to vegetation.

One of the most difficult questions with which Australians have to deal in connection with the subject of irrigation is the best means for the storage of water. There is no doubt that much of the rainfall is of a temporary benefit only, on account of its tropical character, coming, as it does, in vast quantities at a time when it is not needed. The Government Astronomer states that rain fell to the depth of $10\frac{1}{2}$ inches at Newcastle in less than two hours and a half, and that at the South Head, near Sydney, it fell at the rate of 1 inch per hour for more than twenty hours.

The establishment of large reservoirs at the heads of the principal rivers and creeks, and the placing of movable weirs across others in times of flood is recommended by the Commission, as well as sluice-gates to prevent the return of the water to the main stream. Whatever is done for irrigation should be done by high artificial systems of water conservation among the mountains, and by artesian and other wells. Occasionally, in times of flood, water might be preserved, but it could not be depended upon. We should bear in mind that very fair crops can be grown over a large area in New South Wales without the aid of irrigation, and Mr. Harold points out the fact that during the drought of 1885-6, one of the most severe ever known, the average yield of wheat in those parts was $10\frac{1}{2}$ bushels per acre. It is useless to think of irrigation for pastoral purposes in Australia, except upon a limited scale, as the cost would be too great. "It might answer," he says, "where land can be had for almost nothing, but where population increases the land will become more valuable and it will be required to grow food for the people instead of grass for sheep."

The New South Wales Water Conservancy Commission is very decided in the opinion that the riparian rights existing under the common law of England are not at all applicable to the conditions of Australia, and that an attempt to enforce them would be a serious hindrance to the progress of the country, in so far as that progress depends on the conservation of water. In the Colony of Victoria, no such rights can accrue, from the fact that the frontages to all rivers are reserved from sale. The conditions in New South Wales and other colonies are altogether different. Extensive alienations have taken place, which involve the legal rights of ownership to the middle of the beds of the rivers.

A memorandum as to what riparian rights really mean under the common law was prepared by Mr. A. Oliver. He quotes largely from Mr. Justice Storey's opinion in the case of Tyler v. Wilkinson (4 Mason, U.S. reports, 397), in which it is laid down :—

That *prima facie* (*i.e.* the law presumes) every proprietor upon each bank of a river is entitled to the land covered with water in front of the bank to the middle, the bed of the stream, or, as it is commonly expressed, *ad medium filum aqua*. In virtue of his ownership he has a right to the use of the water flowing over it in its natural current without diminution or obstruction. Mr. Justice Storey says that the consequence of this principle is that no proprietor has the right to use the water to the prejudice of another, and that it is wholly immaterial whether the party be a proprietor above or below in the course of the river, the right being common to all proprietors ; therefore, no one has the right to diminish the quantity which will, according to the natural current, flow to the proprietor below or to throw it back upon the proprietor above.

The Commission state that riparian rights, as understood by the common law, are better adapted to England, where the people are more concerned to drain off the water as quickly as possible, than to New South Wales, where the all-important question is how best to retain it.

The Commission does not find fault with the law which enables a riparian proprietor to restrain the action of those who construct works which have the effect of depriving him of participation in the advantage of a flowing stream or who make such a diversion of the water as would inundate his land.

The Commission states : " The position with which we have to deal is not so much with flowing water as with dry channels through which water flows only at long and irregular intervals. It is required that these water-courses should be made to hold water—to be in effect converted into inundation canals ; but this would not be possible under the present state of the law, by which any litigious person could, if so minded, interpose a bar to the erection of weirs or other works."

The Commission further states that there should be no difficulty in superseding the presumption of the English common law by a clear enactment of state ownership, for the common law only gives a riparian owner power to use so much of the water of a river as he requires for his own consumption and that of his own stock, while the object and effect of state ownership would be to increase the supply of water, which now often wholly fails, and to make it permanent.

Several of the Australian Governments have entered into agreements for the transfer of extensive tracts of land to various irrigation companies.

The South Australian Government has recently perfected arrangements with the Messrs. Chaffey Brothers, who have considerable experience with irrigation in California, by which the firm may acquire 250,000 acres of land in that colony. The firm is to have 30,000 acres at once upon the condition that they will, during the first five years, spend the sum of £35,000 ($170,328), during the second five years £140,000 ($681,310), during the third five years £75,000 ($364,988), and during the fourth five years £50,000 ($243,325), or a total of £300,000 ($1,459,500). On spending £1 ($4·86) per acre on the land, inclusive of the first 30,000 acres, they may acquire the fee-simple up to 50,000 acres. This will leave 200,000 acres. When the Messrs. Chaffey Brothers have expended £1 ($4·86) per acre on this area they may purchase it for another £1 ($4·86) per acre, so that altogether it will cost them £600,000 ($2,919,900) to gain the fee-simple of the whole block of 250,000 acres. It is further agreed that all the machinery and pipes shall be manufactured in the Colony, unless the Government determine otherwise.

The Government of Victoria has also concluded an agreement with the same firm by which the Messrs. Chaffey Brothers are to have 50,000 acres in what is known as the mallee country, on the Lower Murray frontage, 11 miles east from the junction of the Darling, with the right of purchasing 200,000 acres hereafter. The fee-simple of the land was valued by the Surveyor-General at 2s. 6d. (60 cents) to 5s. ($1·21) per acre, but the highest rental ever offered for it was 1d. (2 cents) for every 14 acres.

The Messrs. Chaffey Brothers undertake in this agreement to expend the sum of £300,000 ($1,459,950) within twenty years upon 47,000 acres in constructing irrigation works and for building an agricultural college. The land when cleared for settlement is to be cut up in small blocks of not more than 80 acres, if planted and prepared for fruit-growing, and not more than 160 acres if for other products, each to be farmed separately, and no person to be allowed to purchase more than one block. As soon as 100 families are settled there the college is to be opened, in which the principles of agriculture, horticulture, and chemistry, are to be taught. If the additional 200,000 acres are taken up, the sum of £420,000 ($2,043,930) is to be expended in improvements.

This agreement was opposed in Parliament; however, it was finally arranged that the Messrs. Chaffey Brothers should enter upon the occupation of their land.

FORESTS AND FOREST CULTURE.

The Government of New South Wales has for many years been impressed with the necessity of taking steps for the preservation of the useful timber trees of the Colony. The soft, straight-grained woods, such as the pines, except in places as yet inaccessible, are well-nigh exhausted. The white beech and cedar trees are also becoming scarce. The latter trees are now seldom found except in places more or less difficult of access, and it is expensive to convey them to market. Moreover, they are never met with in quantity. In fact, forests of one particular kind of tree, like the pine, spruce, or cedar of the United States, are unknown in this Colony. Such trees, when found, are usually distributed amongst a variety of other kinds,

The forest area of New South Wales would probably not exceed 30,000 square miles out of a total area of 310,938 square miles. The forests proper are mostly confined to the water-shed lying east of the Great Dividing Range or cordillera, which separates the eastern and western water-sheds. This range has seven main branches, the highest peak of which is 7,300 feet.

The country east of the Great Dividing Range is estimated to contain 50,000 square miles, one-fourth of which probably consists of forests.

Pine trees, known as the Moreton Bay pine, *Araucaria Cunninghamii*, Port Macquarie pine, *Frenela Macleayana*, cypress pine, *Frenela Endlicheri*, mountain pine, *Frenela Parlatorei*, and colonial deal, *Podocarpus elata*, together with some others, are found in various parts of this Colony; but this timber is often difficult to reach, the country containing it being very rough, with high ranges and deep gullies. The principal woods of the Colony, "Eucalypti," belong to the natural order *Myrtaceæ*. They are very hard and difficult to work, and are generally known by the name of hardwoods.

Some species of Eucalyptus make good sleepers for railways and piles for bridges and wharves, but it does not at all compete with American timber for ordinary building purposes, where soft and easily worked woods are required. Some of the woods, known as ironbark, *E. siderophloia*, and red gum, *E. rostrata*, are deemed indestructible in moist ground. The red gum is thought to be quite equal in strength and durability to the celebrated "jarrah" of Western Australia, which is also a species of Eucalyptus, *E. marginata*. The "jarrah," like all the hardwoods of Australia, is liable to decay in the centre. The sound trees yield useful and durable timber, and there is talk of exporting it to the United States for cabinet work. The wood is of reddish colour, close in texture, and of slightly wavy grain. It is admirably adapted for docks and wharves. It is impervious to the attacks of the *Teredo navalis* and white ant. The timber of the red gum is characterized by considerable density and hardness. Like the "jarrah," it is of close texture and wavy grain, and is said not to shrink longitudinally. There are fifty-four species of Eucalyptus in New South Wales, and many have lofty stems, thin branches, dull-coloured foliage, and scanty undergrowth. Some of the commonest amongst them are the box, *E. polyanthema*; stringybark, *E. obliqua*, *E. capitellata*, *E. macrorrhyncha*; blue gum, *E. goniocalyx*, *E. botryoides*; red gum, *E. rostrata*; spotted gum, *E. maculata*, *E. hæmastoma*; grey gum, *E. saligna*, *E. tereticornis*, *E. viminalis*; messmate, *E. amygdalina*, *E. piperita*; peppermint, *E. piperita*; tallow-wood, *E. microcorys*; ironbark, *E. siderophloia*, *E. leucoxylon*; and mahogany, *E. resinifera*, and *E. robusta*.

It must be borne in mind that vernacular names for native trees are very loosely applied in Australia, the title "red gum," for instance, being applied to several species of eucalypts, while most species of eucalypt possess several names apiece.

Perhaps the best known species of eucalyptus outside of Australia is the blue gum of Victoria and Tasmania, *E. globulus*; but it is excessively rare in New South Wales. *Eucalyptus amygdalina* (called "mountain ash," "peppermint," "messmate," &c.) is likewise far more common in Victoria and Tasmania than in this Colony. In New South Wales it is confined to the southern portion. The blue gum tree grows to a greater height than any other in the world, and sometimes rises to 200 feet before sending out a branch. It reaches a greater height in Victoria and Tasmania than in New South Wales. The highest ever felled in the latter Colony was 360 feet, while in Victoria one was felled (at Healesville, 37 miles from Melbourne) measuring 480 feet (14 feet higher than the Strasburg Cathedral). The circumference was 100 feet. In Tasmania these trees not unfrequently attain a height of over 400 feet. These giants of the Australian forest do not impress the traveller so much as the big trees of California, on account of the greater bulk of the latter. The Rev. J. E. Tenison-Woods, F.G.S., F.L.S., accounts for the great height of these trees as follows: First, the extreme richness and moisture of the vegetable soil; second, perfect absence of disturbance from the wind; and third, the comparative obscurity, or modified light, which causes the young plant to throw out but few branches or leaves until the light of day is reached, which is often at a height of 100 feet or more above the root. The young leaves fall away and leave the tree still more bare as it grows up.

Mr. Woods says of these trees:—"Long bands of bark hang down from their sides and across their branches, and when set in motion by the wind, keep up a constant rattle and creaking, filling the gloomy forests with the strangest echoes and sounds. The great height of the trees would never be imagined from the aspect they present. As they always grow on very steep slopes, and never crown the summit of the ridges, their height is lost against the adjacent ranges. It is only when standing against their stems, where the roots rise gracefully up around from the buttress-like base, twisting and turning round the bole-like massive moorings, that one gets an idea of their enormous size."

The timber of this tree is strong, heavy, and durable. Its transverse strength is equal to that of English oak. It is used to a limited extent for ship-building purposes, for waggons and carriages, for palings, and for many other purposes.

There are about one hundred different species of acacia in New South Wales. Though the timber they yield is, as a rule, of little value, some species furnish valuable timber. The bark is exported to various countries, where it is highly prized for tanning purposes. These trees are known by the generic name of "wattle." Their gum is utilized to a limited extent for commercial purposes, and the beautiful flowers of one or two species are used in the manufacture of perfume.

In many places after the forest has been burned the "wattle" makes its appearance within a year or two.

With the exception of the Government reserves, which comprise 5,460,125 acres, all forests in New South Wales on Crown lands are common property, except for grazing purposes. The Government reserves are, however, of a temporary character, and are reduced from time to time partly because upon careful examination they are found to contain little or no timber, and partly because the Government yields to pressure to put the land up for sale. The Government also controls large areas of unreserved timbered lands, but when once sold has nothing to do with the timber upon them. In most cases when land is sold the purchaser destroys the timber.

A special license is required to cut timber from Crown lands. The charge for a license is at the rate of 5s. ($1·21) for ordinary timber, and 10s. ($2·43) for cedar. Any person armed with a proper license can cut as much timber as he can remove from the land. No license is required by any one for the purpose of cutting firewood for his own use, if not intended for sale.

Rights to cut and remove timber from blocks within State forests are also sold by auction, or by tender, at an upset price of £10 ($48·66) per block of 640 acres per annum, for a term of one year only, unless circumstances should justify the Government in special cases extending the term to three years, and then, in addition to block rental, a royalty is imposed.

Land can be obtained for grazing purposes from the Government by paying an annual rental of not less than £2 ($9·73) per section of 640 acres. According to the 1884 land law of New South Wales, now in force, the Government can let by tender or at auction, such lands as are not under lease, not to exceed 1,920 acres subject to rental, for the whole year, if tenancy be created at any time of the year prior to the 30th of June, and for the half year's rental, if afterwards.

Lands thus rented, even after renewal, do not bar the area from sale, conditional or otherwise.

Scrub lands may be leased in areas of 10,240 acres maximum, and 640 acres minimum, for a term of fifteen years, subject to clearing conditions from time to time defined by regulations, at a minimum rental of 2s. 6d. (61 cents) per section for the first five years, and 5s. ($1·21) for the second five years, and £1 ($4.86) for the third five years.

Rental during either of the three periods of five years may be remitted upon the recommendation of the Local Land Board. No residence on scrub leases is required by the Land Act.

In the common forest no protection is afforded against the ravages of stock, and some of the edible trees, such as the myall, boree, and the oak, *Casuarina*, will be exterminated, it is said, in a few years, as the stock eat the young seedlings.

The myall is a species of acacia, *A. homalophylla*. It is found on the Salt Bush Plains and on the Murray River, and from the Lachlan to the Barrier Range. The timber is hard, dark, and fragrant. It is suitable for cabinet work, and was formerly used by the aboriginal inhabitants for making spears.

The boree or "Weeping Myall," known to science as *A. pendula*, is a very beautiful tree, attaining to a height of 40 feet, with diameter of 18 inches, though usually of half the dimensions. The foliage is pale or ash-coloured. It is found on the Illawarra and Liverpool Plains, and is said to be the only useful timber tree of the Lachlan morasses. The wood is hard, close-grained, and violet-scented, and in this respect unique. It is highly prized for pipes, fancy boxes, &c., and wood artificially scented is often substituted for it.

The colonial pine, *Araucaria Cunninghamii*, is by far the most suitable and most readily available of the Australian soft woods. It is close-grained, free from knots, and easily worked, and is very generally used for flooring and spars, joiners' and cabinet work. It is shipped to Sydney from the northern districts by sea. The logs measure from 100 to 120 feet in length. Their diameter is from 2 to 3 feet. The greater part of the colonial pine is obtained from lands bordering the rivers in the northern districts. It is abundant on the Crown lands, some distance from navigable water, but has to be drawn by bullock teams over rough country. Boards of this timber sell in Sydney from 12s. ($2·92) to 16s. ($3·89) per 100 superficial feet. Logs from 7s. ($1·70) to 9s. ($2·19) per 100 superficial feet, girth measurement.

White beech, *Gmelina Leichhardtii*.—This timber is one of the most valuable in Australia. It is of a beautiful silvery colour, close-grained, and not liable to shrink or warp. It is used for decks of ships, floorings of verandahs, carving, and wood engraving. It is found on both the northern and southern coast districts, and is conveyed to Sydney in small vessels. Height of tree, 100 to 120 feet; diameter, from 3 to 4 feet. The price of this timber in Sydney is from 14s. ($3·40) to 18s. ($4·38) per 100 superficial feet.

Red cedar, *Cedrela Toona*.—This timber, which at one time was extensively used in Australia, is becoming scarce through neglect and waste. The trees which were cut down years ago were allowed to rot on the ground. The timber is of a dark red colour, light in weight, and very durable; some of it has a lovely figure. It is used for furniture, turning, cabinet-making, and all kinds of fittings in house and ship building, and is still one of the best known timbers in Australia. It is said to be plentiful in Queensland and New Guinea, but is seldom found in New South Wales except in ravines and mountainous country. It is, however, being planted by the Government. The Sydney prices of red cedar vary from 18s. ($4·38) to 35s. ($8·52) per 100 superficial feet, according to quality. Logs bring from 16s. ($3·89) to 25s. ($6·08) per 100 superficial feet, girth measurement.

Native plum, *Achras Australis*.—Is another valuable timber, similar to white pine, and used for the same purposes. It is found in moderate quantities. Height of tree 80 to 100 feet; diameter from 2 to 3 feet.

Blue Mountain pine, *Frenela Muellerii*.—Is a small tree found on the Blue Mountains. The timber is soft and easily worked, but deficient in strength and durability.

White cypress pine, *Frenela robusta v. verrucosa*.—Is found in considerable quantities in the interior. It is strong and durable, and is used for planks, weatherboards, rafters, and telegraph-poles.

Richmond white pine, *Frenela robusta v. microcarpa* is a very valuable timber tree. It is used for general building purposes. The root stock furnishes excellent veneers for cabinet-making, but unfortunately the tree is not plentifully distributed.

There are other species of *Frenela*, some of which are more readily available, and yield better timber.

One of the most valuable of the hardwoods is the black stavewood, *Tarrietia argyrodendron*. It is used for posts, sleepers, piles, and bridges. It is tough, and stands well under water. Height of tree from 80 to 100 feet. The diameter is from 2 to 3 feet.

The Blackwood, *Acacia melanoxylon*, is hard, dark coloured, and often prettily marked. It is easily worked, and is strong and durable. It is used for furniture, fencing, bridges, staves, carriages, pianos, and cabinet work. It is a most valuable timber, exceedingly like American walnut in appearance, and usually employed in this Colony as a substitute for that wood; but it is rather more liable to shrink than walnut. It is fairly plentiful in parts of the southern coast district of the Colony, but it is generally imported from Tasmania.

White box, *Tristania conferta*.—Is another tree, employed to some extent for ship-building, wharves, and bridges. Ribs of vessels built of this timber have kept perfectly sound for over thirty years. The tree attains a height of 150 feet. It has a smooth brown deciduous bark, and a dense foliage. It is found in open and brush forests from the Hastings to the Tweed River.

Red gum, *Eucalyptus rostrata*.—This makes a beautifully grained timber, not unlike the English oak. It takes a fine polish, and is valuable for house carpentry.

Peppermint, *Eucalyptus piperita*.—This tree is abundant in many parts of the Colony. An excellent oil is made from the leaves and is exported to Europe. The tree is found in both the northern and southern districts.

Blue gum, *Eucalyptus globulus*.—This fine tree, peculiar to Victoria and Tasmania, does not grow naturally in New South Wales. It is, however, being extensively cultivated. The timber is heavy, strong, and durable. It is said to be equal to English oak in transverse strength. It is used for ships, house-building, sleepers, shafts, and spokes of wheels. The tree grows rapidly, and has been planted with success in California, Italy, Algiers, Egypt, and other countries. It is said that fever cannot exist in the neighbourhood where it grows. Oil and extracts are made from its leaves. An interesting feature connected with this tree is that it produces two different kinds of leaves. Professor Brioze, an Italian botanist, accounts for this peculiarity on the ground that the original trees grew in totally different climatic situations, and that their leaves were broad and horizontal. Their present vertical position, as well as the various forms of the leaves, especially in the upper parts of older trees, is, he thinks, an attempt to adapt themselves to new conditions by diminishing the leaf-surface exposed to the direct action of solar heat. The size to which these trees attain has been already referred to.

Mountain ash, *Eucalyptus virgata.*—This tree is common in southern New South Wales. It is very durable underground. It is used for palings, shafts, and fencing. Height, from 150 to 180 feet; diameter, from 3 to 5 feet.

Slaty gum, *Eucalyptus bicolor, A. Cunn. (E. largiflorens, F. v. M.)*—Timber very hard, durable, and difficult to split. It is considered almost equal in strength and durability to ironbark, and will not crack when exposed to the sun. It is used for fencing, plow-beams, shafts for drays, and carts. Height, from 80 to 100 feet; diameter, 2 to 3 feet.

Stringy-bark, *Eucalyptus capitellata.*—Timber strong, tough, hard, and durable; largely used for house carpentry, joists, rafters, and fuel. The bark is used for roofing. The tree is plentiful in the counties of Camden and Cumberland, and on the Blue Mountains. Height, 150 to 200 feet; diamater, 3 to 4 feet.

Mountain blood-wood, *Eucalyptus eximia.*—Timber strong and durable, subject to gum veins. It is used for posts, rails, and fuel, and is excellent for waterworks, as it resists decay. Height, 80 to 100 feet. It is chiefly found on the Blue Mountains.

Gray ironbark, *Eucalyptus crebra.*—Timber hard, tough, heavy, inlocked, and durable. It is highly esteemed by coach-builders and wheelrights. Height, from 100 to 150 feet; diameter, 2 to 4 feet.

Red ironbark, *Eucalyptus leucoxylon.* — Timber dark coloured, remarkably hard, heavy, strong, and durable, largely used for girders, beams, poles, bridges, and fences. An invaluable timber, put to innumerable uses.

She ironbark, *Eucalyptus paniculata.*—Timber much valued, hard, tough, inlocked, and durable; used for bridges, sleepers, railway carriages, beams, piles, and spokes. It grows in the northern and southern districts. Height, from 100 to 150 feet. The timber is shipped to Sydney by sea.

Large-leaved ironbark, *Eucalyptus siderophloia.*—Timber dark coloured, hard, heavy, and durable, used for large beams in buildings, stores, and bridges. It is the celebrated Sydney ironbark—the most valuable of New South Wales hardwoods. Its transverse strength is enormous, and there having been such a great demand for this tree for nearly a century it is now becoming comparatively scarce. It is exported to Victoria for public works.

Swamp mahogany, *Eucalyptus robusta.*—Timber strong, hard, and durable, used for shingles, ships, house-building, and rough furniture. Height 80 to 100 feet; diameter, 4 to 6 feet.

Flooded gum, *Eucalyptus saligna.*—Timber light, strong, and durable, extensively used for building purposes, posts, rails, scantling, flooring, ships' planks, naves, and felloes of wheels. It is found in open forests, near banks of rivers and creeks, on rich soil, in both northern and southern districts. This timber is considered one of the best indigenous hardwoods. Height, from 80 to 100 feet.

Boxwood, *Eucalyptus hemiphloia*.—This timber is exceedingly hard and tough, but subject to be attacked by white ants and dry rot. It is used for scantling and house-building, and also for fuel. It burns brilliantly and generates great heat; frequents the southern coast district. Height, from 80 to 100 feet; diameter, 3 to 4 feet.

Woolybutt, *Eucalyptus longifolia*.—Timber hard, tough, and durable, used for felloes, shafts, spokes, house-building, and fencing. It grows on rich alluvial flats in southern coast districts. Height, 100 to 150 feet; diameter, 3 to 4 feet.

Spotted gum, *Eucalyptus maculata*.—Timber strong, elastic, and durable. Used for ship-building, bridges, shafts, and cubes for street paving. It grows in both northern and southern districts. Height, 100 to 150 feet; diameter, 3 to 4 feet.

Tallow-wood, *Eucalyptus microcorys*.—Timber strong, handsome, and durable. It is of a greasy nature, as the name implies, and grows on the northern coast district. Height, 100 to 150 feet; diameter, 4 to 6 feet.

Messmate, *Eucalyptus amygdalina*.—Timber strong and durable. Used for bridge planking, and fencing. Height, 150 to 200 feet; diameter, from 4 to 6 feet. Moderately plentiful in southern districts.

White Mahogany, *Eucalyptus pilularis*.—Timber similar to the preceding but heavier. When planed it has a soft surface and is prettily veined. It is used for building purposes. Height, 80 to 100 feet; diameter, 3 to 4 feet.

Gray gum, *Eucalyptus tereticornis*.—Timber strong, tough, and durable. Used for building purposes; moderately plentiful. Height, 100 to 150 feet; diameter, 3 to 4 feet.

Red mahogany, *Eucalyptus resinifera*.—Timber remarkably strong, hard, heavy, and durable. Used for buildings, fencing, beams, rafters, ships' knees, and shingles. A portion of a Church built of this timber fifty-four years ago was recently pulled down and the rafters were found to be perfectly sound. It abounds in both the northern and southern districts. Height, 100 to 120 feet; diameter, 3 to 4 feet.

Red gum, *Eucalyptus rostrata*.—Timber strong, hard, heavy, close-grained, and durable, impervious to the white ant and cobra; used for ship-building, piles, flooring, railway sleepers, bridges, and wharves. It is one of the most valuable and best known of Australian hardwoods; plentifully distributed; favours river banks and rich flats subject to floods. Height, 100 to 150 feet; diameter, 3 to 5 feet.

Other valuable Eucalypts are—*E. botryoides*, "Bangalay," "Blue gum," &c.; *E. goniocalyx*, "Spotted gum"; *E. macrorrhyncha*, "Stringybark."

Hickory, *Myrtus acmenioides*.—Timber exceedingly strong, tough, and durable. Used for railway sleepers, posts, rails, and fuel. Fence-posts of this timber have kept perfectly sound in the ground for fifty years. It grows in open forest country but is not abundant.

There are a number of other timber trees, but the above are the most important.

About one-fourth of the area of this Colony, east of the dividing range and the main south coast range, is timbered with trees of fair quality, principally hardwood, but very difficult to reach as they are located in very rough country. On the timber reserves, scattered over this area, the natural trees are estimated to number from 6 to 120 per acre.

As before mentioned in no part of Australia are there forests of one kind of trees, as in America. New Zealand has extensive forests of kauri pine, but that Colony does not form a part of the great island Continent.

Appended hereto is a list of some of the best known timbers of this Colony, showing their transverse strength.

TABLE showing the proof transverse strength, modulus of rupture, and weight per cubic foot of New South Wales timber, computed from the results of experiments by Col. E. W. Ward and others.*

Name.	Proof strength.	Modulus of rupture.	Weight of a cubic foot.
			Lbs.
Red-flowering ironbark *Eucalyptus leucoxylon*	401	9,144	73
Grey ironbark *Eucalyptus crebra*	364	8,568	69
Box *Eucalyptus hemiphloia*	350	8,064	73
Green wattle *Acacia decurrens*	317	6,966	45
Red ironbark *Eucalyptus siderophloia*	313	6,858	72
Gray gum *Eucalyptus saligna*	308	7,560	62
Forest oak *Casuarina torulosa*	301	6,930	69
Bloodwood *Eucalyptus eximia*	294	6,930	53
Gray gum *Eucalyptus tereticornis*	285	6,300	71
Flooded gum *Eucalyptus rostrata*	276	6,174	59
Oak *Casuarina stricta*	273	6,048	53
Turpentine tree *Syncarpia laurifolia*	266	5,976	56
Stringybark *Eucalyptus capitellata*	266	5,958	55
Bastard box *Eucalyptus bicolor*	262	5,724	69
Yellow box *Eucalyptus melliodora*	259	5,796	66

* The timber in every case is supposed to by *dry*. Green timber is much weaker, having sometimes only half the strength of dry timber, especially against crushing.

The proof transverse strength is the weight in pounds avoirdupois which a bar of the timber one inch square, supported at two points one foot apart and loaded in the middle, is capable of sustaining without having its fibre and elasticity destroyed or impared in any way. The modulus of rupture is eighteen times the load required to break the bar.

Name.	Proof strength.	Modulus of rupture.	Weight of a cubic foot.
			Lbs.
Flindosa *Flindersia australis*	255	5,922	58
Pencil cedar *Dysoxylon Muellerii*	245	5,724	49
Blackbutt *Eucalyptus pilularis*	245	5,544	56
White gum *Eucalyptus albens*	238	5,040	62
Red mahogany *Eucalyptus resinifera*	238	6,300	70
Mountain ash *Eucalyptus virgata*	231	5,418	60
Woollybutt *Eucalyptus longifolia*	231	5,292	67
Marblewood *Olea paniculata*	231	5,220	63
Messmate *Eucalyptus amygdalina*	224	4,842	68
Light yellow wood *Flindersia Oxleyana*	217	5,346	50
Tea-tree *Melaleuca styphelioides*	217	4,842	66
Apple-tree *Angophora subvelutina*	215	4,446	56
White box *Tristania conferta*	210	4,788	61
Spotted gum *Eucalyptus hæmastoma*	196	5,418	67
Swamp oak *Casuarina suberosa*	196	4,662	52
White gum *Eucalyptus stellulata*	196	4,536	54
Moreton Bay pine *Araucaria Cunninghamii*	196	4,212	48
Native myrtle *Backhousia myrtifolia*	192	4,338	52
Brush cherry *Eugenia myrtifolia*	191	4,788	46
Peppermint *Eucalyptus piperita*	187	3,780	56
Hickory *Myrtus acmenioides*	182	4,914	42
White cypress *Frenela robusta v. verrucosa*	182	3,870	40
Colonial deal *Podocarpus elata*	178	3,960	36
Richmond pine *Frenela robusta v. microcarpa*	174	3,870	39
Sassafras *Doryphora sassafras*	171	3,834	35
Dark yellow-wood *Rhus rhodanthema*	168	3,054	49
Coachwood *Ceratopetalum apetalum*	168	3,744	39
Tea-tree *Callistemon salignus*	168	3,528	44
Red cedar *Cedrela Toona*	140	3,290	28
Silky oak *Grevillea robusta*	....	3,276	35
Beech *Gmelina Leichhardtii*	140	2,898	38
White cedar *Melia composita*	....	2,700	32

Mr. Harrie Wood, Under Secretary for Mines, states that :—A large number of indigenous timbers, collected by the forest rangers, have been supplied since July, 1886, to Professor Warren, of the Sydney University, who has conducted a series of exhaustive experiments with a view to test the strength, by direct compression, tensile resistance, and resistance to shearing, of some of our most useful timbers. The result of Professor Warren's labours, as set out in the annexed report, will no doubt prove of great value to engineers, architects, &c., beside making known the value for various purposes of the timbers tested.

"The strength and elasticity of New South Wales timbers of commercial value : by W. H. Warren, Whitworth Scholar; Member of the Institution of Civil Engineers, London; Professor of Engineering at the University of Sydney.

The following report on the timbers of New South Wales of commercial value has been written to accompany the timber exhibits in the New South Wales Courts at the Adelaide Jubilee Exhibition and the Melbourne Centennial Exhibition :—

The experiments have all been made in the Engineering Laboratory of the University of Sydney.

Although timber is being superseded in permanent works of construction by the use of iron and steel, there are many cases in which these materials are entirely unsuitable, and where timber is the only material which will answer the purpose. Moreover, where either material may be used, timber is generally the cheaper of the two. It appears, therefore, that timber will always be used to a considerable extent in works of construction. Timber in yielding gives more warning than iron, so that an accident can generally be foreseen and prevented. The chief objections to the use of timber in this Colony are its liability to decay from dry rot, and to the attacks of the white ant. Where timber is used in marine works it is liable to the attacks of the teredo. The durability of timber depends to a large extent upon the time when the tree was felled. If a tree be cut down when in full sap it is very probable that in twelve months time dry rot will be found to exist in it. Timber in this Colony is cut all the year round, consequently there is considerable uncertainty in the time which a timber structure may be supposed to last. The experiments described in the following pages have been in progress for the last fifteen months.

SCHEDULE OF TIMBER SENT BY MR. H. WOOD,

Local Name.	Mark.	No.	Date when tree was felled.	Date when tree was cut.	Height of tree.	Diameter of tree.	No. of rings.	Average height of trees in locality.
Tallow-wood	M	1	26-11-86	28-11-86	About 150 feet	About 33 inches	About 90	150 feet
Spotted gum	M	2	do	do	130 ,,	27 ,,	70	130 ,,
Blackbutt	M	3	do	do	150 ,,	30 ,,	80	150 ,,
Red gum	1, 2, 3 M	1, 2, 3	May, 1886	8-2-87	34 ,, to fork.	30 ,,	Not ascertained	80 to 90 ft.
Forest oak	A / A	1 / 0	10-4-87 / 5-5-87	2-5-87 / 5-5-87	74 feet / 62 ,,	15 ,, / 13 ,,	45 / 32	60 to 80 ft. / 50 to 70 ft.
Turpentine	A	2	18-4-87	3-5-87 (All from same tree.)	126 ,,	30 ,,	123	100 to 130 ft.
Flooded gum	A	3	do	do	134 ,,	48 ,,	50	130 to 160 ft.
Stringybark	A	4	19-4-87	do	110 ,,	30 ,,	50 feet	90 to 110 ft.
White ironbark	D	1	18-4-87	4-5-87	100 ,,	24 ,,	103	120 feet
Grey box	D	2	5-85	5-87	90 ,,	20 ,,	123	90 ,,
Pine	D	3	15-4-87	5-5-87	140 ,,	26 ,,	108	140 ,,
Forest mahogany*	D	4	2-87	do	140 ,,	36 ,,	110	110 ,,
Rosewood	D	5	16-4-87	do	70 ,,	15 ,,	100	100 ,,
White beech	D	6	2-5-87	4-5-87	80 ,,	18 ,,	120	120 ,,
Grey ironbark	B	1	10-10-86	11-1-87	90 ,,	30 ,,	130, 30" in diameter	50 to 100 ft.
Red ironbark	B	2	8-12-86	12-1-87	96 ,,	34 ,,	110, 28" in diameter	50 to 100 ft.
Spotted gum	B	3	6-86	22-1-87	100 ,,	28 ,,	80, 20" in diameter	70 to 120 ft.
Blackbutt	B	4	do	24-1-87	110 ,,	36 ,,	92, 30" in diameter	60 to 110 ft.
Woolybutt	B	5	do	do	110 ,,	36 ,,	86, 34" in diameter	80 to 150 ft.
Swamp mahogany	B	6	18-4-87	22-4-87	50 ,,		,,	80	50 to 70 ft.
Mountain ash	B	7	15-4-87	26-4-87	100 ,,	30 ,,	80	80 to 150 ft.
Blackwood	B	8	20-4-87	30-4-87	80 ,,	22 ,,	70	50 to 100 ft.
Blackbutt†	F	1	July or Aug., 1886.	11-5-87	150 ,,	36 ,,	120	120 to 130 ft.
Mahogany‡	F	2	do	14-5-87	120 ,,	33 ,,	110	100 to 120 ft.
Tallow-wood §	F	3	do	12-5-87	130 ,,	31 ,,	115	100 to 120 ft.
Grey gum ‖	F	4	do	20-4-87	150 ,,	33 ,,	90	140 to 150 ft.
Flooded gum ¶	F	5	do	13-5-87	110 ,,	29 ,,	95	110 to 120 ft.

* Those marked with 0, additional, felled some years ago.   † From an old tree decayed at heart 12 inches from the same tree.   § An old tree, 9 inches pipe. Fifteen specimens from the same tree.   ‖ Fairly matured there being no suitable timber left to make the third, 6 x 4, required. The timber having lain in the mill yard

NOTE.—The natural growth and blending of the annual rings into each other renders it impossible to arrive

FORESTS AND FOREST CULTURE.

UNDER SECRETARY FOR THE DEPARTMENT OF MINES.

Average diameter of trees in locality.	Locality whence obtained.	Formation and kind of soil.	Botanical name.
33 inches	Bullahdelah	Altered sedimentary formation; fair depth of soil; slopes and gullies.	Eucalyptus microcorys. F.v.M. Ord. Myrtaceæ.
27 „	do	Same formation; more open lowland soil; generally clayey.	Eucalyptus maculata. Hk. Ord. Myrtaceæ.
30 „	do	Same formation; tops and sides of stoney ridges.	Eucalyptus microcorys. F.v.M. Ord. Myrtaceæ.
30 to 42 in.	Moira State Forest, county of Cadell.	Alluvial; subject to annual inundation; clay, loam.	Eucalyptus rostrata. Schl. Ord. Myrtaceæ.
11 to 13 „ 15 to 20 „		Undulating; sub-soil of yellow clay	Casuarina torulosa. Ait. Ord. Casuarineæ.
18 to 30 „	Cowarra Reserve, parish of Queen's Lake, A. O. Lauriton, county of Macquarie.	Undulating; sub-soil clayey	Syncarpia laurifolia. Jen. Ord. Myrtaceæ.
36 to 48 „		Level; moist and swampy scrub	Eucalyptus saligna. Sm. Ord. Myrtaceæ.
18 to 30 „		Ridges; red soil	Eucalyptus piperita var. Sm. Ord. Myrtaceæ.
24 inches	South Grafton forest ridges.	Ironstone; poor soil, clay sub-soil	Eucalyptus crebra. F.v.M. Ord. Myrtaceæ.
20 „	do	do do	Eucalyptus polyanthema. Schau. Ord. Myrtaceæ.
26 „	West Camp, Nymboida.	Trap; scrub soil	Araucaria Cunninghamii. Ait. Ord. Coniferæ.
36 „	North Arm, Clarence River.	Forest ridges; red soil	Eucalyptus resinifera. Sm. Ord. Myrtaceæ.
24 „	West Camp, Nymboida River.	Trap; scrub soil	Dysoxylum Fraserianum. Benth. Ord. Meliaceæ.
20 „	Alumny Creek Reserve, 200.	Sandstone; alluvial	Not true white beech (Gmelina Leichhardtii); genus and species not identified.
24 to 36 in.	Parish of Benandra, county of St. Vincent.	Slate stony ridges; poor	Eucalyptus crebra. F.v.M. Ord. Myrtaceæ.
24 to 30 „	do	do do	Eucalyptus leucoxylon. F.v.M. Ord. Myrtaceæ.
24 to 48 „	do	Slate formation; poor soil	Eucalyptus maculata. Hk. Ord. Myrtaceæ.
24 to 48 „	do	Quartz and slate; poor soil	Eucalyptus pilularis. Sm. Ord. Myrtaceæ.
24 to 48 „	do	Alluvial; fairly good soil	Eucalyptus sp.? (It is not thought that this is true woolybutt.)
24 to 30 „	Moruya, county of St. Vincent.	Alluvial; and swampy sour soil	Eucalyptus robusta. Sm. Ord. Myrtaceæ.
24 to 48 „	Parish of Monga, county of St. Vincent.	Granite; stony soil	Eucalyptus virgata. Sieb. Ord. Myrtaceæ.
18 to 30 „	Basaltic, stony, porous soil.	do	Acacia melanoxylon, R. Br. Ord. Leguminosæ.
48 inches	Parish of Tanban, county of Dudley.	Clayey soil; decomposed granite formation.	Eucalyptus pilularis. Sm. Ord. Myrtaceæ.
30 „	do	do do	Eucalyptus resinifera. Sm. Ord. Myrtaceæ.
30 to 36 in.	do	do do	Eucalyptus microcorys. F.v.M. Ord. Myrtaceæ.
30 to 96 „	do	Alluvial soil; flooded land	Eucalyptus tereticornis? Sm.
30 inches	do	Clayey soil; decomposed granite formation.	Eucalyptus saligna. Sm. Ord. Myrtaceæ.

pipe. Fifteen specimens, as per size, from the same tree. ‡ An old tree, 6 inches pipe. Fifteen specimens tree, sound, no pipe. Fifteen specimens from same tree. One of these specimens, 5 × 3, is under the size given, exposed since January will account for the numerous sun cracks. ¶ Fully matured tree, 4 inches pipe. at a correct estimate of the number on a rough surface, although this may be done on a polished surface.

In order that the results of the testing should be as valuable as possible for the purposes of comparison, the author decided that the following numbers and sizes of specimens should be used for each kind of timber tested:—

Tension—	2 pieces,	3' 0"	long	x	$2\frac{1}{4}''$	x	$2\frac{1}{4}''$	
Compression—	2	„	6' 0"	„	x	3"	x	3"
	2	„	4' 0"	„	x	3"	x	3"
	2	„	2' 0"	„	x	3"	x	3"
	2	„	1' 0"	„	x	3"	x	3"
Cross breaking—	3	„	4' 6"	„	x	6"	x	4"
Shearing—	2	„	3' 0"	„	x	$2\frac{1}{4}''$	x	$2\frac{1}{4}''$

for cutting up into blocks 6" long, for testing along and at right angles to the grain.

A letter was written by Mr. Warren to the Hon. F. Abigail, Secretary for Mines, requesting that the officers of the Mines Department be instructed to arrange for the collection and naming of specimens of New South Wales timbers, in accordance with the foregoing list of particulars. The request was complied with, and the schedule of particulars given in the preceding table was supplied by Mr. H. Wood, the Under-Secretary for Mines.

The specimens of timber collected by the Department of Mines, were sent to the Government works, Redfern, where they were prepared for testing.

The specimens intended for testing in tension were turned in a lathe.

The specimens for testing in compression were planed square on the four sides and ends. The specimens for testing as beams were planed square on the four sides only. The blocks for shearing along and at right angles to the grain were prepared in the University, and fitted into special apparatus devised for testing them.

An autographic stress-strain apparatus was devised and used for recording the results of the tests in compression and cross-breaking, but was not used in tension.

Description of the Autographic Stress-strain Apparatus used in testing timber.

The apparatus used in drawing stress-strain diagrams consists of a frame, which is rectangular in plan, and which is attached to the cross-head of the testing machine. There are two steel axis fixed to the end plates of frame by means of locknuts. One axis carries a brass drum 12 inches long x 5 inches in diameter; the other axis carries a pulley fixed upon or cast with a brass pipe. A spiral grove is cut upon the pipe, $\frac{1}{4}$ of an inch pitch; and there is also a spiral grove cut upon the drum, which is 2 inches pitch. The two spirals are connected by means of a piece of strong catgut, so that for ten revolutions of the spiral, the drum makes one revolution. The pulley is made to revolve by means of a steel pianoforte-wire attached to the rider from which the poise weight is suspended, and is led round a guide pulley, and makes a complete revolution round a pulley, passing upwards over guide pulleys fixed to ceiling, and terminating in a weight of 14lb. There is a strong clock spring inside the drum, so fixed that the revolution of the drum produced by winding the poise weight along the steel-yard is made to coil up the spring, and by winding the poise weights in the reverse direction the spring uncoils and brings back the drum to its original position. Thus the drum is made to revolve through an angle which is proportional to the distance to which the poise weight has been wound, and therefore proportional to the load on the specimen.

The deflection or compression, as the case may be, is transmitted and recorded upon the revolving drum in the following manner:—A steel rod, square for a portion of its length, slides freely in bearings provided in the end plates of frames, and also at the extremity of an overhanging bracket; the rod carries a slotted link in which slides a small roller which is pressed against the sides of the link by the movement of a lever. There is also a weighted pencil which can be adjusted and fixed to any portion of the square rod between the end plates of frame. The lever is provided with knife edges which are pressed by the forked end of the screwed rod as the specimen yields. The rod slides or is fixed in a bearing which is attached to the test specimen.

In the compression tests the screwed rod is attached by means of a union screw to a steel rod which is connected at its other end with the fixed compression block of the testing machine. The lengths of the rods are arranged according to the length of the specimen tested. Both in cross-breaking or compression the yielding of the specimen is transmitted to the knife edges of the lever as a simple harmonic motion which is reproduced multiplied ten times on the sliding rod carrying the pencil in the manner already referred to.

A piece of sectional paper is wrapped round the drum and clipped, upon which the diagram or diagrams are drawn in the following manner:—The pencil is adjusted to the datum point on the paper by means of the adjusting screw and the adjustable connection of the steel wire with poise weight. The force pump is then worked until the load upon the specimens is sufficient to raise the steel-yard and the poise weight suspended from it, which causes the specimen to yield and the pencil to draw a line parallel with the axis of the drum. The pumping is continued and the poise weight wound along the steel-yard keeping it floating in a horizontal position, and balancing the load upon the specimen.

A diagram is thus drawn, the ordinate of which shows the deflection or compression, and the abscissa the load producing it. The diagram starts with a deflection produced by 2,500lb. in the transverse tests, and at 10,000lb. in the compression tests. The diagram is completed after the paper is taken off the drum, so that it reads from zero both for load and deflection. The effect of the tension on the wire on the poise weight of steel-yard is eliminated by means of guide pulleys, which are so arranged that the moment of the tension on the wire about the fulcrum of the steel-yard is always zero.

The autographic stress-strain apparatus above described was designed by Mr. J. A. M'Donald, A.M.I.C.E., and M.I.M.E., and Professor Warren, and it was made in his laboratory.

Transverse strength and elasticity.

The transverse strength and elasticity were determined in the following manner:—

The beam was fixed in the machine and connected with the autographic stress-strain apparatus. The supports were 48 inches apart, and the load was applied in the centre. The apparatus was first carefully adjusted so that the slightest yielding of the specimen was accurately marked by the pencil on the sectional paper covering the drum, and the beam was first fixed by means of the hand-wheel and screw, which generally produced a slight deflection which was recorded by the pencil moving in a straight line.

The hand-pump was then worked until the load on the specimen was sufficient to raise the steel-yard with 250lb. resting on the figure 10, which showed that the load on the specimen was 2,500lb., the pencil still moving in a straight line parallel to the axis of the drum records the multiplied deflection due to the load. The load is then increased by pumping and balanced by the poise weight in the manner before referred to, and the diagram thus drawn shows the behaviour of the specimen from 2,500lb. to the breaking load. The remainder of the diagram is completed in the manner before described. The yielding of the specimen, however, causes a slight rotation of the drum independently of the winding of the poise weight, which at the breaking load would have caused considerable error only this point is read off the steel-yard and recorded independently of the diagram. The deflection of the specimen within the point where the deflection ceases to be proportional to the load producing it is accurately determined by writing on the diagram the loads called out by the assistant minding the poise weight; but in all these experiments the velocity rates of the apparatus was so adjusted that the loads and corresponding deflections within the limit of elasticity were recorded on the diagram for average specimens, and the difference between this average and the maximum or minimum deflection did not produce an error exceeding 20lb. over or under the true load. The modulus of elasticity was always calculated from the load and corresponding deflection within one-third of the breaking weight, so that an error of 20lb. in recording the load would not produce any appreciable error in the modulus. There is no difficulty in eliminating this error, but it was not considered necessary under the circumstances.

The modulus of rupture is calculated from the formula—

$$f = \frac{3 \, W l}{2 b \, d^2}$$

Where W = Breaking loads in lb.
  l = Span in inches.
  b = Breadth in inches, and
  d = Depth in inches.

The modulus of elasticity is calculated from the formula—

$$E = \frac{Wl^3}{4vb\,d^3}$$

Where W = Breaking load.
  l = Span in inches.
  v = Deflection in inches.
  b = Breadth in inches.
  d = Depth in inches.

l, b, d are measured accurately before the experiment.
W and v are each taken from the diagram.

Compressive strength and elasticity.

The experiments on the compressive strength and elasticity were made on specimens of the following dimensions :—

$$\left.\begin{array}{l}1'\ 0''\\2'\ 0''\\4'\ 0''\\6'\ 0''\end{array}\right\} \times 3'' \times 3''$$

The diagram-drawing apparatus was connected and the length of the rod was varied with the length of the specimen tested. The diagram of load and corresponding compression was drawn in a similar manner to to that described for the specimens tested transversely; the errors, however, which were referred to are much smaller, and may be entirely neglected.

The breaking load is read off the steel-yard, which is divided by the sectional area of the specimen, in order to find the load per square inch.

The modulus of elasticity is calculated from the formula—

$$E = \frac{W L}{K l}$$

Where W = Load producing compression l.
  L = Length of specimen.
  K = Sectional area.

If the curve of compression (as drawn by the autographic stress-strain apparatus) is a straight line, the modulus is calculated from W and l measured off the diagram anywhere in this straight line; if the curve is irregular, the modulus is calculated for W and l at about quarter the breaking load. L is measured before the experiment at the same time as b and d, from which k is calculated thus, K = $b\,d$.

Tensile strength and elasticity.

The tensile strengths and elasticities were determined by fixing the turned specimens in the machine. The autographic apparatus was not used for these tests, but the extensions were marked with steel trammels 10 inches long, and read off with a steel rule divided into hundredths with the aid of a glass.

The diameters of the specimens were carefully measured with vernier callipers.

The breaking load divided by the area in square inches gives the tensile strength per square inch.

The modulus of tensile elasticity was calculated from the formula—

$$E = \frac{WL}{Kl}$$

W and l were taken within $\frac{1}{4}$ of the breaking weight.

The results obtained for tensile elasticity are given as rough approximation, as the method adopted for measuring the elongations can hardly be considered accurate enough for determining the modulus.

Shearing strength.

The shearing strength of the various timbers along the grain was determined by cutting specimens of about 6 inches x 4 inches x 2 inches, and fitting them into the apparatus. With regard to the shearing resistance of timber in a plane at right angles to the lengths of the fibres, the author experimented with a number of specimens, and found that in every case the fracture took place with the grain. It can be proved that wherever there is a tendency to shear in a certain plane, there is an equal tendency to shear in a plane at right angles to it. Hence, in the specimens of timber, although the apparatus was arranged to develop shearing stress in a plane at right angles to the direction of the fibres, there was at the same time developed an equal shearing stress in the plane of the fibres, and since the resistance of the fibres to shear with the grain is less than across the grain, it follows that it is impossible for the timber to shear in any other way than along the grain.

Weight of timber per cubic foot.

The weights of the various timbers per cubic foot were ascertained by weighing each set of three specimens of the timber before testing them for transverse strength, and dividing this weight by the numbers of cubic feet contained in the three pieces.

In this way the column in table has been obtained. The specific gravities of five kinds of timber were determined by Mr. A. Helms, M.A., Ph.D. (Berlin), demonstrator in chemistry at the University of Sydney, in the following manner :—The specimens were prepared as 1-inch cubes, and were kept five days in open air at a temperature of from 15 to 19 degrees C ; they were then dried three hours in a water bath at a temperature of 96 degrees C, varnished and dried one hour in a water bath and kept again three days in the open air at from 15 degrees to 19 degrees C. The specific gravity was taken in each case at a temperature of 17 degrees C. The results are given in the following table :—

Name of Timber.	Weight in air.	Weight in water.	Difference.	Specific gravity.
Grey ironbark	20·0610	3·0714	16·9896	1·1807
Red ironbark	20·0510	2·6620	17·3890	1·1531
Spotted gum	15·1715	1·6790	16·8505	0·9903
Blackbutt	16·0265	0·1410	16·1675	0·9912
Woolybutt	15·7605	0·5200	16·2805	0·9680

The weights per cubic foot have been deduced from the results given in the above, and compared with the results obtained by direct weighing and measuring in the following table :—

Name of Timber.	Weight per cubic foot deduced from experiments made by Dr. Helms, in lb.	Weight per cubic foot, obtained by direct measuring and weighing, in lb.
Gray ironbark	73·79375	73·854
Red ironbark	72·06870	76·522
Spotted gum	56·2687	62·195
Blackbutt	61·9500	65·539
Woolybutt	60·5000	63·895

Both Dr. Helms and Professor Warren consider that the results obtained by direct weighing and measuring are at least as satisfactory as those obtained from the specific gravities, as the want of delicacy in the former method is compensated for by the fact that a better average of the timber is obtained from the large scantlings than from the 1-inch cubical specimens ; and it was, therefore, not considered necessary to find the specific gravity of the remaining specimens. The results are recorded in the summary of tests."

SUMMARY of the Results of Testing New South Wales' Timbers, giving the average values for each kind of Timber.

Local Name.	Number and Letter.	Weight per cubic foot in lb.	Tension Tests. Breaking stress in lb. per square inch.	Tension Tests. Modulus of elasticity in lb. per square in.	Compression Tests. Ratio of length of Column to smallest dimensions. 24 to 1 Breaking stress in lb. per square in.	24 to 1 Modulus of elasticity in lb. per square in.	16 to 1 Modulus of elasticity in lb. per square in.	16 to 1 Breaking stress in lb. per square in.	8 to 1 Modulus of elasticity in lb. per square in.	8 to 1 Breaking stress in lb. per square in.	4 to 1 Modulus of elasticity in lb. per square in.	4 to 1 Breaking stress in lb. per square in.	Bending Tests. Modulus of rupture in lb. per square in.	Bending Tests. Modulus of elasticity in lb. per square in.	Shearing Tests. Breaking stress in lb. per square in. along the grain.
Tallow-wood	F 3	77·06	16,165	2,974,790	6,943	2,222,286	7,721	2,163,360	6,573	1,618,803	7,585	1,663,391	15,257	2,257,732	1,802
Spotted gum	B 3	62·19	14,413	4,383,483	5,499	2,795,579	6,436	2,927,980	6,561	2,028,048	6,753	1,820,432	13,296	2,056,101	1,585
Blackbutt	B 4, F 1	66·69	21,708	3,105,979	6,572	2,343,485	7,736	2,649,063	7,526	1,775,249	7,522	1,734,698	13,728	2,162,761	1,757
Swamp mahogany	B 6	75·98	16,520		5,263	2,524,987	6,113	2,559,386	6,569	1,796,229	6,846	2,491,505	12,124	2,098,701	1,166
Grey ironbark	B 1	73·85	25,080	5,526,400	8,112	3,071,679	9,482	3,354,256	9,112	3,503,090	10,165	1,879,734	17,866	2,484,799	2,187
Red ironbark	b 1	76·52	19,609		7,701	2,770,985	8,760	3,254,172	9,403	1,770,556	9,281	1,612,511	16,275	2,341,802	2,012
White ironbark	D 1	73·55	9,861		6,923	2,450,460	8,103	2,747,581	8,225	1,938,865	8,680	1,314,657	16,932	2,734,020	1,974
Woolybutt	B 5	63·89	19,968	4,495,296	5,542	2,605,892	6,121	2,303,768	7,074	1,325,315	6,951	581,401	12,708	2,140,443	1,729
Red gum	3 M	62·19	8,884	1,292,631	3,370	987,361	4,655	1,498,591	4,651	1,381,447	5,916	6,930	13,492	761,769	2,122
Grey gum	F 4	57·33	20,821	5,010,372	6,492	2,308,678	7,006	2,035,821	7,452	1,753,612	7,243	1,780,029	13,492	2,146,733	1,503
Flooded gum	F 5	77·94	14,887	3,761,988	7,494	2,483,221	8,889	2,129,153	8,700	2,053,027	8,761	1,779,584	17,622	2,341,430	1,976
Mountain ash	A 3	69·34	16,932	2,507,363	7,566	1,864,580	7,786	1,837,792	5,965	2,311,473	5,889	1,333,385	12,025	1,943,328	1,539
Blackwood	B 7	68·57	18,974	2,902,000	5,197	1,962,851	4,903	1,575,852	6,324	1,580,076	5,761	1,359,651	11,527	2,054,227	1,812
Grey box	B 8	70·58	14,883	2,104,400	6,189	1,814,563	7,006	1,929,960	7,100	1,791,961	6,784	1,580,199	10,264	1,908,432	2,033
Pine	B 2	73·62	22,415	2,547,100	7,210	2,606,817	8,031	2,594,558	8,535	2,344,415	8,021	1,753,462	16,209	2,766,485	1,791
	D 3	54·31	15,901	3,263,000	4,448	1,922,626			4,530	1,258,870	4,199	1,181,619	8,823	2,408,367	1,222
Forest mahogany	P 4	72·23	14,115	2,315,400	5,106	2,025,073	6,329	2,095,276	5,386	1,124,000	7,967	1,879,257	13,769	3,010,883	1,607
Rose wood	D 5	74·29	13,578	2,984,750	5,271	1,965,086	5,593	1,773,963	5,371	1,202,261	6,011	1,141,837	10,594	1,937,474	1,722
White leech	D 6	62·03	9,954	2,791,750	4,689	2,072,272	6,528	1,736,143	7,241	1,458,828	8,253	1,229,278	15,607	2,421,119	2,056
Mahogany	F 2	75·06	19,753	3,741,376	7,629	2,451,424	7,902	2,138,100	9,061	2,059,898	7,514	1,588,160	14,500	2,258,372	2,109
Forest oak	A 0, A 1	75·48	17,107, 13,245	4,470,909, 2,207,505	7,270	2,117,461	8,475	2,187,550	8,139	1,742,492	8,325	2,126,210	15,492	2,396,263	1,388
Turpentine	A 2	69·34	16,821	4,077,377	4,917	1,813,631	5,882	1,675,250	5,810	1,382,621	6,364	1,544,477	11,727	1,965,524	1,451
Stringy bark	A 4	71·33	19,399	2,761,812	5,685	2,128,870	5,365	1,810,923	6,575	1,790,161	5,985	1,234,109	13,931	2,353,044	1,942
Australian teak	F 6	62·9			5,648	2,206,857	5,574	2,210,227	6,502	1,883,243	7,030	1,735,887	14,415	2,174,875	1,397

There is a forest conservancy bureau in Sydney attached to the Department of Lands. It has control of all timber-cutting and planting. The field staff consists of 1 inspector, 28 forest rangers, and 10 assistants. It is the duty of the rangers to prevent, as far as practicable, the wasteful cutting of timber below a fixed girth on timber reserves. The Department of Lands has the power to create or revoke timber reserves. Permission to ring-bark timber on Crown lands is granted by the local boards, and under such conditions as may appear advisable. Reports in regard to these matters are made by the rangers.

In an official report it is stated that the cost of a large proportion of the work which it is found convenient should be performed by the Forest Department cannot properly be considered as a charge against the timber revenue, and that the falling off in the revenue in 1885 and 1886 is partly attributed to the lessened demand for New South Wales timber in the Colony of Victoria, and partly to the drought, and to the suspension of public works, the timber for which being usually drawn from the Government reserves. The forest revenue consists principally in the receipts from the reserves subject to royalty and licenses for cutting and ring-barking timber.

The following table shows the revenue and expenditure of the Forest Department for each year from 1877 :—

Year.	Revenue.				Expenditure.	
	Forest Conservancy.		Forest Conservancy and Quarry Licenses.			
	£	s	£	s	£	s
1877			4,325	21,043	4,579	22,284
1878	......	......	5,935	28,883	5,593	27,218
1879	7,310	35,574	7,946	38,670	5,920	28,809
1880	8,328	40,528	8,990	43,750	6,636	32,294
1881	10,156	49,424	10,813	52,621	7,093	34,518
1882	12,327	59,989	13,047	63,493	12,592	61,279
1883	16,001	77,869	16,686	81,202	15,389	74,890
1884	17,565	85,480	18,250	88,814	17,481	85,071
1885	13,144	63,963	13,863	67,464	18,146	88,303
1886	13,935	67,810	14,607	71,085	17,933	87,271

The Forest Department has also charge of the Government operations in the way of forest planting.

The forest rangers have extensive districts assigned to them, and their duties, on that account, are difficult to perform.

An acting ranger has been appointed at Lord Howe's Island, an island belonging to New South Wales, situated about 900 miles from Sydney. There are also several rangers and assistants in the far west. Most of the forest officers are men of large and varied experience, and evince a thorough knowledge of the work they have in hand, whilst some of them possess no little scientific knowledge, although previous to appointment it is not necessary for them to undergo a course of training like that required of those in charge of the large forest estates in Europe and India.

The work of replanting forest trees has not been carried on to any great extent in New South Wales. Indeed, in the year 1886, out of an expenditure of £17,933 ($87,271) by the Forest Department, only £645 17s. ($3,222) was incurred on account of planting.

The experience of the Department in tree planting has mainly been confined to strips of country along the railway lines. The trees chosen for the purpose are usually the wattle (acacia), with a sprinkling of pine and cedar, but such as have been planted are scattered at irregular distances along the routes. The expenses incurred in planting them in this extended fashion, together with their liability to injury, compelled the Department to discontinue the planting, except in particularly favourable localities. In addition to the operations of the Forest Department, the director of the Botanical Gardens, of Sydney, has a tree nursery under his charge at Campbelltown, 34 miles from Sydney. This nursery is used principally for the growth of trees and shrubs to adorn the government reserves, parks, gardens, and grounds, attached to the public buildings. Great care is taken in this nursery to propagate the most useful and ornamental indigenous trees of the Colony, such as the myall, boree, black wattle, green wattle, the waratah, together with various palms, cedars, and figs.

Amongst the indigenous trees to which attention is paid, is the Christmas tree, so called on account of its being so generally used for decorating purposes during the Christmas season. Properly speaking, it is more of a bush than a tree, but it sometimes attains the height of 40 feet and a diameter of 15 inches. In the month of November it is covered with a mass of beautiful white flowers, but towards Christmas the calyces, which are very persistent, change to a bright red colour, or to red mixed with white, which gives the plant quite a different appearance.

Much attention is also given to the cultivation of various kinds of fig-trees, for shade, in the neighbourhood of Sydney and in other parts of the Colony. The two principal species used for this purpose are the long-leaved or Moreton Bay fig *Ficus macrophylla*, and the small-leaved or Illawarra fig *Ficus microphylla*. They frequent the eastern slope. One of the finest species was named by Baron Müller *Ficus columnaris*, and it is said to attain greater perfection in Lord Howe's Island than elsewhere. It originates in the fork of some tree, which it destroys by sending forth strong limbs, from which rope-like shoots descend until they reach the ground, where they take root and enlarge into stems and become the centres from which other stems stretch forth.

The roots of this tree increase so rapidly and at the same time send out such gigantic branches that it is no uncommon thing to see the original tree at a height of 70 or 80 feet peeping through the fig, as if itself were the parasite on the real intruder. Within the angles or walls of the tree there is said to be room enough for a good-sized party to dine comfortably. The rich undergrowth of palms and ferns which find shelter beneath its fantastical branches add greatly to the weird and varied attractions of these trees.

The Forest Department assists the public in regard to tree planting, and when practicable, without interfering with private enterprise, seeds and plants are furnished free of charge, together with much useful information and instructions as to mode of culture. As there is no department of agriculture in the Colony the Forest Branch has to deal with noxious weeds and many other matters which concern more properly an agricultural bureau.

There are no schools of forestry in New South Wales, nor is there provision for the systematic study of the science of forestry. The establishment of model farms in the Colony where the science of forestry can be taught among other branches of practical and scientific farming is much required.

The forests of New South Wales and of other portions of Australia are destroyed in various ways, but principally by ring-barking. This process consists in simply cutting a ring about 6 inches wide round the tree with an axe or tomahawk. The time chosen for this process is in the autumn, when the sap has matured. The destruction of forests in this way has become so great as to seriously attract the attention of the Government. It appears to have begun about thirty years ago in the watershed of the Hunter River, but it did not become general until the inauguration of the system of free selection, by which certain tracts of land were opened up to *bonâ fide* settlers (or to persons who had erected homesteads) at low prices. The free selectors usually chose heavily timbered districts, and the wholesale destruction of forests began. Ring-barking was thought to be the best means for clearing land, not only for small farms but for grazing purposes. According to a paper on this subject, prepared by Mr. W. E. Abbott, for the Royal Geographical Society of New South Wales, the objections urged against this method were that the creeks and rivers would dry up owing to the increased evaporation, and that the rainfall would be reduced by the removal of the large condensing surface offered by the winds when heavily laden with moisture.

Mr. Abbott gave some practical illustrations resulting from his experience. In 1869 and 1870 he ring-barked the greater part of the watershed of two creeks, and the whole of the watershed of a third, being about two miles, and draining a well defined valley shut in by high ridges of basalt. He noticed, as soon as the timber was dead, that one of the creeks assumed the character of a permanent stream, and that the others were very greatly improved. In 1878 all three became permanent streams, and have continued such ever since. Previous to the ring-barking they were dried up during a portion of the year. Mr. Abbott does not think that the destruction of forests will reduce rainfall, but he argues that when there is a large and regular rainfall there is sure to be a heavy forest growth, and that the forest is the result of the rainfall, and not the rainfall of the forest. Mr. Abbott attributed the increased flow of water on his land, first, to the fact that the roots of the trees decaying acted as a sort of subsoil drainage, leading the water down into the subsoil and afterwards allowing it to drain off slowly into the watercourses; second, that a large proportion of the rainfall which was formerly taken up by the roots of the growing trees and evaporated from the leaves was enabled to find its way to the creeks and rivers. Mr. Abbott says: "The fact that the Eucalyptus, so common throughout Australia, is perhaps the most vigorous growing tree known, and that it is used successfully in other parts of the world to dry up swampy land, would seem to support this explanation."

Australian forests are also destroyed by bush fires and natural causes. If the drought lasts long enough, there can be no doubt about its destructive agency, but there are often more effective agents for the destruction of forests than the drought, for during the driest seasons ever known in the Colonies many trees were not affected at all. The injury done to the forests by bush fires is also very much exaggerated. These fires are of course more common during dry seasons than at other times. In the great conflagrations that took place in 1863 and 1865 it seemed that vast tracts of forest country had been fatally injured. The leaves assumed a sickly colour, but the trees, except in a few instances, after two or three years showed marked signs of recovery from the scorching they had received, and large numbers of shoots sprang up from their trunks.

The greatest bush fires ever known in Australia occurred on Thursday, the 6th of February, 1851, called Black Thursday. On that day the thermometer rose in Victoria to 118 degrees in the shade. The northern winds were charged with fearful heat. Vasts forests were in flames. There had been no rain for a considerable period, and fires seemed to break out everywhere. Stations, farm-houses, sheep, cattle, and even human beings were consumed. The wind was so hot that it seemed to bear death upon its wings. A gentleman who reached Melbourne at that time stated that a chain of fire ran on both sides of him even to the margin of the road for a distance of over 50 miles. Like the floods of 1849 the disaster was looked upon as a visitation of Providence.

About thirty years ago vast tracts of forest country were apparently destroyed by fire in New South Wales. The fire seemed to extend in a series of columns from Sydney to Parramatta, a distance of 15 miles. After a period of seven years scarcely a trace of the conflagration was left.

In what are known as bush forests, where the trees are characterized by luxuriance and denseness of growth, fires seldom occur. The bush forests are usually found on the east side of the great dividing range or mountain slopes, where the soil consists of decomposed rocks, or on rich alluvial lands along the courses of rivers. The atmosphere in these forests even during the heat of summer is charged with moisture.

Among the trees common to these forests may be mentioned the cedar, rosewood, pine, tulip-wood, silky oak, white maple, yellow-wood, native laurel, colonial deal, brush cherry, the myrtle, hickory, native tamarind, and othes.

Bush fires occur more frequently among what are called open forests. These forests are composed principally of trees belonging to the eucalypti.

The forests of Australia are occasionally injured by vast multitudes of caterpillars. These insects grow in New South Wales to an extraordinary size, and move in perfect masses, making parallel roads as they eat their way round the trees, destroying both the bark and sap wood.

The chief natural cause, however, of the destruction of forests in Australia is said to be the ravages of the opossum. According to a paper read before the Royal Geographical Society of New South Wales in August, 1885, by Mr. Peter Macpherson, the opossums appear in sufficient numbers to lay waste considerable tracts of timbered country. Mr. Macpherson had been a close observer of the forests for many years. He gave much study and time to the habits of the opossum. He noticed that numbers of these animals flock to the gum trees growing near the waterholes, especially in time of drought. In order to test fully their destructive powers, he captured a few opossums and put them on the trees in his garden. He noticed that a single opossum would eat more than two hundred leaves in one night.

The animals showed great liking for the young sappy leaves of the gum tree, and when very hungry were not averse to cherry leaves, light wood and honeysuckle. They would not touch the tough, leathery leaves of the old gum trees when the young ones were in reach. It was urged against the theory of the destructive powers of the opossum that on account of their heavy weight they could not climb up the slender branches of trees to eat the leaves, but Mr. Macpherson noticed that the large opossums would eat the bark and leaves within their reach, and that the young ones would go out on the branches, and using their fore feet as hands, would bend the branches down towards them and nibble off the leaves. The trees thus destroyed by the opossum assumed a spectral naked appearance, whilst those destroyed by caterpillars and other insects were nothing like so bare, the leaves in the latter case being eaten off in a very irregular and uneven manner. The insects would bite the leaf at the edges and again in the middle, and sometimes in both ways.

Mr. Russell, the government astronomer, in commenting on Mr. Macpherson's paper, said it should be remembered that large patches of forests die off, while all around them there was the usual healthy vegetation. Professor Liversedge, of the Sydney University, is of opinion that the decay of the gum trees in many cases is due to the exhaustion of the soil, although the same soil might support a flourishing growth of other forest trees, and that to obtain the best growth of trees it is necessary to have a rotation, as in farming.

The question of reclamation of sand dunes or waste places by tree planting has not been a pressing one in New South Wales, on account of the sparsely settled condition of the country. With the exception of the work on government reserves, and along the railways, very little has been done in the way of reclaiming waste places, unless, indeed, the reclamation of the sand drifts at Newcastle. The plan adopted at Newcastle consists in the erection of brush or close paling fences running parallel with each other, about 1 or 2 chains apart, from the base to the top of the sand drift, to shelter the trees, and prevent the shifting of the sand by the wind.

The following indigenous trees are for planting in sand dunes or waste places:—

Acacia armata (sometimes called the "Kangaroo thorn"), a small bushy tree with angular branches; leaves reduced to phyllodia; found in the Blue Mountains and in the New England districts. The timber is light and tough, but too small to be of use. The bushes make very good hedges.

Frenela verrucosa.—This tree is valuable not only for its properties for binding coast and desert sands, but for its strong, durable, and easily-wrought timber.

Casuarina.—Most of the species of this genus will grow in exceedingly sandy soil—for instance, the oak, swamp oak, forest oak, dwarf oak, river oak. The latter is sometimes called forest oak; scientific name, *Casuarina torulosa*. It frequents open forests from Illawarra to Richmond River, and westward to Bathurst and New England. The timber is very beautiful, remarkably heavy and strong; used for cabinet work and shingles.

The following list of plants recommended for reclaiming sand dunes, is taken from Mr. J. H. Maiden's new work entitled, "The useful plants of Australia."

Agrostis.	Festuca.	Poa.
Carex.	Imperata.	Rhagodia.
Cynodon.	Lepidosperma.	Spinifex.
Ehrarta.	Mesembryanthemum.	Stipa.
Elymus.	Panicum.	

The government plantations of Catalpa have been successful in various parts of the Colony, especially at Cootamundra and East Maitland.

The following is a list of trees planted at these latter places since 1882:—

At East Maitland.

221 *Catalpa speciosa*. | 221 *Juglans nigra* (black walnut).

At Cootamundra.

613 *Catalpa speciosa*.
121 *Juglans nigra* (black walnut).
61 *Syncarpia laurifolia* (turpentine).
94 *Eucalyptus* (various species).
29 *Grevillea robusta* (silky oak).
225 *Sterculia diversifolia* (kurrajong).
3 *Melaleuca leucodendron* (tea tree).
25 *Tristania conferta* (brush box).
83 *Pinus insignis* (Californian pine).

5 *Eugenia Ventenatii* (water gum).
18 *Quercus ilex* (evergreen oak).
51 *Fraxinus Americana* (American ash tree).
37 *Quercus virens* (evergreen oak).
35 *Laurus camphora* (camphor tree).
24 *Araucaria Cunninghamii* (pine tree).
8 *Olea Europœa* (olive tree).

The Inspector of Forests recommends the following trees and shrubs for planting on swampy land or land subject to inundations.

Blue gum *(Eucalyptus globulus)*.
Red gum *(Eucalyptus rostrata)*.
Flooded gum *(Eucalyptus saligna)*
Swamp oak *(Casuarina suberosa)*.
Scrub she-oak *(Casuarina Cunninghamiana)*.
Moreton Bay Chesnut *(Castanospermum Australe)*.
Brush box *(Tristania conferta)*.
Swamp mahogany *(Eucalyptus robusta)*.
Blue gum *(Eucalyptus botryoides)*.
Blackwood *(Acacia melanoxylon)*.
Turpentine tree *(Syncarpia laurifolia)*.
Alder *(Alnus glutinosa)*.
Bamboo *(Bambusa arundinacea)*.

Weeping willow *(Salix babylonica)*.
Golden osier *(Salix aurea)*.
Huntington willow *(Salix Russelliana)*.
Pampas grass *(Gynerium argenteum)*.
Supple-jack *(Flagellaria indica)*.
New Zealand flax *(Phormium tenax)*.
Cabbage-tree palm *(Corypha Australis)*.
Bangalo palm *(Seaforthia elegans)*.
Red cedar *(Cedrela Australis)*.
Plane tree *(Platanus orientalis)*.
Plane tree *(Platanus occidentalis)*.
Tea tree *(Melaleuca leucodendron)*.
Tea tree *(Melaleuca styphelioides)*.
Tea tree *(Callistemon salignus)*.
Messmate *(Eucalyptus amygdalina)*.

The difficulties in obtaining colonial pine and other easily-wrought home-grown timbers, together with the high cost of same, have induced the people to look abroad for no inconsiderable portion of the timber supply.

Indeed, for several years past the Colony has been obliged to import nearly one-half of the quantity of timber consumed. The quantity of timber returned by the forest rangers during the year 1886 was 62,786,456 superficial feet against 62,669,310 superficial feet for the year 1885. Of the quantity produced in 1886 about two-thirds are classed as hardwoods and cedar.

The total quantity of timber imported into the Colony of New South Wales, exclusive of piles, sleepers, and shingles, for the year ending 31st December, 1887, was 49,814,599 superficial feet, against 64,604,793 superficial feet for 1886.

QUANTITY and value of dressed and undressed timber imported into the Colony of New South Wales for each year from 1878 to 1887, inclusive :—

Year.	Dressed timber.			Undressed timber.		
	Quantity.	Value.		Quantity.	Value.	
	feet.	£	s	feet.	£	s
1878	4,891,272	65,478	318,649	12,747,926	106,144	516,550
1879	5,981,923	61,295	298,292	20,933,969	146,049	710,747
1880	5,565,006	61,620	299,874	14,529,055	106,301	517,314
1881	6,847,336	71,041	345,721	17,140,040	131,200	638,485
1882	14,739,853	183,862	894,764	30,392,919	231,197	1,125,120
1883	16,456,700	176,379	858,348	31,674,757	213,724	1,040,088
1884	16,444,111	159,478	776,100	33,164,714	221,302	1,076,966
1885	19,464,845	176,413	858,514	46,180,779	281,939	1,372,056
1886	23,561,175	201,553	980,858	41,043,618	232,907	1,133,442
1887	14,581,126	122,937	598,273	35,233,473	238,909	1,162,651

QUANTITY and value of timber imported into New South Wales for the years 1886 and 1887, and countries whence imported:—

Dressed.

Countries.	1886.			1887.		
	Quantity.	Value.		Quantity.	Value.	
	sup. feet.	£	$	sup. feet.	£	$
Great Britain	6,404,526	62,952	306,356	4,214,512	38,310	186,436
Victoria	869,540	10,694	52,042	418,366	4,931	23,997
South Australia	346,493	6,186	30,104	823,753	12,013	58,461
New Zealand	5,376,615	39,789	193,633	3,023,488	19,691	95,826
British Columbia	113,577	800	3,893	400,337	2,425	11,801
United States	4,479,598	37,470	182,348	2,327,858	19,288	93,865
Norway	5,762,179	41,535	202,130	3,366,445	26,238	117,687
France	5,288	575	2,798	85	8	39
Germany	171,072	1,300	6,326	....	....	....
Queensland	204	10	49	6,282	33	161
New Caledonia	32,083	242	1,178	....	....	....
Total	23,561,175	201,553	980,858	14,581,126	122,937	598,273

Undressed.

Great Britain	1,519,040	11,645	56,670	780,081	6,109	29,729
Victoria	772,366	7,399	36,007	804,244	6,578	32,012
South Australia	662,426	10,914	53,113	3,615,189	58,327	283,848
Queensland	122,297	850	4,137	486,986	1,396	6,794
Tasmania	64,639	443	2,156	157,255	854	4,156
New Zealand	8,465,653	44,077	214,501	10,560,676	64,001	311,461
Western Australia	30,000	5	24	....	....	....
Hong-Kong	5,338	71	346	12,825	173	842
British Columbia	1,808,416	8,000	38,932	2,682,502	11,691	56,894
United States	25,761,156	137,279	668,068	15,137,529	83,336	405,535
Norway	1,039,042	6,204	30,192	905,315	5,869	28,562
Sweden	513,004	4,200	20,439	....	....	....
Germany	53,696	455	2,214	31,217	253	1,231
Belgium	1,300	5	24	....	....	....
New Caledonia	127,545	640	3,115	960	5	24
New Guinea	4,000	50	243	25,894	215	1,046
Borneo	93,700	670	3,261	....	....	....
India	....	....	....	3,400	17	83
South Sea Islands	....	....	....	8,500	85	414
Total	41,043,618	232,907	1,133,442	35,233,473	238,909	1,162,631

It will be seen from this table that the United States furnishes nearly one-half of the total timber imports, and that New Zealand comes next.

The great bulk of the timber imported into New South Wales from New Zealand consists of kauri pine, a product peculiar to the North Island of that Colony, and not found anywhere else in the world. It is straight grained, soft, and easily wrought. The principal objection to its use is that it is apt to shrink, endways, but this obstacle is avoided by the exercise of care in seasoning. It is, however, a grand timber, and is so generally used in Australasia that New Zealand has developed the largest timber industry in the southern hemisphere. Some of the saw-mills employ as many as 500 hands, and the Auckland Timber Company, in their town and country mills, in New Zealand, give employment to about 1,300 hands. The total annual output of timber for the whole of that Colony is estimated at about 200,000,000 superficial feet.

This Company has recently established a branch saw-mill, at Blackwattle Bay, Glebe, in Sydney Harbour, at a cost of about £30,000 ($145,995), where they carry on an extensive trade in kauri and other timbers; they also import large quantities of Californian redwood, which is in considerable demand for special purposes.

The popularity of American timber in New South Wales is very forcibly illustrated by the extraordinary increase in the quantity and value of the imports. In 1881 the imports of dressed and undressed timber from the United States amounted to only 2,000,197 superficial feet, valued at £22,152 ($107,316). In 1887 they were 17,485,387 superficial feet, valued at £102,624 ($499,420).

The subjoined table shows the quantity and value of the imports of dressed and undressed lumber into the Colony of New South Wales from the United States for each year from 1881 to 1887, inclusive.

Year.	Dressed.			Undressed.		
	Quantity.	Value.		Quantity.	Value.	
	Sup. feet.	£	$	Sup. feet.	£	$
1881	870,082	12,988	62,719	1,129,517	9,164	44,597
1882	2,886,261	38,720	188,431	6,249,246	56,867	276,743
1883	2,859,410	34,843	169,563	8,156,933	60,243	293,173
1884	3,121,896	33,717	164,084	10,653,850	76,248	371,061
1885	3,436,799	35,665	172,667	19,728,436	116,228	565,624
1886	4,479,598	27,470	182,348	25,761,156	137,279	668,008
1887	2,327,858	19,288	93,865	15,157,529	83,336	405,555

The saw-mills of California, Oregon, and Washington Territory rank amongst the foremost in the world, and are equipped with the best and latest improvements in milling and other machinery. The sawn timber of the Pacific slope is often 150 feet in length, and for general building purposes there is perhaps no other that will compare with it. New markets are being opened up every day, and active preparations are being made for its shipment in larger quantities than ever, not only to Australasia, but Japan and other countries.

At a meeting of the saw-mill proprietors, held in Sydney, the chairman stated that the controversy going on as to the comparative merits of Oregon pine and Australian hardwoods had brought a very important subject before the people, and that he thought the weight of the argument was in favour of the hardwoods. He said he had received a number of telegrams from saw-mill proprietors in various parts of the Colony expressing sympathy with the movement to secure an increase of duties, and a leading architect had informed him that the Australian hard woods, if properly seasoned, could be used with better advantage in the construction of certain buildings than any other kinds of timber. It was pointed out at the meeting that the expense of getting colonial timber to the Sydney market was twice as much as it cost to bring lumber all the way from America, and it was said that one of the reasons for this is that the Americans ship their lumber in large vessels, whilst the Australians use small vessels, often steam-boats, which are run at a very heavy cost.

The annual export of timber produced in the colony, although small, has materially increased since 1881. In that year it was only 4,125,896, but in 1887 it was 15,720,792 superficial feet.

The following table shows the quantity of dressed and undressed timber, the produce of the Colony, exported from New South Wales for each year, from 1881 to 1887, inclusive.

Year.	Quantity.	Year.	Quantity.
	Superficial feet.		Superficial feet.
1881	4,125,896	1885	9,981,727
1882	5,834,762	1886	13,389,777
1883	8,829,754	1887	15,720,792
1884	14,559,304		

There are no bounties of any kind upon the exportation of timber from the Colony, and the import trade is severely handicapped with heavy Customs duties. The duties have always been large, but in April, 1886, they were increased. These duties have been continued under the Customs Act of 1887, and have awakened no little opposition, being regarded as presenting an anomaly among a people professing to be wedded to the principles of free trade. The New South Wales timber duties were intended to lessen the imports of the easily wrought foreign lumber, and promote the use of Australian hard wood, but the contrary has been the result, for the home-grown woods are no more popular than before, while the imports of American and other timber have largely increased.

The Colonial Treasurer has, however, intimated the intention of the Government to make very extensive modifications of these duties during the session of 1888.

The various establishments of nurserymen and seedsmen in Sydney will compare favourably with those of the chief cities of Europe and America. Large sums of money have been expended upon improving their grounds and in adding to the number and variety of trees and plants from all parts of the world.

The following are some of the leading nurserymen and seedsmen of Sydney and suburbs:—

Shepherd & Co., Surry Hills.
Anderson & Co., Pitt-street, Sydney.
Graham & Co., Marrickville.
Ferguson & Co., Double Bay, Sydney.
Somerset Nursery, Parramatta.
Searl & Son, Petersham, Sydney.

FORESTS AND FOREST CULTURE.

The only forest laws in New South Wales are included in the Crown Lands Act of 1884. But as the Act is a very complicated and voluminous one, and as the sections referring to forests are scattered amongst other matter in various parts, they are brought together consecutively.

It will be seen from the Act that sections 87 and 88 provide for granting leases of scrub lands at nominal rents, under conditions, enforcing the clearing and destruction of the scrub. Sections 93 to 95 relate to permits for ring-barking timber. Section 98 defines the rights of holders of grazing leases or licenses in regard to cutting timber. Sections 112 and 116, deal with the State forests, timber reserves, licenses, and permits. Section 133 imposes penalties for violation of the regulations. It will be seen by this section that all persons, unless legally authorized, when found in possession of lands, whether of Crown lands, reservations, or dedications, will be liable to a fine of £5 ($24·33) for the first offence, £10 ($48·66) for the second, and £20 ($97·33) for the third or subsequent offence, and that holders of Crown lands under lease or license shall not obstruct any government surveyor or authorized officer from entering at any time on any part or portion of their holdings.

The timber regulations comprise a carefully compiled code of rules for regulating the State forests, timber-cutting, and ring-barking. There are in New South Wales two classes of government reserves for the preservation of timber—one comprising the State forests, and the other the timber reserves. The second class is again divided into three sections.

But although these reserves are systematically arranged, the Minister of Lands, should it be deemed expedient, has the same power at any time to alter the classification, as he also has to close a whole or part of a reserve, if he considers it prudent and beneficial to any part of the country.

With respect to licenses, they are available only for one particular reserve or a subdivision of any reserve, and these certificates may be cancelled at the discretion of the Minister of Lands, or transferred on indorsement of the ranger in charge to another reserve of the same class. Licenses are not transferable, except in special cases upon approval of the Minister.

Restrictions are also laid upon licenses as to the minimum girth of trees at a height of 5 feet from the ground. The prescribed girth for hard woods is as follows:—

Description of Timber.	Girth.	
	Ft.	in.
Black-butt and yellow wood timber	7	6
Red-gum, gray-gum, woolly-butt brush, or white box, and turpentine timber	6	6
Blue-gum, spotted gum, messmate bloodwood, mountain-ash, mahogany (forest), and iron-bark (red, gray, and broad-leaved)	6	0
Peppermint, or red-wood, and swamp mahogany	5	6
Stringy bark	5	0
Blackwood, and yellow and white box	4	0

For soft woods, the minimum girth prescribed is:—

Description of Timber.	Girth.	
	Ft.	in.
Red cedar	9	0
Hoop or Moreton Bay pine	7	6
White beech	7	0
Lilybark and rosewood	6	0
Black, red, or white pine, and swamp oak	3	0
Forest oak	2	3

With the exception of the wattle and ring-barked trees no stripping of bark from standing trees is allowed, and the tops are ordered to be cut off trees within seven days after felling. The kurrajong, quandong, and such other trees as may be specified from time to time, are exempted altogether from operations, excepting in time of drought, when the leaves of the kurrajong may be used as food for stock.

Among other provisions applying to permits and licenses are the regulations : (1) Demanding particulars of quantity, description, and brands of the timber claimed, to be sent to the forest ranger of the district within twenty-one days after January 1, April 1, July 1, and October 1 ; (2) Prohibiting the felling of trees within a chain and a half of any navigable river, unless a particular tree is marked for such a purpose by some one in authority ; and (3) respecting the amount of timber any person is allowed to hold, the stated quantity being 50,000 superficial feet. A separate certificate must be obtained for every portion in excess, although the Minister has power in cases of large contractors, to increase the maximum number of feet. Lastly, lands or timber reserves or State forests that are not leased may be granted as sites for saw-mills to the extent of 10 acres to holders of timber licenses, or permits and areas of 160 acres for the agistment of stock used for drawing timber by licenses.

Extracts from the Crown Lands Act of New South Wales, 1884, referring to forests and timber regulations.

Section 87. Scrub lands may be leased in areas not exceeding 10,240 acres, nor less than 640 acres, and for a term not exceeding fifteen years, to any person, subject to such conditions as to clearing and destruction of scrub as may be defined by regulations, at an annual rental of not less than 2s. 6d. (61 cents) per section of 640 acres for the first five years, 5s. ($1·22) for the next five years, and £1 ($4·86) for the last five years : Provided, that it shall shall be lawful for the Minister, on the recommendation of the Local Land Board, to forego the rent for any period not exceeding five years. Every lessee of any portion of scrub lands shall, within the time and according to the manner prescribed, pay the rent as determined by the Minister, after appraisement by the Local Land Board, into the Treasury, and shall, at the time and in the manner prescribed, satisfy the Local Land Board that he has commenced and is continuing to fulfil the conditions of his lease as to the clearing and destruction of scrub on the leased land ; and if any lessee shall fail to pay his rent or to satisfy the said Board as aforesaid, the Minister, on the recommendation of the said Board, may declare his lease to be forfeited.

Section 88. It shall be lawful for any pastoral or homestead lessee whose leased land contains scrub or other noxious undergrowth to apply in the prescribed manner to the Minister for the conversion of the portion of land under lease containing such scrub or undergrowth into a lease of scrub lands under the last preceding section for any term not exceeding fifteen years ; and if the Local Land Board shall recommend such conversion, the Governor may resume from the lease such portion of land as the said Board shall consider desirable, and may grant a lease thereof to the applicant under the said section : Provided, that the lessee shall be entitled to a proportionate abatement or refund of any rent paid by him under his pastoral or homestead lease for the unexpired portion of any year for which he has paid rent in advance : Provided further, that any applicant for a scrub lease under this or the next preceding section shall pay for the survey thereof : Provided, however, that no pastoral or homestead lessee shall be granted a lease of such scrub land other than within the land held under lease by himself.

Leases may be granted for special purposes.

Section 90. The Governor may lease, by auction or otherwise, for a term not exceeding fifteen years, and in areas not exceeding in any case 320 acres, Crown lands for any of the purposes hereinafter specified, that is to say, for dams * * sawmills * * * * or for any purpose declared by the Governor by proclamation in the *Gazette* to be a purpose within this section, and may determine the upset rent thereof, if let at auction, or the annual rent, if let otherwise, not being in either case less than £10 ($48·86) per annum ; and may annex to any such lease such conditions, reservations, and provisions as he may deem fit : Provided, that leases may be granted at a less rental to contractors of public works for purposes connected with the construction of such works during the term of contract. If it should appear to the satisfaction of the Governor that the land comprised in any such lease is not used and occupied *bond fide* for the purpose for which the same has been made, or that default has been made in any condition, he may declare such lease forfeited, together with any improvements erected on the land and any rent paid in respect thereof.

Section 92. Subject to such conditions as may be prescribed, the Governor may make leases of Crown lands not exceeding 3 chains in width but without limit of length, for irrigation works or for forming and maintaining tramways and crossings, and other necessary approaches and works in connection therewith. And notice of every application for a lease under this section, and of the purpose for which it is proposed to be made, shall be published in the *Gazette* for at least four consecutive weeks before the issue of such lease.

Ring-barking by Lessees.

Section 93. Every lessee of Crown lands desiring to ring-bark trees upon his leasehold land shall obtain a permission to do so from the local land board, and in his application, in the prescribed form addressed to the land agent, shall describe the boundaries and area of the land upon which he proposes to ring-bark ; and in regard to any land not comprised within a timber or forest reserve, the board may, in their discretion, refuse or grant permission for the same after such inquiry and upon such conditions as to them may seem necessary. And any lessee who shall, without such permission, ring-bark trees on a leasehold, or shall cause or knowingly permit or suffer the same to be done, shall, on conviction before any two justices of the peace at the court of petty sessions nearest to such leasehold, be liable for the first offence to a penalty of not less than 1s. nor more than 10s. for each tree so ring-barked, and for a second or subsequent offence be liable to a like penalty, and to the forfeiture of his lease.

Section 94. Whosoever shall ring-bark trees, or strip bark from trees on Crown lands, without holding such permission, or in violation of any condition thereof, or without a written authority under the hand of the lessee of such Crown lands, shall, on conviction as aforesaid, be liable to a penalty for each tree ring-barked or stripped of not less than 1s. nor more than 10s.

Section 95. Every information for an offence under any of the two preceding sections shall be laid by some officer of police or person specially authorized by the Minister. And if, at the hearing of such information, any question shall arise whether any person holds a valid permission to ring-bark, the burden of proof thereof shall be on the person who claims to hold such permission.

General provisions affecting leases, lessees, and licenses.

Section 96. Every lease shall be liable to forfeiture if any rent be not paid within the prescribed period or upon breach of any condition annexed to such lease but forfeiture for non-payment of rent may be prevented by payment thereof with an additional sum equal to 5 per cent. of the amount of rent due within three months of the due date thereof, or of 10 per cent. of such amount within six months of such date ; but no forfeiture shall operate to extinguish any debt to the Crown in respect of such rent.

Section 97. Any sums paid as rent for runs, under the provisions of the Acts hereby repealed, upon unexpired portions of existing leases, shall be credited towards payment of rent or license fee under the provisions of this act, and such sums shall be available for the purposes of refunds under the provisions hereinbefore contained.

Section 98. The following provisions shall govern all leases and licenses granted under this Act and the holders of such leases or licenses, namely :

(I) No lease or license other than special leases shall confer any right to remove material from the leased land, or to sublet such land for other than grazing purposes, or to prevent the entry and removal of material by authorized persons.

(II) Lessees and licensees may take from land under lease or license to them not comprised within a timber or forest reserve such timber and other material for building and other purposes upon the land under lease or license as may be required by them as tenants or licensees respectively.

(III) No lessee or licensee shall prevent other persons duly authorized in that behalf either from cutting or removing timber or material for building or other purposes, or from searching for any mineral within the land under lease or license : Provided, that nothing in this subsection shall apply to a conditional lease as regards the taking or removal of timber or other material for building purposes.

Section 100. If any holder of a pastoral or homestead lease whose rent, in accordance with the provisions hereinbefore contained, has been fixed at the prescribed minimum rate, shall consider that by reason of the inferior grazing capabilities of the land embraced in the lease such rent is an excessive rental for such land, such lessee may, in the prescribed manner, apply to the local land board for a reduction of such minimum rate. And if, upon due inquiry, such Board shall be of opinion that the said rate is excessive it may recommend the Minister to reduce the same ; or, if not of such opinion, may recommend that the said rate be retained. On receipt of any such recommendation, together with any further report from the said Board which the Minister may require, he shall determine the matter of the application and fix the fair annual rental of the land for all purposes of this Act, and shall, upon notification in the *Gazette*, be the rental payable under this Act in respect of such land. But no such reduction shall operate for a longer period than the unexpired portion of the five-year term then current, as hereinbefore provided : Provided also, that no such lessee shall be entitled to make any such application for reduction of such minimum rate unless he shall have duly paid the rent fixed for the current year, pursuant to the provisions hereinbefore contained ; but such lessee shall be entitled to a refund of the amount paid by him in excess of any reduced amount so notified as aforesaid : Provided lastly, that notwithstanding any such reduction so made, the Minister may, on the expiration of the said five-year term for which such reduction shall have been made, direct that the rental shall for the residue of the term of the lease, or for the next period of five years of such lease, be restored to the prescribed minimum rate, or be subject to appraisement by the local land board, and in either case such direction shall be notified to the lessee in the prescribed manner. A return of all rents, if any, reduced under this section shall be laid before Parliament within fourteen days after the commencement of each session. The several provisions of this section shall equally apply to all occupation licenses and their holders and to the license fees paid or made payable in respect thereof.

State forests—timber reserves—licenses—permits.

Section 112. It shall be lawful for the Governor by notification in the *Gazette* to proclaim any areas of Crown lands therein described to be State forests and in like manner to reserve from sale any such areas as timber reserves for the purpose in each case of preserving under regulations in that behalf to be made by the Governor the growth and succession of timber trees, and of preventing as far as practicable the destruction and exhaustion of such State forests.

Section 113. State forests may be subdivided into such blocks as the Minister may think fit. For the purpose of carrying out such subdivision all existing forests and timber reserves may be reserved from sale, lease, or otherwise, as the Minister may think proper until so subdivided.

Section 114. Any State forest or any portion thereof may by notification in the *Gazette* be dedicated or reserved for a specific period by the Governor for the contervation of timber, and upon publication of such notification such forest or portion thereof shall not during the term of reservation be open to timber or other licenses or permits under the provisions of this Act.

Section 115. It shall be lawful for the Governor to frame regulations for the issue of licenses or rights to cut and remove timber on State forests, and also for the issue of permits to cut and remove timber from timber reserves, and also for the issue of wood-cutters' licenses, and of licenses and permits to dig for and remove from State forests, timber reserves, or Crown lands, whether under lease or not, any gravel, stone, clay, shells, or other materials subject to the following provisions :—

(I) The rights or licenses to cut timber on a State forest shall be for one or more specified blocks in such forest, and may be sold by auction at such place as may be determined by the Minister, or by tender, as the Minister may think fit.

(II) Such rights or licenses in State forest shall be for a term not exceeding one year, unless in special cases the Minister may think fit to extend such term, but no such extended term shall exceed three years.

(III) The upset rent shall not be less than £10 ($48·66) per annum for each block of 640 acres, and a proportionate amount for each 160 acres in excess of that area. And every holder of a right to cut timber shall, in addition to his rent, pay such royalty, according to the class of timber cut, at such times and places, and subject to such conditions, as may be fixed by the regulations.

(IV) Permits to cut and remove timber on timber reserves may be issued for a year, or any less term not being less than one month, at an annual fee of not less than £6 ($29·20), and a proportionate fee for shorter terms. Such permits may also be issued for any specified number of trees at a rate to be fixed by regulations for each tree. General permits may also be issued for the supply of saw-mills, for any term not exceeding one year, at an annual rate of £6 ($29·20), and subject to a royalty according to the scale fixed by the regulations.

(V) Licenses may be issued to cut piles or props to be used for mining purposes, for the erection of jetties, wharves, and for other purposes, on such terms and conditions as may be fixed by the regulations.

(VI) All fees or sums of money, except royalty, payable in respect of any rights to cut timber, or in respect of licenses or permits, shall be payable in advance.

And such regulation may prescribe the forms and conditions to be contained in any such right, license, or permit, and may fix the rents or fees to be payable by the holder of any license or permit wheresoever the same shall not have been fixed by this Act, and may provide for the forfeiture of any rights, licenses, or permits for the enforcement of rents, royalties, or fees for the removal of felled timber, for the licensing of sites for saw-mills and the agistment of stock, for the limitation of girth of trees to be felled, for the issue of wattle-bark permits for the marking of logs of felled trees, for the seizure and sale of timber cut without authority or upon which the royalty has not been paid, and for defining the power and privileges conferred by rights, licenses, and permits. And such regulations may also provide for the imposition of penalties and fines for the infringement or violation of any such regulation made under the authority of this act ; but no such penalty shall exceed the sum of £20 ($97·33) exclusive of the value of the material taken or destroyed.

Section 116. The breach of any condition or obligation, or the failure to perform any act or matter specified in any such right, license, or permit issued under the authority of this Act, shall have the effect of forfeiting such right, license, or permit upon a declaration of forfeiture by the Minister.

Section 133. Any person, unless lawfully claiming under any subsisting lease or license, or otherwise under any Act hereby repealed, or under this act, or under any Act in force for the regulation of mining, who shall be found occupying any Crown land or land granted, reserved, or dedicated for public purposes, either by residing or by erecting any hut or building thereon, or by clearing, digging up, or enclosing or cultivating any part thereof, or by cutting timber, other than firewood, not for sale thereon, or by obtaining stone therefrom, or otherwise, or who shall strip or cause to be stripped the bark of any tree thereon, shall be liable, on conviction to a penalty not exceeding £5 ($24·33) for the first offence, and not exceeding £10 ($48·66) for the second offence, and not exceeding £20 ($97·33) for the third or any subsequent offence : Provided, that it shall not be lawful for the holder of any leasehold under this Act to obstruct any Government surveyor or other authorised person from entering upon such leasehold whenever such surveyor or authorised person may require to do so.

COAL.

The coal-mines of New South Wales are by far the most important in the southern hemisphere. The coal is of such excellent quality, and the seams are so extensive and easily worked, that there is every promise for their future. The total area covered by the seams is estimated at 23,950 square miles. They extend from the twenty-ninth to the thirty-sixth parallel of south latitude and penetrate to the water's edge along many miles of sea coast. The seams have been traced 700 miles north of the deposits near Newcastle, and they have been found to be covered and underlaid with the same fossil flora and fauna characteristic of the Newcastle District. These deposits are among the most extensive and valuable in the world. In fact, some of the highest authorities on minerals, both in England and Australia, are very decided in the opinion that the New South Wales coal, in many respects, is superior to English coal, inasmuch as it is better adapted to steam purposes and richer in gas-giving products. The lower beds of the coal series of New South Wales are said by geologists to be older than any worked in Europe, and the upper beds represent the most recent of the European true carboniferous formations. It has been noticed that all the New South Wales seams, from the Silurian upwards, are uniform in their deposits, and this fact has led to the conclusion that this portion of the globe was comparatively free from violent eruptions and disturbances from the Silurian to the Permian period, and that the alternate submergences and elevations of the land were slow and gradual.

Few workable coal seams have been, as yet, discovered in Victoria; but coal exists in immense quantities in various other portions of Australasia, especially in Queensland and in New Zealand, where there are very valuable mines, which last named yielded in 1886 534,353 tons. Indeed, now New Zealand coal only is used by the Government there for their steam vessels, railways, and fuel. Tasmania also has her coal-fields, which only require development.

The output of the Queensland mines in 1886 was 228,656 tons, but the combined products of the whole of the Australasian group are insignificant when compared with those of New South Wales.

The Government have divided the coal-fields of New South Wales into three districts— the northern, southern, and western.

The northern district produces not only the best coal but the largest quantity. The famous Hunter River and Newcastle mines are situated in that district. The shipping facilities at Newcastle are extraordinary, the tonnage of the port being, at times, as large as that of Sydney.

Newcastle, which contains a population of about 30,000, is situated 75 miles north of Sydney, on the banks of the Hunter River, at its mouth, which indeed forms the harbour of the port. The public buildings possess many and varied attractions. The custom-house, post-office, market building, hospital and churches are constructed in approved styles of architecture, and show the taste and wealth of the inhabitants. Large sums have been expended during the last few years in improving the harbour. The depth of water at the wharves is 22 feet.

The machinery used for loading vessels with coal is of very high order. It consists of seven steam cranes and four shoots, belonging to the Government, and five cranes belonging to the Australian Agricultural Company, and two belonging to the Newcastle Company. These cranes have a loading capacity of from 12,000 to 14,000 tons per day. The cranes at Bullock Island Dock have a capacity of 6,000 tons daily. Those erected on the wharf formed by the dyke comprise two of 25 tons each and six of 15 tons each. As much as 250 tons of coal have been put on board ship at Newcastle per hour.

A branch line, with a viaduct over Thorsby's Creek, connects the wharves at Bullock Island with the Great Northern Railway, which now extends to the Queensland frontier.

Naval defence works have been constructed for the purpose of protecting the port in time of war. The fort at Flagstaff Hill, commanding the harbour, has at present three 9-inch guns and four rifled 80-pounders, besides a torpedo and submarine mines armament.

The quantity of coal produced in the northern districts is about 2,200,000 tons per annum—more than two-thirds of the total coal product of the Colony. The mines in the northern district are practically inexhaustible, and it is estimated that at the present rate of consumption they would last for the next seven hundred years.

The publication of the last report of the Royal Commission on the Newcastle collieries reveals many interesting facts in connection with the northern district mines. The report is a very voluminous one.

The commission was composed of gentlemen of large experience in coal-mining, especially in this Colony. They examined many witnesses, and their testimony comprises one of the most valuable and interesting features in the report. The commission gave great attention, not only to the present condition of the mines, but to their prospective workings under the waters of the harbour or the Pacific Ocean. Very careful investigations were made as to the character of the strata, shafts, and underground workings in collieries some miles distant from the harbour but adjoining the Pacific Ocean. The area embraced measures from north to south $7\frac{1}{2}$ miles, and from east to west 4 miles. The report, after mentioning that the district is overlaid with rocks belonging to the Lower Coal Measures, states that the Newcastle seam, the lowest workable coal of this series of carboniferous rocks, as well as the higher and superimposed coal seams, once covered the whole area under review, and which at a subsequent period was denuded in certain portions by the action of the atmosphere, rain, frost, or running water, at a time when the relative height of the land to that of the ocean was different from what it now is. The alteration in the relative position of the land and water may have been caused by the changes in the earth's ecliptic, probably arising from the effects of climate near the poles, or, it may be, but less likely, from the volcanic forces with which the vast insular continent of Australia was assailed during post-Tertiary, or, geologically considered, in comparatively recent times.

Coal in the northern district is pure bituminous coal, with strong coking properties, and contains less ash than that from the southern and western districts, although it is said that many engineers in the British navy and in the merchant-marine service prefer the semi-bituminous coal to the northern, because the disadvantage of the greater proportion of ash in the former is counterbalanced by the fact that it burns more evenly and uniformly than the other; moreover, it does not so readily form into clinkers; but when it is required to get up steam rapidly the northern coal is preferred.

Mr. W. A. Dixon, F.C.S., of Sydney, made a series of analyses of the various coals of the world for the International Exhibition at Sydney, and perhaps a better idea of the character of the New South Wales coals can be formed from his investigations than from any other source. In the work he had in hand he followed the calculation given by Percy, which divides the different kinds of coal into anthracite, bituminous, and hydrous coals; also the conditions laid down by the commission appointed by the Admiralty to investigate the British coals for the purpose of the navy, one of which was that coal should not progressively decay, for in so doing it becomes liable to spontaneous combustion. Another condition was that it should possess considerable cohesion of its particles, so as not to break into small fragments by constant attrition in the vessel. Another point was that it should have considerable density. By comparison, the coal from Newcastle, New South Wales, is much denser than the English Newcastle and very nearly equal to the best Welsh coal.

The following table, prepared by Mr. Dixon, shows the comparative specific gravity and percentage of sulphur, ash, and volatile hydrocarbons, in New South Wales and British coals.

Average Analyses.

Coals.	Number of Samples.	Specific Gravity.	Sulphur.	Ash.	Volatile Hydrocarbons.
Newcastle, New South Wales	14	1,311	0·91	4·07	37·55
Western, New South Wales	9	1,347	1·03	10·31	30·42
Southern, New South Wales.........	7	1,374	0·65	10·25	20·84
Newcastle, England....................	17	1,246	1·24	3·82	36·44
Derbyshire, England	8	1,284	1·06	2·54	39·12
Lancashire, England	28	1,279	1·37	4·04	40·61
Welsh............. , ...	31	1,318	1·34	4·15	21·15

According to this table, a ton of New South Wales coal would occupy nearly 6 per cent less space than an equal quantity of British coal. New South Wales coal contains less sulphur than the British, and consequently is not so liable to spontaneous combustion or to affect the purity of the atmosphere.

COAL.

Proximate Analysis.

Sample of Coal from Australian Agricultural Company's Mine, at Newcastle, N.S.W.

Specific gravity	1.286
Water	1.65
Volatile hydrocarbons	35.45
Fixed carbons	57.84
Ash	4.44
Sulphur	0.62
	100.00

Coke: 63·28 per cent. Ash: reddish.

Analysis of Ash.

Alumina	22·84	
Ferric oxide	15·20	Soluble in acid,
Lime	1·98	43·25
Sulphuric oxide	·97	
Phosphoric oxide	2·26	
Alumina	3·45	
Ferric oxide	trace	Insoluble in acid,
Silica	53·10	56·75.
Undetermined and loss	·20	
	100·00	

Proximate Analysis.

Minmi Colliery, Newcastle.

Bituminous, bright, with a few narrow dull streaks.

Specific gravity	1·28
Moisture	2·59
Volatile hydrocarbons	33·87
Fixed carbon	56·49
Ash	5·61
Sulphur	1·44
	100·00

Coke: 62·10 per cent.; coke bright, dense, with fused appearance, little swollen. Ash: reddish, somewhat fusible.

Proximate Analysis.

Newcastle Coal Company, Glebe, Newcastle.

Specific gravity	1·283
Water	2·14
Volatile hydrocarbons	33·36
Fixed carbon	59·16
Ash	4·76
Sulphur	·58
	100·00

Coke: 63·92 per cent. Ash: buff-coloured.

Analysis of Ash.

Alumina	27·21	
Ferric oxide	11·11	
Lime	1·46	Soluble in acid, 43·30.
Magnesia	1·56	
Sulphuric oxide	·72	
Phosphoric oxide	1·24	
Alumina	6·51	
Ferric oxide	3·02	
Lime	·61	Insoluble in acid, 56·34.
Magnesia	·63	
Silica	45·57	
Undetermined and loss	·36	
	100·00	

Proximate Analysis.
New Lambton Mine.

Specific gravity	1·291
Water	2·61
Volatile hydrocarbons	30·62
Fixed carbon	59·56
Ash	6·72
Sulphur	·49
	100·00

Coke : 66·28 per cent. Ash : reddish-coloured.

Coal from the southern district is of a much duller lustre than the northern, and the structure is not so laminated. It does not coke in an ordinary fire, but will do so if treated in an oven. It has been predicted that the mines of this district will become, in the near future, as important as those of the north. The southern coal is well adapted both for steam and household purposes. Several of the seams extend over a distance of 50 miles. There are five seams at Mount Kembla. The lowest is above the level of the plain, and the others lie superimposed at convenient distances above each other and cropping to the surface. These seams vary in thickness from 4 feet to 17 feet 6 inches. The mine at Mount Keira is worked at an elevation of 500 feet above the level of the sea. The seam descends gradually until it reaches almost to the level of the ocean at Coal Cliff. The mine at the latter place is a very valuable one; coal can be put almost immediately from the mouth of the tunnel there into the bunkers of the vessels.

The method of working these mines is simple and inexpensive. No steam machinery is required. The coal is run down from the mountain by means of revolving drums and wire ropes.

Wollongong, the sea-port of this district, is the third in rank in the Colony. It is situated 66 miles south from Sydney. The harbour has been greatly improved by the construction of a breakwater, and excavations out of solid rock to a depth of 18 feet, and by other improvements. The area of the basins, which now form one, is about 3 acres, and plans are prepared for vastly increasing the basin accommodation. The district in which the mines are situated is noted for its fine wheat and dairy farms. The average price of land in the district is about £20 ($97·33) per acre. The farmers in this district have always complained of a scarcity of labour.

The subjoined table shows the component parts, and specific gravity, of samples of coal from the Southern District:

Locality.	Specific gravity.	Composition per cent., exclusive of water only.						Water, per cent.	Coke, per cent.	Calorific intensity (calculated.)	Water converted into steam by 1 pound coal with calorimeter.
		Carbon.	Hydrogen.	Oxygen.	Nitrogen.	Sulphur.	Ash.				
Nattai	....	91·24	3·60	0·59	....	trace	4·56	3·23	92·37	8,599	Undet.
Mount Kembla ..	1·363	80·07	5·30	1·58	0·70	0·87	10·88	1·50	....	8,276	13·21
Mount Keira ..	1·379	78·82	5·17	3·87	1·33	1·00	9·81	1·15	74·35	7,983	12·02
Berrima	1·364	69·92	4·55	13·09	0·56	1·30	10·58	1·70	64·24	6,653	11·82
Bulli (R. Smith)	1·471	76·35	4·75	5·04	....	0·55	13·31	1·03	74·78	....	12·21
Mean	1·394	79·401	4·675	4·833	0·52	0·74	9·829	1·733	76·436	7,875	12·54

The coals from the western district are much drier than those of the southern district, and contain considerable volatile matter. Mr. Dixon does not think that they will ever be exported in large quantities. He says, however, that they will answer for local purposes quite as well as many coals worked in Great Britain and France.

TABLE showing the average composition of western district coals from nine analyses made by Mr. Dixon.

Constituents.	Average.	Highest.	Lowest.
Specific gravity	1·347	1·400	1·336
Water	2·200	2·900	1·950
Volatile matter	30·420	35·020	25·840
Fixed carbon	55·940	64·340	49·970
Ash	10·310	12·910	9·260
Sulphur......................................	1·310	1·750	0·570

It has been noticed that the ash in western coals was white and dense. In the northern samples it was often buff and red tinted.

From a series of analyses made by Professor Liversedge, of the Sydney University, it appears that the amount of ash of the coals from the northern district was 2·70 to 8·82 per cent., or, upon an average of 5·41 per cent.; from the southern district 4·41 to 13·52 per cent., average 10·02; and from the western district 6·88 to 12·91 per cent., average 9·87 per cent. ash.

The subjoined tables give Mr. Dixon's analyses of samples of coal in the western district:—

Proximate Analysis.

Sample of the whole thickness of a 4-foot seam at Katoomba.

A mixture of a bituminous splint coal, with bright and dull coloured pieces.

Specific gravity	1.343
Moisture	2.71
Volatile hydrocarbons	25.31
Fixed carbon	60.90
Ash	10.84
Sulphur	·24
	100.00

The coke is dense, scarcely swollen, but fairly lustrous; the ash is white. This is a fairly good coal, the low percentage of ash being particularly noteworthy.

Analysis of Ash.

Alumina	35.26	
Ferric oxide	·98	
Lime	traces	Soluble in acid, 37.10.
Magnesia	·30	
Phosphoric oxide	·56	
Alumina	3.23	
Silica	50.58	Insoluble in acid, 62.90.
Undetermined and loss	·09	

Proximate Analysis.
Lithgow Valley Colliery.

Specific gravity	1.340
Water	2.24
Volatile hydrocarbons	28.48
Fixed carbon	58.80
Ash	9.68
Sulphur	·80
	100.00

Ash: Grayish-white.

Analysis of Ash.

Alumina	20·24	⎫
Ferric oxide	1·42	⎪
Lime	·74	⎬ Soluble in acid,
Magnesia	·57	⎪ 23·72.
Sulphuric oxide	·11	⎪
Phosphoric oxide	·64	⎭
Alumina	16·02	⎫ Insoluble in acid,
Silica	60·21	⎭ 76·23.
Undetermined and loss ...	·05	

Other samples of coal from this district have been examined with fully as favourable results. At Wallerawang (western district), 105 miles north-west from Sydney, good coal, hard and compact, has been found. One sample from a seam 17½ feet thick yielded upon analysis 55·74 per cent. of fixed carbon, 33·24 volatile hydrocarbon, water 1·51, and ash 9·50 per cent.; specific gravity, 1·333; coke, 62·25.

Above the lowest seam was one of 6 feet 6 inches, and several others varying from 3 to 4 feet in thickness. There are extensive strata of limestone in the same district. They occur at the junction of the Coal Measures with the Upper Silurian or Devonian beds. Magnetite and brown hematite, as well as clay band ores, are interstratified with the Coal Measures. The magnetite runs approximately north-east and north-west, and the magnetic effect is said to be so powerful as to render the compass useless in the neighbourhood. One vein is 13 feet wide, the ore compact, and accompanied by silicious gangue. It yields about 41 per cent. of iron and is free from phosphorus and sulphur. The brown hematite vein has nearly the same direction as the above, and along the line of its outcrop great blocks of ore are scattered for nearly a mile. At a depth of 40 feet the vein is 18 to 20 feet thick, and the ore is composed of mammilated fibrous nodules. There are four seams of clay-band which lie nearly horizontally, and crop out on both the east and the west sides of the dividing range. The lowest is rather impure, but the others are good, containing from 49 to 56 per cent. of metal and very little sulphur or phosphorus. The seams average from 10 to 20 feet in thickness.

The total output of all the coal-mines in New South Wales during the year 1886 was 2,830,175 tons, valued at £1,303,164 ($6,341,848). The shale product, or boghead mineral, was 43,563 tons, valued at £99,976 ($486,533).

The total output of the coal-mines of New South Wales, since the commencement of coal-mining to 1857, was 1,468,961 tons, valued at £869,391 ($4,230,891); and from 1858 to 1886, 35,553,449 tons, valued at £17,483,277 ($85,082,368).

The total output of the coal-mines in Queensland since the commencement of coal-mining to December, 1886, has been 1,478,238 tons, and in New Zealand 4,052,614 tons.

The following tables, prepared by the Mines Department of New South Wales, show the quantity and value of coal and shale raised in each of the mines there during the year 1886, the number of men employed, also the quantity and value of coal exported to intercolonial and foreign ports to 1886 inclusive.

COAL AND SHALE.

TABLE showing the quantity and value of Coal and Shale won during the year 1886, and the number of Men employed in the Collieries.

Company.	Locality.	Men Employed.			Quantity.	Value.
		Above ground.	Under ground.	Total.		

NORTHERN DISTRICT.
Coal.

Company.	Locality.	Above ground.	Under ground.	Total.	Quantity. (tons.)	Value. (£)
Australian Agricultural Co.	Newcastle	172	803	975	387,084	184,750
Wallsend	,,	180	940	1,120	483,884	240,000
Newcastle Coal Co.	,,	93	400	493	183,573	83,181
Lambton	,,	65	445	510	113,972	56,316
Co-operative	,,	70	442	512	240,274	116,105
Pride of Ferndale	,,	4	17	21	1,500	450
Tighe's Hill	,,	6	17	23	11,596	38,034
New Lambton } New Duckenfield }	,,	83	206	289	71,370	33,455
Greta	Maitland	43	221	264	79,727	39,864
Greta Co.	,,	7	33	40	18,555	9,278
Duckenfield	Newcastle	47	221	268	113,474	54,928
Brown's	,,	58	280	338	114,324	55,309
Waratah	,,	2	8	10	7,142	2,860
South Waratah	,,	25	20	45	1,701	790
East Waratah	,,	36	132	168	37,371	18,752
Goose	,,	1	4	5	4,224	1,689
New Park	Singleton	17	14	31	6,153	3,240
Ellesmere	,,	3	26	29	8,920	4,695
Quarry Tunnel	,,	1	4	5	1,800	810
Sunderland	Four-mile Creek	2	3	5	3,000	650
Brookstown	Newcastle	4	15	19	14,830	7,038
Clay Cross	,,	2	17	19	3,082	711
Dunkirk	,,	4	30	34	12,203	5,990
Hill End	,,	4	8	12	3,271	960
Rix's Creek	Singleton	1	2	3	836	501
Wickham and Bullock Island	Newcastle	19	179	198	55,553	26,229
Morriset	Lake Macquarie.	1	1	2	656	295
Rosedale	Newcastle	2	3	5	1,420	680
Burwood	,,	47	225	272	72,566	39,012
*Lymington Wallsend	,,	18	35	53	......	......
Thornley Colliery	Four-mile Creek	2	7	9	6,613	1,928
†Young Wallsend	Newcastle	2	3	5	......	......
Great Northern	,,	10	9	19	205	72
Hillside	,,	2	6	8	3,494	1,222
Maryville	,,	11	78	89	24,500	12,000
Stockton	,,	40	182	222	84,450	40,121
Homeville and Font Hill	Maitland	3	4	7	2,000	550
Rathluba	,,	2	4	6	2,777	1,090
		1,089	5,044	6,133	2,178,116	1,084,555
						85,277,987

* Sinking. † Sinking for seam.

COAL.

Company.	Locality.	Men Employed. Above ground.	Men Employed. Under ground.	Men Employed. Total.	Quantity.	Value.
SOUTHERN DISTRICT.						
Coal.					tons.	£
*Bulli A.	Wollongong	95	276	371	99,923	22,457
Osborne Wallsend	,,	55	170	225	77,386	28,897
Coal Cliff	,,	40	100	140	56,623	33,040
Illawarra Coal Co.	,,	59	134	193	71,913	28,355
Mount Kembla	,,	40	150	190	51,794	31,076
North Illawarra	,,	30	15	45	......	......
Australian Kerosene Oil and Mineral Co.	Joadja Creek	20	90	110	9,318	4,705
Berrima	Berrima	3	6	9	2,262	897
Broker's Nose	Wollongong	9	6	15	1,611	566
		351	947	1,298	370,830	149,993
						$729,941
WESTERN DISTRICT.						
Vale of Clwydd	Lithgow Valley	6	60	66	51,558	12,649
Lithgow Valley	,,	5	66	71	52,654	12,619
Eskbank	,,	8	68	76	67,774	16,341
Eskbank Old Tunnel	,,	1	12	13	7,500	1,875
Hermitage	,,	...	11	11	9,019	2,064
Zig Zag	,,	10	65	75	60,000	15,000
Coberwull	,,	...	1	1	450	120
Katoomba	Hartley	21	55	76	25,000	6,250
Carlo's Gap	Capertee	1	2	3	250	64
†Great Western		6	...	6	......	......
N. S. W. Shale and Oil Co.		3	15	18	7,024	1,634
		61	355	416	281,229	68,615
						$333,915
Shale.						
Australian Kerosene Oil and Mineral Co.	Joadja Creek	(See	Coal)	...	25,700	64,250
N. S. W. Shale and Oil Co.	Hartley]	30	70	100	17,863	35,726
		30	70	100	43,563	99,976
						$486,533

* On strike since 13th September.   † Boring.

QUANTITY and Value of Coal raised from the opening of the Coal Seams to 1857, inclusive :—

Year.	Quantity.	Average per ton.	Value.
Prior to	Tons.	£ s. d.	£
1829	50,000	0 10 0	25,000
1829	780	0 10 1·23	394
1830	4,000	0 9 0·00	1,800
1831	5,000	0 8 0·00	2,000
1832	7,143	0 7 0·00	2,502
1833	6,812	0 7 6·73	2,373
1834	8,490	0 8 10·00	3,750
1835	12,392	0 8 10·19	5,483
1836	12,646	0 9 1·06	5,747
1837	16,083	0 9 8·81	5,828
1838	17,220	0 9 9·05	8,399
1839	21,283	0 9 9·73	10,441
1840	30,256	0 10 10·86	16,498
1841	34,841	0 12 0·00	20,905
1842	39,900	0 12 0·00	23,940
1843	25,862	0 12 6·54	16,222
1844	23,118	0 10 8·34	12,363
1845	22,324	0 7 10·27	8,769
1846	38,965	0 7 0·46	13,714
1847	40,732	0 6 9·01	13,750
1848	45,447	0 6 3·38	14,275
1849	48,516	0 6 0·45	14,647
1850	71,216	0 6 6·77	23,375
1851	67,610	0 7 6·51	25,546
1852	67,404	0 10 11·33	36,885
1853	96,809	0 16 1·51	78,059
1854	116,642	1 0 5·63	119,380
1855	137,076	0 12 11·96	89,082
1856	189,960	0 12 4·06	117,906
1857	210,434	0 14 0·97	148,158
	1,468,961	0 11 10·72	869,391
		\$2·89	\$4,230,891

COAL.

TABLE showing the Quantities and Average Value per ton of Coal exported to Intercolonial and Foreign Ports respectively, the Quantity of Coal consumed in the Colony, and the Average Price per ton of the total output of the Collieries, from 1858 to 1886 inclusive.

Year	Exports to Intercolonial Ports.			Exports to Foreign Ports.			Total Exports.			Home consumption.	Total Output and Value.		
	Quantity.	Average per ton.	Value.	Quantity.	Average per ton.	Value.	Quantity.	Average per ton.	Value.		Quantity.	Average per ton.	Value.
	tons.	£ s. d.	£	tons.	£ s. d.	£	tons.	£ s. d.	£	tons.	tons.	£ s. d.	£
1858	101,488	0 15 1·07	76,824	12,039	1 0 1·85	12,132	113,527	0 15 6·05	88,956	102,570	216,397	0 14 11·84	162,162
1859	129,586	0 14 6·07	94,312	44,349	0 17 5·27	38,672	173,935	0 15 3·49	132,984	134,278	308,213	0 13 3·14	204,371
1860	140,183	0 14 10·85	104,471	93,694	0 16 11·10	79,290	233,877	0 15 8·67	183,761	134,185	368,062	0 12 2·36	220,483
1861	157,278	0 15 2·25	119,433	50,502	0 16 5·37	41,532	207,780	0 15 5·22	160,965	134,287	342,067	0 12 9·52	218,820
1862	196,427	0 15 0·55	147,019	113,355	0 17 4·03	98,403	309,782	0 15 10·75	245,422	167,740	476,522	0 12 9·73	305,274
1863	213,009	0 13 8·40	146,532	84,129	0 17 6·19	73,649	297,038	0 14 9·30	220,181	135,851	433,889	0 10 10·66	236,230
1864	283,339	0 13 3·74	188,199	98,627	0 14 10·90	66,289	382,466	0 14 4·11	212,488	174,546	549,012	0 10 10·10	270,171
1865	292,664	0 11 11·53	146,129	90,304	0 15 0·79	68,029	382,968	0 11 2·30	214,158	202,546	585,525	0 9 4·13	274,303
1866	344,194	0 9 2·98	158,175	196,711	0 14 4·53	141,413	540,905	0 11 1·57	299,588	233,333	774,238	0 8 4·44	324,049
1867	312,101	0 9 4·95	146,111	161,256	0 13 3·47	107,148	473,357	0 10 8·40	253,259	294,655	770,012	0 8 10·79	342,655
1868	329,652	0 9 5·76	155,975	218,184	0 12 5·29	136,226	548,036	0 10 7·96	292,201	406,495	954,531	0 8 9·08	417,809
1869	340,466	0 8 9·67	149,059	255,087	0 11 8·31	149,136	595,553	0 10 0·35	298,195	324,221	919,774	0 7 6·32	346,146
1870	335,564	0 8 6·92	142,656	242,825	0 10 3·57	125,025	578,389	0 9 3·07	267,681	290,175	868,564	0 7 0·47	316,836
1871	378,891	0 8 6·91	162,470	186,538	0 10 1·22	94,290	565,429	0 9 0·95	256,680	333,355	898,784	0 7 9·92	316,340
1872	394,052	0 8 8·11	170,947	275,058	0 9 11·46	136,914	669,110	0 9 2·42	307,861	343,316	1,012,426	0 7 1·94	396,198
1873	425,937	0 12 9·32	272,110	347,142	0 14 7·59	253,970	773,079	0 13 7·32	526,080	419,783	1,192,862	0 11 1·37	605,747
1874	467,483	0 13 8·90	320,119	405,442	0 15 4·70	312,128	873,025	0 14 5·31	632,247	431,587	1,304,612	0 12 2·06	790,224
1875	518,853	0 13 7·75	354,074	408,154	0 16 6·64	317,409	927,007	0 15 5·84	671,483	402,722	1,329,729	0 12 3·89	819,429
1876	542,952	0 13 8·45	372,045	325,865	0 15 6·45	253,106	868,817	0 14 4·70	625,221	451,101	1,319,918	0 11 2·06	903,300
1877	563,751	0 13 8·14	386,740	351,976	0 14 7·69	262,237	915,727	0 14 2·98	648,977	528,544	1,444,271	0 11 10·74	858,998
1878	624,823	0 13 8·77	427,954	381,607	0 14 7·60	280,452	1,006,430	0 14 0·93	708,406	569,067	1,575,497	0 8 8·28	920,936
1879	621,067	0 13 6·75	421,198	376,962	0 14 6·13	273,509	998,049	0 14 11·66	694,707	585,332	1,583,381	0 11 0·12	950,570
1880	550,072	0 11 2·86	309,004	202,684	0 11 5·70	116,226	753,356	0 11 3·48	425,230	712,824	1,466,180	0 12 6·36	615,331
1881	657,135	0 7 9·34	255,572	372,709	0 8 8·29	161,958	1,029,844	0 8 1·30	417,530	730,753	1,760,597	0 6 9·65	603,248
1882	760,226	0 9 9·54	372,334	501,319	0 11 11·50	274,699	1,261,545	0 10 11·65	647,033	847,737	2,109,282	0 8 11·97	948,965
1883	855,704	0 10 5·75	448,396	656,741	0 11 7·34	381,266	1,512,445	0 11 0·99	829,662	1,069,012	2,581,457	0 9 9·55	1,291,942
1884	994,087	0 10 8·66	532,938	696,676	0 11 5·14	398,107	1,690,763	0 11 0·15	931,045	1,058,346	2,749,109	0 9 5·71	1,303,071
1885	991,924	0 10 7·13	525,443	764,432	0 11 6·32	441,229	1,756,356	0 11 0·09	966,663	1,122,507	2,878,863	0 9 3·72	1,340,213
1886	1,027,775	0 10 7·22	544,824	708,090	0 11 4·31	402,178	1,735,865	0 10 10·93	947,002	1,094,310	2,830,175	0 9 2·53	1,303,164
	13,549,409	0 11 2·9	7,610,023	8,615,041	0 12 9·13	5,496,721	22,164,450	0 11 9·92	13,106,744	13,388,998	35,553,449	0 9 10·02	17,463,277
		£2·73	£7,034,177		£3·10	£6,749,793		£2·87	£6,783,970			£2·39	£85,082,368

67

The following shows, in detail, the quantity and value of coal exported to each place from New South Wales for years 1886 and 1887 respectively:—

Country.	Quantity.	Value.	
	tons.	£	$
1886.			
Victoria	640,655	336,979	1,639,908
South Australia	140,623	73,063	355,561
Tasmania	47,501	26,033	126,690
New Zealand	165,217	90,187	438,895
Queensland	22,053	12,151	59,133
South Sea Islands	815	499	2,428
New Caledonia	9,537	5,201	25,311
Fiji	21,929	12,254	59,634
Hong Kong	100,586	56,148	273,244
China	23,743	14,395	70,053
Chili	41,794	23,787	115,759
Honolulu	23,765	12,816	62,369
Western Australia	11,726	6,411	31,199
Java	33,294	18,606	90,546
Manilla	36,617	19,509	94,941
Peru	5,866	3,335	16,230
Mauritius	6,334	3,602	17,529
Singapore	5,934	3,234	15,738
Ceylon	5,868	3,540	17,227
Burmah	8,155	4,645	22,605
Guam	1,795	991	4,823
Mexico	9,287	5,184	25,228
Bankok	1,885	1,030	5,012
Burrard's Inlet	200	120	584
Panama	3,555	2,025	9,855
New Guinea (British)	600	330	1,606
Maccassar	390	275	1,338
Padang	3,863	2,212	10,765
Petropaulovski	1,750	998	4,857
Cape Town	318	174	847
United States	305,829	176,991	861,327
India	54,386	30,277	147,343
	1,735,865	947,002	4,608,585
1887.			
Victoria	723,676	379,206	1,845,406
South Australia	127,370	62,715	305,203
Tasmania	43,375	23,631	115,000
New Zealand	150,399	81,478	396,513
Queensland	18,613	10,625	51,707
South Sea Islands	1,701	1,053	5,124
New Caledonia	15,153	7,928	38,582
Fiji	21,081	12,067	58,724
Western Australia	13,837	7,429	36,153
United States	299,802	164,983	802,890
India	54,214	30,248	147,202
Hong Kong	86,092	47,448	230,906
Ceylon	1,741	1,300	6,326
Peru	9,368	5,578	27,145
Java	51,974	28,739	139,858
Mauritius	9,916	5,627	27,384
China	23,187	14,301	69,596
Phillipine Islands	38,821	21,355	103,924
Chili	53,133	28,750	139,912
Singapore	32,040	17,807	86,658
Kaisar Wilhelm's Land	909	650	3,163
Mexico	2,310	1,169	5,689
Sandwich Islands	10,720	5,897	28,698
Cape of Good Hope	433	238	1,158
Panama	577	317	1,543
	1,790,442	960,539	4,674,463

The exports of coal to San Francisco and other ports on the Pacific coast of the United States have steadily increased during the last few years. The low rate of freight, and the drawback of 3s. 1d. (75 cents) per ton allowed upon coal imported into the United States for the use of foreign and domestic steamships, are the principal causes of the increase.

TABLE, showing the quantity and value of coal exported to the United States from New South Wales, from 1881 to 1887 inclusive, and the names of ports to which exported.

Port.	Quantity.	Value. £	Value. $
1881.	tons.		
San Francisco	138,772	63,537	309,203
Portland	11,230	4,635	22,556
Total	150,002	68,172	331,759
1882.			
San Francisco	172,958	96,496	469,598
Portland	6,113	3,712	18,064
Total	179,071	100,208	487,662
1883.			
San Francisco	191,184	115,821	563,642
Astoria	1,190	650	3,163
Portland	16,291	9,122	44,392
Total	208,665	125,593	611,197
1884.			
Wilmington, Cal	32,506	21,238	103,355
Astoria	1,481	814	3,961
San Francisco	167,888	98,938	481,482
Portland, United States	5,627	3,411	16,600
Total	207,502	124,401	605,398
1885.			
Wilmington, Cal	31,695	20,224	98,420
San Francisco	171,042	99,503	484,231
Portland	13,720	8,653	42,110
Total	216,457	128,380	624,761
1886.			
San Francisco	218,819	125,870	612,547
Wilmington, Cal	53,488	30,753	149,659
Portland	22,111	12,714	61,873
Astoria	11,411	7,654	37,248
Total	305,829	176,991	861,327
1887.			
San Francisco			
Wilmington, Cal	299,802	164,983	802,890
Portland			
Astoria			

The coal-mine at Greta, near Maitland, in the northern district, is worked at a greater depth than any other in the Colony and that owned by the Agricultural Company, Newcastle, comes next. The former is 450 feet, and the latter 303 feet in depth. Coal has been found, with the assistance of the diamond drill, at a depth of several thousand feet. The greatest depth penetrated with the diamond drill has been on the Sydney Coal mining Company's property, 16 miles from Sydney, were the drill has been sunk 2,308 feet. The samples thus brought to the surface are from the deepest coal deposit which has ever been reached in the southern hemisphere.

The total number of miners at the various collieries in New South Wales during the year 1886 was 7,947; of these 1,531 were employed above and 6,416 below ground.

An interesting feature in connection with coal-mining in New South Wales is its comparative freedom from accidents, such as fire-damp explosions, which render the loss of life so appalling in Great Britain. The total number of accidents in New South Wales during 1886 were seventy-five, and of these twenty-nine were fatal. The greater portion of these accidents were occasioned by the fall of coal.

However, on the 23rd March, 1887, a very serious accident occurred in the workings of the No. 1 or 7-foot coal-seam, at the Bulli Colliery, which resulted in the death of eighty-one miners.

The Bulli Colliery and adjoining village is situated on a portion of the picturesque mountain range of Illawarra that surrounds a small bay about 8 miles north of the sea-port town of Wollongong, and about 35 miles south of Sydney. It is $1\frac{1}{2}$ mile from the Bulli jetty on the sea-coast, from whence the coal is shipped into the Company's steamers and conveyed to market.

The mine was opened in 1863, and up to the time of the explosion, 1,794,685 tons of coal were raised from the No. 1 or 7-feet coal-seam. The coal is won by two adits driven into the coal-seam, facing the Pacific Ocean, on the Illawarra Range, at a height of about 400 feet above sea-level. By means of these adits, which communicate with each other, the miners may at all times pass in and out of the mine. The workings cover an area of 588 acres, and the coal has been wrought by the pillar and stall system. The main tunnels have penetrated $1\frac{1}{6}$ miles from the adit mouth. About July, 1884, the mine or roadway that was being carried through a fault (a dyke of diabase) in the line of the tunnel touched the coal. Much gas, probably "fire-damp," issued from the face, forcing the miners to retire.

The issue of gas from coal contiguous to or from a fault is not uncommon in mining, and special emphasis is laid on this fact on account of the almost perfect immunity the colonial collieries have, until now, enjoyed from the presence of marsh gas or light carburetted hydrogen gas. As gas was present, Davy Safety-lamps were used, and were kept carefully locked. So far as the Royal Commission appointed to inquire into the cause of the explosion could discover, the Regulations under the Mines Acts relating to safety-lamps were adhered to until the mine was closed in September, 1886, owing to a strike among the miners. When work was resumed in February, 1887, these

Regulations were neglected by the workmen, nor were they prevented from taking into the workings matches and tobacco-pipes. The arrangements for firing shots in the mine were also unusual and unsatisfactory.

The Commission were " convinced that the carelessness, want of skill, and the loose and perfunctory manner in which the principal operations in this mine were performed by the majority of the men, and countenanced by at least the overman and deputies, were intimately connected with, and led up to, the occurrence of the final catastrophe, whereby, by the direct negligence of probably one man, eighty other men lost their lives."

Long immunity from accident rendered the miners foolhardy.

This mine is a peculiarly dry one, the coal is friable, and at the end of a busy day the air becomes loaded with impalpable dust—a source of no small danger on the application of an open light. The presence of a dust-laden atmosphere increases the intensity and effects of an explosion.

The Royal Commission " are of opinion that the explosion at Bulli Colliery is one of the most notable instances of this on record"; and they conclude :—" That the exciting cause of the explosion was the flame from an overcharged shot that had been fired in the coal; and that the explosion was intensified, and the force increased and transmitted to a distance by the presence in the atmosphere of the mine of coal-dust in a minute state of division;" and further, they record the statement, " that the whole of the deaths were due, not to the direct effects of the flame of the explosion, but from the effects of after-damp, or the force or impact of the blast." After-damp consists of varying proportions of carbonic acid gas (stytho-choke damp), free nitrogen, and watery vapour in the form of steam, and probably a quantity of carbonic oxide gas (white damp).

It will be interesting to append the following analysis of the coal, as worked at Bulli Colliery, which will convey some idea of its value as a heat-producing agent :—

Analysis of Bulli Coal, by Dr. Pery, London.

Carbon	75·57
Hydrogen	4·70
Oxygen and nitrogen	4·90
Sulphur	0·54
Ash	13·17
Water	1·03
	100·00

For Gas.

Coke	74·78
Volatile gaseous matter	24·19
Water	1·03
	100·00

It has a somewhat singed appearance, is dull and non-lustrous, and, being friable, produces dust by attrition or handling.

Analysis of Coal-dust collected by Members of the Royal Commission.

No.	Description.	Moisture.	Volatile Hydrocarbon.	Fixed Carbon.	Ash.	Sulphur.	Specific Gravity.	Coke. %
1.	From wheel bend of main tunnel, about — chains from entrance.	Fine brown and black coal-dust, and small pieces (¼ inch diameter) of bright bituminous coal, together with small pieces of wood and clay-shale, as though the whole had been scraped up from the ground.	2·15	19·02	48·02	29·30	0·52	1·52	78·31
2.	From top of a fallen prop, – chains from entrance.	Very fine brown and black bituminous coal-dust and a little sand.	2·40	16·30	50·43	30·24	0·63	..	80·67
3.	From main road, 40 yds. from No. 1 heading.	Same as No. 2, with a few stringy splinters of wood.	2·55	16·45	51·27	29·50	0·53	..	80·77
4.	From No. 1 heading from shelf on coal near No. 4 bord.	Fine dust and pieces of bituminous coal up to ¼ inch diameter.	1·40	19·00	55·37	23·70	0·53	..	79·07
5.	From No. 2 bord, No. 2 heading	Dust of bright bituminous coal and pieces of the same up to ¼ inch in diameter, with a little quartz sand.	1·46	19·14	51·94	26·01	0·55	..	78·85
6.	From half-way down No. 2 heading.	Coarse and fine dust of bright bituminous coal and small pieces of clay-shale.	1·43	20·25	51·90	25·81	0·64	1·480	77·71
7.	From recess in coal near face of tunnel, Hill End.	Fine and coarse dust of bright bituminous coal, and a few pieces of the same up to ¼ inch diameter.	1·98	16·87	57·32	23·25	0·58	..	80·57

REMARKS.— All these samples were received in fine powder, and contained much dirt. In one or two of the samples pieces of wood were visible. This will account for the high percentage of ash obtained. The colour of the ashes was from white to gray. Where the specific gravity of the sample is not given there was not a sufficient quantity of the sample left after analysis for that purpose. The samples were rather small for analysis.

The wages paid to miners are from 8d. (16 cents) to 1s. 3d. (30 cents) per hour. The wages and the number of hours the men are required to work have been the causes of frequent disturbances, which in some instances have led to serious rioting and loss of life. These disputes are usually settled by arbitration. They assume a very grave character when the coal companies insist on the employment of non-union men, or blacklegs, as they are called by the miners. As many as 500 to 700 men are out on strike at once, and it is astonishing the length of time they are enabled to hold out. One of the most noted of these occurred when 300 of the men struck at the Lambton mine, in the northern district. The men demanded additional pay as the difficulty of the work increased, and the labour council of their district approved of their course. The miners held out for a period of six months, and during that time they refused to do work of any kind, and were supported by contributions from the various trade and labour organizations. The difficulty was finally settled by arbitration, concessions being made on both sides.

The strike at Mount Kembla and Mount Keira, in the southern district, which began in December, 1886, was of a serious character. The men, after committing several acts of violence, refused every concession offered by their employers, and the dispute, which promised to become still more serious, was not settled until a large number of miners had been engaged from Europe by cable. It was then agreed that the men should resume work on the terms formerly proposed by their employers, and that the European miners should, upon their arrival, be provided with work upon other coal-fields.

KEROSENE.

THE quantity of kerosene imported into New South Wales during the year 1885 was larger than that of any other year in the history of the Colony, and consisted of 1,289,227 gallons. The imports for 1886 were 1,105,771 gallons, and the value £51,631 ($251,263).

The imports of kerosene into the Colony of Victoria are larger than those of New South Wales, as the former Colony does not produce any oil. The import of kerosene into Victoria for 1886 was 1,711,243 gallons, valued at £82,729 ($402,601). A duty of 6d. (12 cents) per gallon is charged on the imports of kerosene into both Colonies.

THE following table shows the quantity and value of kerosene imported into the Colony of New South Wales for each year from 1875 to 1887 :—

Year.	Quantity.	Value.		Year.	Quantity.	Value.	
	Gallons.	£	$		Gallons.	£	$
1875	181,927	13,780	67,060	1882	629,992	39,516	192,305
1876	355,860	29,616	144,126	1883	592,207	33,725	164,123
1877	464,944	45,716	222,427	1884	676,704	38,280	186,290
1878	673,528	47,963	233,412	1885	1,289,227	69,377	337,623
1879	482,669	35,001	170,332	1886	1,105,771	51,631	251,263
1880	485,228	32,094	156,185	1887	932,760	54,484	265,146
1881	493,527	30,737	149,582				

All these imports were of American manufacture, and reached Sydney either direct or by way of other colonial ports.

The Sydney importers of American kerosene complain bitterly against the law in New South Wales for regulating the sale of kerosene. They say that it places them at a great disadvantage in competing for the trade with the local manufacturers. The regulations of the different Insurance Offices in the Colony also require a conformity to the law. The law forbids the imported article from being stored anywhere except in a licensed kerosene warehouse, and provides that no one shall be allowed to keep more than 200 gallons of kerosene on his premises. The Act was passed in 1871 (Statutes of New South Wales, 35 Victoria No. 1). The fourth section of the Act is as follows :—

Storage of kerosene.

4. After 1st January, 1872, no person shall have or keep in any house, store-house, warehouse, shop, cellar, yard, wharf, or any other building or place occupied by the same person or persons, within the boundaries of any town or municipality, more than 200 gallons of kerosene at any one time, unless such house, store-house, warehouse, shop, cellar, yard, wharf, or any other building be situate more than 50 yards from a dwelling-house, or from any building or place belonging to any other person in which goods are stored. And any person acting in contravention of this section shall forfeit all the kerosene so kept in excess of the said quantity, together with the cases or tins containing the same, and be liable to a penalty not exceeding 2s. for every gallon of kerosene so kept in excess : Provided, that nothing in this clause shall prevent the storage of kerosene in any quantity on the premises where it is manufactured.

The local companies are enabled to deliver either small or large quantities of kerosene from their works without incurring the heavy charges for storage; they have also a saving of a certain proportion of railway freight on up country supplies. The American oil is therefore handicapped to the above extent as regards country purchasers. It takes 1¼ American gallons to make 1 imperial gallon, the latter being the measure by which kerosene is sold; there is also the leakage in transit to be considered.

The following table shows the imports of kerosene from the United States of America into the Australasian Colonies during the year 1887. (Each case contains 8 Imperial gallons.)

1887.	Cases.
New South Wales	113,184
Victoria	212,828
Queensland	61,785
South Australia	110,515
New Zealand	115,350
Tasmania and Western Australia	19,322
Total	632,984

The standard tests of New South Wales, and indeed of all the Australasian Colonies, are flash tests instead of fire tests. The commercial meaning of the word test is the fire test, which is usually from 12° to 15° higher than the flashing point. For instance, oil at 130° fire test is equal to about 115° flash test. The directions for applying the flashing test of kerosene oil adopted by the New South Wales Government are as follows:—

The instrument to be employed must be similar in construction to that adopted by the Metropolitan Board of Works for London for similar purposes, and registered W. C. Miles, 36 Great Pearl Street, London, and commonly called the "Metropolitan Petroleum Oil Tester," and the test shall be conducted in a closed room free from current of air.

Sixteen ounces by measure of water shall be placed in the water-bath, of a temperature not less than 70° of Fahrenheit's thermometer.

The oil vessel containing 2 ounces *by measure* of the oil to be tested shall then be placed in the water-bath, and the temperature raised by the means provided in the apparatus. A small jet of flame shall be brought to the prescribed distance from the surface of the oil as indicated by a wire across the mouth of the oil vessel as frequently as may be deemed necessary by the operator, but not less frequently than once for every 5° of heat as shown by the thermometer until a tempearture of 90° is reached, and then once for every 2° until a temperature of 100° is reached, and then the test shall be applied for every degree until the flashing point is reached, that is to say, the temperature at which a flame or flicker of flame first passes from the testing jet to the oil.

The time occupied in performing the test shall in no case exceed *fifteen minutes* reckoning from the time the oil vessel containing the oil is placed in the water-bath.

The bulb of the thermometer shall be immersed half-an-inch in the oil, and the temperature or flashing point to be adopted shall not be less than 110° of *Fahrenheit's* thermometer.

There is a popular brand of Australian oil that bears the test of 200°. It has the same yellowish colour as the low-test oils. The American high-test oils, on the contrary, are always made "water-white." The colonial manufacturers state that the yellow kerosene burns much brighter and better than that made water-white.

The following are, taking an average of years, the current prices for wholesale parcels of American kerosene:—

Brand.	Test.	Price.	
	Degrees.	Pence.	Cents.
Aurora	130	9	18
Devoe's	130	9	18
Diamond	130	9	18
Devoe's Nonpariel	150	12	24
Evening Star	150	12	24
Snowflake	150	12	24
Light of the Age	160	14	28

There are many other brands, but these are the leading ones.

New South Wales has for many years carried on a profitable industry in the manufacture of petroleum and paraffine out of the shale product, which exists in considerable quantities in parts of the Colony. Those interested in the industry state that the decline in price is of a temporary character, and that the industry will rally again, inasmuch as the difficulty of obtaining the mineral at the mines is not so great as formerly, while at the same time the cost of manufacturing it into oil has been materially lessened.

The following table shows the quantity and value of kerosene shale produced during the years 1865 to 1886.

Year.	Quantity.	Average price per ton.			Total value.	Year.	Quantity.	Average price per ton.			Total value.
	Tons.	£	s.	d.	£		Tons.	£	s.	d.	£
1865	570	4	2	5·47	2,350	1878	24,371	2	6	11·40	57,211
1866	2,770	2	18	10·48	8,150	1879	32,519	2	1	1·96	66,930
1867	4,079	3	14	9·21	15,249	1880	19,201	2	6	7·03	44,725
1868	16,952	2	17	7·11	48,816	1881	27,894	1	9	2·59	40,748
1869	7,500	2	10	0·00	18,750	1882	48,065	1	15	0·00	84,114
1870	8,580	3	4	3·18	27,570	1883	49,250	1	16	10·77	90,862
1871	14,700	2	6	3·91	34,050	1884	31,618	2	5	7·86	72,176
1872	11,040	2	11	11·91	28,700	1885	27,462	2	8	11·62	67,239
1873	17,850	2	16	6·55	50,475	1886	43,563	2	5	10·79	99,976
1874	12,100	2	5	1·48	27,300						
1875	6,197	2	10	2·22	15,500		441,242	2	5	1·42	995,413
1876	15,998	3	0	0·00	47,994			$10·98			$4,844,177
1877	18,963	2	9	0·81	46,524						

The heaviest export of shale from New South Wales occurred during 1882, when it reached 35,978 tons, valued at £79,715 ($387,933.)

The following table shows the quantity and value of the export of kerosene shale from the Colony of New South Wales for each year since 1875:—

Year.	Quantity.	Value.	Year.	Quantity.	Value.
	Tons.	£ $		Tons.	£ $
1875	3,527	10,383 50,529	1882	35,978	79,715 387,933
1876	8,154	21,314 103,725	1883	22,657	47,345 230,404
1877	4,667	14,163 68,924	1884	12,804	29,970 145,846
1878	12,202	34,063 165,768	1885	14,456	40,606 197,609
1879	11,436	29,275 142,467	1886	21,086	60,621 295,012
1880	10,880	24,189 117,788	1887	21,418	62,320 303,280
1881	17,846	38,231 186,002			

It has been predicted for many years that the oil-bearing districts of the United States would soon become exhausted, and that the bulk of the world's supply must be looked for in Russia and Australia. Although we cannot reasonably hope for such unlooked for development as was shown by some of the wells of Pennsylvania and New York in 1882, nevertheless nothing as yet has occurred to indicate that the United States will not continue for many years to furnish the great bulk of the world's supply of kerosene.

The kerosene shale in New South Wales covers a vast area. It is found at Lake Macquarie and Greta, in Cumberland County; at Mount Megalong and Mount York, in Cook County; at Joadja Creek, Cambewarra ranges, Broughton Creek, and Toonali River, Burragorang, in Camden County, and at Blackheath, the Vale of Hartley, and other places in the Blue Mountains. The mineral was known to exist in New South Wales as early as 1827. In that year D. P. Cunningham, of the British navy, describes a species of coal found at Bathurst resembling Scotch cannel coal, "being nearly as light, and breaking with a similar fracture."

The Rev. W. B. Clarke, in an able report directed the attention of the New South Wales Government to this mineral in the year 1849. Mr. Clarke stated in his report that he had examined the mineral in 1841 and was then greatly impressed with its peculiar properties. Count Strzelecki, in a work entitled "Physical Description of New South Wales," published in 1845, gives a brief description of the mineral. The Count at first thought it belonged to the Newcastle basin, but that theory was invalidated from the fact that the seams overlapped masses of pure bitumen, a characteristic not found with Newcastle coals. Mr. Clarke stated its specific gravity was 1·204, and that it was found in masses from 6 to 12 inches in thickness. In a subsequent edition the London editor without Mr. Clarke's knowledge, omitted to use the matter referring to the existence of this coal. Mr. Clarke afterwards said, that while this undeserved act concealed from the English reader a valuable discovery it did not prevent the colonists from bringing their product under the notice of manufacturers.

Professor Liversidge, one of the highest authorities on minerals in Australasia, does not think that the name "kerosene shale" is a proper one for the New South Wales mineral, for the reason that the substance does not possess the properties of a shale; that is, it has not the characteristic lamellar or fatty structure, but the reverse, being very compact and breaking with large, smooth, conchoidal surfaces with equal readiness in every direction, and without any tendency to follow the planes of stratification. Professor Liversidge states that when the mineral is in large blocks there are occasional evidences of stratification, but even then they are mainly rendered visible by the presence of layers or films of earthy matter. The mineral does not differ very widely from cannel coal and torbanite. Like cannel coal it usually occurs with ordinary coal in the form of lenticular deposits, and when of good quality it burns readily without melting, and emits a luminous smoky flame. When heated in a tube it neither decrepitates nor fuses. In colour it varies from a brownish-black with greenish shade to full black. When struck it emits a dull wooden sound. The surface of the joints is often coated with a film of white clay, and for this reason it is sometimes called "white clay." The mineral at Hartley Vale and Murrurundi is only slightly soluble in alcohol.

The Vale of Hartley mine is situated in one of the most picturesque and romantic parts of the Colony, about 83 miles north-west of Sydney, in the center of the Blue Mountains, at an altitude of 3,118 feet above the level of the sea. The "zig-zag" railway up the mountains has aided greatly in the establishment of a number of important industries in the District. Iron works at Eskbank are carried on successfully, and the coal deposits are inexhaustible. The kerosene shale found there is said to be the richest in the world. Considerable quantities of it are used in the large cities of the Colonies for the purpose of enriching gas. It is also exported for the same purpose to Holland, Java, and the States on the Pacific slope of the United States. Only the better quality of the mineral is exported, the scraps and inferior portions being retained for the extraction of oil. The seams are from 6 inches to 30 inches in thickness. It is much more difficult to mine than coal. It does not run down readily into blocks, but has to be separated piece by piece and splintered off into sharp thin pieces. It is easily lighted with a match, and burns with a steady flame like a candle, and emits a strong odour of kerosene. The company working the mine has a capital of £100,000 ($486,650), in £1 ($4·86) shares. Besides their operations at the mine they have extensive oil works at the suburb of Waterloo, where they manufacture paraffine and gasolene.

The Joadja Creek mine is situated 95 miles south of Sydney by Railway and 15 miles from Mittagong. The property, consisting of 1,944 acres, belongs to the Australian Kerosene Oil and Mineral Company. The plant was erected at considerable cost, and is one of the best in the Colony, the machinery being of the most improved patterns. The stationary engine for the purpose of winding the mineral out of the valley is an object of especial interest, and much can be said in favour of the company's method of separating the shale through their improved coal-cutters, run by compressed air. Mr. W. H. Lyne, in a valuable work entitled the "Commerce and Resources of New South Wales," has given a charming account of the Joadja Creek mine. He describes it as being situated "in the midst of a circle of mountains in a lovely valley, the extent of which in any direction would not exceed the range of a rifle shot." The approaches to it are almost inaccessible. The huts of the village can be seen in the distance like toys, and a little further off is seen the manufacturing works, and above and beyond them on the mountain side the mine from which the shale is taken. At night, standing on the ridge immediately above the village, and between the place and Mittagong, the valley seems a tremendous abyss of darkness with nothing to relieve the intensity of the gloom but the faint glimmer of a few window or fire lights. The shale seams are believed to be the same as those worked in the Hartley District, although much thinner. The Joadja mine shows first a freestone roof and next about 8 inches of soft coal, then the top shale, which is from 9 to 11 inches in thickness, capable of yielding 100 gallons of crude oil to the ton; below this is the bottom shale, ranging in thickness from 12 to 16 inches, and then is found a seam of hard inferior coal about 16 inches thick. Professor Liversidge states that the shale contains impressions of glossopteris and of the vertebraria. These fossil plants are best seen in the outcrops of the poorer portions of the shale, and especially where they have been exposed to the weather. The glossopteris fronds are generally found between the laminæ; the vertebraria runs across them. The company working the mine has given much satisfaction to the shareholders. They claim that their product is the best hitherto supplied in the Colony, and that is fully 25 per cent. richer than the best samples of the Scotch Boghead mineral. They furnish shale to the gas-works in Sydney and elsewhere. The method of using it is to break it into small bits, and mix from 3 to 6 per cent. of it with the ordinary charge of coal according to the quality of the gas required. The Manager of the mine states that it is not desirable to retort the shale by the usual process, from the fact that its extreme richness causes the heat to fall off and a large proportion of the volatile matter to recondense in the hydraulic main. When mixed with ordinary coking coal 3 per cent. will yield gas of 18 candles, and 6 per cent. with the same coal, 22 candles. The use of the shale prevents the deposits of naphthaline—the chief obstacle in the way of making gas.

Professor Liversidge examined two specimens of shale from the Joadja mine, which upon analysis yielded the following results:—

Constituents.	No. 1.	No. 2
	Per cent.	Per cent.
Hydroscopic moisture	·44	·04
Volatile hydrocarbon	83·87	82·13
Fixed carbon	8·03	7·16
Ash gray	7·17	10·34
Sulphur	·58	·33
	100·00	100·00

Another specimen examined by Mr. Charles Watt, when Government Analyst, gave the following analysis :—

Constituents.	Per cent.
Volatile matter	85·2
Fixed Carbon	8·2
Ash	6·6
	100·00

It may here be observed that coal seams to the north of Sydney are less bituminous and more anthracite in their character than those which have been worked near the coast south of Sydney.

Mr. W. A. Dixon, F.C.S., obtained a number of specimens of this mineral and found it much lighter than the Boghead shale of Scotland, the specific gravity being 1·098 against 1·20. The yield of hydrocarbon he said was much greater than that obtained from picked specimens of Boghead, whilst the ash was only half as great.

One sample yielded the following :—

Constituents.	Per cent.
Moisture	·41
Volatile hydrocarbon	77·07
Fixed carbon	12·13
Ash	10·27
Sulphur	·12
	100·00
Coke	22·30

Mr. Dixon found the coke to be bright and lustrous in colour, and the ash white. He said that on account of the very large proportion of volatile hydrocarbon in the mineral the yield of gas or coal from it ought to be very great. That its low specific gravity, together with the small quantity of sulphur it contained, warranted the conclusion that the product would be easy of purification and of high illuminating power. The shale has been used for several years with much satisfaction at the North Shore Gas Works, Sydney. At the Sydney Gas Works some thousands of tons per annum are used with great success. The Manager stated that its percentage of ash was unusually low.

In London the mineral attracted much attention, and the question arose as to whether it was a Boghead coal or a mineral shale, and whether or not it should be subject to the city dues on coal. It was, however, determined to be coal on the authority of Charles Heisch, F.C.S., and Professor Ramsey, director of the geological surveys of Great Britain. A similar discussion took place a number of years ago in the celebrated case of E. W. Binney against the Clydesdale Chemical Works for the infringement of patents for the manufacture of paraffine from bituminous coal. The case was tried at Edinburgh, but the result showed a wide difference of opinion in regard to the character of the mineral. Professor Graham and Dr. Penny pronounced it coal. Hugh Miller called it an inflammable shale. Professor Chapman was positive that it was a bituminous shale, and Professor Anderson was equally positive that it was very far from being anything of the kind. Professor Brande said it was a new, peculiar mineral, and Dr. Wilson called it clay impregnated with bitumen. Three microscopists testified that it exhibited no trace of organic structure, and four others stated that there was the strongest possible evidence of vegetable structure. Mr. Dixon said that nothing clearly was settled by the trial, and that while the mineral examined partook of the nature of coal, it differed from it in so many essential particulars that it should be classed as a different substance, and that it must be borne in mind that when we distill coal the product is tar, and when we distill the so called kerosene shale the product is oil. Dr. Heisch, in his report upon the New South Wales Joadja mineral, showed that its gas-producing power was extraordinary. The following is the analysis of the specimen:—

Result of analysis by Charles Heisch, F.C.S., late professor of chemistry in the Medical College of Middlesex Hospital; public analyst of the districts of Lewisham and Hampstead, London.

Specific gravity	1131·13
Ash	10·1
Moisture lost at 212°	3·56
Moisture lost at 250°	3·72
Coke	25·65
Gas-tar and volatile matter	67·07
Total carbons	64·72
Total hydrogens	4·65
The ash contains:—	
Silica	7·4
Alumina with traces of iron	2·27
Lime, &c.	0·43
Worked as in practice, it yields:—	
Gas .... cubic feet per ton	16,200
Coke .... cwt. per ton	4·46
Tar .... gallons = 257 pounds	19

The gas is too rich to test in our photometer; it is certainly over 50 candles. When the mineral is put into the retort the gas comes off so quickly as to make it almost impossible to work on the large scale without mixing it with some other mineral.

The tar is very fluid. It yields hardly any benzole, much light oil fit for rubber solvent, little or no anthracene, but a larger quantity of pitch than might have been expected from the fluidity. The coke is very light and friable.

It yields but little water or ammonia during carbonizing.

Mixed in small quantity with ordinary coal it is valuable, as it increases the illuminating power of the gas very much. It is one of the substances on the borderland of coal, but taking all its properties, chemical and mechanical, into consideration I believe it to be coal. It is certainly as much coal as many of the Bogheads, and both equitably and commercially I think must be considered coal.

Mr. Robert Martin, engineer of the London Gas-Light Company, found the mineral to give 15,428 cubic feet per ton, of 44·7 candles and that a mixture of 5 per cent. of it with 95 per cent. of Penrith coal gave 11,480 cubic feet per ton, of 18·35 candles.

A report furnished by Alfred Kitt, engineer to the Gas-Light and Coke Company, Pimlico, London, states that a quantity consisting of 200 tons received from four different ships gave the following practical results:—

Gas made per ton of shale .... cubic feet	14,057
Illuminating power in standard sperm candles	43·13
Hydrocarbon absorbed by bromine .... per cent...	21·0
Oil and tar per ton of shale .... gallons...	40
Ammoniacal liquor of 3½ ounce strength ...... gallons...	24
Coke or refuse ....cwt. to the ton ...	4

The illuminating power ranged from 39·10 to 46·5 sperm candles.

NOTE.—As standard candles burn 120 grains of sperm per hour, whilst 1 pound weighs 7,000 grains.

$$\frac{17,267 \times 46 \cdot 04 \times 120}{5 \times 7,000} = 2,733 \text{ pounds sperm.}$$

That is to say, the mineral converted into illuminating gas gives out on consumption more light than its own weight of sperm. Ordinary bituminous coal yields about 11,000 cubic feet of gas of about 16 candle power, so

$$\frac{11,000 \times 16 \times 120}{5 \times 7,000} = 592 \text{ pounds sperm.}$$

So that the shale is 4·6 times as valuable as coal for gas making.

It may be mentioned that the works of the Australian Kerosene Oil and Mineral Company at Joadja alone have an area of about 7 acres, while its operations there support a population of over 1,000 souls.

The discovery of kerosene shale at Capertee, near the Mudgee line of railway, a few years ago, attracted much attention throughout the Colony. A valuable report was made upon this mine by Mining Surveyer Seaver, in August, 1883, accompanied by a map showing the mode of occurrences of the shale and coal seams as determined by aneroid measurement. Although a company was organised for working the mine and operations conducted with every appearance of success, work was suspended from some unexplained cause.

Mr. Seaver states that the formation of the country in which the mine is located is hilly, and that the coal measures are capped by from 300 to 500 feet of Hawkesbury sandstone and conglomerates, which are occasionally surmounted by basalts rising above the intervening valleys from 1,200 to 1,600 feet. The formations in the valleys consist of slate and limestone beds. The Hawkesbury sandstones and conglomerates form bold escarpments to the summits of hills, consisting of cliffs and precipices. In some places the tops of the hills are worn by meteoric forces. In other places the table tops rise into low hills composed of broken bluestone. Immediately below the base of the Hawkesbury sandstone, which is about 2,900 feet above sea level, the coal measures commence. These measures for about 40 feet consist of clay bands, sandstones, iron bands, and light-gray slates, and at 2,900 feet a coal seam of about 5 feet 6 inches thick, with narrow clay bands running through it, then about 7 feet of clay bands much stained with iron oxide, and then another clay band and 40 feet of sandstone and another coal seam about 3 feet thick. At about 150 feet below the last seam is found the seam of cannel coal varying from about 3 feet to 6 inches in thickness. Two tunnels have been constructed, one of which is 100 feet in length and the other 300 feet. The mine is situated within 3 miles of the railway.

F

The following analyses of shale found in the neighborhood of Capertee were made by Mr. C. Watt, while government analyst :—

Locality.	Hygroscopic moisture.	Volatile hydrocarbons, &c.	Fixed carbon.	Ash.	Total.	Specific gravity.
	per cent.	per cent.	per cent.	per cent.	per cent.	per cent.
Mudgee line of railway	2·20	28·40	18·60	50·80	100	......
Neighbourhood of Capertee ..	1·04	72·56	18·40	8·00	100	......
Do	0.75	68·25	20·48	10·52	100	1·11
Do	0·44	57·16	17·00	35·40	100	......
Glenowlan, near Capertee	0·34	48·56	8·70	42·40	100	1·37
Capertee	0·75	67·09	8·66	23·50	100	1·18
Do	1·30	33·26	33·62	31·82	100	1·42

Professor Liversidge gives the following valuable tables, in which the kerosene shale of New South Wales is compared with that of some of the most celebrated mines in Europe and America :—

Tables comparing New South Wales kerosene shale with that of some of the most celebrated mines in Europe and America :—

Locality.	Moisture.	Volatile hydrocarbons.	Fixed carbon.	Ash.	Sulphur.	Specific gravity.	Analyst.
Joadja Creek	0·71	87·42	5·17	6·17	0·53	....	W. A. Dixon.
Joadja Creek	0·44	83·861	8·035	7·075	0·520	1·054	Liversidge.
Hartley Vale	....	82·50	6·50	11·0	......	....	B. Silliman.
Joadja Creek	0·04	82·123	7·160	10·340	0·337	1·220	Liversidge.
Hartley Vale	....	82·24	4·97	12·79	......	1·052	Do
Joadja Creek	0·41	77·07	12·13	10·27	0·12	1·098	W. A. Dixon.
Do	1·16	73·364	15·765	9·175	0·536	1·103	Liversidge.
Cannel coal, Mold Flints....	....	72·08	21·91	6·01	......	....	Percy.
Murrurundi...............	1·165	71·882	6·467	19·136	0·540	....	Liversidge.
Torbanite, Torbane Hill	....	71·17	7·65	21·18	......	1·170	How.
Cannel coal, Scotland	....	60·77	10·43	19·78	......	....	Percy.
Torbonite, Torbane Hill	9·720	69·095	9·045	20·540	......	1·316	Liversidge.
New Caledonia (Hartley's) ..	0·55	64·62	8·71	26·12	......	1·238	Do
Greta mine	0·48	61·18	25·13	13·21	......	....	Do
Albertite, New Brunswick ..	....	57·490	42·086	0·424	......	1·100	Do
Greta mine	1·475	53·798	27·046	15·870	0·011	1·130	Do
Cannel coal, Wigan	1·464	45·000	45·510	7·117	......	1·250	Do

The following table, was prepared by Professor Chandler, Columbia College, New York, to compare the Hartley Mineral with Grahamite and Albertite, both of which are used for enriching gas:—

Locality.	Volatile matter.	Fixed carbon.	Ash.	Gas per ton of 2,240 pounds, in cubic feet.	Candle power of gas.	Coke per ton of 2,240 pounds.		Gas purified by 1 bushel of lime in cubic feet.
						lb.	Bush.	
Grahamite, West Virginia	53·50	41·50	2·00	15,000	28·70	1,056	44	......
Albertite, Nova Scotia	57·70	41·90	0·40	14,784	49·55	806	16	......
Hartley mineral, New South Wales	82·50	6·50	11·00	13,716	131·00	424	....	5,086

The Australian Kerosene Oil and Mineral Company, and the New South Wales Shale and Oil Company manufacture lubricants, candles, and a very fair article of axle oil, which is extensively used by the Public Works Department of the Colony. Until recently all the axle oil used was imported from Europe. Mr. Downe, Superintendent of Locomotives, while on a visit to the United States, observed the use of a superior axle oil on the railway carriages, and obtained samples of it for the purpose of introducing it here. Its use gave much satisfaction, and large quantities of it were imported from time to time from America. Samples of this oil were at Mr. Downe's suggestion submitted to Mr. Fell, in Sydney, for the purpose of having a similar oil manufactured out of the native shales. Mr. Fell, after a series of experiments with the colonial shale, succeeded in producing an oil very nearly as good as the imported article and at about the same cost. The oil has been so much improved that it is now used on the tram cars, motors, and railway stock.

DIAMONDS.

Although diamonds have been known to exist in various parts of Australia for the last thirty or forty years no effort has been made to conduct any systematic mining operations for them except in the Colony of New South Wales. For a considerable period no importance was attached to the discovery, on account of the small size of the stones. There was also a prevailing opinion that they were not diamonds but a species of colourless topaz.

The Rev. W. B. Clarke, in an interesting and valuable paper on the resources of the Colonies, makes mention of the discovery of diamonds on the Macquarie River in New South Wales in the year 1860. No mention, however, is made as to their size or value or of the conditions under which they were found. In 1867 attention was directed to the discovery of diamonds on the Cudgegong River, about 20 miles from Mudgee and 170 miles from Sydney. About that time the discovery of diamonds was reported at Beechworth, Victoria, and in various localities amongst the gold-bearing reefs of South Australia. Professor Liversidge, of the Sydney University, has devoted much study to the subject of diamonds, and especially to their occurrence in Australia. He visited the mines at Bingera in 1873, and has since taken the deepest interest in the progress of mining there.

A very valuable paper, entitled "The Occurrence of the Diamond near Mudgee," by Mr. Norman Taylor, of the Victorian Geological Survey, and Professor Alexander M. Thomson, states that diamonds were first seen in the Mudgee district, 190 miles from Sydney by railroad, at a place called Two-mile Flat. Little attention, however, was paid to the discovery until the spring of 1869, when the search was taken up briskly by the Gwydir Mining Company, and by several independent parties. The localities producing the diamonds are situated along the Cudgegong River, beginning at the junction of the river with Waldra Creek and extending to Hassall's Hill, a distance of 7 miles. The gems are said to be more numerous in outliers of an ancient river bed.

These outliers occur at various distances from the present channel, and at elevations of about 40 feet above it. Mr. Taylor and Professor Thomson state that these outliers of drift are capped by hard, compact, and in many instances columnar basalt, and that they have all the characteristics of the widespread deposits in Victoria, which the geological survey there assigned to the older pliocene. The paper states that the patches of diamond-bearing drift (older pliocene), with their protective coverings of basalt, though once forming parts of a continuous deposit, have been isolated by extensive denudations. The point of eruption from which the basaltic flow emanated appears to lie to the eastward, but it has not hitherto been detected; its remnants can be followed up for at least 17 miles along the river, in some spots still showing a thickness of 70 feet, which proves the igneous outburst to have been of considerable magnitude, and sufficiently to alter materially the physical aspects of the river valley. The following is a list of the gem stones and heavy minerals found in the drift :—1st, black vesicular pleonaste ; 2nd, topaz ; 3rd, quartz : 4th, corundum ; 5th, zircon ; 6th, tourmaline ; 7th, black titaniferous iron sand ; 8th, black magnetic iron sand ; 9th, titanic acid, probably brookite, in flat red transparent or reddish white translucent plates ; 10th, wood tin ; 11th, garnet ; 12th, iron hagly fragments slightly rusted metal ; 13th, gold, fine scaly and occasionally fragments enclosed by quartz : 14th, the diamond itself is found distributed irregularly through the older pliocene river drift.

At Hassall's Hill thirty-three loads from one claim yielded 306 diamonds. Another claim yielded at the rate of eight diamonds to the load. Out of 5,000 or 6,000 diamonds found, very few were of any considerable size, the largest being a colourless octahedron, weighing 5 3-5 carats. It was found in the river, between Two-mile Flat and the Rocky Ridge at a spot where the older pliocene drift had been discharged in gold-washing. A large majority of the stones were pellucid and colourless ; many were straw-coloured, and a few dark, green and black. The method adopted in washing for the diamonds, when water could be obtained, consisted in screening the drift so as to separate the larger stones. The coarser portions of the clay were then raked aside, so that the gold and finer matter could be carried away by a stream of water flowing through an iron grating on the water blankets below. One of Hunt's machines was used to separate the heavier from the lighter material that passed over the blankets. After the reduction of the material by this process the diamonds could be readily distinguished. Water is now said to be more abundant than formerly in the Mudgee district, and a new company has been formed for the purpose of conducting operations. The new company, it is said, will be supplied with the latest improvements in machinery and diamond mining appliances.

The Bingera diamond-mines are located on the Gwydir River, 8 miles from the town of Bingera and 354 miles north-west of Sydney. The route there is by railway to Glen Innes 324 miles and the remainder of the journey is performed by coach.

According to Professor Liversidge, the Bingera diamond deposits are situated in a kind of a basin or closed valley amidst the hills. The basin is 4 miles long and 3 wide and opens towards the north. Running into the valley are various spurs of basalt covering portions of the drift. The drift is 30 or 40 miles in length and is thought to be the old bed of the river Horton. The rocks upon which the diamond drift rest consists of *Argillaceous shales*. In one part of the ground the shales are joined by siliceous conglomerates, and there the diamonds are the most abundant. The pebbles and boulders consist of various coloured jasper white quartz, black flinty slate. The following list of gem stones associated with diamonds at Bingera is supplied by Professor Liversidge. Tourmaline, or jet stone occurs as rolled prisms usually from $\frac{1}{4}$ to $\frac{3}{4}$ of an inch long. They retain the triangular section, but occasionally no trace of crystalline form is left, and they appear merely as more or less rounded black pebbles often with a jetted surface totally unlike the usual appearance of tourmaline ; the blow-pipe decides their character at once. These black jet stones are invariably found with the diamond, and are regarded by the miners as one of the best indications of its presence. Zircon, occurs in small crystals of red and brown colours also nearly colourless, but more commonly as rolled pieces of a brown shade. A cleavage plane is usually to be seen. Sapphire, generally in small angular pieces and usually of a pale colour. In many the blue tint does not overspread the whole of the fragment. The ruby is present, but very rare. One fragment showed the faces of an acute hexagonal pyramid and basal pinacoid. The lower half of the crystal had been fractured. The fragments of sapphire are far less in size than those found at Mudgee and in other places, and far less rolled. The major part often appears to have undergone no rounding at all, thus showing a broad distinction between it and the gem sand at Mudgee. Topaz, as rounded fragments and sometimes with rough crystalline outline. They are generally of a dull yellowish colour. Garnet, in small rough looking illformed crystals of a dull red shade. Spinelle, not very common, generally in small red or pinkish fragments. Quartz, small prisms capped with the pyramid, more or less rolled, transparent, of a pale red smoke colour. Amongst the jaspar pebbles are some of pale mottled tints of yellow, pink, drab, brown, and bluish grey. These are termed morlops by the miners and are regarded by them with much favour as they say that they never find one of them in the dish without diamonds accompanying it. The average specific gravity of the morlops is 3·25, nearly the same as that of the diamond, hence the reason of their being found together. They are oval in form, smooth, and rarely exceed a $\frac{1}{4}$ of an inch in length. The miners are unable to tell how the name originated and there is no mention of it in any work in mineralogy. Brookite, small flat fragments, very rare titaniferous iron, rather common. Magnetic iron ore, in small grains showing an octahedral form under the microscope, coated with hydrated sesquioxide of iron easily removed by the magnet. Wood-tin, rare in small rolled particles. Gold, fine grains and scales present, but in small quantity, and the greater portion attached to the magnetite, hence the magnet was used for the purpose of removing it. Osmiridium, in small brittle plates rare. Diamonds, small size, clear, colourless and transparent, while others have a pale straw or yellow tint. One or two small size of very dark colour have been seen, also a greenish one. Nineteen specimens were examined and their specific gravity found to be 3·42, that of the Mudgee being 3·44. In some the crystalline form is distinctly shown, but a number of others have rounded faces.

The following table shows the yield of the Bingera diamond drift to the ton:—

6 tons of drift	41 diamonds.
4½ ,,	143 ,,
6 ,,	88 ,,
6 ,,	125 ,,
6 ,,	163 ,,
Refuse from Machines	41 ,,
	601 diamonds.

In 1873, diamonds were discovered at Bald Hill in the Touron district. The stones obtained there were sent by the Minister for Lands to Professor Liversidge for examination. The Professor, in reporting upon the same, said that the largest stone was in the form of a six-faced octahedron rather flattened owing to four of the groups of faces being more highly developed than the other four. The faces and edges were rounded somewhat, but Professor Liversidge did not think that the roundness was caused by attrition from the fact that the diamonds not unfrequently crystalise with curved faces and rounded edges. The stone was clear and colourless and perfectly free from all visible internal flaws. It possessed a specific gravity of 3·58, and weighed a little over three carats. The diamond next in size possessed the same crystallographic form but was less compressed. Its weight was $1\frac{1}{2}$ carats. The third specimen weighed about half a grain and was of high lustre but imperfect in colour. Accompanying the diamonds were two small boxes of gem sand. None of the gems contained in the sand, except the diamonds, were of any commercial value.

Mr. Wilkinson, the Government Geologist, states that he is fully convinced that diamond mining will form an important industry in the Colony. The mines, he says, would have been developed earlier, but for the want of water. He commends very highly the prompt action of Messrs. Falk and Co. in sinking for water at Bingera. Mr. Harrie Wood, Under Secretary for Mines, fully agrees with the views expressed by Mr. Wilkinson in regard to the prospects of the industry. Mr. Wood states that the Australian Diamond-mining Company obtained at Doctor's Creek, Bingera, 1,193 diamonds, weighing 254 carats, when the water gave out. They raised 5,000 tons of drift, but were unable to wash out more than 400 tons. The drift was found by Messrs. Powell and party. The Craddock party had a small wash of about a half a ton, which yielded seventeen diamonds. Messrs. Demsey and Co. also obtained a number of diamonds, but had to abandon the drift on account of the scarcity of water. Mr. Wood reports the discovery of diamonds at Tingha, near Big River, Auburn Vale, and at Berrima and Inverell. At the latter place sixty loads of washdirt from the New Banca Mine, yielded 1,951 diamonds, weighing 288 carats, and 110 loads from the Pine Ridge Company's ground yielded 1,450 diamonds, weighing 280 carats.

Diamonds have also been found in the Mittagong, Wellington, and the Uralla districts. Those found at Auburn Vale and Berrima were said by London experts to be of the very best quality, superior in every way to those of Cape Colony, South Africa. Mr. Wood is of opinion that the mines at Tingha will eventually prove the richest in Australia. The Australian Diamond-mining Company about eighteen months ago purchased a lease of 40 acres, for which they paid £4,000 ($19,466). They have also incurred considerable expense in erecting machinery. As yet no stones of large size have been found by the company, but even at the celebrated Kimberly Mines in South Africa one large stone in 10,000 is the general run, and one half a carat per ton of drift is considered a good result for a diamond-mine. Mr. Wood received a telegram from the manager of the Australian Diamond-mining Company at Bingera stating that they had cleaned up eighty-seven loads of drift yielding 1,139 diamonds, weighing 209 carats. This is the best yield the company has had. Some of the stones were larger than any which have hitherto been found, and six men only were employed for a period of ten days in breaking up, carting, and cleaning the drift.

The Department of Mines has tested thoroughly by actual trial the utility of the New South Wales diamonds for drill purposes. Mr. Slee, the Chief Inspector of Mines, made a valuable report upon the subject, and at Heathcote, near Coalcliff, a Bingera diamond stood the test of boring 1,267 feet through thick layers of hard sandstone and conglomerates, the latter being especially injurious, and yet without the slightest fracture. Professor Liversidge forwarded to the Indian and Colonial Exhibition in London, a very valuable collection of diamonds, among which are the following:

1 diamond, tetrahedron, Lachlan River, N.S.W., at ·415 grammes.

9 small diamonds, Bingera, N.S.W., at ·335 grammes.

1 diamond, dark, incetohedron, Bingera, N.S.W., at ·290 grammes.

1 black diamond, Mudgee, N.S.W., at ·735 grammes.

also a few Cape Colony diamonds for the purpose of comparing the matrix.

A parcel of Bingera diamonds placed on the London market in September, 1886, averaged £1 12s. ($7·78) per carat, whilst the highest average of the Cape diamonds during the same months was only 18s. ($4·38) per carat. Another parcel of New South Wales diamonds, weighing 126 carats, brought in London £1 10s. ($7·29) per carat. These were obtained from 127 tons of drift, averaging nearly 1 carat per ton. A few months previous to this shipment another parcel was sent to London, weighing 80 carats, obtained from 40 tons of drift, equal to 2 carats per ton. The manager of the Australian Diamond Mining Company estimates the cost of washing for diamonds at 2s. 6d. (61 cents) per ton of drift. He states that they can wash easily with one machine 200 tons of drift per day, and even if the average should be no higher than ¾ carat per ton, the net profits would be considerable. He is very decided in the opinion that the quality of the Bingera stones is far superior to those of the Cape.

It will perhaps be of interest to mention here that the geographical position of Bingera is almost identical with that of the celebrated Kimberley Mines of South Africa, both being situated on the 30th parallel of south latitude. Another striking coincidence is that the coast lines of Bingera and Kimberley bear from north-west to north-east at precisely the same angles. There is also a dividing chain of mountains in both places at about the same distance from the coast-line, and, moreover, the diamonds are located within mountains in each case at an equal distance from the coast-line. The production of the South African diamond mines during the month of July, 1885, was in round numbers 170,000 carats, valued at 18s. 5d. ($4·48) per carat. In October, 1882, the production was 211,746 carats, which realised £1 13s. 7d. ($8·16) per carat. From this it will be seen that the tendency of the price of South African diamonds is downward. The production, it is said, has also been affected by serious falls of reef. The Kimberley Mines during the last fifteen years have produced more diamonds than all the other mines in the world were able to produce for two centuries previous to 1870. The steady decline in the price of diamonds has led to the conclusion that the South African Mines have been allowed to produce too rapidly, and it is more than probable that this over-production has forced the amalgamation of the principal diamond companies both at the Cape and in Brazil.

The diamond, although the hardest and most beautiful and brilliant gem known, is composed of the simplest substance, being nothing more nor less than crystallised carbon. It occurs principally in gold-bearing rocks or in sands derived from them. It doubtless originated, like coal or mineral oil, from the gradual decomposition of vegetable or animal matter.

The diamond when placed under the blow-pipe burns without leaving any residue. It is so hard that it will scratch all other jewels, and remain unscratched by them. Indeed, a diamond is the only substance that will cut a diamond. Another interesting fact about it is, that unlike any other crystal, it exerts little or no action on polarised light. It occurred to scientists that if some means could be devised whereby the element of carbon (which will not dissolve in liquid or vaporise in flame) could be rendered soluble or gaseous it could be recovered in crystallised forms. In 1853 M. Despretz showed in a series of experiments that carbon free from every trace of mineral substance, prepared from crystallized sugar-candy, could be made to deposit microscopic crystals in black octahedrons, in colourless, translucent octahedrons, in colourless and translucent plates, possessing all the hardness of natural diamonds, and which would burn without leaving any residue. The crystals, however, being in powder, it was impossible to separate and measure them. Similar experiments were made from time to time, the most important of which are detailed in the "Transactions of the Royal Society of London." In March, 1879, a paper was read before that body, prepared by J. B. Hannay, F.R.S.E., and James Hogarth, a Scotch chemist, "On the solubility of solids in gases." It described a series of experiments in which various solids and gaseous solvents (such non volatile solids as iodide of potassium, chloride of cobalt, and bromide of potassium) were dissolved in alcohol and again crystallised. It was maintained that the experiments furnished abundant proof of the continuity of the liquid and gaseous states and of the solubility of solids in gases. The paper, amongst much other interesting matter, directed attention to the fact that many natural crystals contain small cavities filled with a liquid. This liquid requires very great pressure to retain it, being, in fact, a gas under ordinary circumstances. So great is the pressure exerted by this liquified gas that such crystals frequently burst in this way.

Mr. Hannay, in a second paper, described at length his researches for a suitable solvent. He first tried hydrocarbon, then the dissociation of hydrocarbon by means of a metal was attempted, and at last successfully, by submitting hydrocarbon in the presence of a nitrogenous substance to pressure and heat. On opening the tube in which the experiments were made, a number of crystals of diamonds were found. Professor Maskelyne, of the British Museum, subsequently announced that the experiments were of the most satisfactory character, that the stones produced stood every test, that they scratched deep grooves on the polished surface of sapphire, and were nearly inert in polarised light like natural diamonds. He fixed the angle of their cleavage faces at 79 degrees and 29 minutes, that of the real gem being 79 degrees and 30 minutes. He said, however, that the task of exact measurement was one of great difficulty on account of the minuteness of the stones.

The Under Secretary for Mines states:—"Some time ago I called attention to the difficulty experienced by miners in finding a ready market for their diamonds, and suggested that advantage might be taken of the exhibit of our diamonds at the Colonial and Indian Exhibition to obtain through the Agent-General some information concerning the prospect of a market in London for the products of our mines. The Agent-General was good enough to obtain and forward the following valuable reports":—

REPORT ON NEW SOUTH WALES DIAMONDS.

To Sir Saul Samuel, K.C.M.G., C.B., Agent-General for New South Wales.

Sir,   London, 16 November, 1886.

In response to your request that we should examine and report to you on the collection of diamonds in the New South Wales Court of the Colonial and Indian Exhibition, we have the honor to inform you that we have carefully examined the 285 crystals comprising it, and have fully gone into the literature bearing on the occurrence of the diamond in New South Wales, so far as known to us.

The mode of occurrence, physical characters, accompanying gems, and the general history of the diamond in New South Wales have been so ably treated by Messrs. Norman Taylor and the late Professor A. M. Thomson (*Trans. R. Soc. N. S. Wales for* 1870, p. 94), Mr. Norman Taylor (*Geological Magazine*, 1879, vol. vi., pp. 399 and 444), and Professor A. Liversidge (*Trans. R. Soc. N. S. Wales for* 1873 [1874], pp. 91 and 102; *Quart. Journal Geol. Soc.*, 1875, xxxi., p, 489), and the equally full description of the deposits yielding the gem, given by the same authors, and Mr. E. F. Pittman (*Annual Report, Dept. of Mines, N. S. Wales for* 1881, p. 141), that it is quite superfluous for us to do more than briefly refer to these parts of the subject.

With regard to the crystallographic form, we have recognised all those described by Messrs. Taylor and Thomson and Professor Liversidge. When compared with those of South Africa, we find that the New South Wales forms are more varied, *i.e.*, the crystals partake more of the dodecahedral with its numerous modifications, than of the octohedral habit, which is so marked a feature in those from the Cape. In this respect the New South Wales stones bear a remarkable resemblance to those from Brazil, and also differ from the Indian gems. Another peculiarity of the Cape diamond is the large proportion of cleaved stones, or "cleavage," which appear to be entirely absent in the parcel submitted to us from the Crown Jewel Mine. Speaking of those from Bingera generally, Professor Liversidge says, "no fractured specimens have been detected;" whilst among those from Cudgegong Mr. Taylor remarks, "it is very rare to meet with fractured stones." Again, amongst the Cape diamonds a fairly large number of "macles," or twinned-crystals, are met with, and these, as we have elsewhere pointed out, are found to present difficulties in cutting through the planes of contact. Now, in the present collection, these macles appear to be exceptional, but Mr. Taylor has described twinned-crystals from the Cudgegong, although not obtained in any quantity. Flattened octahedra, known in the trade as "flats," appear to be rare, although we have noticed a few. They are converted into "rose diamonds," a form of cutting formerly much practised in oriental countries, but only used in the case of imperfect stones. It naturally follows that the comparative absence of stones with these crystallographic characters will tend to reduce the cost of preparation, loss of material, and necessity for the production of a less saleable gem.

The black specks so frequently met with not only in the Cape, but also in Brazilian diamonds, appear in those from Inverell to be more or less confined to the surface planes, not extending to any depth within the crystals, and would doubtless be eliminated in the cutting without detracting to any great extent from the value of the stones as gems. On the other hand, speaking of the Cudgegong diamonds, Messrs. Taylor and Thomson say that "black specks within the crystals are not uncommon," and Professor Liversidge remarks on those from Bingera, "it is rather common to find them with . . . . internal black specks." The above observers have fully described the various colours characteristic of the New South Wales diamond, but in the present parcel we have only noted the colourless, shades of yellow, and a peculiar light yellowish brown, or light cinnamon colour. A small number are so slightly tinged as to practically come within the term "byewaters," whilst a very considerable proportion are of that straw-yellow tint known as "off-colours," but it is satisfactory to note that, as we have elsewhere stated, these off-colour stones far eclipse, when seen by artificial light, those regarded as of pure water.

On analysing the colour of 275 stones from Inverell, we find the following proportions:—

Colourless	100
Straw-yellow ("off-colours")	126
Slightly tinted yellow ("byewaters")	39
Cinnamon-yellow	6
Dirty gray hue ("rejections")	4
	275

Messrs. Taylor and Thomson, Mr. Taylor separately, and Professor Liversidge make particular mention of shades of green as sometimes occurring. Mr. Taylor speaks of "light or dark bottle green" stones, and Professor Liversidge mentions "light green" gems. We have no information what proportion such colours occupy in comparison with the others just enumerated, but we would point out that the commercial value of stones so tinted is enormously augmented, if of any size, and we cannot impress too strongly on those engaged in diamond mining the importance of this point.

We are likewise unfurnished with information as to the quantity of "Boart" yet obtained in the Colony, but considering the numerous uses to which this variety of the diamond has been put of late years, more particularly as applied to the diamond drill, and considering the important part this machine is now playing in water borings throughout the Australian Continent—we would strongly recommend this variety to the attention of the mining community. Several crystals of a dirty gray hue, and known in diamond circles as "rejections," are present in the collection, and these with a few irregular malformed crystals may be taken as types of stones which could be successfully used for this purpose. "One or two opaque black" diamonds are mentioned by Mr. Taylor, and Professor Liversidge cites an example of Boart, which was exhibited in the New South Wales Court, and is said to have been found at Mudgee. In another place (Liversidge, *The Minerals of New South Wales*, 2nd Edition, p. 122), this is stated to have come from Bathurst. It is described as black in colour, and with graphitic lustre, of the size of a large pea, and with a few small crystallographic processes projecting from the surface, 7·352 grains in weight, and Sp. Gr. 3·56, at 70° F. This description strongly recalls to mind the true Brazilian Boart, which is in such request for diamond drills, and as distinguished from that of the Cape Diamond Fields. The latter consists simply of badly crystallised and dark coloured stones, similar to those previously referred to as of a dirty gray hue from the Crown Jewel Mine. The importance of these facts will be at once preceived when it is remembered that the true or Brazilian Boart consists of more or less spherical aggregations of acicular crystals, radiating from a centre, and possessing an external aspect with which Professor Liversidge's description seems to correspond. We have examined the stone in question, and beyond exhibiting a smoother surface it appears to us to fulfil these conditions. We need not say more on this point than by reminding those interested that the true Boart is now worth 7s. 6d. ($1·82) per carat, and the Cape or false Boart, 3s. 6d. (85 cents).

The lustre of the crystalline faces, which is not to be differentiated from that of Brazilian stones, is chiefly adamantine, but at times somewhat dull, but this in no way detracts from their beauty when cut, the exterior crystal irregularities having little or no connection with the structure below the surface. The dullness appears to be partly due, as pointed out by Mr. Taylor and Professor Liversidge, to certain crystallographic irregularities, and certainly is not owing, as suggested by some, to abrasion or attrition. The rounding of the faces, visible on many of these crystals, is entirely due to the well-known peculiarities of diamond crystallisation, and that it is not due to attrition is evident by the sharply defined character of the edges bounding these rounded faces.

The equally noticeable pitting of the surfaces of the crystal planes is characteristic of the diamond in all hitherto known localities, and cannot therefore be used as a means of comparison with those of one field as against those of another. The pitting is very irregular both in position and shape, more so in fact than is generally seen in examples from other fields. The colourless stones are not only pitted to a greater extent than the yellow, but the crystal planes are more unequally developed, imparting to the crystals a much more distorted appearance. The brilliancy of the white and yellow stones when the gems are good is about equal, and before cutting this feature is more pronounced the nearer they approach the octahedron in form, a fact holding good both for the yellow and white stones, and one quite in accord with theory.

Some of the colourless are very beautiful stones, and the quality quite justifies the manner in which parcels have been brought into the London market, a fact to be referred to hereafter.

Amongst the stones cut for you by Messrs. Ford & Wright is one of a very peculiar, and, so far as we know, original structure, to which our attention was drawn by their Manager, Mr. L. Atkinson. The prepared facet exhibits triangular markings which appear to correspond with some of the surface pittings. These markings, so far as we were able to judge, seemed to extend through the whole of the crystal, and unless removable by polishing, stones of a similar structure to this, judging from a trade point of view, would be of little value, but we are of opinion that this is an isolated instance of a peculiar crystallographic growth.

Hardness is a physical feature upon which much stress is laid by lapidaries and diamond-cutters, and it is stated by Messrs. Ford & Wright that the New South Wales diamonds are much harder than those from the Cape, judging by the time necessary for the preparation of the facets. But, as a matter of fact, in other precious stones the relative hardness depends, to a great extent upon the direction in which a stone is cut with regard to its crystalline form, and until many more careful observations are recorded, we hesitate to pronounce any opinion as to the value of this. If proved, we would call attention to the necessary increase in the cost of cutting the diamonds from your Colony, but, as a set-off to this, the probable increase in brilliancy. One thing is quite apparent, when cut, some of these stones produce most exquisite gems.

Messrs. Taylor and Thomson, and Professor Liversidge also, have determined the specific gravity to vary between the limits of 3·42 (Bingera) and 3·44 (Mudgee), but with an average of 3·42. We find the mean of a series of experiments with the Crown Jewel diamonds to be 3·46. The following table of specific gravities gives a comparison with that of those from Brazil, India, and Borneo, the data of the latter being taken from Mr. Harry Emanuel's work, and that of M. M. Jacob and Chatrain:—

Country.	White Stones.	Yellow Stones.
India	3·524	3·556
Brazil	3·442	3·520
Cape	3·520	
Borneo	3·492	...
N. S. Wales	3·42	

The analogy in density between the white Brazilian stones and those from New South Wales, irrespective of colour, is at once apparent.

The average weight of Mudgee stones was estimated at 0·23, or nearly 1 carat grain each, by Messrs. Taylor and Thomson, and this has received corroboration from Mr. C. S. Wilkinson in the case of diamonds from the Borah Creek Tindrifts (*Mines and Min. Statistics, N. S. Wales, for* 1874, p. 79). On the other hand, those from Bingera are said by Professor Liversidge to be "for the most part small in size." We have made two series of determinations of the weights of the Crown Jewel Mine diamonds, with the following results:—

20 1st size stones	(a) = ...	$16\frac{1}{2} + \frac{1}{10}$ carats	Mean	$\frac{3}{4} + \frac{1}{8}$
,, ,,	(b) = ...	$12\frac{1}{4} + \frac{1}{8}$	,,	$\frac{5}{8} + \frac{1}{8}$
20 medium stones	(a) = ...	$10\frac{1}{4} + \frac{1}{16}$	,,	$\frac{1}{2} + \frac{1}{16} + \frac{1}{32} + \frac{1}{64}$
,, ,,	(b) = ...	$8\frac{1}{2} + \frac{1}{16} + \frac{1}{64}$	,,	$\frac{1}{2} + \frac{1}{16}$
20 small stones	(a) = ...	$3\frac{1}{2} + \frac{1}{8}$	,,	$\frac{1}{8} + \frac{1}{16}$
,, ,,	(b) = ...	$2\frac{1}{2} + \frac{1}{8} + \frac{1}{32} + \frac{1}{64}$	,,	$\frac{1}{8} + \frac{1}{64}$

Mr. Harrie Wood, in the Annual Report of the Department of Mines for 1885 (p. 40), gives the total weight of this parcel as $104\frac{3}{4}$ carats. He states that "280 ranged from $\frac{1}{4}$ to 1 carat each in weight, and five from 1 to $1\frac{1}{2}$ carat."

As a fair average of the diamonds found in the Cudgegong field, Messrs. Taylor and Thomson give the following statistics :—

106 diamonds weighed $74\frac{1}{2}$ carats, the largest $1\frac{3}{4}$ carats.
81 ,, ,, 19 ,, ,, $1\frac{1}{4}$,,
110 ,, ,, $26\frac{1}{4}$,,
16 ,, ,, 6 ,,
700 ,, ,, $151\frac{1}{4}$,,

Large diamonds appear to be quite the exception in New South Wales; at any rate, definite data are wanting on this branch of the subject. The largest stones of which we have been able to find reliable record are the following:— Messrs. Taylor and Thomson give the largest found at $5\frac{3}{4}$ carats, a perfectly colourless octahedron, discovered in the Cudgegong River, between the "Two-mile-Flat" and the "Rocky Ridge"; another of $3\frac{1}{4}$ carats at the former locality. Two very excellent stones were lately exhibited in the New South Wales Court by Mr. R. H. D. White, weighing, respectively, in the cut form 3 and $3\frac{1}{2}$ carats. Professor Liversidge states that at Bald Hill, Hill End, one stone slightly over 3 carats, and another $1\frac{1}{4}$ carat, were obtained. On the other hand, Mr. C. S. Wilkinson records the discovery, in the stream-tin washings of the Borah Tin and Diamond Mining Company, Borah Creek, of a diamond weighing 5·5 carats, and another 7·5 carats at the Bengonover Mine, in the same creek. From the Crown Jewel Mine the largest stones we noticed were the following :—

1 large colourless stone = $1\frac{1}{4} + \frac{1}{16}$
,, ,, = $\frac{3}{4} + \frac{1}{16} + \frac{1}{32}$
,, yellow stone = $\frac{3}{4} + \frac{1}{8}$
,, ,, = $\frac{1}{2} + \frac{1}{16}$

As compared with the stones of other localities, the size is somewhat small, although it is stated that Brazilian diamonds frequently take from 15 to 20 to weigh a carat. This smallness of size is compensated, however, by the fact, as we are informed by an excellent trade authority, that medium sized diamonds are now more in request than large ones, for mounting in conjunction with other gems such as rubies and sapphires. In form, size, and physical character, the New South Wales diamonds appear to agree better with those of the country just mentioned than of any other; but, of course, they cannot vie in size or quantity with Cape stones. In brilliancy and fire when cut, they are, however, stone for stone, quite able to hold their own with those from the latter Colony. In fact, it appears, from information gathered through most reliable sources, that a large proportion of New South Wales gems have found their way to the London market as Brazilian stones. Otherwise we would ask what has become of the 12,000 which are officially returned as found up to the end of 1885, especially when it is distinctly stated by Mr. E. F. Pittman, Chief Mining Surveyor for New South Wales, that in 1872-73, the Sydney jewellers declined to buy Bingera stones. We are quite aware that some small parcels have reached certain eminent firms in London, in a genuinely open manner, as New South Wales diamonds; but we believe that the other course has been more frequently adopted. If this be the case, what more satisfactory certificate could be adduced in favour of the diamonds yielded by the tertiary drifts of New South Wales.

Whilst preparing the present Report, we have been asked on several occasions two very pertinent questions—questions which appear to us to have a very important bearing on the future development and permanency of the diamond industry in New South Wales. The first of these was, what is the area of the diamantiferous ground, and the approximate thickness of the drift in the several fields? The second and equally important question related to the yield of stones. Unfortunately, beyond the general statement that 12,000 diamonds have been found, we are unacquainted with any official return dealing with such details, and even until within the last two years this subject does not appear as one of the items in your excellent "Reports of the Department of Mines"; and the same remarks may be applied to the question of area. Many statements have appeared in the public press on the first of these points, but they are so utterly unreliable as to be quite useless for statistical purposes.

With the view of pointing out how difficult it is for an estimate to be formed, even within several degrees of accuracy, the following brief and imperfect description of the diamantiferous deposits may not be out of place, abstracted from the several excellent authorities we have before referred to.

The diamond in New South Wales occurs in outliers of drift and cement representing old river accumulations of more than one geological age, lying at various distances from the present river channels, and once forming portions of widespread and continuous deposits, resting on the bed rock of the country. The older drifts have been protected from total destruction by cappings of basaltic rock, but the isolated condition of these clearly shows the enormous amount of denudation which has gone on, and the quantity of diamantiferous drift removed. The latter is usually loose and coarse, but in places passes into a compact conglomerate. There are six of these drifts at Mudgee, occupying different levels, resulting from the successive denudations of one another, and we believe all diamond-bearing. At Bingera, on the other hand, the drift is described as a "small-grained siliceous brecciated conglomerate, strongly agglutinated together by a ferruginous cement." The younger drifts have in every case been derived from the destruction by fluviatile agencies of the older. Mr. Taylor describes the older drift as a "coarse and heavy deposit—some boulders in it weighing several hundredweights—for the most part loose, but portions of it united into a compact conglomerate. It varies greatly in thickness, from a few inches to 30 feet . . . The *newer* drift derived from the above is composed of the same contents as the *older* drift, with the addition of boulders of greenstone and basalt . . . The newer drifts (upper and lower) comprising the present river bed, and older and deeper channels, contain pebbles, boulders, and shingle of the neighbouring sandstones, slates, &c." Throughout these drifts the diamonds are described as occurring in rich patches. The drift at Bingera is said by Professor Liversidge to vary from 3 to 60 feet.

It will be readily understood from this that without a detailed official survey of *all* the likely diamond-bearing drifts, it would be impossible to give even an approximate idea of the areas capable of yielding the precious stones; but that such deposits are numerous throughout New South Wales, is itself evident to any one who has perused the able geological reports of Mr. C. S. Wilkinson and his assistants. It can naturally be roughly ascertained from the geological maps prepared by these gentlemen, but we believe it would greatly stimulate diamond-mining if a detailed report could be prepared furnishing the information in question. As an indication to parties interested, we can only refer to what has been done, and for this purpose we quote certain of the ascertained areas of the Cudgegong (Mudgee) Diamond Field, as given by Messrs. Taylor and Thomson, thus—

Name of Claim.	Area in Acres.	Thickness of Drift.
Two-mile Flat	70	
Jordan's Hill	40	18 feet.
Miller's Claim	..	12 ,,
Junction of Reedy Creek with Cudgegong River	100	
Rocky Ridge (older drift)	40	
Horseshoe Bend do	20	
Hassal's Hill do	340	? 12 to 30 feet.
	610	

DIAMONDS.

Touching the second point—the number of diamonds found—the following reliable data are extant :—

Claim.	Diamonds.	No. per Load.	Carats.	Authority.	Date.
Australian Diamond Mining Company (Mudgee)	1,765	From 1 to 2 loads, to 4 or 5 in 1 load.	...	Taylor......	1867
Messrs. Scott & Allen (Mudgee.)	700	8 to 12 or 15 loads.	...	,, ...	,,
Messrs. Cooney & Party (Mudgee.)	1,000	1 to 15 to 1 load, average 5.	...	,, ...	,,
Falk & Co. (Bingera)	400	From 100 loads...	...	Wood	1883
Gwydir Diamond Company (Bingera.)	690	,, 34½ ,, ...	...	Liversidge.	1873
Australian Diamond Mining Company (Bingera)	1,193	,, 418 ,, ...	254	,,	1884
Craddock & Party (Bingera)	17	,, ½ ,, ...	...	Wood	,,
Australian Diamond Mining Company (Bingera)	1,134	,, 87 ,, ...	209	,, ...	1885
Crown Jewel Mine (Tingha)	285	....	104⅝	,, ...	,,

These, of course, represent but a small proportion of those found, and the numbers are only quoted as indicating the relative richness of average claims. Had all the statements been accepted to which we have had access, doubtless the total of 12,000, given in the New South Wales official catalogue, Colonial and Indian Exhibition (p. 149), could be much exceeded.

The distribution of the diamond throughout New South Wales is widespread. It has been recorded as occurring at the undermentioned places :—

	Authority.	Date.
Turon River	Stutchbury	1851
Reedy Creek, near Bathurst	Hargraves	,,
Burrendong	Clarke	1859
Pyramal Creek	,, ...	,,
Calabash	,, ...	1860
Suttor's Bar, Macquarie River	,, ...	,,
Cudgegong River (Mudgee)	Taylor and Thomson	1867
Bingera	Liversidge	1873
Bald Hill, Hill End	,, ...	1875
Borah and Bengonover Tin Mines	Wilkinson	,,
Trunkey Creek, Tuena	Taylor	1879
Brook's Creek, Gundaroo, near Goulburn......	Liversidge	1882
Lachlan River......	,, ...	,,
Monkey Hill, and Sally's Flat......	,, ...	,,
Big River, Auburn Valley, Tingha......	Wood	1884
Berrima District	,, ...	,,
Crown Jewel Mine, Inverell	C.I.E.	1886

The diamond has likewise been found at a few localities in Victoria, chiefly in Gippsland, and it is said by the late Dr. J. J. Bleasdale to have also been discovered at the Echunga diggings in South Australia (*Colonial Monthly*, 1868, vol. II, p. 436). At the latter place it is reported to occur in "Itacolumite," but from the description given the matrix is evidently an ordinary auriferous drift.

We have seen it stated that certain claims at Bingera show "good wash of the proper kind, and of the same sort as yields well in South Africa." Now a statement of this kind, if true, would naturally do more perhaps for diamond mining in New South Wales than any other fact which could be adduced in its favour. On the other hand, if erroneous, a corresponding amount of harm will be done by inducing investors to speculate in the hope of obtaining similar gratifying results. We have neither seen or read of any diamantiferous soil from New South Wales having even the faintest resemblance to the peculiar rock forming the matrix of the diamond at Kimberley and neighbouring mines, nor occurring in a like manner. We presume the Kimberley deposit is referred to in such a paragraph as we have quoted, and not the Vaal diggings, which are now comparatively worked out. We cannot too strongly condemn such statements, as having no foundation in fact. We have already briefly described the diamond matrices in New South Wales, which are *drifts*, widely distributed horizontally. In South Africa, on the other hand, the origin of the diamantiferous rock has given rise to much speculation, and is still a subject for discussion, although it probably results in a great measure from a peculiar form of hydrothermal action. Instead of a wide-spread distribution it occupies restricted areas, having no semblance to drift deposits at all, but is an agglomerate filling strange pipe-like depressions, or elliptical cavities extending vertically to unknown depths, the exact nature of which have yet to be explained. This is the celebrated "blue" of the South African miners, and it is a "distinct agglomerate, consisting of fragments of all shapes and sizes of many rocks which vary much in mineral composition, enclosed in a base of serpentinized material, which appears to have largely resulted from the alteration of enstatite and olivine. The enclosed rocks, or some of their mineral constituents, have partaken, to a considerable extent, of the same chemical alteration. The texture varies very much, and depends upon the size and abundance of the enclosed fragments; sometimes it resembles a breccia, sometimes a conglomerate, and sometimes partakes of the character of both. In some parts the blocks are very much rounded, and present the aspect of water-worn pebbles; this is especially the case in many of the doleritic rocks, though we have seen blocks of mica-schist in it which it was difficult to believe were not true pebbles. In others the fragments are more angular, but all that we have seen appear to have had their sharp edges more or less removed by some mode of attrition." No such rock has ever been described to our knowledge from New South Wales, diamantiferous or otherwise, and to say therefore that the conditions are similar in the two countries is both misleading and erroneous. With the view of showing the relations of the New South Wales diamond matrix, we here append a list of some of the more frequent rocks and minerals constituting those of Brazil, India, Borneo, and the Cape, from which the resemblance it bears to the two former will be at once apparent.

Brazil.—Gold, lydian stone, quartz, red ironstone (siliceous), cassiterite, topaz, spinel, garnet, lazulite, chrysoberyl, carbonado, tourmaline, andalusite, beryl, rutile, anatase, brookite, tantalite, hæmatite, kyanite.

India.—Quartz, jaspers, hornblende, corundum.

Borneo.—Mostly red clay, which contains pebbles of serpentine, diorite, and quartz, interbedded with marl, containing fossils, magnetite, platinum, black quartz.

New South Wales.—Quartz, quartzites, cassiterite, jasper, lydian stone, topaz, sapphire, ruby, varieties of zircon, spinel (varieties of), gold, tourmaline, flinty slate, shale, sandstone, illmenite, magnetic iron sand, brookite, rutile (Bald Hill), garnet, osmiridium (newer drift of Mudgee).

Cape.—Garnets, green, ruby-red, and brown; smaragdite, bronzite, enstatite, olivine, illmenite, zircon, vaalite, hornblende, zeolites, calcite, opal, staurolite, iron pyrites, pegmatite, talc schist, mica schist, augite rock, amphibolite, eclogite, serpentine, gneiss, peridotite, granite, dolerites, basalt, melaphyre (with agates) and others, amounting to over eighty in number.

With regard to the source of the diamond in New South Wales we do not see any other course than to unhesitatingly accept the explanations offered by Mr. Norman Taylor, so far as the facts bearing on this branch of the subject have been yet gathered. He believes that they were chemically formed in the older tertiary drifts, and in support of this view adduces the following cogent reasons:—

1. The older rocks of the various diamantiferous districts have not been proved to be diamond bearing.
2. The older tertiary drifts or cements are derived from the denudation of these, and contain diamonds.
3. The younger drifts are only diamantiferous when resulting from the destruction of the latter, and similarly the recent alluvium again from them.
4. The natural conclusion is that the diamonds have been formed in the drifts, and not derived from any pre-existing rocks.

Mr. Taylor was further of opinion that the "fluctuating yield, small average size of the gems, the expense in extracting the drift from beneath the basalt, cartage to water, and washing effectually, are the drawbacks which have hitherto stood in the way of the successful investment of capital in this direction." We imagine that some of these difficulties will in the future be overcome by stricter attention to the details of at least two of these points. For instance, we have it on record that in certain claims, when chiefly worked for gold only, the lower portions of the drift, or that near the "gutter" was removed, leaving what was perhaps the richest diamond-bearing portion behind. Mr. Taylor distinctly states that the gems do not appear to occur much on the bottom with the gold, and also from the fact, in the Cudgegong field, at least, they appear to be found in "runs" or "veins," at various levels in the drift. It is not improbable, therefore, that in a number of the tertiary deposits which have been explored simply for gold, diamonds have unconsciously been overlooked. We think that a remark of Messrs. Taylor and Thomson's to the effect that—"the mere fact of the not unfrequent discovery of diamonds on the waste heaps round old shafts which were sunk for gold, is enough to suggest that the diamonds may occur in the higher portions of the deposit, since the bottom layer has been invariably carted to the river for gold-washing," to some extent proves this, and even opens up the far wider question touched on in the preceding paragraph. The small average size of the stones, as we have previously pointed out, ought not to militate against a successful prosecution of the industry, under present circumstances. On the other hand, the expense of mining and question of water supply are so entirely matters of local detail as to be quite out of place in the present remarks.

Washing effectually can only be carried out by thoroughly good machinery, and there is evidence to show that such is now being introduced. In all probability the machine best suited to the diamond drifts of New South Wales would be a slight modification of the "Washing Gear and Pulsator," as used by the Griqualand West Diamond Mining Company, Dutoit's Pan, in 1885, a model of which was exhibited at the late Exhibition.

In bringing our report to a termination we beg to emphasise the following conclusions, which the foregoing remarks bear out:—

1. The diamonds of New South Wales in their physical characters are more nearly allied to those of Brazil than any other country.
2. They have been very largely sold in London as such.
3. As regards colour, they differ pratically but little from those of other fields.
4. The general absence of "cleavage" and "macles" is a point much in their favour.
5. Stones of the rarer colours assumed by the diamond should be particularly sought for.
6. The greater hardness of the New South Wales gems will probably raise the cost of cutting, but this will be compensated for by their extra "brilliancy."
7. "Boart" should be eagerly sought for.

G

8. Detailed statistics of the area and thickness of drifts likely to prove diamantiferous, and the number hitherto found so, should be prepared officially.

9. All auriferous drifts should be prospected for diamonds.

10. The matrix of the diamond in New South Wales bears no resemblance to that at the Cape.

We are, &c.,
THOS. DAVIES, F.G.S.
R. ETHERIDGE, JUNR.

A REPORT TO THE NEW SOUTH WALES GOVERNMENT UPON ITS DIAMONDS.

THE four Australian diamonds selected by myself in the New South Wales Court at the Colonial and Indian Exhibition by the request of Sir Saul Samuel, K.C.M.G., C.B., to make a report upon after being cut and polished, during which process I had thoroughly and closely investigated them, with this result, that :—

No. 1 parcel contains one diamond, which had the ordinary dodecahedron crystallisation, the crust or coat of the stone was perfectly naturally polished, with very few indentations, and no indication whatever of triangular indentations or markings as so frequently found in the African diamond; it was cut into the shape most suitable to show to the greatest advantage, and on the polisher commencing to put the first facet on it called the table, it was found on careful examination that there was a triangular formation which is generally found on the outer coat or crust, but very rarely indeed right inside the stone, and it is so remarkable that on the heads of the Mineral Department of the British Museum hearing of it, and after examining it, expressed a strong desire to possess the stone, as being of such a wonderful and interesting formation; therefore I thought it advisable to stop the polishing process of it and submit the stone for inspection with the desire of the Mineral Department of the British Museum, South Kensington.

No. 2 parcel contains the diamonds which were most carefully selected by myself out of the 286 Australian diamonds exhibited in the New South Wales Court at the Colonial and Indian Exhibition, that they might be as near a match as it is possible to get in every respect such as size, shape, colour, and appearance. One has been cut and polished and proves a brilliant of the finest water; the other diamond is left in its natural rough shape just as it was found, so as to show at once the practical difference between the two diamonds.

No. 3 parcel contains one diamond, which, in its rough state, weighed $1\frac{1}{2}$ carats, the crystallisation, a hexakis octahedron of a dull white colour after being cut and polished; it now weighs the $\frac{1}{2}$, $\frac{1}{8}$, $\frac{1}{16}$ of a carat, and is about as fine a brilliant as it is possible to get, be it from Golconda, Borneo, Brazil, or Jaggersfontein.

The market price of the Australian diamonds in the rough state is liable, like all other diamonds, to great fluctuations, and on the whole are generally lower than the African diamond, for this important reason that they are a great deal harder to cut and polish; as, if it were possible to pick out an Australian and an African diamond exactly the same size, weight, shape, and appearance, and given to one man to polish, the African stone would be finished in six days, whilst the Australian stone would take eight days, with this vastly important difference that the Australian diamond would be of greater brilliancy and refracting power than the African stone; and might I suggest that these cut stones might be handed over to some skilled gentleman who would carefully test in every way the refracting powers and polarization of light in comparison with an African diamond.

There is always a great market open for Australian brilliants, as although they are at present small in size in comparison to the African diamond, with regard to colour in proportion to their production, Australia finds the most white diamonds, and there is always a great demand for fine white stones, and always will be, as being small they are the most suitable to set round all other coloured gems and different kinds of ornaments and decorations connected with jewelry, more especially for the future, as China and Japan are commencing to introduce diamond jewelry into their countries.

The market price at the present time for parcels of diamonds, containing such stones as the one cut and polished in No. 2 and also No. 3 parcels, varies from £8 ($38) to £9 ($43.8) per carat.

There is another very great market open for all inferior diamonds, especially rounded stones, commonly called ball boart, as it is used now so universally in large quantities for rock drilling, mill dressing, and for turning all hard metals and stones, and the supply at the present time is not sufficient for the demand, as the inferior diamonds from Africa rarely answer the purpose, being of a softer nature than the Brazilian diamond, which on careful examination, I have come to this most important conclusion, is the same in every respect with the Australian diamond. Australia has a very important market open for its diamonds that are too small to cut and polish, as natural stones are largely used for glass cutting and china drilling, &c.

In examining the different collections shown in the New South Wales Court at the Exhibition, I found one piece of carbon which is the hardest mineral known, and is greatly needed, for which there is an immense market. I believe that on the diamond mines in Australia being thoroughly and properly worked with the immensely improved machine that we have now, there will be found paying quantities of this stone, and I am also firmly convinced that the deeper the mines are sunk, not only a larger quantity, but finer, and most important of all, the diamonds will be found larger in size.

After thoroughly and exhaustively going into the matter, I am so satisfied that there is a large and wealthy industry to be developed in Australia that, although I am in a good position, still if the Government would offer on certain conditions I would willingly go out to the Colony and enter thoroughly into the whole matter, as, having been connected practically with the cutting and polishing of diamonds for fifteen years, and being the expert and sole manager in directing the whole of the diamond washing at the Exhibition, I know exactly what ground the diamonds are to be found, and could at once see to proper machinery being erected, and I am perfectly satisfied that the result would be a great development of a new industry and a source of wealth to the Colony.

LEWIS ATKINSON,
33, Brook-street, Grosvenor Square, London, W.

GOLD.

The total yield of the Australasian Gold Mines for the year 1886 is estimated at 1,365,981 ounces against 1,443,660 ounces for the year 1885. With one or two exceptions the yield has steadily declined in every one of the Colonies for the last ten or twelve years.

The output of Victoria for 1886 was smaller than that of any previous year since the discovery of gold in that Colony. The yield was 70,412 ounces less than that of 1885, and nearly 300,000 less than in 1876. The yield in New Zealand was 10,272 ounces less than in 1885, and 90,288 ounces less than in 1876. The yield in New South Wales declined from 100,647 ounces in 1885 to 98,446 ounces in 1886. South Australia, however, increased her yield from 18,327 ounces in 1885 to 21,115 ounces in 1886. There has also been an increase in Queensland, from 308,348 ounces in 1885 to 341,551 ounces in 1886. The total yield of gold in Australasia, since the opening of the mines in 1851 to the present time, is estimated at 80,808,981 ounces, valued at £316,500,000, ($1,540,247,250.) This is an enormous yield, but it is not so large as that of the United States, since the discovery of gold in California, by £29,200,000 ($142,101,800.) The United States produce one-third of all the gold in the world, and more than one-half of the silver.

During the years 1882 to 1886, the value of the world's annual product of gold has been about £20,000,000 ($97,330,000), the United States taking the first rank, Australasia the second, and Russia the third.

The subjoined table shows the quantity of gold produced in each of the Australasian Colonies for each year since 1876:—

Year.	New South Wales.	New Zealand.	Queensland.	South Australia.	Tasmania.	Victoria.
	oz.	oz.	oz.	oz.	oz.	oz.
1876	155,156	318,367	374,776	9,858	11,107	963,760
1877	122,629	371,685	353,266	11,811	5,777	809,653
1878	117,978	310,486	283,592	10,746	25,240	775,272
1879	107,640	284,100	281,552	14,251	60,155	758,947
1880	116,751	303,315	228,120	13,246	52,595	829,121
1881	145,532	250,683	259,782	16,976	56,693	858,850
1882	129,233	230,893	230,000	15,668	49,122	898,536
1883	122,257	222,899	193,994	15,938	46,577	810,047
1884	105,933	246,392	261,824	21,455	42,340	778,618
1885	100,667	222,732	308,348	18,327	41,241	735,218
1886	98,446	227,079	341,551	21,115	31,015	665,196

It will be seen, from this table, that Victoria surpasses all the other Colonies in the production of the precious metal.

Although gold was known to exist in various parts of Australia as early as 1823, it was not acknowledged to have been found in workable quantities until 1851, about three years after the discovery of gold in California.

As far back as 1781, it was reported that gold had been found in Australia, and although little faith at that time was placed in the reports, it is now believed that the discovery was then made, but that the authorities refused to encourage a further search for the metal, fearing it might interfere with the proper government of the then but little known territory.

In 1839, Count Strzelecki found auriferous pyrites in the Wellington District, New South Wales, but was unable to prevail on the Governor to issue a proclamation declaring the discovery. In 1841, the Rev. W. B. Clarke found gold *in situ* in the granite formations of the Vale of Clwydd and in the Macquarie valley. Sir R. Murchison in 1844, stated in the journal of the Royal Geographical Society, that there were gold-bearing veins in Eastern Australia smiliar to those of the Ural Mountains. 1848, Mr. F. W. Smith, of Sydney, found gold and offered to reveal the locality to the Government upon the payment of £250 ($1,217). The Governor, although not accepting the offer, stated that if Mr. Smith would rely on the liberality of Government his reward should be in proportion to the value of his discovery. In February 1851, Mr. E. H. Hargreaves, who had recently returned from California, as he stated, expressly for the purpose of searching for gold, succeeded in finding that metal at Summer Hill Creek, and other places in New South Wales. Mr. Hargreaves at once revealed the localities to the Government, and was rewarded for his services.

In the same year gold was found in payable quantities at Clunes, Ballarat, Mount Alexander, and other places in Victoria. The Select Committee of the Legislative Council of that Colony, appointed for considering the claims for rewards for gold discoveries, reported that the Honorable William Campbell found gold in March, 1850, but concealed the fact until 5th July, 1851, the date upon which gold was found in the same Colony by Mr. James Esmond, a Californian miner.

About the same time the famous gold-fields at Ballarat were discovered, and one of the effects of the discovery of the precious metal upon the population, was that Victoria increased, within a period of fourteen months, the number of her inhabitants from 55,000 to 260,000.

The first large nugget found in Australia was called the "Brevner Nugget," and weighed 364 ounces, but this was shortly afterwards eclipsed by the discovery of the famous "One Hundred Weight Nugget," at Ballarat. This nugget was in three pieces, each of which weighed sixty pounds. The total yield in the three pieces was 106 pounds troy of gold or 1,272 ounces. In 1858, a large nugget was found near Burradong, New South Wales, weighing 1,182 ounces 7 dwt., valued at £4,389 ($21,359). To the Colony of Victoria, however, belongs the credit of having produced the largest nugget ever found. It was called the "Welcome Nugget," and weighed 2,217 ounces 16 dwt., valued at £10,500 ($51,098), and was found at Ballarat in 1858. Other nuggets are:—

- The "Viscount Canterbury Nugget," at John's Paddock, Berlin, Victoria, 31st May, 1870; weight 1,106 ounces.
- The "Precious Nugget," at Catto's Paddock, Berlin, Victoria, 17th April, 1871; weight 1,018 ounces.
- The "Schlem Nugget," at Dunolly, Victoria, 11th July, 1872; weight 538 ounces.

The greater part of the gold obtained in the Australasian Colonies is from quartz or reef mining. In Victoria the portion obtained from that source is nearly two-thirds more than from alluvial mining. The Victorian Statistician, Mr. Hayter, states that in proportion to the number of miners engaged in quartz and alluvial mining, the yield of gold from the former is frequently more than twice as large as that from the latter. It should be remembered, however, than only one-fifth of the steam mining machinery of the Colony is employed for alluvial workings, the remaining four-fifths being used for working in quartz reefs. Quartz-mining in New South Wales is not as profitable as in other parts of Australia, indeed, with the exception of a few localities, the veins in New South Wales have not been worked to any great depth. The mining heretofore carried on has been principally confined to the working of creek and river beds and shallow alluvial diggings. The poor success which has often attended the working of quartz veins in New South Wales is attributed to inexperience and the absence of the right kind of ore separator, and other mining appliances. The deepest gold mine in New South Wales is at Adelong, and is not more that 900 feet deep. The reef is about 18 inches wide, but the yield is only 2 or 3 ounces to the ton. In Victoria there is a mine 2,409 feet deep, and fifteen or twenty others are worked at depths of over 1,700 feet. The most productive gold mine has been the Long Tunnel Mine, Walhalla, Victoria. Since it was found, in 1867, the total quantity of stone crushed has been 302,670 tons, and the product 473,275 ounces of gold. The mine is the only one in Australasia that has paid over £1,000,000 ($4,866,000) in dividends.

In one quartz mine in New Zealand the yield of gold to the ton has been as much as 600 ounces. It is believed that now the gold yield is largest in Queensland. With regard to the gold-mines in New Zealand the value of such a reef as the one already quoted, according to Sir J. Hector, Director of the Geological Survey of that Colony, may be best understood by those not acquainted with the subject, when it is stated that one half ounce to the ton is in most cases a profitable return. Gold-mining in New Zealand is still in its infancy, and only awaits the judicious expenditure of capital to extend to vast proportions. The same observations apply, with perfect truth, to gold-mining in New South Wales, where gold is reported to be present over so large an area of country, and it is only when rich alluvial "finds" are reported that attention is attracted to reefs containing the precious metal.

In the Colony of Victoria, at Stawell, the yield of gold from 2,306 tons of quartz, from a depth of 1,200 feet, averaged about 8 dwt. per ton; 8,273 tons at Ballarat, at depths varying from 590 to 1,205 feet averaged from 5 dwt. to 8 dwt. 19 grains per ton,; 87,347 tons at Sandhurst, at depths between 500 and 1,306 feet, from 7 dwt. 1 grain to 2 ounces 6 dwt. and 14 grains per ton ; 20,521 tons at Castlemaine, at depths varying from 300 to 745 feet, yielded from 6 dwt. 11 grains to 6 ounces 18 dwt 1 grain per ton; 31,987 tons at Maryborough, at depths from 300 to 820 feet, gave a yield from 5 dwt. to 3 ounces per ton ; 22,727 tons, at Stringer's Creek in Gippsland, at depths varying from 300 to 723 feet, yielded from 17 dwt. 23 grains to 1 ounce 17 dwt. 1 grain per ton, and 5,224 tons, at Beechworth, at depths varying from 300 to 600 feet, yielded from 4 dwt. 17 grains to 17 dwt. 3 grains of gold per ton.

Gold is believed to exist in vast quantities in Western Australia, the largest colony of the group, but as yet very little has been done to develop gold mining there. The "rush" to the Kimberley diggings in 1885 was unprecedented since the influx to the Palmer gold-fields in Queensland, but unfortunately the mines did not turn out as well as expected, and much suffering was entailed upon the ill-advised persons who flocked there. Mr. R. T. Hindman, one of the Government geologists who has travelled in the Kimberley country, has prepared a sketch map showing the geological features of about 10,000 square miles of the country. He states that the wide-spread area of the carboniferous rocks is of the highest interest to geologists, and that he was fortunate enough to discover a formation hitherto unknown in Western Australia, namely, the Devonian. These rocks, resting on the metamorphic beds of the Silurian, cover a very large space. Another very interesting discovery was an immense mass of basaltic rock, which was traced for more than 100 miles, forming an extensive plateau 2,000 feet above the level of the sea, and covering an area of 3,000 square miles. The auriferous country he passed through comprises an area of 2,000 square miles, and is watered by the Margaret, Mary, Elvira, Panton, and Ord rivers. The formation is principally Lower Silurian slate and schist of various kinds, intersected by an enormous number of quartz reefs. The river valleys and flats are in many places covered with extensive quantities of quartz gravel and drift. The quartz being derived from the denudations of the reefs. He says, further, that he has never failed to find amongst the gravels good colors of gold, and of an encouraging character. Very often good colours of gold were obtained in every pan washed. Nuggets averaging from 3 to 190 ounces had been found. More than 2,000 ounces of gold were obtained from the Barrett workings in the course of three months.

The gold mines of South Australia are undeveloped. Drought and the want of capital appear to be the principal obstacles in the way. Important discoveries of the metal were made in 1886 at Kangaroo Island in that colony. The stone averaged 16 dwt. of gold to the ton. Both quartz and alluvial gold-mining are carried on at Blackwood Gully Myponga, Manna Hill, &c.

The Gold-fields of Tasmania require development. According to a report by the Under Secretary for Mines in that Colony the indications are favourable. The gold of Tasmania is said not to be of such uniform quality as in other parts of Australasia. The product of the Beaconsfield field is worth £3 15s. ($18·25) per ounce, at Golconda and Denison £3 10s. ($16·03) per ounce, while that from Sepoy Fingal is worth £4 ($19·47) per ounce. A nugget weighing 48 ounces was unearthed on the West Coast in 1886. The largest ever produced in the Colony was found in 1883. It weighed 243 ounces 1 dwt.

The conditions under which gold is found in Australasia are precisely the same as in other countries; the Australasian metal, however, is believed to be of a higher standard than that produced elsewhere, and in some places—for instance, at Mount Morgan mine, Queensland—it may be said to be nearly pure. It has been stated by Lock, Percy, Liversidge, and other authorities on metals, that gold is not found in nature unalloyed with silver, but Dr. Leibius, of the Sydney Mint, states that considerably over 60,000 ounces of gold from the Mount Morgan mine has been found to be free from silver, with the exception of a minute trace. He says, further, that it assayed 99⁷⁄₁₀ per cent. of gold : the remaining ³⁄₁₀ was copper with a trace of iron.

The Mount Morgan gold is the richest native gold hitherto found. Some of the gold from Victoria comes next to this, and assays 96 per cent. Mr. F. B. Miller, the inventor of the chlorine process for refining gold, is very decided in opinion that the nearer we go northward in Australasia the less pure the gold becomes. He cites in support of this theory the statement that the average fineness of Victorian gold is 96 per cent., that of New South Wales 93 per cent., and Queensland 87 per cent. The Mount Morgan gold forms a striking exception to this rule.

The Mount Morgan is the most valuable mining property in Australasia. It is situated near the summit of Mount Morgan, about 1,125 feet above the sea, on the Dee Creek 26 miles S.S.W. from Rockhampton, and 420 miles N.W. of Brisbane. The place where the gold is found is in the centre of what has been a hot spring or geyzer. The stone is simply quarried out of the mountain, and is treated by the chlorinating process. It returns from 3 to 12 ounces of gold to the ton, and it is estimated that there is more than half a million tons of ore at the mine accessible for treating. The mine was discovered in 1882 by three brothers, the Messrs. Morgan, from whom it takes its name.

There were 47,801 miners employed on the various gold-fields of Australasia at the close of 1885. Victoria gave employment to 26,194 ; New Zealand, 11,178 ; Queensland, 7,160 ; New South Wales, 5,911 ; South Australia, 1,190 ; Tasmania, 868 ; West Australia, 300 miners. Their wages average from 7s. to 10s. ($1·70 to $2·43) per day. The miners usually live in tents or bark huts, erected on land belonging to Government or to their employers. They provide their own food.

The manufacture of mining machinery and mining appliances is carried to great perfection in Victoria, but the bulk of the requirements of the other Australasian Colonies is met by imports from Melbourne and Great Britain : a large proportion is, moreover, imported from the United States. Within the last two or three years quite an impetus has been given to the trade in American mining machinery through the success attending the operations of various kinds of American steam engines, furnaces, smelters, ore separators, pumps, pumping gear, and rock drills. Messrs. Park and Lacey, of Sydney, have imported from San Francisco during the last six months of 1887, over £20,000 ($97,330) worth of mining machinery, against £3,000 ($14,599) worth imported during a like period in 1886. The estimated value of all kinds of machinery and mining appliances used on the gold-fields of Australasia is £3,917,182 ($15,234,491). About one-half of this amount is invested in Victoria alone. The number of steam engines used in gold-mining in Victoria is estimated at 1,085, of 26,627 horse-power.

Among the various processes employed in Australasia for extracting gold from pyrites is the Newbery-Vautin system. This process is said to have given much satisfaction at Mount Morgan, in Queensland, and at Sandhurst, Ballarat, and Maldon, in Victoria. The following is a description of the method of working this process:—

The usual mode of roasting the pyrites is adopted to free them from arsenic, sulphur, and other foreign substances, and then the calcined pyrites are mixed with water, and brought to the consistence of a thin paste, and placed in a revolving iron cylinder lined with lead, where they are mixed with 1 per cent. of chloride of lime and 1 per cent. of sulphuric acid, and rotated at a moderate speed after air has been pumped into the cylinder to a pressure of 60lb. to the square inch. The metallic gold, attacked by the chlorine gas, is converted into a chloride, which is readily soluble in water, and, after the air is blown off, the contents of the cylinder are tipped into a filter, which is an iron cylinder having a percolating false bottom, out of which the air is exhausted by a vacuum pump, and water being freely poured upon the superincumbent pyrites the result is that this is sucked through with marvellous rapidity, carrying the gold in solution. This process has hitherto occupied some twenty-four hours, but now three washings, taking half an hour altogether, are sufficient to treat the contents of the cylinder above, now rotating with a fresh charge. The false chamber is filled with a series of slanting cross pieces, which enable the exhausted solids to be tipped out after being discharged into the bottom receptacle from the upper part of the cylinder. The auriferous stream is raised by a pump constructed of composite metal, having no affinity to gold, into a vat, where the sediment is allowed to gravitate, and it is then run into another, tested for gold with sulphate of iron, and run through a bed of charcoal, which attracts all the gold in a metallic form, and allows the water to escape. The charcoal, when thoroughly impregnated, is brown in colour, and on being gently scraped with a knife shows that it is saturated with gold, and which assumes its usual colour. The charcoal is then burnt, and the pure gold remains.

The history of the establishment of a branch of the Royal Mint at Sydney is interesting. The colonists had for some years been much inconvenienced from the want of a proper circulating medium. At one time coin of all kinds was so scarce in Australasia that the Governor of New South Wales, the only colony of the group then existing, issued a proclamation fixing the values of the various kinds of coin at considerably higher rates than were allowed for them by the Imperial Treasury.

A guinea was declared to be worth £1 2s. ($5·34); and a half-crown 2s. 8½d. (66 cents); a shilling (24 cents) was proclaimed to be worth 1s. 1d. (26 cents). Copper coin was also made a legal tender to the amount of £5 ($24·33), and the recipient of that sum was obliged to carry home with him 37½ lb. weight of metal. At a later period the Governor adopted the plan of permitting the issue of promissory notes by private individuals, payable on demand in copper coin. No one was allowed to dispose of these notes at a less sum than the value on the face of them. The appreciation of coin at that time can very well be illustrated by the statement that a Spanish dollar, worth 5s. ($1·22), was made to take the value of 6s. 3d. ($1·52), by punching out of the centre a circular piece which was called a "dump," and valued at 1s. 3d. (30 cents), while the remaining part of the coin, dignified by the name of a "holey dollar," circulated for 5s. ($1·22).

After the discovery of gold in Australia there was a still greater demand than ever for a proper metallic currency, and in their desire to remedy the inconvenience the coinage of gold was ordered by some of the Colonial Governments, without waiting for authority to do so from the British Government. No objection was, however, made to this infringement on the prerogative of the Crown, for at that time probably no better expedient could have been adopted. The first coins made were sovereigns, and were issued at Adelaide, South Australia. They were alloyed with silver instead of copper, and weighed 135 grains, instead of 123·294 grains, British standard. The Australian coin bore on the obverse side the figure of a Royal Crown, with the words "Government Assay Office," and on the reverse side "Weight, 5 dwt. 15 grs.; value, 1 pound; 22 carats." In 1853 the Imperial Government finally consented to the establishment of a branch of the Royal Mint at Sydney. It was first agreed that the coin of the Branch Mint should not be a legal tender out of the Australian Colonies, but afterwards the privilege of circulation was extended to the colonies of Mauritius, Ceylon, and Hong Kong, and in 1866 the circulation was legalized throughout the British Dominions.

The Sydney coinage was at first attended with considerable pecuniary loss, as there was not gold enough in New South Wales to utilize the machinery erected at the Mint. The difficulty was in time removed by a regulation permitting the coinage of the produce of other colonies at reduced rates, and Victorian gold was attracted to Sydney. Subsequently, in 1872, a Branch Mint was established at Melbourne. Gold is the only metal coined at the Australian Mints, the silver and bronze coinage used in the Colonies being obtained from London. About three-fifths of the Australian coinage finds its way to the Bank of England.

The following tables, taken from the Royal Mint returns, show the weight and value of gold received for coinage at the Sydney and Melbourne Mints, from the opening of the Mints to 31st December 1887:—

At the Sydney Mint, from 14th May, 1855.			At the Melbourne Mint, from 12th June, 1872.		
Year.	Gold received for Coinage.		Year.	Gold received for Coinage.	
	Weight.	Value.		Weight.	Value.
	oz.	£ s. d.		oz.	£ s. d.
1855 to 1876	10,787,761·07	41,571,393 15 2	1872	190,738·14	764,917 6 9
			1873	221,870·44	887,126 15 6
			1874	335,317·62	1,349,101 17 3
1877	438,385·50	1,608,248 2 8	1875	489,731·59	1,947,712 14 3
1878	365,173·89	1,308,898 1 5	1876	543,198·59	2,149,480 17 6
1879	394,606·76	1,434,871 3 2	1877	378,310·33	1,491,819 4 9
1880	406,291·87	1,487,678 12 10	1878	569,932·17	2,267,430 10 0
1881	465,584·70	1,702,102 7 2	1879	656,555·84	2,637,738 8 9
1882	401,559·69	1,477,134 7 9	1880	758,720·84	3,061,820 7 5
1883	374,141·20	1,353,665 9 6	1881	692,213·29	2,792,985 6 2
1884	475,053·41	1,713,843 19 9	1882	818,905·42	3,310,970 8 6
1885	422,160·20	1,510,061 10 3	1883	785,715·82	3,158,419 19 9
1886	475,166·21	1,712,244 8 5	1884	945,429·23	3,802,228 18 2
1887	597,706·82	2,173,305 19 8	1885	836,168·89	3,350,736 15 10
			1886	756,248·88	3,028,374 3 8
			1887	769,897·05	3,074,222 14 9
Total	15,603,591·32	59,053,447 17 9 $287,383,605	Total	9,748,954·14	39,075,086 9 0 $190,158,906

RETURN showing countries where the gold was produced which was received.

Country.	At the Melbourne Mint.		At the Sydney Mint.	
	During the year 1887.	Since the opening of the Mint.	During the year 1887.	Since the opening of the Mint.
	oz.	oz.	oz.	oz.
Victoria.....................	595,087	7,072,357	49	1,438,144
New South Wales	799	8,095	105,269	7,099,404
New Zealand	98,717	1,426,381	53,101	2,113,503
Queensland	184	4,507	426,110	4,717,601
South Australia	31,746	183,901	5,626	47,549
Tasmania	31,861	387.238	5,633	11,789
West Australia	1,659	2,259	1,694	14,153
Natal		1,731		
India	......	1		
Unknown	9,844	62,484		
Other countries' coin ...	......	......	225	161,448
Totals.........	769,897	9,748,954	597,707	15,603,591

ESTIMATE of the amount of coin in New South Wales at the close of 1886.

Where held.	Gold.	Silver.	Bronze.	Total.
	£	£	£	£
In private hands	3,027,220	309,857	24,827	3,361,904
In Banks......................	4,230,792	206,488	2,462	4,439,742
Total............	7,258,012	516,345	27,289	7,801,646

The process adopted at the Australian Mints for refining gold and silver, is the invention of Mr. F. B. Miller, formerly one of the assayers at the Sydney Mint, and now Superintendent of the Bullion Office, Melbourne. It consists simply in passing chlorine gas through the metal.

The process was commenced in Sydney in 1869, and in Melbourne in 1872. The total amount of gold operated upon at both Mints since the introduction of the process has been about 16,200,000 ounces.

It was believed for many years, that previous to Mr. Miller's discovery, the use of chlorine gas for refining gold was altogether unknown, but the fact is, it was successfully employed by Duroche and others, in Paris, many years previously. Mr. Lewis Thompson, in a communication to the Society of Arts, London, in 1838, said of this process:— "The plan for assaying and purifying gold is no less simple in execution than certain in effect, and is founded upon a circumstance long known to chemists, namely, that not only has gold at red heat no affinity for chlorine, but that it actually parts with it at that temperature, although previously combined." Professor Aiken, about the same period, published the results of a series of successful experiments in purifying gold by means of chlorine gas. These experiments were, however, conducted upon a small scale and should not affect in the least the credit to which Mr. Miller is justly entitled, for there is no evidence to show that he had ever heard of these experiments. Dr. John Percy and other scientists, who have investigated the history or origin of the invention, are of opinion that Mr. Miller was the first to show that the process was fully practicable, more especially with the object of saving the silver combined with gold.

The process appears to have given general satisfaction at the Sydney and Melbourne Mints. Indeed, the Bank of New Zealand has the process at work in their Bank at Auckland, having purchased the right to use the process in New Zealand, from Mr. Miller. The process has been satisfactory principally because the Australasian gold is so largely impregnated with silver. The latter metal often running as high as 40 per cent. It is admitted, however, that when auriferous silver occurs, as well as argentiferous gold, that the process of dissolving out the silver with acids is much more economical than the chlorine process.

The furnace used in the Miller process differs very little from that commonly used in melting gold. The flue is brought near the top, so that the crucible holding the molten gold can be placed high up in the furnace without being cooled by the draught. The crucibles are made of clay, and are capable of holding about 700 ounces of gold. They are provided with loosely-fitting covers, made of the same material, each having two small holes bored through them. The crucibles are first filled with boiling borax, for the purpose of glazing their interior surfaces, and rendering them impervious to melted chloride of silver. The pipes through which the chlorine gas passes are also made of clay. The jars for generating the chlorine gas are of the best glazed stoneware, and hold from 10 to 15 gallons each. The chlorine gas is conducted from the generator into a leaden pipe fitted with branches for the several furnaces respectively, all intermediate connections being formed by means of vulcanized rubber tubing. The crucibles are slowly heated, to a dull red color, and the gold, in the form of what is known as the "slipper-shaped ingot," is introduced, the narrow ends of the ingots being placed downwards. As soon as the gold is melted, a small proportion of molten borax is poured upon it. The end of the clay pipe is then introduced to the bottom of the crucible, and the gas bubbles up through the molten gold, without causing any projection of globules. Hydrochloric acid is, from time to time, introduced into the generator, to keep up a rapid supply of chlorine.

When the gas first passes through the molten gold, fumes escape from the holes in the covers of the crucibles. These fumes consist of the volatile chlorides of the baser metals, and not of the chloride of silver. So long as any of the silver remains in the gold, the whole, or nearly the whole, of the chlorine continues to be absorbed. When the operation is nearly over, fumes of a darker color than those produced at first make their appearance, and the end of the operation is indicated by the color of the flame or vapor, which, at first, is of a bright yellow and then a dull reddish brown color.

The quantity of chlorine gas employed in the process depends upon the quality of the gold operated upon. The time required to deliver sufficient chlorine to refine about 600 ounces of gold, assaying 900 parts in 1000, is usually about two hours.

As soon as the operation is over, the gold is cast into bars. The chloride of silver is re-melted—in the clay crucibles, coated with borax—together with eight to ten per cent. of laminated metallic silver. When the contents are thoroughly heated, the crucibles are withdrawn from the furnace, and, after standing a few minutes to settle, the still liquid of chloride of silver is poured into moulds and cast into slabs. Any gold that may have remained in the chloride of silver, alloys with the metallic silver and remains, in the form of a cake, at the bottom of the crucible.

SILVER.

The recent introduction of American and other appliances for smelting and refining silver ores in this Colony has given a new impetus to the mining interests of Australasia. Silver has been known to exist for many years in various parts of New South Wales, but until the discovery of the mines at Boorook, in the New England district, it was not found in workable quantities. Mr. Wilkinson, the Government geologist, has repeatedly expressed the opinion that the silver deposits would eventually prove to be great sources of wealth to the Colony. These deposits are not only rich in character but extend over a vast area.

The cause of their having been neglected hitherto is attributed principally to want of knowledge as to the proper methods for treating the various kinds of ores. Some of the chief silver-bearing lodes of the Colony are situated in the Barrier ranges of the Albert district, and are believed to extend to a considerable distance toward the interior of South Australia. Silverton, the chief mining town of the silver country, is about 590 miles from Sydney and 257 miles from Adelaide, with which city it is connected by railroad and tram-line. Mr. Wilkinson describes Silverton as occupying a convenient position upon the main road from Adelaide to Wilcannia, and near the western margin of broken, hilly country, called the Barrier range. The country is almost entirely surrounded by open salt-bush plains, and extends 150 miles in a north north-east direction, and varying in width up to 110 miles. Nearly the whole of this country consists of metalliferous formations, but it is chiefly on the south-western portion that the silver lodes have been discovered. The deepest shaft in the Albert district is about 327 feet. The lodes vary, but are in some places over 10 feet wide. About 8 miles distant other shafts have been sunk, with very favourable results. At Brade & Nickel's mine, in the same neighbourhood, considerable quantities of ferruginous carbonate of lead containing horn silver have been found. An assay of one piece of this mixed ore gave 3,240 ounces of silver per ton. Further north is the Christmas mine of Hawser & Collins, from which specimens have been obtained assaying horn silver at the rate of 11,073 ounces to the ton. Valuable lodes have also been opened at Stephens' Creek, 23 miles from Silverton. At a place called Thackaringa, thirty silver-bearing lodes have been discovered within a radius of 4 miles.

The Government geologist examined eighty-one lodes in the Silverton country, and the examination led him to the following conclusions:—

1. That the geological formations which contain the argentiferous lodes of the Barrier Range Silver-field are mica-schists, clay-slates, and sandstones, traversed by numerous quartz-reefs and intrusive masses and dikes of coarsely crystalline granite (pegmatite) and diorite. Nearly all the lodes occur in the mica-schists, and they have been found over a tract of country 70 miles long and 30 miles wide, which has been only partly prospected, so that many more lodes will probably be discovered. But the metalliferous formations are known to occupy a much larger area, and extend to Kooringbury on the north, and on the east as far as the Eight-mile Tank, on the road to Silverton, about 38 miles from Wilcannia.

2. That the lodes, with the exception of those of the Broken Hill and Pinnacles, which are chiefly composed of ferruginous quartzite, all consist either of brown iron ore (gossan) containing argentiferous carbonate of lead and galena in bunches, and sometimes chloride and chloro-bromide of silver, and carbonate of copper, or rarely of argentiferous carbonate of lead and galena alone; quartz is sometimes, though not always, present, It is evident that the oxides, carbonates, and chlorides have resulted from the decomposition of the sulphides, and perhaps arsenides of iron, lead, silver, and copper, which will be met with in their original condition below the water level. Sulphide of lead (galena), and in two instances iron pyrites, are even found above the water level. I did not notice any distinct sulphide of silver, iodide of silver, or antimonial ores in the lodes. Mr. J. Cosmo Newbery, C.M.G., reports having found "chloride, bromide, and iodide of silver, with brown iron ore, carbonate and sulphide of lead, oxide and sulphide of antimony, and traces of bismith" in the ore from the Christmas mine. It is stated that 12 cwt. of this ore treated at the Victoria Pyrites Smelting Company's works yielded 2,575 ounces of silver. In one mine the water level has been reached at a depth of 133 feet, in another at 72 feet.

3. That the lodes, without exception, are very inconstant in thickness, both in longitudinal and vertical extent, and many of them thin out entirely within a few yards. A surface plan of the numerous lodes would resemble the shrinkage cracks upon the surface of a dried piece of cross-grained wood; in fact, as before mentioned, the lode-fissures were shrinkage cracks formed by the contraction of the rock mass after the intrusion of the igneous rocks.

At present fuel has to be brought a very considerable distance, at a cost of about £5 ($24·33) per ton. The Government geologist recommends the establishment of a railway from Silverton to Menindie, a distance of 90 miles, where fuel and water are plentiful. The construction of this railway, besides lessening the cost of the reduction of the ore, would open up a valuable and interesting part of the country. At present much of the ore is sent to Adelaide for treatment.

So much attention has of late been drawn to the unprecedented richness of the Broken Hill Silver Mines in the Silverton country that authentic information from official sources will doubtless prove acceptable.

Mr. Harrie Wood, Under Secretary for Mines, Sydney, says:—"Notwithstanding the failure to treat successfully the ores obtained in some of our silver-mines, and the depression consequent thereon in certain quarters, it is very cheering to find that the result of our operations in 1886 shows an increase of more than a quarter of a million in excess of the preceding year. In view of the fact that the treatment of silver ores is new to us, it is no wonder that attempts to treat some of the more difficult ores have not been successful, and it would not be surprising if some of the mines now regarded with disfavour should, as our experience and appliances increase, prove exceedingly valuable."

"In the Silverton Division satisfactory progress was made during the year, though most of the mines are in their infancy. The magnificent results obtained by the Broken Hill Company have induced a considerable amount of prospecting. During the year this Company raised and treated 14,750 tons of ore, from which 36¼ tons of silver, valued at £228,519 ($1,112,088), were obtained. To the end of 1886 this Company had paid £64,000 ($311,456) in dividends. Work has been resumed at the Pinnacle's mine, and it is thought that with the aid of concentrating machinery, which is being erected, the Company will be able to treat the refractory ores effectively, and then, with the improved water supply, this mine will be second only to the Broken Hill. This Company had 450 tons of ore left from 1885, and raised during the year 800 tons; of this, 88 tons were sold for £1,100 ($5,353), and 511 tons were smelted, yielding 18,937 oz. of silver, valued at £3,800 ($18,493), leaving 651 tons of ore. At the Day Dream the men were engaged prospecting the mine at a greater depth, and they have met with fair success. The Umberumberka Company may now be regarded as established as a first-class mine. This Company raised during the year 1,389 tons of ore, which was sold for £31,026 ($150,988), and added 1,246 tons of second-class ore, to their stock. Several of the small chloride veins which are to be found all over the field, especially in the vicinity of Purnamoota, have been steadily worked during the year.

There are seven smelters on the field.

The Warden at Silverton, Mr. Brown, reports:—

The declared value of the mineral exports from this field for the year 1886, is as follows:—

					Value.	
					£	$
Refined silver	410,256 oz.				81,910	398,615
Silver ore	1,711 tons	2 cwt.	3 qr.	16 ℔.	67,233	327,189
Argentiferous lead	2,556 ,,	11 ,,	1 .,	12 ,,	188,486	917,267
,, via Menindie	474 ,,	4 ,,	0 ,,	5 ,,	32,725	159,256
Tin ore	2 ,,	1 ,,	0 ,,	0 ,,	69	336
Total value of export					£370,423	$1,802,663

In addition to this, there is a large quantity of ore still remaining at the different mines, which has been raised during the past year, but not yet sold or treated, and would add considerably to the total amount of ore won.

I estimate the value of plant and machinery now at work on the field at £45,000 ($218,993).

As the Broken Hill Proprietary Company's mine is the most extensive and valuable silver mine in Australia, a short *résumé* of its history may not be out of place:—

"In September, 1883, Charles Rasp, then a boundary-rider on Mount Gipps station, marked out an area of 40 acres, believing the outcrop of manganese to be tin. On reaching the station at night, he informed Mr. McCulloch, the general manager of the station, also his mates, of what he had done, when it was determined to form a syndicate of seven persons, all station hands, each putting £70 ($341) into the venture. The first thing done was to apply for a mineral lease of the land taken up by Rasp, together with six other 40-acre blocks on the same line. These seven blocks now constitute the Broken Hill proper, and were originally applied for by G. McCulloch, G. Urquhart, C. Rasp, J. Poole, P. Charley, D. James, and G. M. Lind. Work was commenced, and assays made for tin, but with no beneficial result. It was then decided to sink a shaft, and prospect for silver, which, by this time, had been proved to exist in the district. The country being hard, and the sinking not showing encouraging prospects, coupled with the fact that the small amount of capital that had been subscribed was exhausted, caused some of the original shareholders to sell to others, Lind being the first to retire, his interest being taken by McCulloch and Rasp, Urquhart being the next to give in. It was now determined to increase the syndicate to fourteen, for the purpose of raising funds for further prospecting. This arrangement was carried out, and the work continued until the latter part of 1884, when chlorides were first found in Rasp's shaft, at a depth of 100 feet. Shortly after rich chloride ore was found in the cap of the lode, at a different part of the mine. The cap of this lode is discernible through the seven blocks owned by the Company, being about 1¾ mile in length, and rising in places fully 50 feet above the surface, while in the workings below it has been proved, in places, to be considerably over 100 feet wide. In 1885 it was determined to offer a portion of this enormous property to the public, and on the 10th August, 1885, the present Broken Hill Proprietary Company was floated. The prospectus issued was to form a Company of 16,000 shares, of £20 ($97·33) per share, the fourteen shareholders receiving 1,000 shares each, paid up to £19 ($92·46), the remaining 2,000 were offered to the public at £9 ($43·80) per share paid on allotment, and then to be considered paid up to £19 ($92·46), after which all shares alike were liable to a call of 20s. ($4·86) on formation of this Company. £3,000 ($14,599) was to be paid (in addition to the shares) to the original proprietors, for expenses previously incurred. Thus, on the formation of the present Company, only £15,000 ($72,998) was available for all purposes. Extensive operations were now commenced, machinery erected, and the first two smelters put in blast in May, 1886, and the result may be considered highly satisfactory. £64,000 ($311,456) has been paid in dividends, and another of £1 (4·86) per share is payable on the 19th January, 1887. Machinery and supplies of coke, firewood, explosives, &c., now on the mine, exceed in value several thousands of pounds; substantial stone buildings have been erected, for manager's residence, offices, and other purposes. All this has been paid for by the value of ore won from the mine whilst sinking shafts and driving levels, which, in ordinary cases, would be considered dead work. The supply of ore is, apparently unlimited. The market value of the mine on 1st January, 1888, was £8,000,000 ($38,932,000), the latest quotations being £365 ($1,776) per share. In 1884, a one-fourteenth in this property was worth about £100 ($486), some shares being sold for less than that amount. Of the seven original proprietors four retain an interest in the Company, viz., Mr. G. McCulloch, P. Charley, C. Rasp, and D. James, the former gentleman retaining the whole of his fourteenth interest.

By the printed report submitted to the shareholders on 18th January, 1888, the result of a twenty-four weeks' run, ending 30th November, was as follows:—Ore treated, 28,799 net tons, for 1,267,699 oz. silver and 6,511 tons of lead, the average of silver being 44·11 oz. per ton of ore. The profits from the mine for the six months, from 1st June to 30th November, were £120,201 ($584,958). The average cost of smelting the ore was £2 12s. 4d. ($12·73) per ton. The total employés on and in the mine are 898. The manager (Mr. W. H. Patton) receives a salary of £4,000 ($19,466) per annum. He was formerly manager of a group of the celebrated Nevada Comstock mines.

Mr. W. H. J. Slee, Inspector of Mines, reports:—

In October, 1886, I started from Sydney for the purpose of making a thorough inspection of the silver and other mines in the Silverton district. The first mines inspected by me were those of Broken Hill.

The Broken Hill Proprietary S. M. Co.'s mine is at present the best dividend-paying and the most extensive silver mine in New South Wales, and on the future development and skilful management, both in the working of the mine and the reduction and treatment of the ore, will greatly depend the prosperity of this rich and extensive mineral district.

The hill on which this mine is situated rises about 150 feet above the level of the plains which stretch on each side, the lode forming the crest of the highest peak of a rugged ridge, and can be traced with an occasional break for about 2 miles, after which it runs into several lodes or branches. Course of lode north-east and south-west, and consists of iron coated with manganese, carbonates of lead, gossan, felspar, quartz, quartzite, and ferruginous drifts.

Chlorides of silver in payable quantities are being raised from several parts of the mine ; it is also well distributed in the southern part of the mine through the kaolin formation. In the northern part of the mine, out of a shaft known as Rasps, carbonate of lead is being raised from an extensive deposit, and is associated with very high percentage of carbonates, oxides, and grey sulphides of copper ore, which occur in the shape of boulders, and which may be estimated to contain from 40 to 50 per cent. of copper, in addition to silver. The lode, as far as opened out, forms a striking similarity to those top levels of the Great Cobar Copper Mine, with the exception that the Broken Hill is argentiferous, whereas the Great Cobar deposit is cupriferous. No correct estimate can at present be formed as to the real value of this undoubtedly rich mine.

The first furnace started to work on the 6th May, 1886, and was run for sixteen weeks, after which two furnaces have been running. Up to the date of my inspection, the first week in November, 8,612 tons of ore had been raised and treated, yielding 1,734 tons 15 cwt. of lead, and 740,480 ozs. (22¾ tons) of silver, to the value, in round numbers, of £148,000 ($720,242). Several furnaces have since been completed and set to work, resulting in a large increase in the yield of silver.

There are five shafts and two tunnels on the mine, and the lode has been opened in different parts from north to south, a total length of 2,092 ft., viz., Rasp's to M'Culloch's, 440 ft. ; M'Culloch's to Broadribb's, 1,148 ft. ; Broadribb's to Jamieson's, 308 ft. ; and Jamieson's to Knox's shaft, 196 ft. The whole of these shafts are, however, not as yet connected with each other. Nearly the whole of these shafts are down on the water-level. Rasp's shaft is 288 ft. ; M'Culloch's shaft, 327 ft. ; Broadribb's, 132 ft. ; Jamieson's, 212 ft. ; and Knox's, 196 ft. in depth. The contour of the country makes the apparent difference in depth of water-level.

Machinery.—The Company has steam boilers equal to 100 h.-p., and eight steam engines equal to 72 h.-p.; also four steam pumps equal to 24 h.-p. They have also excavated a large tank, from which they obtain their water-supply. They have also erected substantial buildings, covering about 12,000 ft. ; and their reducing plant is now equal to about 1,200 tons per week. About 500 men, inclusive of some boys, are directly employed on or about the mine and furnaces. This is exclusive of fuel getters, carriers, &c. The mine was inspected by me on the 8th and 9th November, and I found ladder-way, and everything in connection with the mine in as safe a state as could be reasonably expected, considering that the rough timber in use for the securing of the mine cannot be obtained nearer than Menindie on the Darling, a distance of 90 miles.

The works and machinery have been greatly increased since the above authentic report was written.

Disputes and litigations concerning the titles to land in the Silverton country have done much to retard progress, but these disputes are in a fair way of being settled. Mr. J. H. Maiden, of the Technological Museum at Sydney, stated in 1885 that the Silverton district will turn out a second Nevada. He thinks the district especially rich in horn silver. He writes, I have been fortunate enough to secure for the Museum a piece of almost pure horn silver weighing about 3 lb. It is one of the richest specimens ever found. The Government geologist did not see anything so rich on his recent tour.

The ores, however, of the Silverton country vary greatly in character. Samples sent from there recently, assayed at the mint from 39 oz. to 18·912 oz. of silver per ton, and specimens of galena yielded 16 per cent. of lead, 17·730 oz. of silver per ton; 45 per cent. of lead and 15 oz. of silver per ton; 82½ per cent of lead, 198 oz. of silver per ton; 14½ per cent. of lead, and 9·175 oz. of silver per ton.

Mr. Warden Gower, of Wilcannia, supplies the following list of assays from some of the claims at Silverton and Thackaringa:—

Name.	Holder.	Lead.	Silver.	Lead.	Silver.
		Per cent.	Oz. to ton.	Per cent.	Oz. to ton.
Robert Burns...........	Kitto..	......	......	55½	23
Hercules Company	....	32	79	......	......
Pluck Up Company ...	....	......	......	......	2,993
Gipsy Girl	Brigham	61¼	46	48	61
Hen and Chickens ...	Crispe	......	......	......	......
Gipsy Girl	Brigham	75	94	70½	191
Lubra	Crispe	......	......	......	......
	Collins and Hawson.	......	......	......	......
	Sinclair............	......	......	41	164
	Nicol and Anderson.	......	......	......	......
	Dawes	45	15	49	38
Chanticleer..............	Meech	74¾.	158	82½	198
	Purcell	......	......	......	......
St. Thomas..............	Thomas.........	25	1,919	22¾	1,402
Norwood Lads	McMahon..............	......	......	......	......
Consolation	Stewart	56	4,859	......	......
Black Prince	White	55½	849	53¼	181
Jo' the Marine	.. ..	......	......	......	......

Name.	Holder.	Lead.	Silver.	Silver.	Silver.	Silver.
		Per cent.	Oz. to ton	Oz. to ton	Oz. to ton	Oz. to ton
Robert Burns	Kitto	40	136	628	......	......
Hercules Company.	....	......	......	......	......	......
Pluck Up Company	....	......	2,858	4,083	9,869	470
Gipsy Girl	Brigham..............	72¾	80	......	......	......
Hen and Chickens..	Crispe.................	......	......	3,442	......	......
Gipsy Girl	Brigham.......	66	62	......	......	......
Lubra	Crispe.................	......	......	1,670	15,921	......
	Collins and Hawson	......	......	15,859	18,921	......
	Sinclair	14½	9,175	10,890	......	......
	Nicol and Anderson	......	......	18,148	6,112	310
	Dawes.................	......	......	......	......	......
Chanticleer	Meech.................	28½	69	......	......	......
	Purcell	......	......	39	10,151	......
St. Thomas	Thomas	16¾	1,739	......	......	......
Norwood Lads	McMahon	......	......	8,030	6,868	......
Consolation	Stewart	......	......	......	......	......
Black Prince.........	White.................	43¼	78	469	142	......
Jo' the Marine	....	......	......	4,887	10,724	......

Barrier Ranges.—Embolite, from 31 feet level, Broken Hill, lode, 17 feet thick.

Analyses:—	Chloride of silver..................................	81·67
	Bromide of silver	10·19
	Oxide of iron, silica, &c..........................	8·14
		100·00

Barrier Ranges.—Chloride of silver, in micasious schist, 7,872 oz. 13 dwt. silver per ton.

Barrier Ranges.—Ferruginous lode stuff, with galena, from Rockwell Paddock, lode 12 feet wide, 159 oz. 10 dwt. silver per ton.

Silver in workable quantities was discovered in 1878, at Boorook, near Tenterfield, in the New England district. This district is one of the most important in the Colony, and consists of a vast area of high table-lands. It is remarkable both for its agricultural and mineral products.

The country surrounding Boorook is very mountainous, and its geological formation consists of sandstone, granite, and slate, the last of which contains marine fossils. The argentiferous reefs are near the junction of the slate and granite. One of the reefs was first worked in 1871 for gold. Specimens of the ore being sent to Sydney the gold was found to be associated with a large percentage of silver. The stone becoming poorer, the lode was deserted about the time of the opening of the tin-fields in 1872. In 1879 stone was found at a depth of 130 feet, which assayed 830 ounces of silver to the ton. One claim with limited power produced in one week 889 ounces of silver. The Boorook metal is in part an antimonial one, mixed with the chloride, sulphide, and perhaps arsenide of silver. Associated with this mixed ore are found native gold, iron oxide, iron pyrites, chlorite, quartz, and other minerals. Mr. Lamont Young, one of the Government geological surveyors, states that the lodes are situated in belts of feldspar porphyry, between beds of altered and fossiliferous shales. Some of the fossils indicate the Upper Devonian formation. The ore itself is generally found in quartz, and the surface of the veins is usually covered with small crystals and much stained with oxide of iron, while the quartz is often very friable. The treatment adopted at first was similar to that for auriferous quartz, the discoverers having at hand a small battery for reducing the stone, and a Berden amalgamating machine. This process had to be abandoned, as considerable quantities of silver were carried away in the tailings.

The Golden Age Mine is one of the most promising in New England district. According to the mining inspector the work is carried on in stopes connected by shafts. The geological formation to a depth of 200 feet is of black slate lightly impregnated with iron pyrites, and mineral crystals of galena, silver, and blende. At the 200-foot level a lead of hard greenstone, about 30 feet in thickness, with layers of pipe-clay, was met with, beneath which the slate again occurs to the depth of 280 feet, when a syenite stratum makes its appearance. The ore as far as it has been proved is richer in the slate than in the greenstone or syenite formation. There are two distinct lodes in this mine—The Golden Age proper, which has an underlay to the west of 57 degrees, and a strike of 29 degrees east, and the Addison Contra lode, which is perpendicular except at the junction with the Golden Age lode, where there is a slight underlay. The strike of the Addison Contra lode is due north. It is at the point of junction where the largest and richest deposits of silver ores have been discovered. The Addison Contra lode averages only 6 ounces of silver per ton, but the Golden Age varies from 40 to 600 ounces per ton. The silver occurs in a variety of forms. At a depth of 75 feet from the surface it was found as chloride and bromide. From this point to the 140-foot level it was argentiferous iron pyrites, and blended with sundry spots of silver glance, but below this level it occurs principally in a state of flexible sulphide, of which some magnificent specimens have been obtained. The silver is extracted by the chlorination and amalgamation process. The ore is sorted by hand at the mine and carted to the works in parcels of 20 to 30 tons, containing from 70 ounces to 140 ounces of silver per ton. It is then dried, crushed, and mixed, and passed through the roasting chlorinating furnace. When cold enough the chlorinated ore is passed through a circular sieve of 2,500 holes to the square inch so as to separate the grit, which is again crushed and passed through fine gratings, recalcined, and taken to the amalgamators. The poorer ores are crushed by means of a Marsden fine crusher and concentrated in the ordinary hand giggers.

The Sunny Corner is one of the most important mines, formerly the premier silver mine, in the Colony. It is situated on the Mitchell Gold Field, about 127 miles from Sydney and 25 miles east of Bathurst (the third city in New South Wales) and only 15 miles north of Rydal on the Great Western Railway. The land occupied by the mine was originally applied for as a "mineral lease," for the purpose of mining for copper, but it was subsequently worked as a gold mine with variable success, and a considerable quantity of silver was allowed to remain unextracted in the tailings. The geological formation of the country is paleozoic (Siluro-Devonian) and consists of more or less altered slates and sandstones forming steep mountain ranges and deep valleys. Only a few of the numerous lodes which occur in these ranges have been more than superficially prospected.

The lode in Sunny Corner Mine proper is irregular in width and occupies a series of fissures or cavities along a "line of fault," which occurs in the axis of an anticlinal curve. Another lode to the north is worked by the Nevada company, and has been found to contain a good proportion of galena and copper pyrites. Several shafts have been sunk north of Sunny Corner on a mineral lode 2 or 3 feet in thickness, and apparently a continuation of the lode in Sunny Corner. A tunnel is driven to intersect the lode sunk on the hill. This tunnel is 170 feet in length. A lode of black-jack was struck at the end of the tunnel, intermixed with malleable or native copper. The Inspector of Mines states that in removing the black lode in the face of the tunnel, water made its appearance, and a beautiful sight met the eye, for, as the water forced through the black slate, narrow, horizontal quartz veins became visible, containing a large percentage of native copper. This copper had no doubt been in a solution coming from some copper deposits higher up the hill, and was gathered by the action of silicate and the natural backing up of the water against the black lode. About 120 feet up the hill there is a large quartz reef, said to contain 6 pennyweights of gold per ton by crushing, and still higher up is the mineral lode, to intersect which the tunnel is driven. Out of one of the shafts in this lode, and 30 feet deep from the surface, the inspector tried a a prospecting dish full of stuff, and it was found to contain 2 grains of gold. The lode is 9 feet thick.

The following extract from the Annual Report of the Government Geologist tend to prove the permanency of the silver bearing lodes which occur at Sunny Corner :—

The primary or oldest formation of the district consists of sedimentary rocks, altered sandstone, and shales. These have been upheaved and intruded by igneous rocks composed of quartzitic elvan and quartz porphyry, which have burst through the sedimentary strata in various directions, but principally north and south, as masses 20 chains wide or as narrow dykes only 4 feet thick, consequently the line of junction between the formations is most uneven and irregular. After the eruption of the igneous rocks, fractures or displacements in the rocks took place on at least two different occasions, resulting in the opening of irregular fissures from a few inches to 40 ft. wide, in which were deposited the gold and silver-bearing sulphides of iron, copper, lead, zinc, and arsenic and quartz, constituting the lode-stuff now worked.

Evidence of these displacements in the rocks may be seen in the Sunny Corner mine. A dyke of the elvanite has been split in two and the fissures filled with clay, showing that the fracture took place after the intrusive rock had solidified. Then again, the sedimentary formation has in places been displaced from its contact with the igneous rock, appearing to have moved bodily over the igneous rock, causing, where the original line of junction was uneven, the projecting surface of the one formation to abut on portion of the other, the intervening concave surfaces forming the irregular cavities now filled with lode-stuff, and, of course, where the line of junction was even or straight, the upper formation has moved upon the other without producing any cavity, consequently where this occurs the so-called lodes pinch out, though a well defined fissure joint continues, containing a thin seam of clay fluccan.

In the Great Western Mine the two different sites of fissures are very clearly seen. We here see that along the line of fracture the surface of the rock has been grooved by the friction of one rock upon the other, and the fissure filled with fragments of the crushed rock. In this fissure-deposit argentiferous sulphides of lead, copper, iron, and zinc, have been found in patches. The fissure then opened again and became filled with clay, which in one place is 20 feet thick. Then shrinkage cracks formed in the clay-lode and were filled with carbonate of lead, probably derived from the decomposition of the galena in the breccia lode.

On account of the irregular manner in which the intrusive rock has been intruded, it is of course impossible to indicate where the middle line of juncture between the formations is uneven, and therefore, the whereabouts of any cavities filled with lode-stuff can only be ascertained by actual prospecting along the lines of fracture. But we have a general guide in that the sliding movement of the upper formation has taken place towards the north-west ; for the ore deposits already discovered occur chiefly upon the north-western slopes of the intrusive formation. This is an important feature, for it affords us assurance that in a north-westerly direction, below the deposits already opened, other similar irregular lodes are likely to be found. From the nature of the formation of the lodes, it will be apparent that there is no probability of the occurrence of *one main lode* in this district, but only of such of those which are at present known, and which are so variable in extent and thickness, notwithstanding that they are true fossil lodes.

The Sunny Corner Mine, is the oldest and most productive of the silver mines. The lode, consisting of porous siliceous gossan, was worked for gold as far back as 1875, and though at that time the ore was known to contain a good percentage of silver, it was not until the Pacific smelters were introduced upon the field, by Messrs. Lamont and Kahlo, in 1885, through the enterprise of Messrs. Newton and Co., that mining for silver commenced. Since then this mine has produced 1,169,454·164 oz. of gold and silver bullion, of which 562,987 oz. were obtained from 27,231 tons of ore smelted during the year ending 31st October, 1886. The lode varies considerably in thickness, and has been opened at five different levels, by tunnels driven in a southerly direction from the northern slope of the hill. At the top, or No. 5 level, which is about 190 feet above the lowest or No. 1 tunnel, a large excavation open to the surface has been made in the lode, which here attains a thickness of 40 feet of gossan, covered in places with gold-bearing porous quartz, and passing downwards through No. 4 level into undecomposed sulphides, or "base ore," 19 feet thick. From some of the gossan rich specimens of native silver, in beautiful arborescent forms, have been obtained; specimens of it have been presented to the Mining and Geological Museum, Sydney. In No. 3 level, 147 feet above No. 1, richer ore has been struck, yielding, it is said, 70 oz. of silver per ton, and averaging 2 ft. thick; it consists of galena, with iron and copper pyrites. But this ore will be found to vary much in its yield; for one sample gave on assay 12·74 per cent. lead, 0·85 per cent. copper, and 4 oz. 18 dwt. of silver per ton. No. 2 level, 75 feet above No. 1, has been driven along the line of lode, which in one place is from 7 ft. to 15 ft. thick, then narrowing opens again at the end of the tunnel to 2 ft., consisting of finely crystalline galena and pyrites. An assay of a sample of this ore gave:—Copper, 1·65 per cent.; lead, 14·60 per cent.; silver, 37 oz. 10½ dwt. per ton; gold, 4 dwt. per ton. The hanging wall dips W. 10° S. at 58°. This ore should be followed down.

In No. 1 tunnel no defined lode has been found, but a block of good sulphide ore, 7 feet thick, was struck, the hanging wall dipping W. 10° S. at 58°, which is almost the same angle of dip as that in No. 2 level. It is probably due to the greater regularity in the walls of the fissure that it has here not formed large cavities, such as those formed in the higher levels, where the containing walls of the fissure are very uneven.

Larger ore deposits occur in the higher levels than in the lower, which, as above mentioned, appears to be due to the fissure walls being more regular or even in the latter than in the former. As it is unlikely that the regularity has continued for any considerable distance there is every probability that in following the fissure walls other large and valuable ore deposits will be discovered from time to time. The most favourable places for searching for them are on the north-western and western face of the elvanite rock; that is where the line of junction between the igneous and sedimentary rocks curves round from a southerly course to the west.

At the Sunny Corner Mine, which is under the able direction of Mr. Thos. Eyre, mining manager, smelting operations are very successfully carried on by means of "water-jacket" furnaces; but the large Probert furnace at first erected has been discarded in favour of the smaller furnaces which are much more conveniently worked. Mr. Woodgate, the smelting manager, has, by judicious fluxing, succeeded in reducing the loss of silver in the slag to an average of 1 oz. 17 dwt. per ton for four months run, as against an average loss of 2 oz. 19 dwt. for the previous five months run. He is also successfully smelting in the "water-jacket" furnace the base ores into "matte," and from experiments he is at present conducting further improvement in the reduction of the base ores is anticipated. It is said that ore yielding 16 oz. of silver per ton can be profitably worked by the present process. During the half-year ending October 31st, 11,647 tons of ore were smelted at these works, giving an average yield of 23·56 oz. of gold and silver bullion per ton; the bullion is worth on account of the gold contained in it about 5s. per oz. The Sunny Corner Company has recently erected an amalgamation plant for treating the old tailings from the battery, which are said to contain an average of 35 oz. of silver, and about 2 dwt. of gold per ton.

It will thus be seen that the primary formation of this district consists of siluro-devonian sandstones and shales, which have been upheaved and penetrated by elvanite and quartz porphyry; that, subsequently, movements of the rocks took place, resulting in the production of the fissures in which the metalliferous ores were deposited, chiefly about the line of junction of the sedimentary and igneous rocks; that these movements having affected the rocks to a considerable extent, the fissures will continue to great depths, though, owing to their irregular form, the ore deposits in them will vary much in thickness; that as these lodes are explored in depth, similar large patchy deposits to those already discovered, are likely to be found; that the gossan or oxidized portions of the lodes occurring within about 100 feet from the surface, must soon be exhausted; that the less easily worked unoxidized or sulphide ores will be the permanent class of ores to mine; and that, as these are usually less rich in silver than the gossan ores, weight of ore considered, special appliances for concentrating the sulphides must be employed, especially as the ores are not rich in silver and will necessitate the most economic methods of treatment, not only for the extraction of the silver, but also of the lead and copper which are sometimes present to a large extent in the ore.

In conclusion, I consider that silver-mining on this field will be a permanent and important industry; but its development, which must necessarily be gradual, must to a large extent depend upon—1st, the concentration of the sulphide ores, for they are generally of low grade; 2nd, more economical methods of smelting the sulphides, which will be the permanent class of ore to operate upon; judicious exploration of the lodes, for as the ore deposits are very irregular in thickness, having originated, as I have already described, in fissure cavities of varying extent, it will be necessary that the prospecting of the lode should be kept well in advance. The gossans or oxidized portions of the lodes, occurring within 100 feet from the surface, must soon be exhausted, but the depth to which the undecomposed sulphide ores may be found is practically unlimited.

Old methods of smelting silver ore have been abandoned and the American process is adopted at many mines. Probert (American) and other furnaces have been erected. The Probert furnace has been successfully employed at Sunny Corner and elsewhere, and met with so much success that Mr. E. F. Pittman, the chief mining surveyor of the Colony, wrote a very elaborate description of it. This process, so well known to those engaged in mining pursuits in the United States, consists in fusing the ore by means of a suitable flux and with the addition of lead when that metal is not found in sufficient quantities in the ore.

One of the essential requirements of the process being the presence of a certain proportion of lead, by which the silver and gold are carried down, and from which they are subsequently removed by cupellation, it becomes necessary to add lead if the ores do not contain a sufficient quantity of that metal. The flux used is limestone, which, with the silica and iron in the tailings and ore, make a fusible silicate of lime and iron, and the fusion is assisted by some of the old slag. If the ore does not contain iron, a sufficiency of that metal is added in the form of scrap iron. The fuel used is prepared Newcastle coke which costs about £4 (19·46) per ton. The furnace, said to be capable of smelting about 50 tons of ore per day, stands upon a sunk base of brick work, inclosed in a casing of cast iron, which is constructed of sixteen flanged sections, 5 feet in height, bolted together and having a cast-iron plate at the bottom. The crucible, which is situated just above the surface of the ground, is built in the centre of the brick work, and is made of the best Stourbridge fire-brick. It is cup shaped, and has a diameter of 7 feet and a depth of 21 inches in the centre. The walls of that portion of the furnace within which the smelting takes place are constructed of vertical water jackets, with loose-hinged covers. These water jackets are made in ten disconnected sections, 4 feet 6 inches high, 2 feet 6 inches wide, and about 6 inches through. They are made of the best wrought iron, and are strapped together at the top and bottom. The water is conveyed to the bottom of each of them by a rubber pipe and escapes by spouts from the top into a trough which surrounds the furnace; from here it flows into a well, when, after cooling, it is again available, being pumped up into a reservoir. A continual circulation of water thus takes place, and the consumption is small, as there is very little loss by evaporation. The inner surface of the wall of the furnace (water-jacket) being cooled by the circulation of water, speedily becomes covered with a coating of slag, which effectually protects it from corrosion, and in this manner the wear and tear of the furnace wall is reduced to a minimum. The water-jackets are pierced by nine tuyères. The nozzles of five of these are flush with the inner face of the water-jackets, while the remaining four (which are water tuyères) extend further inwards, their nozzles being about 20 inches from the centre of the furnace. Above the water-jackets the furnace is lined with fire brick for a height of 18 inches. For the first 6 inches the bricks are uncovered, but above that they are protected by a wrought-iron covering. The uncovered space is necessary for the purpose of removing any of the water-jacket sections for repairs, &c. Above the fire-bricks the furnace is formed like an inverted cone, lined with ordinary brick and having a dome-shaped roof. In the sides of the cone, at a height of 11 feet 9 inches above the crucible, are three feeding holes, where the charges of fuel, ore, and fluxes are thrown in. From the centre of the dome-shaped roof springs a vertical cylinder of wrought-iron, closed at the top but having a small trap-door. Just above the dome a horizontal wrought-iron flue leads from the vertical cylinder to a brick condensing chamber, at the base of a high stack. Attached at intervals to the lower side of this horizontal flue are a number of small V-shaped chambers, closed at the bottom by slides. These are for the purpose of catching the bulk of the condensed fumes, and as the latter contain both silver and lead they are returned to the furnace. The blast is supplied by a "Baker blower," size 5 feet by 4 feet, which is driven at the rate of about 100 revolutions per minute, and which forces the air into a windpipe, about 1 foot square in section, surrounding the furnace above the water-jackets. The air is thence conducted by canvas pipes to the tuyères. The ore when it comes from the mine is first broken to the size of walnuts in a Dodge crusher (of a similar type to the ordinary alligator-jaw crushers). It is then ground fine in a Dodge pulverizer, which consists of a revolving, horizontal cylinder, covered with screens, and protected on the inside by iron laths. The pulverizing is effected inside the cylinder by from twenty to fifty cannon balls, the number being varied according to the hardness of the ore. If the ore does not contain sufficient lead it is now subjected to treatment in the "lead bath," which necessitates its being thoroughly dried. For this purpose it is removed to a long drying furnace, which is so constructed that the flame returns over itself, thus providing three drying floors where the moisture is thoroughly expelled. It is then introduced into the "lead bath," which consists of a cast-iron cauldron filled with molten lead, to the bottom of which the powdered ore is forced by means of a plunger working in a cylinder. The ore as it rises to the surface is coated or mixed with litharge and shots of metallic lead. It is skimmed off the surface and is then ready to be mixed with the fluxes. Should the ore contain sufficient galena in the first instance, the treatment in the pulverizer, drying furnace, and lead bath would be omitted, and it would, after being roasted, be taken direct to the mixing floor. The ore is now weighed and mixed with the requisite proportion of limestone, broken to the size of walnuts, slag dust from the condensing flues, and, if necessary, scrap iron.

The furnace, being in blast, is fed continuously as the contents subside, with successive charges of coke and mixed ore and flux. The coke is used in the proportion of 1 ton to every 5 tons of ore. The lead bullion, containing the silver and gold, as it collects in the crucible, escapes by means of a siphon to a heated basin outside the furnace, whence it is ladled into ingot moulds, each holding about 80 pounds of metal. The slag is tapped at intervals from tap-holes situated immediately over the surface of the metal in the crucible. A certain proportion of the slag, as before stated, is used for flux; the remainder is carried away in basin-shaped molds attached to wheels.

The ingots of lead bullion are now assayed to ascertain the proportion of silver and gold contained in them. They are then introduced into cupelling furnaces. The cupels are made by tamping bone ashes with a rod, and each cupel occupies one man twelve hours in making. The frames are somewhat oval-shaped, but wider at the end nearest the front of the furnace. Each frame weighs about 125 lb., being made of cast iron, and holds about 350 lb. of bone ash. Through an aperture in the back of each cupel furnace a jet of steam plays over the surface of the molten lead or bullion. It is claimed that the steam aids in the more rapid oxidation of the lead, besides tending to blow the litharge forward into the channel which is cut across part of the wider ends of the cupel and which communicates with a small hole by which the litharge escapes to the floor beneath the surface.

The metal now left in the cupels consists of silver and gold, with traces of copper. It is next treated in the refiners—small open firebrick-lined furnaces, circular in section and sufficiently large to allow coke room, round moderately large plumbago crucibles. The metal is smelted in these with a flux consisting of borax and nitre. The oxides of the baser metals rise to the surface, forming a scum, which is removed, and the purified bullion is run into ingots, which upon assay yield 996 to 999 parts of silver and gold in 1,000.

The American furnace erected by Messrs. Hudson Brothers at their works at Clyde is called the "Gifford," after the patentee, and differs from the Probert in having no brick-work lining above the crucible, the whole of the furnace walls being constructed of water-jackets. This modification would appear to be an improvement, in so far as it tends to lessen the necessity for repairs to the inside of the furnace. In other respects the principle of the two furnaces is the same.

Until American smelting machinery was introduced the bulk of the silver product of this Colony was obtained during the process of refining gold by passing chlorine gas through it.

The following table shows the quantity and value of the silver exports:—

Year.	Silver.		Silver and Lead Ore.				Total Value.	
	Quantity.	Value.	Quantity.		Value.			
			Ore.	Metal.				
	oz.	£	s	Tons cwt. qrs.	Tons.	£	s	£	s
Up to 1881	726,779	178,405	868,208	191 13 0	..	5,025	24,454	183,430	892,663
1882	56,618	9,024	43,915	11 19 0	..	360	1,752	9,384	45,667
1883	77,065	16,488	80,239	136 4 0	..	2,075	10,098	18,563	90,337
1884	93,650	19,780	96,259	9,167 11 1	..	241,940	1,177,401	261,720	1,273,660
1885	794,174	159,187	774,684	2,095 16 0	190	107,026	523,762	266,813	1,298,445
1886	1,015,133	197,544	961,348	4,802 2 0	..	294,485	1,433,111	492,029	2,394,459
1887	177,307	32,458	157,957	12,530 3 2	..	541,952	2,637,409	574,410	2,795,366
	2,923,036	612,886	2,982,610	28,935 8 3	190	1,193,463	5,807,987	1,806,349	8,790,597

The approximate number of persons engaged in mining for silver during the year 1885 was 929, and in 1886, 1,297. The rise in the silver mining stock consequent on extensive discoveries of new and rich deposits of silver bearing ore in the Broken Hill, Silverton Districts, will give an impetus to silver mining during 1888. Already considerable excitement prevails and silver mining claims are being "taken up" in various parts of the Colony where silver bearing rock is known to exist. Companies are being floated in all directions. Lately the prospectus of a company called the "White Rock Proprietary Silver Mining Company," with a proposed capital of £1,000,000 ($4,866,500), has been issued in Sydney, to acquire and work silver bearing land at Drake, near Tenterfield, a mining town of the New England district.

The Geological Branch of the Mines Department has lately issued a most valuable and exhaustive memoir, with maps, of the geology of the Vegetable Creek (now Emmaville) tin and silver mining district, and this, being information upon which reliance can be placed, has, in a great measure, tended to attract the attention of investors to the untold mineral wealth of that portion of this Colony.

COPPER.

The copper-mines of Australia are amongst the most famous in the world. The ores are so rich that they produce a metal in many respects quite equal to the best lake copper of the United States, and cheerful testimony to that fact is given by some of the foremost metallurgists in Europe and America. The Chief of the Division of Mining Statistics and Technology, at Washington, D. C., says that the Australian mines, in a certain sense, are competitors with the American ones. He is also of the opinion that lowering of the price of copper would not affect seriously the supplies from Australia. At one time South Australia took the lead of all the other Colonies in the production of copper, but now New South Wales is the first in the list.

During the year 1886, New South Wales produced 3,969 tons of metal and 58 tons of ore, valued at £167,665 ($815,942), while South Australia produced 3,636 tons of metal and 14,782 tons of ore, valued at £230,868 ($1,123,519). The great bulk of the South Australian ore is sent abroad for smelting, while that of New South Wales is refined at the mines.

Copper exists in various parts of Tasmania, but as yet very little has been done toward developing the industry. Land, however, has been leased by several companies for the purpose of mining for this metal, but the low price of copper checked the operations. In Queensland, where copper also exists in large quantities, the development of the mines await the price of copper to advance to something like its normal value. Queensland produced 900 tons of copper in 1886. A number of valuable copper lodes have also been opened in New Zealand, those in the district of Nelson proving especially rich, but as yet little progress has been made with them. The value of the exports of copper from New South Wales, since the opening of the mines to December, 1887, reached £5,163,352 ($25,258,848.)

It would be difficult to form anything like a just estimate of the cupriferous formations of Australia from the fact that such a small extent of the country has been fully explored.

The known cupriferous area of New South Wales alone amounts to nearly 5,000,000 acres. In South Australia the lodes are distributed wherever the metamorphic and paleozoic rocks occur. As many as forty mines have been opened in the latter Colony; but few of them continued to be worked on account of the low price of copper. The principal mines are the Hamley, Moonta, Wallaroo, Blueman, Victory, and Burra Burra. A shaft has been sunk at Moonta to a depth of 1,320 feet, and another at Wallaroo to 1,020 feet. In New South Wales the most valuable lodes occur in silurian slates. These ores consist principally in carbonates, metallic copper in films, red oxide, and grey and yellow sulphides.

The Great Cobar Copper-mine, in the county of Cobar, is one of the most important in New South Wales. It is situated 497 miles west of Sydney, in the centre of the vast plains which lie between the Macquarie and Bogan Rivers. The ore is so rich and abundant that the industry has been a profitable one until a recent period, notwithstanding the great distance of the mine from the settled portion of the Colony, and the still more important fact of the country for miles around being almost wholly destitute of water. The produce of the mine has to be hauled by waggons a distance of 80 miles to Nyngan, the nearest railway station. The industry caused a settlement to spring up at Cobar, and it is estimated that within a radius of 3 miles the population is between 2,000 and 3,000. There are in the town two banks, several hotels, two churches, a newspaper, and a public school, with an average daily attendance of 130 pupils.

The Great Cobar Mine gives employment to about 500 persons. The plant is the best in Australasia. The company, however, experience great difficulty in getting the copper to market. Sometimes they have as much as 500 tons of metal waiting for teams to carry it to the railway station. During the year 1886 the number of miners employed in the Cobar district was 804. The amount of refined copper produced was 2,044 tons. The value of the plant at the Great Cobar Mine alone is £85,000 ($413,653). This plant embraces 3 forty horse-power engines, 2 stone-breakers, 1 cracker, 1 jigger, 3 eight horse-power engines, 1 Chilian-mill, 2 pug-mills, 2 air-compressors, 8 rock-drills, a tramway 11 miles in length, 6 locomotives (4 imported and 2 made in the Colony), and 84 trucks. During the year 1886 the Great Cobar Company raised 25,887 tons of ore.

The greatest depth obtained by sinking the main shaft in the Great Cobar Mine is 664 feet, from which diamond drills have been driven 60 feet farther. The lode at this depth, according to the report of Mr. W. H. H. Slee, Inspector of Mines, exhibits a thickness of 40 feet of fair, yellow, sulphide ore. Stoping is carried on in various parts of this mine. "Stoping" is a mining term for the drives that are made to reach the wall on each side of the lode. The drives are the tunnelings from the shafts. The miners work upwards from the levels, the object being to exhaust the whole of the lode, and as fast as a stope is worked out it is filled in and another drive made. With the exception of the 54-fathom level the ores obtained are carbonates, oxides, and grey ores, which average about 16 per cent. of copper. A new discovery of ore has been made between the 29 and 26 fathom level, which yielded 14 per cent. of fine copper.

Mr. Slee states that independently of this new find, it will take years to work out the different copper ores in sight and known to exist in the mine. The average thickness of the lode on the 29-fathom level is 110 feet.

The capital of the Great Cobar Copper-mining Company is £80,000 ($389,320) in £1 ($4·86) shares. The quantity of ore at this mine on the 1st of January, 1886, was 10,697 tons.

The Nymagee Copper-mine is next in importance to the Great Cobar. This mine is situated near the town of Nymagee, in the Cobar district, about 440 miles west of Sydney, and 70 miles south-east of Cobar. The town has a population of about 1,500 persons, composed principally of miners, 300 of whom are employed at the Nymagee Mine. This mine raised during the year 1886, 14,782 tons of ore, yielding 1,478 tons of copper. The width of the lode is from 4 to 12 feet. Stoping is carried on in different parts of the mine. Mr. Slee reports that some of the shoots of ore stoped upon contain large masses of rich copper. Some of this ore is raised and broken at the small cost of 4 shillings (97 cents) per ton. Large quantities of carbonates are obtained near the surface, which are mixed with yellow sulphides in smelting. A prospecting shaft has been sunk on the brow of a hill, on which there is a large outcrop of hematitic iron. The shaft is 147 feet in depth. A drive of 293 feet has been driven south of the shaft, and at the end of this drive a winze of about 40 feet in depth has been sunk.

During the year 1886 several new furnaces were erected. The total number of furnaces now in operation at the mines is fifteen. The yellow sulphide ore is crushed, and forced through a wire screen, ten holes to a square inch, after which it is taken on the tramlines to the calciners. By the calcining process the ore is reduced in weight fully 25 per cent. and increased in percentage 3 to 4 per cent., which enables the smelters to mix nearly two-thirds of sulphides in a charge of 21 cwt. of ore.

The capital of the Nymagee Copper-mining Company is the same as that of the Great Cobar, viz., £80,000 ($389,320.)

The New Mount Hope Copper-mine is the third in rank, and it is also in the Cobar district, 90 miles south of the Great Cobar Mine.

The main lode in the New Mount Hope Mine is ferruginous sandstone. The shaft is 340 feet deep. The width of the lode is from 10 to 50 feet. The lode consists of shoots and bunches of rich oxides, carbonates, and grey ores. These deposits occur in altered sandstone and belts of sandstone formations. It is said that there is no other mine in New South Wales which produces such interesting geological specimens of copper ores. Pieces varying from a few pounds to a ton in weight can be procured containing all the different carbonates, oxides, and sulphide ores.

The Great Central Copper-mine is situated 4 miles south of New Mount Hope, on a high hill, in porphyry formations. The ores are of high quality. There are seven shafts, varying in depth from 82 feet to 206. The deepest level is 150 feet, and the widest part of the lode is 13 feet. It has been proposed to open up other levels on different parts of the lodes. There are a number of other mines in the Colony that promises very favourable results. The Cheshire Copper-mine at Cudgegong shows a shoot of ore 46 feet wide, yielding 8 to 10 per cent. of copper. This ore appears in shoots, not in a continuous lode. At Blayney, a new copper lode, 2 feet in width, has been found within 1 mile of the town containing rich grey ore. The Boone West Copper-mine has a lode 6 feet in width. About half a mile west is the Big Ben lode. The lode at Nowendoc, which was abandoned a few years ago, has been started again. Satisfactory assays have been made from the lodes at Sernby Bush, Sounding Rock near Trunkey, Glanmire near Bathurst, and Burraga.

Mr. Harrie Wood, Under Secretary for Mines, has supplied the following assays of copper ores :—

Locality.	Description of Mineral.	Copper. Per cent.	Gold. Per ton. oz. dwt.	Silver. Per ton. oz. dwt.
Bombala	Iron pyrites and carbonate of lead and copper, from 80 miles south-west of Bombala.	26·4	....	2 9
Do	Ferruginous grey and yellow sulphide and green carbonate of copper, from 18 miles from Bombala.	28·45	....	2 9
Barrier Ranges	Grey sulphide and traces of green carbonate of copper	57·35	....	2 9
Do	Do do with gypsum	48·85	....	3 5
Bermagui River	Copper pyrites and quartz and traces of green carbonate of copper.	28·25	....	10 6½
Cobar	Blue and green carbonates of copper, from 3 miles from Cobar.	32·05	....	....
Do	Green carbonate of copper (fibrous malachite), from 70 miles west of Cobar.	55·2	....	....
Fairfield	Crushed sample of copper and iron pyrites, coated with a thin film of black oxide of copper.	36·75	1 19	6 4
Do	Ferruginous grey sulphide of copper, from Kelly's claim.	53·84	0 4	3 5
Gulgong	Ferruginous carbonates and sulphides of copper, old Gulgong reefs.	27·55	....	4 18
Gundagai	Red oxide of copper and a little quartz and green carbonates of copper.	72·05	....	....
Molong	Earthy lodestuff, 60-feet level	21·75	....	....
Do	Yellowish earthy felspathic lodestuff, with carbonates of copper.	20·5	....	1 12½
Do	Do do do	25·3	....	2 14½
Mitchell	Lodestuff from Tonkin's mine	45·6	0 3	22 1
New England	Green carbonate and grey sulphide of copper, from Lottery Creek.	39·9	0 3	14 14
Razorback	Ferruginous copper gossan, from 6 miles from Razorback.	37·85	....	1 12½
Shoalhaven River	Quartz and grey sulphide of copper	33·85	....	....

Rich specimens were found at Wellington, 240 miles north-west of Sydney. The town of Wellington is situated at the junction of Macquarie and Bell Rivers, 1,000 feet above the sea, at the foot of a mountain range. Wellington, together with the township of Montifiore, on the opposite side of the Macquarie River, contains about 2,500 inhabitants. The district in which this mine is located is a rich agricultural one, and at the same time is noted for the large number of auriferous reefs it contains. The reefs, however, have not been worked, and little more than prospecting has been done with the cupriferous lodes.

There are a great many varieties of copper ores distributed throughout the Colony, but the sulphides, carbonates, and oxides are those principally relied upon for the production of refined copper.

Professor Liversidge, in his valuable work on the minerals of New South Wales, states that the variety of copper pyrites known as peacock ore, from the splendour that it acquires, is found in nearly all the metalliferous districts—at Cobar (county Robinson), Bingera, Elsmore (county Murchison), Clarence (county Clarence), Wiseman's Creek and Oberon (county Westmoreland), Wellington district; with zinc blende, steatite, quartz, and asbestos; Ophir, Carcoar, Cow Flat, and Mitchell's Creek (county Bathurst), Wallabadah (county Buckland), Cargo and Molong (county Ashburnham), Peelwood (county Roxburg), at Tuena; with gold, Kiandra (county Wallace), Gordon Brooke (county Richmond), Snowball mine (county Clarendon), Dundee (county Gough), Goodrich (county Gordon), Cootalantra mine and Belmore mine (county Auckland), Nymagee (county Mouramba), Solferino (county Argyle), and at Malline Creek, between Goulburn and Braidwood. Professor Liversidge mentions that crystallized native copper is by no means rare in New South Wales, but that large and well-developed crystals, as elsewhere, are uncommon. It is found in plates, in threads, wires, and arborescent forms, and contains traces of silver, lead, bismuth, and other metals. In nearly all cases it is associated with cuprite malachite, and other oxidized copper ores. Red copper ore is found in various places in the Colony, and is abundant at Cobar, both in massive and crystallized forms. It is also met with in Richmond, Vernon, Phillip, Argyle, and other counties. Black oxide of copper is also frequently met with in the form of black powder. Massive or sporadic green carbonate of copper (malachite) occurs in various forms, massive and crystals, the various layers often possessing different shades of colour, forming a beautiful stone for ornamental and inlaying purposes. Professor Liversidge states that the crystals found at Cobar are particularly beautiful, the silky lustre being very remarkable. The capillary crystals are sometimes several inches long, and compacted together into fibrous bundles. Malachite is found in most of the upper workings of the copper-mines. Blue carbonate of copper is also found in various parts of the Colony, the best specimens coming from Cobar. Atacamite also occurs in the Cobar mines. A specimen of a dark translucent green colour, with vitreous lustre and apple-green streak, gave the following analysis:—

Water lost at $105°$	·536
Combined	13·955
Copper oxide	64·709
Copper chloride	13·218
Silica and insoluble matter	7·599
	100·017

Blue vitriol, or copper sulphate, is often met with in a form of efflorescence or incrustation. Copper glance is found both in the massive and crystallized state. Silicious redruthite, a peculiar copper ore, occurs at Carcoar. It is of a dark, almost black, colour. It resembles redruthite, but is of a duller lustre, and is very much harder. Purple ore and gray copper ore are not uncommon there.

TABLE showing the quantity and value of Copper, the produce of the Colony, exported from the Colony of New South Wales, from 1858 to 1887.

Year.	Ingots.		Ore and Regulus.		Total.	
	Quantity.	Value.	Quantity.	Value.	Quantity.	Value.
	Tons.	£	Tons.	£	Tons.	£
1858	....	....	58	1,400	58	1,400
1859	30	578	....	....	30	578
1860	....	....	43	1,535	43	1,535
1861	....	....	144	3,390	144	3,390
1862	....	....	213	5,742	213	5,742
1863	23	1,680	114	420	137	2,100
1864	54	5,230	....	....	54	5,230
1865	247	15,820	22	545	269	16,365
1866	255	18,905	23	1,885	278	20,790
1867	393	30,189	....	5	393	30,194
1868	644	23,297	172	4,000	816	27,297
1869	1,980	74,605	104	2,070	2,084	76,675
1870	994	65,671	6	60	1,000	65,731
1871	1,350	87,579	94	1,297	1,444	88,876
1872	1,035	92,736	417	13,152	1,452	105,888
1873	2,795	237,412	51	1,690	2,846	239,102
1874	3,638	311,519	522	13,621	4,160	325,140
1875	3,520	297,334	157	4,356	3,677	301,690
1876	3,106	243,142	169	6,836	3,275	249,978
1877	4,153	307,181	360	17,045	4,513	324,226
1878	4,983	337,409	236	7,749	5,219	345,158
1879	4,107	256,437	36	915	4,143	257,352
1880	5,262	359,260	132	4,799	5,394	364,059
1881	5,361	350,087	132	4,975	5,494	355,062
1882	4,865	321,887	93	2,840	4,958	324,727
1883	8,873	574,497	84	2,704	8,957	577,201
1884	7,286	415,601	19	578	7,305	416,179
1885	5,745	264,905	1	15	5,746	264,920
1886	3,969	166,429	58	1,236	4,026	167,665
1887	4,464	195,752	299	3,350	4,763	199,102
	79,133	5,055,142	3,760	108,210	82,892	5,163,352 $25,258,848

The vast increase in the output of the copper-mines of the United States during the last few years has completely revolutionized the price of copper. The refined copper of the United States has more than a restricted home market, and is finding its way into various parts of the world. The American refining works are unsurpassed. Those of Pope, Cole, & Co. of Baltimore, the Oxford Sulphur and Copper Company of New York, the Jersey Extraction Works at Elizabeth, N. J., the Phœnixville Works, Pennsylvania, and the Chicago Copper Company of Chicago, Ill., have now a world-wide reputation.

The fluctuation in the price of copper somewhat checked the industry in Australia, at present, prices are higher than they have been since 1880, and there seems to be a general impression that this state of affairs will continue. In January, 1888, the price of South Australian copper had risen to £74 ($360) per ton.

The metal is such a useful one, and enters into such an infinite variety of manufactures that the constantly increasing demand for it must of necessity occasion an advance in its cost. Those who think to the contrary, point to the fact that the introduction of new and improved machinery has materially lessened the price of the metal and will lessen the cost of production still more in the near future.

In the United States in the year 1875, the cost of the production of Lake Superior copper at many of the leading mines was as high as 11d. (22 cents) per pound; now it is less than 3½d. (7 cents) per pound.

It should also be remembered that the United States, from being the third in the list, has risen to the position of the greatest copper-producing country in the world, producing more than 30 per cent. of the whole copper supplies of the world, as compared with only about 15 per cent. in 1879.

The bulk of machinery used in Australia for smelting copper is imported from Great Britain, very little coming from the United States. The American machinery is generally acknowledged to be superior to all others, but it is almost an impossibility to overcome the prejudices of the Australasians in favour of purchasing all kinds of mining machinery in Europe. Many of the furnaces used are the ordinary old-fashioned cupola ones, and with them the process of smelting copper is both tedious and expensive.

From time to time the managers of the principal mines in the Colony have expressed the opinion that some other and more economic process will have to be adopted for the treatment of copper ores, and especially of sulphurets. Indeed, the manager of the Nymagee Mine stated that the falling off in the output of the mine was to be attributed to the method of smelting refractory ores. He said that in treating large quantities of sulphides it is necessary to produce a low percentage regulus, which is very difficult to work up into refined copper by the old process. Hundreds of tons of regulus have been made at Nymagee, which would not assay more than 35 per cent., and which could not be avoided in the absence of other ores.

Several reducing furnaces are employed, and even with them the regulus accumulated; and it has been determined that some change was necessary, in order to make the work profitable. A cold blast of air has been introduced into the reverberatory furnace, on the surface of the liquid metal, the motive power being a duplex engine and Root's blower. The furnace is charged in the usual way with 10 or 12 tons of regulus, and fired on until the whole mass is liquefied, after which the blast is applied, and by this means one furnace can be made to do the work of three in the ordinary way of working. An objection was made to the effect that the blast was driving small particles of copper into the stack; but it is said that this difficulty could be overcome by the construction of a large culvert and stack some distance from the furnace.

The Great Cobar and Nymagee Mines introduced a process for smelting copper like that at the Parot Silver and Copper Mining Works in Montana, U.S.A. This process has not given as much satisfaction as was expected; nevertheless, the principle has been shown to be good.

In the process, the ores are subjected to a simple fusion in a blow-blast or cupola furnace, for the purpose of obtaining a regulus or matt and slagging away the earthy matter. The converter is constructed after the model of a Bessemer one, with blast holes only on one side. Cog-wheels and a crank incline the converter in such a way that the molten mass can be blasted at any desired level. Hitherto the attempts at blasting copper have all failed, for the reason that, the blast going through the whole mass, the melted copper got chilled. In the new process the copper produced is collected at the bottom, when by a turn of the crank the blasting takes place on a higher level. Gradually in this manner, till the end of the operation, the blast passes through matter containing combustible elements, the metal is not chilled, and the blast holes do not get choked. The copper produced by this converter, it is said, is almost pure, containing 98 to 99 per cent. of pure metal. The whole operation lasts from fifteen to forty-five minutes, according to the purity of the matter introduced into the converter, the ore having been previously melted in a cupola furnace without any preliminary calcination. It is stated that by this process only two operations are required where formerly eight were used, and that the saving in fuel, labour, and time is remarkable.

The cost of freight on copper ore, or ingots, from Sydney to London, is usually nominal. From March to November it is required by sailing vessels and steamers for ballast, and in some cases a small premium is paid for it. During this period the only charge made by steamers is from 1s. (24 cents), to 2s. 6d. (61 cents), per ton. It forms an admirable ballast for cargoes of wool. When hides can be procured, copper is not so much in demand, as a sufficient quantity of hides will enable ships to dispense with ore as ballast.

Consequent on disorganisation as the result of the unsettled state of the copper market, the stocks of copper at the end of January, 1888, were 45,692 tons, as against 61,375 tons in 1887, and 58,589 tons in 1886.

TIN.

The large and steady annual increase in the export of tin ore and ingots to the United States from Sydney, has directed attention to the condition of the tin-fields. Although tin was discovered in New South Wales as early as 1849, mines were not opened until 1872, and since then 80,408 tons of ingots, and 16,480 tons of ore have been exported, valued at £7,402,456 ($36,024,052).

Twenty years ago the total tin product of the world did not amount to more than 15,000 tons per annum. In 1886 New South Wales alone produced 4,968 tons, and the whole of Australia considerably more than that. With the exception of gold, New South Wales takes the lead of all the other Colonies in the production of minerals, and although the value of her gold product declined from £366,388 ($1,783,027) in 1885 to £355,600 ($1,730,527) in 1886, there was during the same period a large increase in the value of the other mineral products. The aggregate value of all the mineral products of New South Wales for 1886, including gold, silver, coal, shale, copper, iron, antimony, asbestos, bismuth, and mixed minerals, was £2,928,427 ($14,251,190).

Tin, although one of the best known and most useful of metals, is produced in workable quantities in very few countries. For a long period the principal supply came from the county of Cornwall, in England, where very great skill is employed in tin mining. A royalty of £4 ($19·46), was charged on every ton of tin raised in Cornwall, the proceeds of which went to the revenue of the Dukedom of Cornwall, one of the titles held by the Heir Apparent to the British throne. In 1837, when Queen Victoria succeeded, an Act of Parliament was passed abolishing the royalty, but granting to the revenues of the Dukedom an annuity equal to the average amount of the royalty.

The mines of Bohemia and Saxony rank next in value to those of Cornwall. Then those of the Malayan Peninsula. The mines of Perak for a long time yielded a very large supply, and are still profitably worked, on account of the low cost at which labor can be obtained.

The most promising tin mines in the United States are in California, Dakota, Colorado, and Alabama. Very favorable results are expected from the Broad Arrow Mine in Clay County, Alabama. Tin is also found in quantities near Chesterfield and Goshen, Mass., and in Jackson, N.H. Tin mining in the United States has, however, been greatly neglected, from the fact that mining for silver and gold has proved more attractive.

In 1872 the total tin product of New South Wales was only 896 tons. In the year following it was 4,571. In 1875 it was 8,180 tons. In 1876 the quantity fell to 6,958 tons, but rose in 1877 to 8,054 tons. It declined again in 1880 to 6,159 tons.

The price of tin in London has varied from £120 ($584) to £170 ($827) per ton, and it has fallen to about £59 ($287) per ton, the tendency of the market, however, is towards high quotations. A singular fact connected with the price of tin is that it is not always regulated by the supply and demand.

The phenomenally, the marvellously, rapid rise in the price of tin is engrossing at the moment the whole world's attention. £100 ($485) to £105 ($510) was generally looked upon as good enough money, but when £110 ($535), even up to £120 ($584) to £150 ($730) was talked of, holders were spoken of as mad enthusiasts. But now, when a £170 ($827) market has been climbed up to, with no one rash enough to determine any present limit of values, who will venture to say that the £200 prophesied may not be reached? Few persons are aware of the importance of the Australian tin trade—a trade of growing importance as better prices prompt further developments. Of course, Australia's staple exports are wool and gold; but in the first six months of 1887 she sent to Great Britain alone—to say nothing of her American exports—3,214 tons of tin, valued at £326,808 ($1,590,311); her copper export value for the same period being £111,011 ($540,235). The violence of the movements in the market during recent years may be seen from the following figures of the highest and lowest prices of Straits tin in London :—

Year.	Price per ton.		Year.	Price per ton.	
	Highest.	Lowest.		Highest.	Lowest.
	£	£		£	£
1888 1st Feb.	170	102	1879	96	59
			1878	65½	52½
1887	166	116	1877	76	64½
1886	106½	100	1876	81	70
1885	97	74	1875	96½	76
1884	87	72½	1874	121½	87
1883	98½	82½	1873	149	114½
1882	114½	86½	1872	159	130
1881	110½	85½	1871	155	124
1880	102	68½	1870	134½	104½

The *Statist*, foretelling the future of the tin market, said :—" Of tin there are two main sources of supply, exclusive of English tin—the Straits and Australia. The first, which is growing, did not until 1879 reach 10,000 tons a year, but latterly it has grown to over 16,000 tons a year. The Australian supply was at its best in 1883, when it amounted to 9,500 tons. The two combined have, however, grown considerably in the past decade. In 1876 they aggregated 16,400 tons, and in 1886 they were rather more than 25,000 tons. The Cornish supply has during the same period been very regular; it ranges from 9,000 to 10,000 tons per annum. Operators in tin, therefore, can easily reckon with Cornwall. It is a safe quantity, and fluctuations in price do not disturb it much. They can also tell pretty well what becomes of the Cornish tin. About half of it is exported, and the other half consumed at home. Our imports of foreign tin follow, as a rule, the same principle of division. In exceptional years, like 1883 and 1884, the re-exports have been nearly 15,000 tons out of 25,000 tons or 26,000, but the average is 12,000 tons a year. Tin has of late fluctuated in price more than any other metal. It has been going through an alternative course of plunges and jumps. About the end of 1884 it was sold as low as £73 10s. ($357·70) per ton. By the end of

1885 it had risen to £93 5s. ($454); in the autumn of 1886 it got up to £102 11s. ($499), and it was done within a fraction of £105 ($511). The statistical conditions were not greatly different in 1883, when tin was £73 10s. ($357·70), from what they are, when it is £90 ($438) higher."

The tin market is, in fact, controlled by syndicates in Paris and London, who raise and lower the prices at pleasure, regardless of the quantity on hand or the demand. The price of tin has been known to decline suddenly in London, without any apparent cause, at a time when the stocks were the lightest and the most satisfactory accounts were being received from the markets elsewhere. The tin market is much more easily controlled by a syndicate than that of copper, from the fact that the supply of the former metal is much smaller than the latter.

Since 1878 the bulk of the tin shipped from New South Wales has been in ingots instead in the ore, which shows that great progress has been made in smelting the ore in the Colony. The heaviest shipment of the ore occured in 1873, and it is extremely probable that the exports of the ore will soon cease altogether.

The following table shows the quantity and value of the export of tin ingots, the produce of New South Wales since 1872.

Year.	Tons.	Value.		Year.	Tons.	Value.	
		£	$			£	$
1872	47	6,482	31,545	1880	5,476	440,615	2,144,253
1873	911	107,795	524,584	1881	7,590	686,511	3,333,906
1874	4,101	366,189	1,682,687	1882	8,059	800,571	3,895,979
1875	6,058	475,168	2,317,272	1883	8,680	802,867	3,907,152
1876	5,449	379,318	1,845,951	1884	6,316	506,726	2,533,630
1877	7,250	477,952	2,325,953	1885	4,658	390,458	1,900,164
1878	6,085	362,072	1,762,023	1886	4,641	449,303	2,186,533
1879	5,107	343,075	1,669,574	1887	4,669	509,000	2,477,258

An ingot of tin weighs about 70 pounds, and it is said not to have changed in weight and very little in shape from the earliest record we have in British history to the present time. Strabo, Diodorus, Pliny, and other early historians make mention of the commerce in tin carried on between the Phœnicans and the Britons.

The subjoined table shows the quantity and value of native tin ore shipped from the colony of New South Wales for each year from the opening of the tin fields in 1872.

Year.	Tons.	Value.		Year.	Tons.	Value.	
		£	$			£	$
1872	849	41,337	201,167	1880	682	30,722	140,509
1873	3,660	226,641	1,102,949	1881	600	37,492	182,455
1874	2,118	118,133	574,894	1882	611	32,890	159,050
1875	2,122	86,143	419,215	1883	475	21,685	100,664
1876	1,509	60,320	293,547	1884	349	14,861	72,321
1877	824	30,558	148,711	1885	535	25,168	122,480
1878	1,124	33,750	164,244	1886	327	18,350	89,300
1879	814	29,274	242,462	1887	292	16,411	79,864

The tin deposits of New South Wales are estimated by the Colonial Geologist to cover an area of 5,440,000 acres, but the area is probably much greater than that, as new finds of tin are being reported every day. Both mine and stream tin are found in localities hitherto unlooked for, and, besides, very few of the lodes have been worked, the great bulk of the tin being the produce of the alluvial mines. According to Mr. Harrie Wood the lodes that have been opened at Tingha, Elsmore, and Newstead, New South Wales, occur chiefly in euritic and micaceous granites. Gold, wolfram, metallic bismuth, and carbonate and sulphide of bismuth, are occasionally found with the tin ore, the sulphide of tin occurring very rarely. The concretionary variety of tin oxide called toadseye is found in the Pliocene gold drifts at Grenfell and on the Grampian Hills, New South Wales.

Professor Liversidge, F.R.S., mentions as an interesting fact that all the minerals found associated with tin stone in England, Germany, France, Russia, and the United States are combined with this mineral in New South Wales. The matrix of the tin stone of this colony is sometimes composed solely of topaz. Malachite, copper and iron pyrites, garnets, and schorl crystals are often associated with the ore. Rolled wood tin, which is the same as the toadseye, except that the pebbles are much larger, is found at Abbington and other places. At Mudgee, and Bathurst and Inverell diamonds are not unfrequently mixed with this variety.

There are two distinct drifts of alluvial tin in New South Wales, the older and the newer. The former are more compact and are often cemented together into a hard conglomerate. The stone is rounded and much water-worn. In the newer drifts the metal is very bright and has undergone little attrition. Some of the fragments weigh many pounds. The richest tin mines in the colony are located in the Vegetable Creek, now Emmaville, district, New England, about 25 miles from Glen Innes and 380 north from Sydney. New England lies in the north-eastern part of the colony, and has an area of 13,100 square miles. It forms an immense table-land, at an elevation of 3,000 feet above the sea. The climate is mild and genial, although in the winter frosts occur. The population is about 17,000. A railway, which bisects the district, has been constructed to the Queensland border, and much of the produce reaches Sydney by that route. Tin ore is very abundant in Queensland, and it is thought that the fields become richer as they advance northward. In both colonies the ore occurs in the granite formation of the great dividing chain of mountains that stretches throughout the whole length of the eastern and north-eastern coast of Australia. This great dividing chain forms the chief watershed of the country.

Tin is believed to be more completely associated with the older forms of rock than any other metal to any series of rocks. Granite usually consists of very old rock, but it must be borne in mind that there are several kinds of granite. First, there is the Paleozoic; then there is the Mesozoic or Secondary, and the Cenozoic or Tertiary. Granite is a compound rock, consisting of quartz, feldspar, and mica.

Tin is supposed to have been very finely disseminated in the shale of which granite is formed, and under the effects of heat, pressure, and water it has been forced, by a process of segregation, to combine with oxygen gas, and thereby formed the oxide of tin. The Australian tin fields differ in some respects from those of Perak. For instance, the ore in the latter country is usually found in the granite formations, overlaid with lime and sandstone, whereas in Australia no tin has been discovered under similar conditions. At first it was thought that the tin ore in New England district was confined to existing shallow streams, and that it was useless to look for it at any considerable distance below the surface. It has since been discovered at various depths from a few inches to 250 feet.

The first deep-stream tin found at Emmaville (Vegetable Creek) was in 1873. The lead was traced along a distance of from 400 to 500 yards, and at a depth of 50 feet very heavy deposits were found, under basaltic rocks. Several other leads were afterwards struck at a greater depth, running almost parallel with the first. It is now believed that tin ore exists throughout the old river beds and valleys of the district. Some of the deposits are covered with immense masses of basaltic rock, which will require a heavy expenditure of capital to remove; but the ore is so rich and abundant that the outlay can very easily be afforded. There is reason to believe, however, that many years will elapse before the surface mines are exhausted. During the year 1883 the Vegetable Creek Tin Mining Company obtained 2,000 tons of ore from an area of five acres. The Secretary for Mines states that the flow of basalt and other geological formations in New England district indicates that stream tin will last for many years.

Emmaville is the centre of a very large tin mining district, and is situated about 25 miles to the north-west of Glen Innes. Tin ore was first discovered at Tent Hill, about 3 miles to the north-east, in 1871, where some very heavy deposits of stream tin were obtained, and soon after smelting works were erected by the Glen Smelting Company, and the works have been constantly employed in reducing the ore to a metallic state up to the present time. During the year 1886, over 1,000 tons of metal were dispatched to Sydney from ore raised and purchased locally by the above company.

As the shallow workings became exhausted, capital was directed towards the discovery of the deep leads that were supposed to exist in the district, and it was not long ere the lead was struck, and heavy deposits of ore obtained at depths ranging up to 200 feet deep, the yield from which rapidly repaid the original outlay of prospecting, and continues to return handsome profits. A considerable area of the known deep leads still remains to be worked.

Much capital and labour have been spent on the numerous lodes which exist in the neighbourhood, notably the "Ottery" "Dutchman" "Torrington" and "Butler" line of lodes. The out-put from the "Ottery," which is situated about 1 mile from the Glen Smelting Company's works, has kept a ten-head battery continuously going in crushing the stone for the past 3 years, and there does not appear to be any falling off in the supply. The stone does not contain a high percentage of ore, but the large quantity of payable stone, which is easy obtainable, give payable returns for the capital and labour invested. The Ottery is principally worked by wages men, who receives £2 10s. ($12·16) per week of forty-six hours labour. The "Dutchman" also keeps a ten-head battery going, but it is worked wholly on the tribute principle, and at times the tributors make as much as £5 ($24·33) per week each, and seldom less than the current rate of wages.

At the Torrington, the ore occurs in very rich quantities and handsome returns are obtained, great quantities of the stone crushed yielding from 20 per cent. to 30 per cent. of black ore.

The Glen Smelting Company is the largest employer of labour in the district and upon the field, whilst Mr. A Cadell has the greatest amount of mining land, which is wholly worked by tribute.

At the "Gulf" a great quantity of ore has been obtained and continues to be obtained by the miners in that vicinity. The want of some means of conserving the rainfall has a tendency to retard this portion of the field, as often many months are occupied in stacking the wash-dirt to await a fall of rain and enable the miner to get returns for his labour.

Professor Liversidge, F.R.S., gives the following analysis of a specimen of dark-coloured, almost black, stream tin stone from the Jupiter mine, Emmaville, New South Wales:—

Tin oxide (SnO_2)	89·92
Titanic acid (TiO_2)	·69
Alumina	6·75
Silica	·80
Iron sesquioxide	2·30
	100·46

The specific gravity of the stone was 6·629.

The tin that has recently been discovered in Dakota, United States, is said to bear a very close resemblance to the products of the Jupiter mine.

In the Temschal Range, California, about five hundred claims for tin mining have been located, but only a few of them have been worked.

An analysis of the Temschal ore, made by Dr. F. A. Genth, gives:—

Silicic acid	9·82
Tunstic acid	·22
Tin oxide	76·15
Copper oxide	·27
Oxide of iron, manganese, lime, and alumina	13·50

Professor Liversidge has some specimens of ore from Tuscany containing 92·40 per cent. of oxide of tin, and a specimen from Carabuco, Bolivia, which yields 93·33. Dr. Genth has recently published the following analysis of two specimens from the San Jacinto mine, California:—

Constituents.	First specimen.	Second specimen.
Tin oxide (SnO_2)	82.00	76.15
Wolfram trioxide (WO_3)	1.08	.22
Silica (SvO_2)	7.20	9.82
Copper oxide (CuO)	.32	.27
Other constituents*	9.40	13.34
	100.00	100.00

* Consisting of iron, manganese, aluminium, magnesium, calcium, bismuth, and other oxides.

The subjoined assays of tin ore from various districts in New South Wales were made by Mr. C. Watt, late Government Analyst :—

Metallic Tin.	per cent.
Tin ore and Pyrites from near Glen Innes	49.4
Tin ore from Bungonia	74.9
Tin ore from new discovery, table-land, New England	26.4
Tin ore from new ground in neighbourhood of Inverell	64.9
Tin ore from Wagga district	24.1
Tin ore from new discovery, Glen Innes district	34.0
Tin ore from new discovery, Glen Innes district	63.1
Tin ore from new discovery, Glen Innes district	58.4

Upwards of fifty tin-bearing lodes have been opened in New England district, New South Wales, and in several places the American diamond drill has been successfully employed. The majority of the veins, however, are small. There are, of course, exceptions to the rule—for instance, in the Carr, Butler, and one or two other mines. The lodes, however, are variable; sometimes the ore is found in quartz, and at others it is found in feldspar, greisen, and chlorite.

The uncertainty in the mode of the occurrence of the ore will necessitate some special appliances for its treatment. Fifteen lodes have been opened in the Inverell district, but they are chiefly narrow quartz and feldspar veins, containing the ore distributed irregularly through them. The ore, however, is found in quantities at the Elsmore, the Ding Dong, and the Pheasant Creek mines. At Stannifer, Bischoff, it is disseminated in separate crystals through porphyritic granite.

Several improved crushing machines, with concentrators, have recently been erected at the last-named mines.

The number of miners, inclusive of the Chinese, employed in the various tin-fields of the colony in 1886, was 2,814. The number in the New England district alone is about 1,500, and more than one-half are Chinese. The latter class of miners are very steady and economical in their habits, and through their patience and industry they have been enabled to derive large returns from mines which have been abandoned as worthless by Europeans.

There are two methods of working the tin fields—by tribute and by wages.

The tribute system is the most popular. By this method the men contract with the owner of the field to win the ore for so much per ton. The men not unfrequently net large gains, and the owner has his mine worked cheaply and expeditiously.

One of the most important uses to which tin is applied is in the manufacture of tin-plates, an industry now attracting much attention in America. It is a remarkable fact that the United States up to the year 1886 did not possess a single tinplate manufactory. Various companies have been formed at different periods for the establishment of such an industry, but every one proved a failure. The absence of an import tax on the plates, and the low price at which they can be obtained in England, are said to be the principal reasons why the industry has not been successful in the United States. Not long since a

New York firm proposed to engage in the manufacture of tin-plates, but expressed a doubt as to the success of the enterprise unless the Government placed an import duty of 2 cents. (1d.) per lb. on all tin-plates imported into the country. Mr. J. Jarrett, secretary of the American Tin-plate Company, said in a recent letter that the duty on tin-plates should be $2\frac{1}{2}$ cents. ($1\frac{1}{4}$d.) per lb. He pointed out the fact that the maximum rate on galvanised iron—that is, on all guages between 25 and 30—is $2\frac{1}{2}$ cents. ($1\frac{1}{4}$d.) per lb. He said that the minimum duty on tin should not be less, from the fact that tin-plates run much lighter in gauges than galvanised iron. He said also that the crosses in I. C. (common No. 1) are higher in price, while the cost of galvanised iron increases as the gauges run lighter, galvanised iron being sold by the gauge and tin-plates by the box. A box of tin containing 225 plates should weigh exactly 112 lbs. Mr. Jarrett cited comparative statistics for the purpose of showing the importance of the industry, and what might be expected from it in the future. In 1870 the United States produced 620,000 tons of steel rails. In 1883 the products were 1,360,694 tons, an increase of 119 per cent. At the close of 1870 the United States had 58,984 miles of railroad in operation. At the close of 1883 it had 127,925 miles, an increase of 117 per cent. The amount of tin-plates imported in 1870 was 75,469 tons, while in 1883 the imports were 240,000 tons, an increase of 218 per cent.

There is no reason why the manufacture of tin-plates should not prosper fully as well as that of steel rails. The latter industry is doing remarkably well, for the number of Bessemer steel works in the United States is constantly increasing.

Notwithstanding the large number of tin-plate factories in Great Britain, that country consumes only a small portion of her tin-plate product when compared with the quantity used in the United States.

It is said that over £2,400,000 ($11,679,600) per annum are expended for wages alone in the various factories in the United States using tin plates, whilst the sum paid for similar work in Great Britain would not amount to £1,000,000 ($4,866,500) per annum. Moreover, the work turned out in the United States is very much lighter and more artistic in construction than that made in England. Great Britain has not yet adopted the process of stamping or pressing tin, especially for the manufacture of cans for preserving fruit. The vast consumption of tin plates will necessitate their manufacture in the United States.

A great impetus was given to the tin industry in Great Britain through the invention of Mr. Payne's method of rolling iron for the manufacture of tin plates. The process consisted of working the metal over several times and drawing it into bars and plates. The latter were repeatedly doubled and passed through rollers, and then re-heated and doubled again until the required thickness was obtained. This method was further improved by Mr. Daniel by putting $2\frac{1}{2}$ cwt. of the refined metal in a charcoal finery, and taking it out in one lump. It was next placed under a hammer and then passed through balling rolls and reduced to bars 2 feet 6 inches long and 6 inches square. It was next cut into pieces 12 inches long,

6 inches in width, and 2½ inches in thickness, which were again heated, and afterwards rolled to a still smaller size and drawn into plates. Great improvement has been made recently in preparing the plates for the purpose of receiving the coating of tin. It is said that the plates made of steel bars are better and cheaper than those made from iron bars, from the fact that a greater number of plates can be made from a ton of steel bars than from a ton of coke-iron bars, and that, in consequence of the greater closeness of grain and even surface of the steel plates, a much smaller quantity of tin is required to make a steel plate look equal to one of iron. The introduction of the Moewood rolls has quite revolutionized the system of coating, as they render it much more equal, while considerably less tin is wasted than by the old process. By regulating the speed of the rolls the maker can arrange the exact amount of tin to be deposited on each plate.

The tin ore shipped from Sydney to the United States is packed in bags, each containing 100 pounds. The ingots are placed loose in the hold of the ship. The price of freight on either the ore or ingots to the United States is in most cases nominal. It is generally shipped as ballast, it being well suited for that purpose on account of its great weight and the small space it occupies. If a charge is made at all, it rarely exceeds more than 12s. 6d. ($3·04) or 16s. 6d. ($4·02) per ton.

Considerable quantities of tin are shipped to the United States by way of London, and the charge is about £2 ($9·73) per ton, which, of course, is inclusive of the cost of transhipment at London to the American ports.

The excessively high prices to which tin has risen, have so stimulated production, that according to Messrs. Strauss & Co., the visible supply at the end of January, 1888, was estimated at 20,034, as compared with 12,013 tons at the same date in 1887, and 13,589 tons in 1886.

AGRICULTURE.

The New South Wales agricultural returns for 1887 indicate a more bountiful harvest than that of the previous year.

In wheat, the principal crop, there was an increase of 3,135,711 bushels; oats increased by 321,785 bushels, barley by 47,343 bushels, hay by 161,526 tons, potatoes by 7,108 tons. The grapes, for wine, increased equal to 46,427 gallons over the produce of 1886. There was, however, a decrease in the maize crop from 4,336,163 to 3,825,146 bushels, or 511,017 bushels. There was also a decline in the yield of sugar-cane, the decline being from 239,347 to 167,959 tons, or 71,388 tons for 1887. The tobacco crop for the same period declined from 2,570,064 lb to 1,676,640 lb, or 893,424 lb.

The following tables show the yield of some of the principal crops in New South Wales, with the number of acres of land under cultivation, and the yield per acre for each year from 1878 to 1887, inclusive:—

Wheat.

Year ended 21 March.	Area of crop.	Produce.	Yield per acre.	Year ended 31 March.	Area of crop.	Produce.	Yield per acre.
	acres.	bushels.	bush.		acres.	bushels.	bush.
1878	176,686	2,445,507	13·84	1883	247,361	4,042,395	16·35
1879	233,252	3,439,326	14·74	1884	289,757	4,345,437	15·00
1880	233,368	3,613,266	15·48	1885	275,225	4,271,304	15·52
1881	253,137	3,717,355	14·69	1886	264,867	2,733,133	10·45
1882	221,887	3,405,966	15·35	1887	337,730	5,868,844	17·37

Maize.

Year ended 31 March.	Area of crop.	Produce.	Yield per acre.	Year ended 31 March.	Area of crop.	Produce.	Yield per acre.
	acres.	bushels.	bush.		acres.	bushels.	bush.
1878	105,510	3,551,806	33·66	1883	118,180	4,057,635	34·33
1879	130,582	4,420,580	33·83	1884	123,634	4,538,604	36·71
1880	135,034	4,761,856	35·26	1885	115,600	3,389,505	29·67
1881	127,196	4,518,897	35·53	1886	132,709	4,336,163	32·67
1882	117,478	4,330,956	36·87	1887	146,957	3,825,146	26·01

Barley.

Year ended 31 March.	Area of crop.	Produce.	Yield per acre.	Year ended 31 March.	Area of crop.	Produce.	Yield per acre.
	acres.	bushels.	bush.		acres.	bushels.	bush.
1878	5,055	99,485	17·70	1883	6,473	133,050	20·55
1879	6,152	132,072	21·46	1884	5,081	106,496	20·95
1880	6,130	131,541	21·45	1885	7,036	148,869	21·15
1881	8,056	163,395	20·28	1886	5,298	85,606	16·15
1882	6,427	135,218	21·03	1887	6,079	132,949	21·87

Oats.

Year ended 31 March.	Area of crop.	Produce.	Yield per acre.	Year ended 31 March.	Area of crop.	Produce.	Yield per acre.
	acres.	bushels.	bush.		acres.	bushels.	bush.
1878	18,581	358,853	19·31	1883	24,818	617,465	24·86
1879	22,129	447,912	20·24	1884	17,810	376,635	21·14
1880	23,883	516,937	21·64	1885	19,472	425,920	21·80
1881	17,923	356,121	19·86	1886	14,117	279,107	19·76
1882	16,348	356,566	21·81	1887	23,947	600,892	25·09

Potatoes.

Year ended 31 March.	Area of crop.	Produce.	Yield per acre.	Year ended 31 March.	Area of crop.	Produce.	Yield per acre.
	acres.	tons.	tons.		acres.	tons.	tons.
1878	13,862	34,957	2·52	1883	14,462	43,461	3·00
1879	16,724	53,590	3·20	1884	14,954	36,977	2·47
1880	19,271	62,228	3·23	1885	12,417	31,335	2·52
1881	19,095	52,112	2·73	1886	15,166	38,695	2·55
1882	15,944	44,323	2·78	1887	17,322	45,803	2·63

Sugar-cane (productive).

Year ended 31 March.	Area of crop.	Produce tons of cane.	Yield per acre.	Year ended 31 March.	Area of crop.	Produce tons of cane.	Yield per acre.
	acres.	tons.	tons.		acres.	tons.	tons.
1878	3,332	99,978	30·01	1883	6,362	169,192	26·59
1879	2,950	104,192	35·28	1884	7,583	204,547	26·90
1880	3,675	126,119	34·31	1885	6,997	105,523	15·05
1881	4,463	121,612	29·47	1886	9,583	230,347	24·97
1882	4,984	128,752	25·83	1887	5,915	167,959	28·39

Wine.

Year ended 31 March.	Area under vines for wine making.	Produce.	Average per acre.	Year ended 31 March.	Area under vines for wine making.	Produce.	Average per acre.
	acres.	gallons.	galls.		acres.	gallons.	galls.
1878	3,027	708,431	234·04	1883	2,629	543,596	206·76
1879	3,024	684,733	226·43	1884	2,660	589,604	221·65
1880	3,091	733,576	237·38	1885	2,405	442,612	184·04
1881	2,907	602,007	207·09	1886	2,876	555,470	193·13
1882	2,597	513,688	197·80	1887	3,131	601,897	192·23

The Australian Continent measures 1,970 miles from north to south, and 2,400 miles from east to west. Its total area is 2,944,628 square miles, or 1,884,561,920 acres, being twenty-four times as large as Great Britain and Ireland, fifteen times as large as France, and only about one-sixth smaller than the whole of the United States of America. The Colony of New South Wales is situated in the choicest part of the Continent, between the parallels 28 deg. 10 min. and 37 deg. 38 min. north latitude, and between the meridians 153 deg. 37 min. and 141 deg. east longitude, the total area being 310,938 square miles, or 199,000,320 acres.

Mr. Russell, the Colonial Astronomer, directed attention to the fact that New South Wales is no exception to the general deduction of science, that southern lands are cooler than those at corresponding latitudes in the north. It is only during the hot winds, which are rare in New South Wales, that the temperature runs to extremes. A comparison of the latitudes with those of the United States would place those of the Colony within the limits of Washington and New Orleans. The mean temperature at Washington is 55 deg., and at New Orleans 68 deg., while that of Eden, New South Wales, is 60 deg. If the mean temperature were a complete test of climate, New South Wales would be hotter than the corresponding latitudes in America; but mean temperature is not enough, and we should compare the summer and winter temperature. For instance, the summer at Washington to 76 deg., and at Eden to only 67 deg., being 9 deg. cooler. At New Orleans the summer is 82 deg., but at Grafton it is 77 deg. Moreover, it is said that 82 deg. does not fairly represent the summer heat at New Orleans; for during at least three months there the temperature is over 80 deg., a temperature only reached on the coast during hot winds. At Washington the winter temperature falls to 37 deg., and at New Orleans to 53 deg. At Eden it is 53 deg., and at Grafton 56 deg. It will be seen from these figures that the heat is less in New South Wales in summer and greater in winter than in America. The rainfall along the coast of New South Wales ranges from 45 inches at Eden to 70 inches at the River Tweed; at Sydney it is 50 inches; among the mountains it is from 30 inches to 40 inches, and over the flat country from 10 inches to 20 inches.

Independent of the area of land held under the pastoral occupation laws, consisting of 142,927,360 acres, or 223,324 square miles, for which the rent received in 1886 amounted to £304,344 ($1,481,090), there were 36,726,169 acres of land in New South Wales held for cultivation, against 18,210,796 acres in 1877, an increase of 18,515,373 acres in the ten years; but there was not a corresponding increase in the number of acres actually under cultivation. The increase of the latter during that period was from 513,840 acres to 972,496. These figures show that while large tracts of land were taken up for the purpose of cultivation no such purpose was carried out, and agriculture has not advanced in spite of the activity shown in taking up the land.

The average yield of wheat in New South Wales in 1887 was 17·37 bushels per acre, against 10·45 bushels for 1886. The average for New South Wales, while not nearly so high as that of New Zealand (26·09 bushels), and not quite so high as that of Tasmania, is considerably more than that of Victoria or any other portion of Australia.

In oats New South Wales averages 25·09 bushels per acre, and Victoria 20·23 bushels. New Zealand, however, takes the lead in the average of oats as in all other grain. The average of oats in that Colony for a term of ten years was 32·51 bushels per acre.

The average yield of barley in New South Wales in 1887 was 21·87 bushels per acre, in Victoria it was 20·86, and in New Zealand 30·38 bushels. In some of the wheat growing districts in Australia the yield per acre is as large as in any part of the world, and it is said that the most fertile land in Australasia is to be found in New South Wales along the margins of the rivers, particularly the Clarence, Macleay, Manning, Hunter, and Hawkesbury. This fertility is counterbalanced by the frequency of floods, often at times when the crops are ready to be harvested. As the means of communication are extended wheat will be more profitably grown on the high tablelands of the interior, at from 2,500 to 3,500 feet above the level of the sea.

The conditions under which wheat is farmed in New South Wales differ very little from those in the other Australian Colonies. The wheat growers in these Colonies have many difficulties to encounter. The season for sowing is uncertain. It extends through April and May, and in some districts seed is sown as late as June. At the Roseworthy Model Farm, South Australia, the Purple Straw wheat which was sown on 13th May, 1886, was harvested on 10th December following. Of course, much depends on the state of the weather. When rain does not fall during the month of April there is delay. In relation to this, it is well to bear in mind that, Australia being south of the Equator, the seasons are directly opposite to those of Britain and the United States. The autumn in Australia begins in March instead of September; therefore, sowing time (April) in this part of the globe corresponds with October in North America.

When wheat cannot be sown in April there is always danger of red rust, the great enemy of wheat in Australia, and especially in New South Wales and Queensland. As a matter of fact, the sowing season is often too dry and the harvest time too wet. Hence the frequency of light and thin crops for want of early rain, and the terrible destruction by rust when rain comes upon the ripening grain; but when the spring season is moist and other conditions favorable, there is perhaps no better wheat land in any other part of the world. This opinion appears to be strongly indorsed by the best authorities on wheat in the Colonies, and is emphasised with great force by Mr. Angus Mackay in a series of valuable and interesting papers on Australian agriculture.

It is estimated that over one-sixth of the total area of New South Wales is capable of growing wheat. It must, however, be understood that only a small part is capable of growing wheat profitably, on account of the high cost of labour and the difficulties in the way of transit to market. The cost of freight by railway in all the Australasian Colonies is nearly 100 per cent. higher than in the United States; but even if freights could be obtained on better terms than at present, it is exceedingly doubtful whether it would pay farmers to grow wheat at a less price than 3s. 6d. (85 cents.) per bushel.

Wheat farms in New South Wales seldom exceed 80 acres each. The rotation is to allow the land to grow indigenous grass or to take a crop of corn (maize) or of potatoes or other produce from it. The very best American and European machinery is in general use, not only in New South Wales, but throughout Australasia.

Wheat is the staple food of the inhabitants of Australasia—even the aboriginals prefer it to any other food. The consumption of wheat per head in Australasia, however, is not as great as in the United States. According to a series of calculations, extending through a period of fourteen years, the consumption of wheat per head is given at 5·30 Winchester bushels. A Winchester bushel is 1-32nd part smaller than an Imperial English bushel. The average quantity of wheat consumed per head in New South Wales during that period was 4·36 bushels. Mr. Hayter, the Government Statist in Victoria, gives a valuable table, showing the consumption of wheat per head in Victoria, from 1840 to 1885. An examination of this table shows that in 1840 the population of the Colony was 8,056, and the quantity consumed as food was 66,491 bushels, equal to 8·25 bushels per head. He estimates that during that year 3,880 bushels were used as seed, making the total quantity available for consumption 70,371 bushels. In 1850 the population was 71,191, and the consumption per head 7·36 bushels. In 1860, population 534,055, consumption per head 6·62 bushels. In 1870, population 713,195, consumption per head 7·06 bushels. In 1880, population 850,343, consumption per head 4·55 bushels. In 1885, population 975,040, quantity available for consumption 6,687,161 bushels, quantity used for seed 2,040,164 bushels, for food, 4,646,997 bushels, equal to 4·77 bushels per head. The average consumption during the whole period of forty-six years is given at 5·74 bushels per head, but during the five years prior to 1885 (an exceptional year), the average was 4·64 bushels. Considering the present population of Victoria, it may be fair to assume that from $4\frac{1}{2}$ to $4\frac{3}{4}$ bushels per head, irrespective of the quantity required for seed, are amply sufficient to supply the wants of any given year. Mr. Hayter cites the fact that the high price of animal food in Great Britain compels the inhabitants to use such food more sparingly than in Australia; hence the consumption of breadstuffs in proportion to the numbers of the population is somewhat higher than it is here. He gives

K

the population of Great Britain for 1886 at 36,519,700, and the number of bushels of wheat available for home consumption as 206,887,000 equal to 5·67 bushels per head.

The quantity of seed used per acre in New South Wales is about 1½ bushel. The wheat crop cannot be said to be reliable on account of the uncertain seasons and the frequency of red rust. Professor Custance is of opinion that the best means to be used for getting rid of rust is to obtain a new variety of seed wheat, but first to grow root or fodder crops which can be fed off by sheep and cattle as a preparation for the wheat crop. Rust is the great enemy to wheat in Australia. It is, however, comparatively unknown on the tablelands of New South Wales, and especially in the New England district.

If it were not for rust, wheat would be more profitable than cattle raising in Australia. It is generally admitted that the export of frozen meat to Europe does not pay at the present prices. Moreover, there is a want of technical knowledge as to the proper means of dealing with the meat after it arrives in Europe. The expensive freezing chambers fixed upon the various steamers plying between England and these Colonies have not been profitable investments; and it is said that the method of constructing them will have to be very greatly improved before the export of meat can be made to pay, notwithstanding the low price of cattle in the colonial market.

Many are of the opinion that the proper method of growing wheat in Australia is to combine the industry with that of sheep farming. In cases where the farms are of sufficient size, Professor Custance, of the Roseworthy Agricultural College, South Australia, strongly recommends this course, especially if the price of wheat is low. He says, that a farmer holding 1,000 acres of land could very well keep from 500 to 600 ewes, as a permanent flock. Feed, however, as a rule, has to be found for the sheep during some part of the year. The Professor says further, that wheat land requires occasional enriching, and that sheep folded on a root or green crop improve the land in the cheapest possible way. This is an important point worthy of the consideration of farmers, for by such a system as this the land is improved, and made capable of producing increased crops. By management, a succession of crops—for instance, some thousand headed kale or drumhead cabbage—could be ready by November, and, with a run in a lucerne paddock occasionally, would last through November and December. Then a few acres of mangels previously sown on a portion of a wheat paddock would be ready when the sheep are turned into the stubble. By the time this is finished, the second crop of kale would be sufficiently advanced to commence feeding off the second time. Some kohl-rabi, mangel, or red clover might be reserved for the latter end of summer. Mr. Mackay, in commenting upon this method of farming, does not recommend it where the object is to produce high-class wool, for as a rule the carcase is of secondary importance to the sheep farmer. However, the turning of sheep upon grain stubble with sufficiency of root or green crops to keep them going until they manure the land is an effectual system of ensuring fertility.

The most favourable results have been obtained by a system of mixed agriculture in the Riverina district, where it was said wheat would not grow. The farmers there who adopted this system were enabled in 1886, (the year after the driest season ever known in the colonies), to realize, even on poor land, from 10 to 12 bushels of wheat to the acre, and on good land from 25 to 35 bushels. Mr. Harold states:—"After travelling over the great wheat-growing districts in Europe, America, and Australasia, I am proud to be able to give the highest meed of praise for wheat cultivation to a few energetic men in the Cootamundra, Young, and Grenfell districts of New South Wales. These men know very little of the theories of agriculture, and their method of farming is one acquired by experience only, and it is encouraging to everybody to see how well they have succeeded." He says further, that these men usually possess from 500 to 3,000 acres of land, and that their plan is invariably to crop every alternate year, and to permit sheep to graze on the land in the intervening year. They plough their land in the autumn, as soon as possible after the sheep have gone through the stubble. This kills the weeds and opens the soil to the winter rains and the atmosphere. The land has never been exhausted, and consequently there are few inferior weeds; and in ordinary seasons an abundance of green and succulent herbage makes its appearance, and sheep and cattle are turned in to eat it down. The first ploughing is shallow, then it gets a deeper ploughing in spring, and then when sowing time comes the seed is put in with a cultivator or perhaps another shallow ploughing. Mr Harold states that the successful farmers in the dry districts of Australia shallow plough in their seed—that is, they sow their seed on the surface of the soil, and shallow plough to a depth of about 3 or 4 inches. Farmers who follow this plan are enabled to grow much more wheat than their neighbours.

A clay soil is best adapted to wheat, for the reason that it contains a sufficient quantity of alumina and potash. The following table shows the component parts of the average wheat soil of Australia, the analysis having been made upon the basis that an acre of soil six inches in depth weighs 2,000,000 lb. worked out on that proportion with acid test:—

	lb.
Water of constitution	61,100
Organic matter	81,520
Equal to nitrogen	1,149
Oxide of iron	134,540
Alumina	220,220
Lime	7,380
Magnesia	5,380
Potash	4,460
Soda	2,320
Sulphuric acid	5,420
Carbonic acid	nil
Phosphoric acid	1,140
Silica soluble in alkali	358,880
Insoluble silicious residue	988,320

The soil from which this analysis was made by Dr. Augustus Volcker was a very stiff dark chocolate-brown, almost black. It contained, like most clay soils, much alumina and a fair proportion of potash. It appears, however, to be very poor in phosphoric acid, and also in lime. If lime or chalk, or chalk marl or calcareous sea or shell sand, could be applied to this land, such application would have a beneficial effect. Doubtless wheat has been grown for years upon the land from which the soil was taken, which would account for its being poor in nitrogen and phosphoric acid. Dr. Volcker recommends deep cultivation for improving its productiveness.

The growing crop, on account of the early rains in April, has shown fairly well. In many districts the farmers have taken more care than usual in sowing and selecting the seed. Several varieties of American seed, such as the "Defiance" and "Champion" were used. Both are very well adapted to the Australasian climate on account of their earliness and rust-resisting properties. The Defiance is a favourite seed, both here and in south Australia. It is beardless white chaff wheat, with heads often measuring 5 in. in length, very closely set with large grains. About 1½ bushel of seed to the acre is considered a fair quantity for sowing purposes. Some farmers use as much as 3½ bushels per acre. Such cases are, however, exceptional, but the proportion used depends both upon the quality of soil and seed. Other varieties of seed wheat for Australian soil are the Purple Straw, the New Zealand Purple Straw, White Tuscan, Talavera, and Early Bart. The so called Mexican wheat, which was distributed in 1885, through the agency of the Department of Agriculture, in Victoria, and from which so much was expected on account of its reputed earliness and rust resisting qualities, proved a failure in many districts. The variety turned out to be the common red Indian wheat, which has been known in these Colonies for many years. Its straw is very weak and slender, and when grown on rich soil, falls down and cannot be harvested without great difficulty.

The most successful farmers seem to place more reliance upon the Purple Straw variety than any other, although very fair results have been obtained from the White Tuscan and Early Bart.

The price of wheat generally depends on the quantity afloat in the Colonies; but it is not infrequently affected by the conditions of the London market. For instance, when there are indications of a European war, wheat is almost certain to have an upward tendency. The quantity of wheat at present afloat in Sydney is unusually small. The price of wheat sufficiently advanced in 1886 to induce shipments to Sydney from California.

The following table shows the average prices of wheat in Sydney for each year since 1880 :—

Year.	Price per bushel of 65lb.	
	s. d.	$ c.
1880	4 3½	1·04
1881	4 3½	1·04
1882	5 3	1·28
1883	4 0	·97
1884	3 8	·89
1885	3 4	·81
1886	4 5	1·67
1887 September	3 9	·91

AGRICULTURE.

New South Wales has for many years been unable to grow a sufficient quantity of wheat for home consumption, much less for export. Wheat, of course, appears in the list of exports, but very little is the produce of the country itself, the great bulk being consigned here for transhipment to other Colonies, Victoria usually receiving the largest portion. In Victoria it is made into flour and shipped again to this market.

The following table shows the quantity and value of wheat imported, and the countries whence imported :—

Country.	Quantity.	Value.	
1885.	bushels.	£	$
New Zealand	270,618	40,876	198,923
South Australia	154,105	31,236	152,009
Victoria	120,684	23,433	114,037
Queensland	8	1	5
Tasmania	8	1	5
Totals	545,423	95,547	464,979
1886.			
Victoria	285,721	57,729	280,938
South Australia	3,223	853	4,150
Queensland	1,964	491	2,389
Tasmania	2,054	457	2,221
New Zealand	437,486	86,668	421,468
United States	356,005	70,835	344,733
India	18,626	3,314	16,128
Totals	1,105,079	220,287	1,072,027
1887.			
Victoria	181,659	34,050	165,304
South Australia	65,681	11,388	55,420
New Zealand	24,766	3,476	16,916
United States	5,885	939	4,570
India	114	25	122
Totals	278,105	49,878	242,732

It will be seen that the imports of wheat were larger during 1886 than those of any previous year. The imports of other breadstuffs were also in like proportion.

The imports of flour into New South Wales are increasing steadily in both quantity and value. The finest and best flour comes from South Australia.

Mr. G. M. Pitt, an authority on the flour trade in Sydney, states that the products of the mills in Adelaide, South Australia, are by far the best that reach this market, and quite equal to those of any other country. The quality of Australasian flour has very greatly improved since the introduction of the roller system. Some favorite brands of Victorian flour command very nearly as good prices as those of South Australia.

The following table shows the quantity and value of flour imported, and the countries whence imported:—

Country.	Quantity.	Value.	
1885.	tons.	£	$
Victoria	30,222	291,999	1,421,013
South Australia	21,807	219,320	1,067,321
New Zealand	1,246	11,301	54,996
Queensland	109	1,296	6,307
Fiji	15	150	730
Tasmania	10	137	667
Great Britain	10	97	472
South Sea Islands	1½	15	73
Totals	53,420½	524,315	2,551,579
1886.			
Great Britain	8	70	341
Victoria	36,564	384,037	1,868,916
South Australia	15,668	172,299	838,493
Queensland	77	927	4,511
New Zealand	6,671	66,658	324,372
United States	2,504	25,381	123,516
Totals	61,492	649,372	3,160,149
1887.			
Victoria	36,824	364,107	1,771,927
South Australia	30,474	308,805	1,502,800
Queensland	102	1,248	6,071
New Zealand	863	8,617	41,935
United States	1	9	44
Great Britain	14	115	560
Tasmania	128	1,284	6,249
Hong Kong	3	32	156
Germany	10	100	486
Austria	2	25	122
Totals	68,421	684,342	3,330,350

The wheat exported from this Colony consists principally of purchases made in other Colonies for transhipment at the port of Sydney. The exports for 1887 amounted to 135,920 bushels against 120,306 bushels for 1886, and 47,647 bushels for 1885.

The exports of flour from New South Wales materially increased during 1887. In 1882 they amounted to 16,669 tons, in 1887 to 21,205 tons.

The following table shows the quantity and value of flour exported, and the countries to which exported in 1885-6 and 7 :—

Country.	Quantity.	Value.	
1885.	tons.	£	$
Queensland	7,035	69,314	237,317
Victoria	1,032	10,397	50,597
New Caledonia	566	5,062	24,634
Fiji	200	1,948	9,480
South Sea Islands	139	1,348	6,560
New Zealand	48	471	2,292
Ceylon	30	290	1,411
Great Britain	20	195	900
Hongkong	18	178	866
South Australia	10	100	487
Other countries	21	201	978
Totals	9,139	89,504	435,522
1886.			
Victoria	1,649	17,043	82,940
South Australia	180	2,119	10,312
New Zealand	14	162	788
Queensland	4,987	53,923	262,416
South Sea Islands	66	733	3,567
New Caledonia	476	5,412	26,337
Fiji	156	1,749	8,512
Western Australia	150	1,696	8,254
Kaiser Wilhelm's Land	20	11	53
Totals	7,679	82,848	403,180
1887.			
Victoria	1,074	10,463	50,918
Queensland	17,984	180,617	878,973
South Australia	78	785	3,820
New Zealand	19	200	973
New Caledonia	1,383	13,858	67,440
Western Australia	28	288	1,402
Other countries	639	6,444	31,360
Totals	21,205	212,655	1,034,886

The harvest is over in all the Australian Colonies by the end of March, and in many districts much earlier than that. The yield of wheat in South Australia was much larger in 1887 than in 1886, but no statistics for the former year were collected. The harvest for 1886 was the worst in the history of that Colony. There was a deficiency of over 300,000 tons of wheat alone, according to estimate.

The returns for 1887 in Victoria show a marked increase in all the cereals over those of 1886. The yield of wheat was 12,100,036 bushels, against 9,073,327 for 1886.

Western Australia produced 288,516 bushels for 1887, Tasmania 632,573, New Zealand 6,297,638, Queensland 21,221 bushels.

There is no doubt that the Australians prefer ploughs of their own manufacture to any other kind, although they are much more heavy and clumsy, and more expensive than those made in the United States. The ploughs most generally in use are the ordinary two and three furrow ploughs, made wholly of iron. The Australian farmer has a decided objection to the use of ploughs with wooden handles.

Several St. Louis and Louisville firms have succeeded in building up a trade in their ploughs, especially in this Colony and Queensland; but their implements have been manufactured solely for the Australian market from plans furnished by their agents who have visited the Colonies and remained sufficiently long to understand the requirements of the Australian farmer. The American harrows are very popular, especially the Disk harrows, for with them the farmers are enabled, in some cases, to dispense with the use of ploughs.

In reapers and binders the Americans have heretofore had a decided advantage, but English manufacturerers now make improvements and close imitatations, and competition for the trade in these articles is very keen. In some portions of the Colonies the Australian stripper is preferred to the reaper and binder. The stripper, although usually called an Australian invention, is in reality an adaptation of an American machine which has been in use for many years in California and other Western States of the Union. It not only cuts the grain, but dispenses with the necessity of thrashing it. The stripper is worked like the reaper and binder, only it is fitted in front with a combing apparatus which catches the heads of the grain, and, stripping them off, passes them into a box, from which they are discharged and put through a cleaner. The machine is able to cut from 5 to 9 acres of wheat per day, according to the condition of the crop and the weather.

In damp weather or in early morning it does not act well. Some of the machines are fitted with ordinary thrashing drums, which thrash any heads not stripped. These machines are called "damp weather strippers." The stripper was first manufactured in South Australia, where it is more popular than in the other Colonies. Recently, however, facilities have been afforded for its manufacture in Melbourne and Sydney.

The introduction of the American reaper and binder did not, at first, interfere with the supremacy of the stripper, more especially in South Australia; but in time the American machine became a very formidable rival, not only in Victoria and New South Wales, but also in South Australia. It must be remembered, however, that in some localities— as, for instance, where straw is regarded as of little value—the stripper is almost sure to be preferred; besides, harvesting with the stripper is generally admitted to be an economical process, from the fact that there is only one loss of grain, instead of several, as are sure to occur more or less in the different processes of binding, stooking, carting, and thrashing. In addition, there are districts in Australia where the crops grown are thin and short, and they cannot well be harvested with the reaper and binder. The practice of burning the straw on the field is said to render the land more fertile, an advantage which cannot be utilzed when the reaper is employed. Nevertheless, it cannot be questioned that the reaper is coming more into use, and especially near the cities and towns, or in districts where there is a demand for straw.

In the South-eastern district of Victoria and along the Goulburn the reaper is invariably used. According to the *Melbourne Argus*, all the American reaping and binding machines in the market in 1886 were purchased, and more would have been used had they been available. It has been recommended that a system of farming be adopted combining both kinds of machines, from the fact that reaping and binding can be commenced some days earlier than stripping, and that stripping can be carried on long after reaping would be possible. By this means all hurry at harvest can be avoided. The wheat harvested by the stripper can also be sent to an earlier market if necessary, while that which has been reaped can the more easily be allowed to wait for shipment.

The stripper is, however, capable of very great improvement, and it is a matter of surprise that manufacturers of agricultural machinery in England and the United States have not invented a machine upon the same principle which will be better suited to the general requirements of the Colonial markets. The California combined reaper and cleaner, while admirably adapted to the States on the Pacific Slope of America, is too cumbersome for Australian farms.

The machine which seems to be required is a lightly-constructed reaper and cleaner that could be worked with four horses.

The present land law of New South Wales is believed by the farming community to be a serious obstacle in the way of agricultural progress. The law is said to have been made more for the benefit of the wealthy "squatter" *i.e.*, sheepowner, than for the agriculturist, and there is a loud clamour for the amendment of the law.

It is certainly very difficult to obtain land except for pastoral purposes in New South Wales. The land laws of the other Colonies are more liberal in this respect ; but it does not appear that agriculture has advanced in any Colony to the extent that it has in countries less favoured by climate and soil.

South Australia is the only one of the group where growing grain for export has been made a speciality, but even there the results have not been as satisfactory as the people anticipated.

As far back as 1843, or long before the wheat-fields of California and of the Great North-west were thought of, wheat was cultivated for export in South Australia ; and it is perhaps not generally known that California for many years obtained the bulk of her supply of seed wheat from that Colony. Now, however, the Australian Colonies, with an area very nearly as large as the whole of the United States, are unable to produce as much wheat as the State of California.

The total yield of wheat in all the Australian Colonies is seldom more than 35,000,000 bushels per annum, while California, besides supplying her own requirements, has not unfrequently considerably more than that quantity available for export.

One of the chief obstacles to wheat cultivation in many parts of Australia, is the heavy cost connected with clearing the land and preparing it for crops. Moreover, the freight charges on the Australian railways are more than double those in America. Another obstacle to agricultural progress in Australia is the vast areas of country taken up for sheep farming.

In Riverina district there are plains so extensive that a man on horseback feels as if in a ship at sea. As far as the eye can reach there is the vast level, unbroken by a single obstacle, save perhaps where a few trees outline the meandering of some sluggish watercourse. The formation of the country is lacustrine, of unknown depth, and the plains gradually slope to the west at the rate of about 1 foot per mile. An unlimited supply of water exists in this district at an average depth of about 80 feet. At present this magnificent domain is almost entirely under sheep pasture, affording the "squatter" a return of about 6s. ($1·46) per acre, or one sheep to the acre. Considerable areas in this district have been purchased, but a much larger proportion is owned by the Government, and is leased for pastoral purposes at rents varying up to 2d. (4 cents.) per acre per annum. Rabbits devastate many parts of this district, in numbers estimated at hundreds of millions. The "squatter" receives a subsidy from Government for the scalps of the rabbits, and it is some times questioned which pays the best—killing rabbits or raising sheep.

Wheat of excellent quality, averaging from 20 to 30 bushels to the acre, could be grown on some of the land in these districts if the land could be obtained.

The uncertainty of the rainfall in Australia is perhaps the greatest difficulty with which the Australian farmer has to contend. The drought, which is more or less severe in the northern and western divisions on account of the great heat, is often prolonged for several years. The rain, when it comes, is almost sure to come at a period when it is not needed. The late very general droughts in Australia have been so destructive that much interest has been aroused in the question of irrigation as a means of increasing or ensuring crops. A number of gentlemen of acknowledged ability, including the Hon. Alfred Deakin, Minister for Agriculture in Victoria, have recently visited the States on the Pacific Slope, for the purpose of reporting on the system of irrigation employed there, and the advantages to be derived from its adoption in Australia.

The main difficulty however in the Colonies is, that all the rivers and streams are below the level of the lands suitable for irrigation. Pumping or other means of water-lifting has therefore to be resorted to, and this, as a matter of course, increases the cost of irrigation. Very little, however, has as yet been done in any of the Colonies in the way of irrigation, but the little that has been done has given satisfaction, and the system adopted is certainly extending. Some of the large land owning companies in the interior of New South Wales are either irrigating by means of centrifugal pumps, or are arranging for the erection of such like machinery.

The ancient English riparian rights, which prohibit the turning of watercourses into dams or in any way interfering with the natural flow of water, form an important obstacle to irrigation in Australia.

It is likely, however, that the Colonies interested will adopt a law which will be intercolonial, making all watercourses, creeks, and rivers, the property of the respective Governments, so that water can be stored in suitable places for irrigation. It is estimated that fully 5,000,000 acres of land could be supplied with irrigation water. The cost would however be enormous, but the results would more than justify the expenditure.

WOOL.

An interesting fact in connection with the Australasian Colonies is that every one of them is especially adapted to the production of wool. Indeed, the wool industry has reached such vast proportions in so short a period that we may well be amazed at the promise of its future.

The mining industry for a time overshadowed all other pursuits, but the people have found out that there is more gold in wool than in all the varied mineral products. And what is the most astonishing thing connected with the subject is that the industry has been of such short duration. It is true that sheep were introduced into the Colonies soon after settlement, but it does not appear that they existed in any great number until the year 1860. At the beginning of the present century there were only 6,000 sheep in Australasia; now the number is 86,352,020. In 1816 there were only 97,402; in 1821 the number was 182,468; in 1841 the number had increased to 6,721,786; in 1860 it was 21,898,626; in 1870 it was 41,593,612; and in 1881, 65,171,401. In 1882 the quantity of wool exported from Australasia was 344,046,910 lb.; in 1886 the exports amounted to 406,729,436 lb., and they reached 429,782,000 lb. in 1887.

Among the many reasons assigned for the vast increase in the wool product is the suitability of the soil and climate for rearing sheep. Indeed, it is said that the climatic condition of the Colonies is precisely the same as that of the most celebrated wool-producing countries in the Old World.

In the Prize Essay on wool, in the Australian Year Book, edited by Mr. E. Greville, Sydney, it is stated that the merino is the only branch of the numerous divisions of the great ovine tribe whose history can be traced for many centuries. The merino sheep were introduced into Europe and Asia Minor by the ancient Greeks, and through them transmitted to Italy shortly after the foundation of Rome, where they were brought to a high state of perfection.

According to Pliny, "the best wool of all others was that of Apulia, and the next that grown further south about Tarentum." Pliny further states that the whitest wool was grown on the Po and in Lombardy. The Romans introduced the merino into Spain, where it fared quite as well as in its native homes. Strabo (50 B. C.) mentions that the rich fabrics of the wealthy Romans were manufactured from the produce of the flocks which roamed over the plains of Truditania, in Spain. All accounts seem to agree that the merino remained exclusively in Spain and preserved its distinctive features through a period of seventeen and a half centuries. Since then these useful animals have been distributed all over the globe, and they seem to adapt themselves to various kinds of climate without losing the purity and vigor of their blood.

The history of Australasian wool is traced in Mr. Greville's Australian Year Book, from the discovery of the Australian continent down to the present time, and states that when Capt. Arthur Phillip established the first Australian settlement, on the 26th January, 1788, at Port Jackson, where the city of Sydney now stands, there was not a single specimen of the ovine tribe amongst the imported stock. Before the close of the year (1788) about thirty sheep were bought from Bengal, and these were of the true East India breed, having long legs, fat rumps, large heads, pendent ears, Roman noses, arched backs, and narrow shoulders. Their fleeces were thin and poor, of a coarse, hairy type, and of little commercial value. The climate and pastures, however, of the country were so fine that the colonists were quite surprised at the improvement in both the wool and carcasses. A few years later small additions were made to the flock by the importations of several Leicesters and Southdowns and some high-class sheep from the Cape of Good Hope. Captain McArthur, of the 102nd Foot, has the credit of forming the first pure flock of merinos in the Colonies. In 1797 he was fortunate enough to secure some superb Spanish merinos which had been bred by Colonel Gordon from sheep that had been sent originally from Holland. In 1801 Captain McArthur visited England and exhibited samples of Australian wool grown by him to the London brokers, who pronounced it of excellent quality, and this, together with an unbounded faith in the unlimited production of wool in Australia, led him to petition Lord Hobart, then Secretary of State for the Colonies, for assistance, with the result that a grant of 10,000 acres of land was conferred upon him.

Mr. McArthur, when returning to Australia, took with him some high-class sheep purchased from the estate of King George III at Hampton Court. An extract from the auctioneer's catalogue of the first public sale of Hampton Court merinos, August, 1804, showing the price of the sheep, the weight of the fleece, and the name of the purchaser, at this sale, is appended :—

Lot.	Weight of fleece at last shearing.	Price.				Purchaser.
	lb. oz.	£	s.	d.	$	
1	3 4	6	15	0	32·85	McArthur.
6 (not weighed)	....	11	0	0	53·53	Do.
11	3 12	15	15	0	76·64	Do.
13	3 4	16	16	0	81·75	Do.
15	4 12	23	2	0	112·42	Do.
23	4 8	22	1	0	107·30	Do.
30	7 12	28	7	0	137·96	Do.
41 (not weighed)	....	11	11	0	56·21	Do.

After the great drought of 1813 the discovery of the well-grassed plains in the interior led to the breeding of sheep on a more extensive scale. The next stimulus to sheep farming was the discovery that Tasmania, with its salubrious climate and suitable pastures, was equally, if not more, adapted than New South Wales for breeding high-class merinos, the bracing atmosphere of the more southern colony having the effect of clothing the sheep with a fleece of greater density, without prejudicing its quality or style.

In studying the condition of the climate of Australasia it must be borne in mind that the Colonies are situated south of the equator and that the seasons are reversed, and that the heat increases toward the north, while the further south we go the colder it becomes.

The Australasian farmers availed themselves of every opportunity to improve the condition of their sheep. In 1859 a number of the celebrated Rambouillet or French merino sheep were introduced into Australia. The first lot came to the order of Messrs. Desgraves & Co., of Melbourne, who used them on their large property at Coliban Park, Victoria. The next lot was imported through the agency of Messrs. R. Goldsbrough & Co. In 1861 a consignment of 50 rams of this breed averaged, at a sale of Messrs. R. Goldsbrough & Co., £83 ($403) per head. In 1863 the flocks were still further improved by the importation of some superb American merinos from Mr. George Campbell's farm in the State of Vermont. These were descended from old Spanish stock, introduced into America in 1802 by Colonel Humphries, then United States Minister to the court of Madrid.

The Australian farmers found the merino sheep to do well in their new homes, and that their fleece increased in size and weight, due partly to the large percentage of yolk or grease. In addition to a naturally hardy constitution, these sheep are vigorous and productive and extremely well woolled all over, the head, belly, and points being especially well covered. Dr. Randall, a high authority on American sheep, says, "The Vermont merinos have a short, thick body, good fore and hind quarters, and short, thick heads. All have dewlaps and neckfolds. The fleece, which is long and even all over the body, opens freely and is of good lustre and style." There is, however, a prevalent opinion amongst the Australasian farmers that the large proportion of yolk in the American merinos has a tendency to make the wool coarse, and they argue that in increasing the weight of the fleece by the American method of breeding, the wool loses its fineness and lustre. Some authorities state that the American fleece loses 80 per cent. in the scouring. This may be true in some instances, but there is no denying the fact that the weight of the fleece remains very heavy after the scouring. There are instances of merino rams giving each 8 or 9 lb. of scoured wool, and in all cases the proportion of wool to the weight of the sheep is unusually large. Vermont rams weigh about 120 lb. of live weight and yield 30 lb. of wool in the grease; the amount of greasy wool to the live weight ranges from 20 to 24 per cent. Objection is made to the wrinkles on the American sheep, which give trouble in shearing. It is maintained that in breeding for wrinkles the evenness of the wool is destroyed. The Vermont Breeders' Association, in one of their reports, make no objection to the wrinkles and folds, and in regard to the yolk, state that breeders cannot dispense with any of the average amount of yolk or grease without running a risk of serious loss from the deterioration in the amount of wool, as well as the strength, lustre, fineness, and evenness of fibre.

The Vermont sheep in Australia do not need housing nor grain feeding, and there is abundant evidence to show that the amount of yolk they possess is necessary to insure a heavy growth of wool. It is certain that the samples of Vermont merino grown in Victoria and sent to Melbourne last year showed no greater percentage of shrinkage than any other Australasian wools.

It is now a common practice for the sheep farmers of Victoria and New South Wales to purchase stud sheep in New Zealand and Tasmania. The rich pastoral lands of these Colonies and the genial climate, together with the equal distribution of warmth and moisture, have led to the production of distinct types of sheep, the wool of which is remarkable for its fineness, density, lustre and great length of staple.

During the last few years auction sales of wool in Sydney, Melbourne, Adelaide, and Brisbane, have been of sufficient importance to induce a large number of buyers to come here from various parts of Europe and the United States. Heretofore nearly all Australasian wool was shipped to London for sale. This, however, is no longer the case, for about one fifth of the product of this season (1887-8) will be sold direct in this market to the English, continental, and American manufacturers. Under these circumstances the day is not far distant when the whole wool crop of Australasia, like the cotton crop of America, will pass the hammer before shipment. It is worthy of note that the large wool broking companies of Australasia have recently erected in Sydney, Melbourne, and Adelaide, some of the most spacious and magnificent warehouses in the world. The advantages of local sales are very great, both to the buyer and seller. By selling locally the growers realize the full value of their wool at once, and are saved the risk and anxiety attendant on a distant and uncertain market, while the manufacturers, on the other hand, can obtain a full selection from the choicest clips. The American buyers can ship their wool to their factories in the Eastern States, by the San Francisco Mail Steamship Company, at low rates of freight, within thirty days, and the European manufacturers can deliver their wool at their own mills, through the large steamship lines going through the Suez Canal, in about six weeks from the date of purchase. They are thus enabled to place their new goods on the market two months earlier than if they waited for the London sales to supply their requirements.

Notwithstanding the vast pastoral area of New South Wales, only about one seventh of the wool product is suitable to the American market. The kinds of wools desired by American manufacturers are those of fine fibre, elastic, sound, full stapled, and free from burrs and grass seed. They should also be of light condition, with only a small proportion of yolk. No heavy or fatty wools could be profitably exported to the United States, on account of the high duties there.

The area of New South Wales, where wool suitable to the American market is produced, is situated on the western slope of the main mountain range, stretching from the border of the Colony of Victoria to that of Queensland. The area embraces the districts of Albury, Wagga Wagga, Murrumburrah, Yass, Young, Inverell, and a part of New England. The wool from Albury and part of that of Wagga Wagga, on account of being near Victoria, finds its outlet at Melbourne. The condition of the wool depends in a great measure on the character of the season. In a favourable season fully 50,000 bales of wool suitable for the American market could be produced on the plains of the western slope. In a season of drought, which, however, is uncommon in the districts named, the wool becomes impoverished on account of the heat and dust, and is very tender, with a dry, wasty top. Droughts are more frequent in the districts remote from the mountains, and the result is that the wools generally are of a medium to low class. Even in good seasons on account of the heat, the wools grown there do not rank high. It is now very well understood that sheep carrying plenty of yolk are best adapted to dry climates. The sheep farmers on the dry plains in order to increase the yolk in their wool have recently imported a number of American rams with very favourable results.

On the table-lands of New England and Monaro droughts are almost unknown, and although the wool produced there is sound and well grown, it is generally too heavy and greasy for the American market.

About nine-tenths of New South Wales wool is shorn in the grease. In many districts there is not water enough to wash the wool on the sheep's back, and there is always great difficulty in keeping the wool clean between the washing and shearing. The wool, however, intended for the American market is not washed on the sheeps' backs, even in districts where water is plentiful, from the fact that wool washed in that way is not desired in the United States. Moreover, the duty on washed wool is almost prohibitory. In very dry districts where there is sufficient water the wool is scoured after shearing, so as to save the expense of cartage. In a bad season much of the wool loses about 80 per cent. in scouring. The bulk of the wool offered for sale in Sydney in 1885-6 season was very tender, musty, and seedy, on account of the drought; nevertheless it brought better prices than at the London sales.

One of the most remarkable features in connection with the wool clip for 1886-7 was the decided improvement in the quality of the fleece over that of the previous season. This fact is mainly due to the improved condition of the natural grasses through the copious rains in almost every part of Australia. The evil effects of the drought which seem to have extended over a period of three or four years, have almost wholly disappeared except in very few places. The wools of Riverina District are said to have recovered their former superiority. In some districts the felting power of the clip has never been surpassed.

The Victorian wools sold in London during the months of November and December, 1886, attracted no small amount of attention on account of their superb quality and lustre. The New Zealand wools, which arrived a few weeks later, were remarkable for their fineness and great length of staple. A marked improvement was noted in the condition of the clip from every one of the Australasian Colonies.

Mr. F. H. Bowman, F.R.S., a wool expert, who examined the samples sent to the Colonial and Indian Exhibition, expressed the opinion that no previous collection of Australasian wools ever equalled it. He commented especially on the samples sent by Messrs. R. Goldsbrough & Sons, many of which, he said, presented the highest state of perfection to which wools are capable of being grown. He described the New South Wales wool as being better suited for the fine clothing trade, but possessing less lustre than those from Victoria.

The total number of bales exported from all the Colonies during the year ended the 31st of May, 1887, was 1,161,571, against 1,112,172 for the corresponding period of the previous year.

The subjoined table shows the number of bales shipped from all the Colonies up to the 1st June, 1887, compared with the same dates for 1886 and 1885:—

Colony.	1887.	1886.	Increase.	Decrease.	1885.
	Bales.	Bales.	Bales.	Bales.	Bales.
New South Wales	328,441	340,090		11,649	287,615
Victoria	327,931	309,366	18,565		328,290
Queensland	63,081	70,801		7,720	70,260
South Australia	147,554	129,905	17,649		151,297
West Australia	16,373	14,343	2,030		13,222
Tasmania	18,621	16,281	2,340		17,268
New Zealand	259,573	231,386	28,187		218,163
Total	1,161,574	1,112,172			1,086,115

The average weight of a bale of Australasian wool may be taken as 400 pounds.

It will be seen from the preceding table that New South Wales heads the list in the export with 328,441 bales, and that Victoria comes close to it with 327,931 bales. The exports, however, from Victoria show an increase of 18,565 bales over those of 1886, while the New South Wales exports show a decrease during the same period of 11.649 bales. The cause of the decline in the New South Wales shipments was not occasioned by any falling off in the quantity produced, but was due to the rainfall, in that the rivers on the borders had become navigable, thereby enabling growers to send their wool direct to Melbourne, who in seasons of drought send by railway to Sydney.

New Zealand increased her exports from 231,386 bales in 1886 to 259,573 bales in 1887. While the exports of New Zealand are not as heavy as those of Victoria, nevertheless she is the second wool-producing Colony in Australasia, New South Wales, of course, taking the first rank.

The total annual value of the wool product of Australasia for 1886–7 is £20,533,309 ($99,925,348). Of this amount New South Wales furnishes £8,895,556 ($43,265,891); New Zealand, £3,879,620 ($18,879,170); Victoria, £3,342,509 ($16,266,320); Queensland, £1,889,504 ($9,295,296); South Australia, £1,823,431 ($8,873,727); Tasmania, £453,167 ($2,206,797); and West Australia, £249,255 ($1,212,999).

The consignments from the Mudgee District of New South Wales are stated on the authority of the New Zealand Loan and Mercantile Agency Company in Sydney to have been splendidly bred. One well-known brand brought 12¼d. (24½ cents) in the grease, the highest price of the season. The New England and the Upper Hunter clips were this year conspicuous for elasticity, fineness, and clearness of staple.

The demand for steamer freights to London has been throughout the season unprecedented, and such as to give rise to some apprehension concerning the future utilization of sailing vessels for the wool trade. Sailing vessels labour under great disadvantages owing to the times of the sales in London being so fixed that no sooner have steamers completed their loading for one series than shippers find it is then too late to think of catching the next series by sailing vessels, and they consequently have recourse to steamers.

The direct export of wool to the United States has been very small. The absence of the usual number of buyers on American account was noticed at all the Colonial sales, especially in Sydney and Adelaide. The few who were present showed little disposition to bid against the French and German buyers for the kinds of wool desired for the American market. Indeed the only effect of the presence of Americans at all was to excite the competition between the Continental buyers, which was throughout keen and sharp, and formed the mainstay of the market. The only direct shipments to America consisted of 14,969 bales from Melbourne and 169 bales from Sydney.

The following table shows the quantity of Australasian wool exported direct to the United States during the last four years, the only points of shipment being at Melbourne and Sydney :—

1883-4	......	Melbourne,	14,863 bales.	Sydney,	7,712 bales.
1884-5	......	,,	6,621 ,,	,,	...... ,,
1885-6	......	,,	20,161 ,,	,,	4,296 ,,
1886-7	......	,,	14,969 ,,	,,	169 ,,

It was noticed both at the London and Colonial sales that, notwithstanding the advance in the price of wool, the advance was confined principally to cross-breds, medium, and the lower sorts. Mediums, particularly at the Sydney sales, were relatively the strongest. The light-conditioned wools at the January and February sales, brought even lower prices than in 1886. Up to the 14th February, 1887, only about 1,000 bales were purchased at the London sales for the American market. The reason given for this was that considerable quanities of Australasian wool purchased last season were still held over in New York and Boston. A change for the better occurred in March and April. The advance was particularly marked in extra merinos. Cablegrams from America are to the effect that the American demand was increasing, and that prices were rather higher than at late sales.

There has been a decided improvement in the direct trade between Australasia and the Continent of Europe. The recent establishment of two splendid lines of steamers, under heavy subsidies from the French and German Governments, it is thought will do much towards stimulating the wool trade. The French line, the Messageries Maritimes, notwithstanding the steady demand for steamer freights, seldom charged more than $\frac{3}{4}$d. ($\frac{3}{4}$ cents) and $\frac{1}{2}$d. (1 cent) per lb. The highest rates reached for freight by steamers during the season were- 1$\frac{1}{4}$d. (2$\frac{1}{4}$ cents) per lb. This, however, was exceptionable. The German line, the Norddeutscher Lloyd, carried freight at fully as low rates as those of the French line.

The direct shipments to Marseilles during the season of 1886-7 were —4,731 bales, against 3,323 bales for 1885-6. Those to the German ports showed a much greater increase, the figures being 40,968 bales for

1886-7, against 15,888 for 1885-6. These figures, however, only represent the direct shipments, as considerable quantities of Australasian wools reach the continental centres by way of Liverpool and London. The subjoined table shows the quantity of wool shipped from Australia direct to each of the European ports for the last three years :—

	1884-5.	1885-6.	1886-7.
	Bales.	Bales.	Bales.
Shipments to Antwerp	39,526	15,888	36,247
,, Hamburg			2,268
,, Dunkirk	nil.	2,539	2,107
,, Bremen	nil.	nil.	2,452
,, Marseilles	6,149	3,323	4,731
	45,675	21,750	47,805

The extraordinary decline in the price of wool, up to the March and April sales of 1886, was attributed to the general depression of trade, in the leading articles of consumption all over the world. Such a depression had not been known for a period of fifteen years. As compared with the opening of the previous season, the decline in the price of wool was startling. Combing wool brought fully 3½d. (7 cents), and washed 4d. (8 cents) per lb. less than in 1885. Between the close of the second and the opening of the third series of London sales the reaction set in, and large private transactions took place in London, at prices showing an advance of 1d. (2 cents) per lb. on March rates. The June sales opened with an advance of 2½d. (5 cents) on greasy merino, and 4d. (8 cents) per lb. on seconds, and the sales closed very firm, greasy merino being 30 per cent., and crossbreds 15 per cent., and seconds 25 per cent., higher than in April.

All through the next interval purchases by private contract were being made, and the September sales opened with an excitement without parallel in the history of the London wool sales, greasy wool being 1½d. (3 cents) to 2d. (4 cents), and second 2½d. (5 cents) to 4d. (8 cents), higher than the closing rates of the previous series. Prices, however, were somewhat irregular, and towards the close a slight relapse took place; but there is no doubt that at the highest point of this series the Australasian staple was 50 to 60 per cent. dearer than at the lowest point in April, some five months before. In fact several large clips of faulty New South Wales wool sold at double the money similar clips brought in the second series, when wool was at its lowest. Cross-bred wools, of the finer quality, have fluctuated throughout the season, in sympathy with the various changes in the value of merinos. Coarser qualities and Lincoln wool, on the other hand, have sold steadily at figures showing little variation on those current during sales of the preceding season.

The following table, shows the fluctuation in the prices of Lincoln, half-bred, and fine cross-bred wools at the Sydney and Melbourne sales for each season, from 1882-3 to 1886-7 inclusive:—

```
1882-3.
Lincoln .....................  6d. (12 cents) to  8d. (16 cents) per lb.
Half-bred ..................  8d. (16   ,,  ) to 10½d. (21  ,,   )   ,,
Fine cross-bred ........... 11d. (22   ,,  ) to 18½d. (38  ,,   )   ,,
     1883-4.
Lincoln .....................  6d. (12   ,,  ) to  8d. (16  ,,   )   ,,
Half-bred ..................  8d. (16   ,,  ) to 10d.  (20  ,,   )   ,,
Fine cross-bred ........... 10½d. (22  ,,  ) to 13d.  (26  ,,   )   ,,
     1884-5.
Lincoln .....................  5d. (10   ,,  ) to  7½d. (15  ,,   )   ,,
Half-bred ..................  8d. (16   ,,  ) to 10½d. (21  ,,   )   ,,
Fine cross-bred ........... 11d. (22   ,,  ) to 13½d. (27  ,,   )   ,,
     1885-6.
Lincoln .....................  6d. (12   ,,  ) to  8d. (16  ,,   )   ,,
Half-bred ..................  8d. (16   ,,  ) to 10d.  (20  ,,   )   ,,
Fine cross-bred ........... 10½d. (21  ,,  ) to 12d.  (24  ,,   )   ,,
     1886-7.
Lincoln ..  ..................  7d. (14   ,,  ) to  8½d. (17  ,,   )   ,,
Half-bred ..................  8½d. (17  ,,  ) to 10½d. (21  ,,   )   ,,
Fine cross-bred ........... 10½d. (21  ,,  ) to 12d.  (24  ,,   )   ,,
```

The wool season for 1887-8 opened in the Colonies about the middle of October; up to the 3rd February, 1888, the following are the quantities of wool offered and sold :—

Since opening of season, 196,707 bales catalogued and 139,195 bales sold.
Same period for 1886-7, 158,608   ,,   115,357   ,,

The total exports from Sydney and Newcastle have been ----

1887-8.	1886-7.	1885-6.
298,690 bales.	243,904 bales.	271,573 bales.

Sales opened at values about 20 per cent. lower than the opening rates in 1886-7, and as a consequence there was a great difficulty in getting growers to accept the ruling rates, although there is little prospect of improved prices.

The clip this season (1887-88) is bulky and well grown; grass seeds and burrs (both Bathurst and trefoil) were present in most of the early wool grown on the dry western plains in greater quantity than usual. This is a consequence of the very favorable season. The price of wools so affected is seriously depreciated, and some of the worst are quite neglected. On the other hand light conditioned wools free from faults sell readily. The wool from the western slopes and also from the table lands, was sound and well grown and comparatively free from faults, but rather yolky. The very best price of the season has been obtained for a wool of that description from near Berrima. It was deeply skirted and realized 10½d. (21 cents) per lb., being bought for America.

The news of a weakness at the sales which lately opened at Antwerp, still further unsettled the market, and sales have been in consequence made more difficult to effect.

Wool sales have been held at Newcastle, the second port of New South Wales, but as very few buyers attended it is unlikely that any further effort will be made to sell at that port.

The season continues all that could be desired from a pastoralist's point of view. Rain has fallen at seasonable intervals, and both grass and water are everywhere abundant.

The past year's lambing has been one of the best ever known in New South Wales, and the increase is 7,518,555.

The returns collected by Government, in January, 1888, show the sheep in the Colony as numbering 46,687,859. The lambing for this year (1888) is also pretty well assured.

It is estimated that the wool clip of 1887–8 for Australasia will show an increase of about 50,000 bales over the previous season, while that of 1888–9 will be 100,000 bales in excess of the 1887–8 clip.

Mr. A. Bruce, the Chief Inspector of Stock for New South Wales, returns the number of sheep in the colony at the close of March, 1887, at 39,169,304, against 37,820,906 for 1886, and 21,521,662 for 1877. During the year 672,903 were sent to Queensland. The subjoined table, prepared by Mr. Bruce, shows the number of each kind of sheep in New South Wales at the close of March, 1887.

(1) Merino.

Combing.

	Rams.	Ewes.	Wethers.	Lambs.	Totals.
Pure and stud –					
Superfine	41,233	613,915	144,018	145,452	944,618
Ordinary	108,735	2,289,751	1,430,715	1,312,012	5,141,213
					6,085,831
Pure and stud –					
Medium	64,463	844,117	369,755	443,322	1,721,657
Ordinary	159,485	4,847,472	3,304,493	2,378,227	10,689,677
					12,411,334
Pure and stud –					
Strong	78,292	688,034	354,194	356,204	1,476,724
Ordinary	84,141	3,310,312	2,429,052	2,118,453	7,941,958
					9,418,682
Total, Combing					27,915,847

Clothing.

	Rams.	Ewes.	Wethers.	Lambs.	Totals.
Pure and stud					
Superfine	9,658	145,301	82,187	79,444	316,590
Ordinary	42,104	497,183	353,674	219,528	1,112,489
					1,429,079
Pure and stud					
Medium	25,716	258,102	157,775	118,423	560,016
Ordinary	124,703	2,198,484	1,436,558	1,137,980	4,897,725
					5,457,741
Pure and stud					
Strong	62,805	280,370	135,160	140,778	619,113
Ordinary	40,735	1,069,898	1,025,332	509,729	2,645,694
					3,264,807
Total, Clothing					10,151,627
Total number of Merino Sheep					38,067,474

(2) Long-woolled Sheep.

	Rams.	Ewes.	Wethers.	Lambs.	Totals.
Pure and stud—					
Lincoln	2,838	31,514	23,401	21,685	79,438
Ordinary	3,184	67,633	40,664	31,045	142,526
Total, Lincoln				...	221,964
Pure and stud—					
Leicester	1,987	27,341	21,695	12,938	63,961
Ordinary	1,903	20,951	17,092	15,683	55,629
Total, Leicester				...	119,590
Pure and stud—					
Downs	413	3,307	957	2,000	6,677
Ordinary	1,260	7,285	7,712	3,710	19,967
Total Downs				...	26,644
Pure and stud—					
Romney Marsh	10	100	154	19	283
Ordinary	428	4,466	3,715	1,293	9,902
Total, Romney Marsh			...	...	10,185
Total number, long-woolled Sheep					378,383

(3) Crosses.

	Rams.	Ewes.	Wethers.	Lambs.	Totals.
Crosses of the above breeds (long-woolled) with Merino principally	3,180	301,116	249,865	169,286	723,447
Total, crosses		...	...	...	...	723,447
Grand total			...	...	39,169,304

The bulk of the stud sheep introduced into New South Wales are from Tasmania. Out of a total import of 1,656, Tasmania furnished 1,536, South Australia 54, Queensland 32, and California 35. These sheep were quarantined for eighteen days, and received one dipping in a solution of tobacco and sulphur. The laws of all the Australian Colonies forbid the importation of sheep except under stringent quarantine regulations. On account of these restrictions the importation of high class sheep from America has seldom proved profitable to the shippers. Of the total number of stud sheep brought to New South Wales in 1886, 953 were unshorn and 639 were shorn in Sydney before dipping. After reaching the various sheep stations they were all examined again by the inspectors, who were instructed to report on their appearance and the effects of the dipping. Of the unshorn sheep, 1 ewe and 2 lambs were dead and 35 sheep were injured. Of the shorn sheep, 1 ram died, and several were injured by the dipping. The inspector thinks that no loss or injury would occur if the sheep were kept in quarantine after dipping a sufficient time to permit them to become thoroughly dry before removal.

A conference of representatives from the Australian Colonies was recently held in Sydney for the purpose of endeavouring to assimilate the regulations in force in the Australian Colonies relating to stock.

Much interest in the subject was taken by the delegates to the conference from Tasmania, where the mild and genial climate, together with the unparalleled richness of the natural grasses, have enabled that favoured colony to reach a degree of perfection in the production of high class sheep. The summers are never excessively hot and the winters are not cold enough, even on the high table lands, to put a stop to the operations of the pastoralist.

West Australia, with a territory larger than that of any of the other Colonies, carries very few sheep. The number for 1886 is estimated at 1,753,000.

There are very few districts in Australasia where sheep will not thrive; in fact, throughout the whole of this group of Colonies, the climate is so mild that neither sheep nor cattle require the same amount of housing they would receive in America or Europe. It is only natural under the circumstances that sheep farming should receive so much attention.

Mr. Bowman, in his report on Australasian wools, says that the wool-growers cannot keep up their reputation for high class wools without a careful system of selection in breeding, and the introduction of fresh blood from other countries. He says that certain classes of sheep are more adapted to certain regions of the earth's surface than others, and that in many cases the environments of sheep tend in the course of generations under careful management to produce a special character which becomes permanent and may be retained as a pure special breed. He therefore contends that certain characteristics of wool, such as lustre in the long wool breeds, can only be retained permanently by the reintroduction of fresh blood from time to time, and especially in those countries approaching the equator.

This lustre, for which he considers a certain degree of temperature and moisture is necessary for its permanency, is retained longer in New Zealand and on the Southern Coast of Australia than anywhere else. He accounts for the deterioration of Australasian sheep in South Africa from the fact that the herbage of that country is not fitted to the requisite conditions for the better class of sheep.

The high scale of wages demanded by sheep-shearers in Australasia, together with the repeated strikes amongst them, and the difficulty of supplying their places with skilled workmen, have led to various attempts in Sydney and Melbourne to invent an instrument for shearing sheep by machinery.

Such an invention was believed to be impossible. Two difficulties at once presented themselves: the first was the employment of some means to control the animal while being shorn, and the second was to construct the instrument for shearing it.

These difficulties have been wholly overcome by Mr. F. Y. Wolseley, of this Colony, who, some years ago, conceived an idea of constructing such a machine, which has culminated in the invention he has patented. During the past shearing season it has been successfully tried in various places. Trials were given at some of principal wool-brokers' establishments in Sydney and Melbourne, and there were present at the trials representatives of all parties interested. They united in the opinion that the machine did the work which its inventor claimed for it in the most satisfactory manner. The apparatus is a very simple one, being made on the same principle as the cutter of a mower or reaper, and the knives are worked by means of rods within the handle, which in their turn are moved by a core within a long flexible tube, kept in a rotary shaft, and which is driven by some stationary motive power. The comb is in the form of the segment of a circle, about 3 inches in diameter, provided with eleven conical-shaped teeth. Each machine is worked by a man—not necessarily an experienced shearer—and as he moves the comb along the skin of the animal, the fleece is cut much closer than it can be cut by any shearer, and without the possibility of the most inexperienced person injuring the skin of the sheep. One of the principal advantages of the machine is that it does not require a skilled person to use it; any ordinary hand on a sheep station can be taught to use it in a couple of days.

The Chief Inspector of Stock is of opinion that this machine will soon come into general use. He thinks it admirably adapted for the small farms. There has been recently more or less discussion in the various agricultural journals of the Colony as to the economy of its use. While all agree that it is a labour-saving machine, it is said that the work can be done quicker by the ordinary process of shearing. The advocates of the machine claim that it effects a saving of fully 10 per cent. The first cost of the machine and the cost of the motive power are more than counterbalanced by the efficiency of the work done by it. For instance, it takes off the whole of the wool at one cut and leaves the sheepskin absolutely intact, whereas by the old method the sheep are often cut by the shears, which is always the case should a person attempt to shear a sheep who is not accustomed to use the shears. It is sufficient to observe that the machine can be run with either a steam or gas engine, or by ordinary horse motive power, and that the apparatus does not easily break down; all the parts are interchangeable, and in the event of one getting out of order it can be replaced without trouble by a duplicate piece. Moreover, the cutter, is inexpensive, and will shear several sheep without sharpening.

The machines are being fitted up in sheep-shearing sheds in various parts. Those exhibited at the stores of the New Zealand Loan and Mercantile Company, Sydney, did not perform the work as rapidly as a first-class shearer would do, but there can be no question as to the superiority of the work done. The number of sheep shorn at the first trial was at the rate of 60 a day of 10 hours, whereas 80 is a fair day's work for a good shearer with a pair of shears, but on the other hand every sheep shorn by the machine yields from 4 to 10 ounces additional wool at the first shearing with the machine, and the skins of the sheep are not injured by being cut. The machine cuts the full natural length of the wool, nor are there any "ribs" left on the skins or any tufts of uncut wool.

Another shearing machine has been patented by Mr. Suckling, of the Hunter District. The motive power is compressed air, but the cutting arrangements are similar to those in the Wolseley machine. 11,000 sheep have been shorn by this method. The machine did good work at the Sydney Centennial Agricultural Show, in competition with Wolseley's. It is probable both will be brought into use.

The American trade with Australasia is insignificant when compared with that enjoyed by Great Britain. This unfortunate state of affairs is believed to be principally due to the high protective tariff of the United States, which virtually excludes wool, the chief product of Australasia, from the American markets.

The people of Australasia have always evinced a strong desire to trade with the United States, and there is abundant evidence to show that the average Australian has a decided preference for articles of American type and manufacture over those of other countries, but he will not purchase goods and wares from a country which imposes such heavy penalties upon his own raw products.

The Bill introduced into the United States Congress in 1886, providing for the removal of the wool duties, attracted no little attention here, and it was sincerely hoped that it would become law. It is said that the sole cause of the rejection of the measure was the proposition to admit woollens as well as the raw material, free of duty, and that of course secured the opposition of the manufacturers, who were principally interested in the admission of the raw product.

It has been frequently pointed out that the wool-farmers of America received better prices for their wool for a term of years when the duties were the lowest, for the reason that wherever there is a demand in the United States for foreign wools, there is also a demand for the home grown wool.

People argue that the United States is the only country in the world which levies a duty upon raw products, and that if the Americans wish to perfect their manufactures, they should do so by removing the restrictions from the raw material.

It is further said, that the woollen industry of the States, both on the Atlantic and Pacific coasts, is allowed to languish for want of cheap wools, and these the manufacturers could easily obtain if it were not for the Customs' tariff; also, that the reason why the French and Germans make such superb woollens, is because they have access to Australasian wools. The mill-owners of California have repeatedly stated that the reason why they cannot make the woollen industry pay on the Pacific slope is because they cannot obtain Australasian long stapled wools to mix with their own of shorter growth. In California the wools are of two growths. One growth is from April to September, and the other from September to April. In Australasia there is but one growth. Of course manufacturers have an advantage who use the long stapled wools, for cloth made with them has a smoother and brighter finish, without rough points protruding, as in goods made with short stapled wools. If such wools could be mixed with Australasian wools, it is contended, that Californian manufacturers would soon be enabled to produce cloth of better quality than the French and German, and at a lower price.

Colonel W. Harney, who is largely interested in the woollen industry of San Francisco, says, that if it were not for the tariff the Californian woollens would be preferred to all others. He has himself used several lots of New South Wales wools to advantage in the manufacture of blankets and other articles. Some of these articles found their way to Sydney market and attracted much attention. Indeed, they were very generally admitted to be superior to any of the kind ever imported, the price alone preventing extensive orders. Colonel Harney, in his evidence before the Central and South American Wool Commission, which met at San Francisco about two years ago, said, "In California we are prepared to suit every taste, if we can get the trade, or the taste of any nation or people. That is we can manufacture anything in the shape of woollen goods made by any foreign establishment, and do it successfully." Colonel Harney's views were strongly corroborated by Mr. Donald M'Lennan, and other gentlemen who gave evidence before the Commission. Mr. M'Lennan said, "If we could use the wools of Australasia in conjunction with American wools, not only would the value of Californian wools be enhanced, but we could manufacture just so much and so many more yards of goods than we can now, that the extra consumption of Australasian wools would enhance the value of domestic wools, that is, give a larger market to domestic wools by combining them with foreign wools." Mr. Mitchell, of the Chamber of Commerce, Sydney, highly commended the views of Colonel Harney and Mr. M'Lennan, and it is no wonder that such opinions should attract attention in Sydney, a city offering so many advantages for direct trade with the Pacific Coast of the United States. The fact that the Australasian wool trade with France and Germany is increasing, while that with the United States is decreasing, should be a note of warning to Americans. If Congress will not remove the Customs duties on wool, it certainly ought to modify the duties on the kinds of wool which cannot be produced in the United States, such as the soft, fine long staple wools of Victoria, New South Wales, and New Zealand. These wools are remarkable, not only for their softness and smoothness, but also for their elasticity and brilliancy.

SUGAR.

The production of sugar is one of special interest at this time on account of the system of bounties adopted by the various Governments in Europe. International conferences are being held for the purpose of settling the vexed questions which are said to effect seriously the sugar trade of the world.

In the face of many difficulties sugar production has become firmly established in Australia. At present the trade is depressed, but it is not any worse in that respect than the same interest in other countries. There is overproduction of the article, and though that state of affairs does not extend directly to Australia, the low prices of sugar in Europe and America have affected the industry here. Never before has the price of sugar been so low, nor is there much prospect of an immediate change. It has also been said that the continuance of the present bounties for five years would break up three-fourths of the Australian sugar plantations. Mr. E. Pulsford, the Secretary to the Free Trade Association, Sydney, however, contends that more injury has resulted to the cane sugar industry from the improvements in beet culture than from the payment of bounties. He cites the fact that the beet now yields 12 per cent. of saccharine matter instead of 4 per cent. as formerly. Thus, when formerly 100 tons of beet-root yielded only 4 tons of sugar the same quantity now yields 12 tons. Other authorities give the yield at much higher figures.

Unfortunately for the sugar interest here each one of the Australian Colonies has its own special tariff. This diversity of tariffs not only awakens jealousy between the Colonies, but occasions a conflict of interests. For instance, sugar from Queensland, the largest sugar producing Colony in the group, cannot be admitted into New South Wales except upon the same terms as that imported from the Straits Settlements, China, Mauritius, and other countries, and the result is Queensland often finds a more profitable market for her product elsewhere. The efficient shipping facilities between Queensland and London, Glasgow, and other British ports, together with the low cost of freights, are further inducements for shipping to the European ports. Planters obtain such low rates of freight that the cost of exporting sugar to London from Queensland is seldom more than £1 10s. ($7·29) per ton, and moreover it is said that they can obtain even in China and Japan from £2 ($9·73) to £3 ($14·59) more for their sugar than in Australia. There is also an effort being made here to find a market for Australian sugar in the Pacific slope of the United States. The trade between the Colonies and San Francisco is steadily increasing.

As the production of sugar increases here the desire to export to America will increase.

It is a curious subject of observation and inquiry that two countries like Australia and the United States, which have so many interests in common, should continue to confront each other with hostile tariffs, but as long as the Colonies themselves are unable to establish anything like a free interchange of products with one another it is hardly reasonable to expect them to perfect reciprocal relations with foreign countries.

The customs regulations of New South Wales approach nearer to free trade than those of any of the other Colonies, but, notwithstanding so-called free trade principles, they impose a very heavy tax upon American products. People here complain that Australasian sugar and wool and other raw products are virtually excluded from the United States markets, but at the same time they show no disposition to remove the heavy colonial tax on American tobacco, kerosene, and other articles; indeed they are constantly agitating for an increase of duties. The import duty on sugar into New South Wales is 6s. 8d. ($1·62) per cwt. for refined and 5s. ($1·21) for raw sugar.

The impression seems to be gaining ground that the American duties on sugar and other raw products of Australasia will shortly be repealed, and the fact that the United States has not been able with the help of her high protective tariff to produce more than 12 per cent. of the sugar she consumes is frequently cited by the Sydney press. Attention has also been directed to the fact that sugar industry in the States is not as large as it was thirty or forty years ago.

In 1853 the total sugar product of the United States amounted to 449,324 hogsheads, but in 1884 it was only 170,431 hogsheads, being 279,893 hogsheads less than in 1853. One of the most astonishing facts in connection with the matter is, that the present American tariff on sugar is fully six times more than the tariff of 1853, therefore it is argued that the industry was far more prosperous under a low tariff, than under the present high one. It is conceded that there is a marked difference between the conditions of labour at the two periods, but the labour question, although an important one, does not form the chief factor in the production of sugar, and it is thought that the cost of labour is higher in Australia than in Louisiana and other sugar-producing States of the American Union.

Although New South Wales was the first of the Australian Colonies to engage in the cultivation of cane for the production of sugar, Queensland appears to have made the first decided advances towards the establishment of the industry. Sugar-cane was first grown at Port Macquarie, in New South Wales. Governor Darling, writing from Port Macquarie in 1828, said, "Both sugar and tobacco are now cultivated successfully in this delightful country." At a later period sugar-cane was tried in the botanical gardens at Brisbane, Queensland, with very favourable results. No attempt, however, was made to crush the cane until about twenty years ago, when the late Mr. T. Scott, of Brisbane, made a series of successful experiments in crushing sugar with such mechanical appliances as were at his command. These experiments furnished abundant evidence that the industry could be carried on in the Colonies profitably. The price of sugar at that time was more than double what it is at present, and the sugar brought to Australia was a very indifferent sort of raw muscovado, which would to-day be regarded as fit only for refining purposes.

Between the years 1865 and 1872 a number of plantations were established in the north of Queensland and in the Macleay and Clarence districts of New South Wales. The most extensive plantations, however, were established in the Mary and Mackay districts, Queensland. In the latter district great skill and powerful machinery were brought to bear upon the industry, especially at the Yengarie factory, where the business was conducted upon a system similar to that of the beet-root factories in Germany and other European countries. The sugar made at Yengarie factory was of a fine white grain and rich in saccharine matter. A few years afterward the Colonial Sugar Refining Company erected powerful crushing-mills upon the banks of the Macleay, Clarence, and Richmond Rivers, and from that time to the present this company has been in advance of all others in Australia in regard to everything in relation to the production of sugar.

From the outset the company have experienced much difficulty in obtaining suitable labour for the cane fields. In New South Wales the cane has always been cultivated by white men, and generally upon their own land. At first, and indeed up to the close of last season, the farmers sustained considerable losses in attempting to make sugar with defective machinery, but that plan is now abandoned, and the farmers sell their cane to the large companies. In Queensland the planters have had to depend mainly upon coloured labour, and they have had to undergo much abuse on account of the manner in which such labour was obtained. A great hue and cry was raised in England against what was called the "Queensland labour traffic," and the planters were charged with encouraging horrible outrages and crimes. It is certain that the natives of the South Sea Islands were in many instances forced on board the labour vessels, and that while this recruiting was going on many horrible massacres occurred. There is, however, not a particle of truth in the statement that the natives were badly treated after they once reached Queensland.

The most searching investigations by the Government failed to convict a single planter of inhuman treatment of his employees. The Government nevertheless resolved to put a stop to the introduction of coloured labour, and this awakened much opposition on the part of the planters. The latter complained that the industry was being destroyed, and that the Government did not understand the difficulties they had to encounter. These complaints were followed by a persistent agitation for the separation of northern portions of Queensland. The Premier, Sir S. W. Griffith, visited the sugar districts with the view of allaying the hostility. He made conciliatory speeches, in which he spoke of the evils that would follow separation, and dwelt upon the advantages to be derived from the introduction of white labour. He admitted that the planters had many grievances, but thought that a satisfactory settlement could be reached through the exercise of patience and forbearance on both sides. In the meantime, the agitation continued, and there is reason to believe that a separate Colonial Government may be established in Northern Queensland. In 1875 the Queensland Government commissioned Mr. Angus Mackay, now instructor in agriculture at the Technical College, Sydney, to visit the West India Islands, the United

States, and other sugar producing countries, for the purpose of investigating and reporting upon the systems of labour, of cane cultivation, sugar manufacture, sugar machinery, and generally concerning the sugar industry in those countries. Mr. Mackay's reports, which had an extensive circulation, furnished conclusive evidence that a great change was going on in the sugar industry, and that to make the business profitable it is absolutely necessary to separate cane growing from sugar making. During the year 1876 Mr. Mackay visited the factories in the French West India Islands, and his reports are exhaustive and instructive. During the same year he visited Jamaica, San Domingo, Cuba, and other sugar growing countries. After studying the industry in those places he went to the United States, and visited the various plantations on the banks of the Lower Mississippi. His reports upon these plantations are elaborate, and form, in many respects, the most valuable contributions ever published upon the sugar industry of the United States.

These reports are exceedingly complimentary to the enterprise, skill, and industry of the American sugar-planters.

Mr. Mackay found much to commend in their system of draining and farming the lands that are below the level of the waters of the Mississippi River. From Belair plantation, owned by Mr. John Diamond, of New Orleans, Mr. Mackay shipped to Queensland sugar-cane of the Creole variety, now extensively cultivated in both Queensland and New South Wales. Mr. Mackay was aware that out of forty or fifty varieties of cane grown in the Colonies very few of them yielded much sugar. The farmers usually selected the best looking canes, but many of these, such as the Bourbon and the Cherrybon, although splendid in appearance, would not stand the sugar test. Mr. Mackay observed that the Creole variety was of rapid growth and, although of small size, yielded a large percentage of juice. The Creole cane is of a dark purple colour, heavy in weight, with the eyes coming very close together. Mr. John McDonald, superintendent of the St. Helena plantation, Moreton Bay, Queensland, obtained samples of it through Mr. Mackay, and found it to do extremely well. In the State of Louisiana, where the sugar cane has only between six and seven months of hot, growing weather, the Creole variety comes to maturity before the approach of cold weather. It is usually cut in November, on the first appearance of frost. Its yield is about 20 tons to the acre. Mr. Mackay stated in his reports that the production of sugar in Australia, in order to become a large and profitable industry, should be conducted on the plan adopted in America. He said that the American planters, in selling their cane to the sugar companies possessed of sufficient capital to employ the necessary machinery and skill, realised about 60 per cent. more than the Queensland farmers were enabled to do with their feeble little crushing-machines. The first official returns of the sugar product in Queensland were published in 1868, and they showed that during that year six mills were in operation, which produced 168 tons of sugar and 13,100 gallons of molasses. The industry has increased ever since.

The subjoined table shows the number of mills and number of acres of cane crushed, and the products of sugar, molasses, and rum in Queensland for each year, from 1868 to 1887 inclusive:

Years ended 31 March.	Sugar Mills.				Rum Distilleries.	
	No. of Sugar Mills	Sugar Cane Crushed.	Sugar Manufactured.	Molasses Manufactured.	No. of Distilleries.	Rum Distilled.
		Acres.	Tons.	Gallons.		Proof Galls.
1868	6	...	168	13,100	2	12,045
1869	10	...	619	68,622	6	35,599
1870	28	1,238	1,490	137,598	8	74,483
1871	39	2,188	2,854	177,656	10	124,665
1872	55	3,078	3,762	219,694	11	112,979
1873	65	5,018	6,266	357,619	9	161,473
1874	66	5,380	7,978	442,253	10	164,413
1875	71	6,978	12,108	651,259	11	217,701
1876	66	7,668	6,322	438,950	14	343,244
1877	70	7,245	8,214	416,415	12	183,243
1878	59	8,043	12,243	490,200	10	196,001
1879	68	10,702	13,525	570,301	12	216,395
1880	70	11,409	18,714	641,486	9	238,710
1881	83	12,306	15,564	602,960	9	201,111
1882	103	15,550	19,051	753,658	7	157,325
1883	120	16,874	15,702	663,825	6	149,428
1884	152	25,792	36,148	1,071,413	6	144,073
1885	166	29,051	32,010	804,613	7	133,768
1886	166	40,756	59,225	1,784,266	9	159,122
1887	160	36,104	56,859	1,510,308	10	97,376

It will be seen from the returns for the year ended 31st March, 1887, that the average yield per acre of cane crushed is 1·69 tons.

There are ten distilleries in Queensland manufacturing per annum 97,000 gallons of rum from molasses. These distilleries are owned by the large sugar companies. The smaller mills do not utilise the molasses, but allow it to run to waste. The Inspector of Distilleries in Sydney is of opinion that this material could be utilized by the introduction of improved distilling machinery from Europe and America.

The distilleries make less rum than they did ten years ago, when their production was 183,000 gallons.

The distillation of rum from molasses in New South Wales, like that in Queensland, has made little progress. In 1877 the number of gallons distilled was 150,737 from 26,531 cwt., and in 1886 it was 202,420 gallons from 41,098 cwt. of molasses. Some of this rum is exported to New Caledonia as white spirit.

SUGAR.

The following table shows the number of acres of cane and the production of sugar cane, and the number of mills and quantities of sugar molasses, and rum manufactured in New South Wales in each year from 31st March, 1877 inclusive :—

Year ended 31st March.	Area in Sugar Cane.		Production in tons of cane.	Number of Sugar Mills.	Quantity of Sugar Manufactured.
	Productive.	Unproductive.			
	acres.	acres.			cwt.
1877	3,524	3,231	99,430	50	93,960
1878	3,331	3,735	99,978	50	150,744
1879	2,949	4,489	104,192	59	163,203
1880	3,675	4,102	126,119	65	153,833
1881	4,465	6,506	121,616	65	146,003
1882	4,983	7,184	128,752	76	159,048
1883	6,362	7,176	169,192	86	270,000
1884	7,583	7,401	204,547	93	280,000
1885	6,997	10,520	105,323	98	230,000
1886	9,583	6,835	239,347	102	360,280
1887	5,915	9,202	167,959	64	275,000

Year ended. 31st March	Quantity of Molasses Manufactured.	Number of Sugar Refineries.	Quantity of Sugar Melted.	Number of Distilleries.	Material used - Molasses.	Rum distilled.
	gallons.		cwt.		cwt.	proof galls.
1877	273,480	...	...	...	...	...
1878	345,543	2	259,650	2	26,531	150,737
1879	532,825	2	324,480	2	20,576	124,156
1880	440,506	3	388,480	2	32,592	128,285
1881	269,092	2	414,400	2	20,882	110,063
1882	354,402	3	514,400	1	14,399	74,377
1883	560,000	2	470,000	20	25,035	118,066
1884	580,000	2	468,000	10	31,596	152,766
1885	450,000	3	370,000	8	34,523	160,403
1886	635,000	4	384,000	7	39,380	193,343
1887	507,000	2	510,000	6	41,098	202,420

The following table shows the quantity and value of sugar imported into the Colony of New South Wales for each year, from 1877 to 1887 inclusive :—

Year.	Raw Sugar.			Refined Sugar.		
	Quantity.	Value.		Quantity.	Value.	
	Tons.	£	s	Tons.	£	s
1877	22,841	570,818	2,777,886	317	12,277	59,746
1878	27,458	697,234	3,393,089	215	7,457	36,289
1879	35,108	834,916	4,063,119	233	8,422	40,986
1880	19,765	539,953	2,627,081	157	5,435	26,449
1881	27,164	655,722	3,190,505	295	11,948	58,145
1882	32,491	838,256	4,079,373	142	5,285	25,719
1883	27,527	743,374	3,666,290	98	3,715	18,079
1884	33,579	843,385	4,152,998	458	14,523	70,676
1885	27,362	500,084	2,433,659	366	10,077	49,040
1886	29,981	478,992	2,331,015	218	5,646	27,564
1887	25,994	475,958	2,316,250	298	6,897	33,564

The subjoined table shows the quantity and value of raw and refined sugar exported from the Colony of New South Wales for each year, from 1877 to 1887 inclusive:—

Year.	Raw Sugar.			Refined Sugar.		
	Quantity.	Value.		Quantity.	Value.	
	Tons.	£	$	Tons.	£	$
1877	403	14,040	68,325	4,070	140,469	683,592
1878	502	15,608	75,956	4,228	170,323	828,877
1879	1,522	42,309	205,897	5,281	170,638	830,410
1880	1,779	57,625	280,432	5,265	171,413	834,181
1881	688	20,521	99,861	3,655	116,944	569,108
1882	830	24,685	120,130	2,438	77,258	375,976
1883	778	21,902	107,586	2,014	61,429	298,944
1884	1,284	32,543	158,371	1,229	37,725	183,589
1885	1,846	36,667	178,440	111	3,366	15,894
1886	5,818	108,877	530,850	23	745	3,626
1887	5,803	110,024	535,432	18	501	2,438

One of the most extensive sugar works in Australia is that of Messrs. Cran & Co., at Bundaberg, Queensland. It has a frontage of 200 feet and a depth of 225 feet, with a "smoke stack" 135 feet high. One of the engines is of 250 horse power, and about 90,000 gallons of cane juice are daily extracted.

From the factory pipes are laid under-ground, connecting with crushing mills on plantations in every direction for a distance of 10 miles. The cane-juice is specially prepared by treatment with lime for transit through the pipes. This method is found to be very successful, as it saves the cost of carting the material from the mills to the refinery. The planters usually get 10s. ($2·43) per ton for cane of a density of 8 degrees.

Capitalists, stimulated by the success of the various sugar-refineries in Victoria, New South Wales, and Queensland, undertook the establishment of a similar enterprise in Auckland, New Zealand, to be, in fact, a branch of the Colonial Sugar Refining Company of Sydney and Melbourne. A bonus had been offered by the Government in aid of the work, and efforts were made to secure it by Auckland, Christchurch, Dunedin, and other cities. The prize, however, was won by Auckland. A company was formed there in 1882, and secured 189 acres of land near Northcote, immediately opposite Auckland. The refinery was begun in January, 1883, and on the 30th of August, 1884, it was opened to the public for inspection. Viewed from the harbour the buildings appear to be massed together in one large square block, which is the case, the workshop and general store being the only ones detached, and between them the space is small. This is unusual in sugar refineries in Australasia, as these buildings are generally remote from the refinery. The purpose of the Company in placing the buildings so close together was to save labour in handling the raw material. The refinery proper is 90 feet long and 60 wide, and has two sides of brick and two of iron. This building, like all the others, is covered with a galvanized iron roof. It contains the blow-up pans, bag-filters, bag-washing tanks, vacuum pans, heaters, vacuum engines, centrifugals, and a steam railway. The char department is entirely of heavy brick-work, and is 90 feet high and 60 feet square. It contains twenty large cast-iron cylinders, 30 feet in circumference, with a depth of 18 feet. Each cylinder, when filled with water or other liquid, weighs 50 tons. The char-kiln house is of brick and iron; it is 60 feet in length and 42 feet in breadth. It has eight kilns, said to be the largest in the southern hemisphere. The char filters weigh 300 tons. The works produce 400 tons of refined sugar per week. Each vacuum pan contains 300 feet of solid drawn copper coils, and produces at every skipping 7 tons of dry sugar. In this building are the engines. The steam, after actuating the engines, is used for all the cleansing and boiling work of the refinery. Outside of the refinery there are five 30-horse-power steam boilers, a number of patent fuel economizers, a chimney stack 126 feet high, with an internal diameter of 7 feet, and several retorts for making animal charcoal, and gas to light the works. There is also a workshop with lathes, planing-machine, drilling-machines driven by a Tangye engine and boiler. The machinery was made by Merilees, Watson, & Co., of Glasgow, Blake, Barclay & Co., and M'Lean, Angus, & Co., of Greenock. The boilers were furnished by Joseph Clayton, of Preston, England, and the engines and tools by Tangye Bros. The timber used in the buildings cost about £40,000 ($194,660). The works are well supplied with fresh water, a necessary consideration for a refinery, as a ton of sugar requires in its various processes fully 1,000 gallons of water. The creek furnishing the supply runs upon both sides of the estate. The lower dam which feeds the boilers is about 2 acres in extent. There are two wharves, each 211 feet in length, with an outward jetty of 330 feet. The wharves stand on solid rock and have a depth of water of 21 feet at low spring tides.

The shipping wharf is provided with a long jibbed hydraulic crane and hydraulic jigger capable of discharging cargo at the rate of 200 tons per day.

At the end of the jetty and close to the sugar stores is a large size weigh-bridge over which all sugar, both inward and outward, is run. The bond which contains the raw sugar as it is landed from the ships is an unusually large one, and is capable of holding 10,000 tons. The bond is 38 feet in height, and on every side pockets of sugar are stacked up to a height of 32 feet. Between the refinery and the bond is an elevated floor to which is connected a hydraulic cage which lifts 2 tons of sugar at every lift on to the floor. This floor, which resembles a draw-bridge, is called a "cutting-in platform," from the fact that the pockets of sugar are cut open on this platform. About 100 tons per day are lifted from the bond to the elevated floor. As soon as the pockets are cut open the contents are shot through a trap-door into the melting pans, when the first operation of the refining process takes place. The pans are circular, and hold 6 tons of sugar, and are filled every half-hour. After the sugar is melted the filtering process begins, which is done by means of flaxen bags. The bag filters are provided with run-off valves and gutters, steam coils inside, and steam connections outside. From the bag filters the purified liquor is conducted by cast-iron receivers into the cellar, from which it is pumped into other receivers at the top of the char cylinders. Then it passes through various processes until it is ready for crystallization. The boiling ranges from 90 degrees to 170 degrees Fahrenheit. The pans must be perfectly air and steam tight. The boiling must be performed in vacuum, as the slightest excess of heat may prevent the proper crystallization. Leading from the upper dome of each pan there is a large pipe communicating with a condenser into which cold water is continually rushing. The cold fluid intercepts the vapour from the boiling liquid into the pan and condenses it. The art of the sugar boiler is shown by the uniformity of the crystals which he can produce. After leaving the boiling-room the sugar passes into the "fine-sugar store," which is made of brick and contains four cast-iron columns. The floor is of Kauri pine, and is divided into bins to separate the different qualities of sugar, each bin holding from 30 to 40 tons. The sugar falls from these bins through a chute into packing bags on the floor underneath, and thence on to the delivery floor at the bottom, where it is stacked and ready for shipment.

The New Zealand Sugar Company manufacture much of the raw products of the various sugar mills in the Fiji Islands. In addition to the products of their own mill at the Ba, they obtain those of the enormous mill of the Colonial Sugar Refining Company, built at the junction of the Suva and Rewa Rivers, Fiji. The Colonial Sugar Refining Company has large plantations and mills in Queensland, besides their refineries in Sydney and Melbourne.

There are several large sugar mills in Fiji in addition to those mentioned. One, on the Rewa River, belongs to the Rewa Sugar Refining Company and another on the Nauva, the property of Stanlake, Lee, & Co. The Pioneer Mill, on the Island of Mango, just completed by Mr. Leicester Smith, is another large establishment, and there is still another large mill belonging to Billyard Brothers, at Taviuna. These mills are located either on or near the sugar plantations. This appears to be absolutely necessary, for, if the crushing power were not close at hand, fermentation would set in soon after the cane was cut and destroy it. The soil of Fiji is so well adapted to the growth of the cane that many other mills, it is said, will shortly be established. Land, which now sells at £5 ($24) an acre, would bring from £15 ($73) to £20 ($97) an acre if crushing power in the vicinity were available.

Mr. Thomson Leys is of the opinion that Fiji will develop in the near future one of the largest sugar industries in the southern hemisphere. This industry is one that requires a large outlay of capital. Some idea of the extent of the operations of the various companies in Fiji may be formed from the following statistics in reference to the Colonial Sugar Company, the first ever established there. This company during the season of 1886, employed 2,980 men, of whom 120 were Europeans, 2,650 coolies, 160 Polynesians, 50 Fijians. During the crushing season, from May to December, two steam-tugs, four steam-launches, and forty iron punts, capable of carrying from 50 to 100 tons each, were continually employed, and forty additional punts have been constructed for this season's work. The mill has also been increased from a capacity of 50 tons to 100 tons per day.

The Governor of Fiji expressed the opinion that the depression in the sugar market of the world was a sign of overproduction. His fears are groundless. The United States consumes fully one-fourth of all the sugar product of the world, and the demand for it increases in proportion to the reduction in price.

The Queensland Government has recently voted the sum of £50,000 ($243,325), for the purpose of establishing central sugar-mills, with the condition that European labour shall be employed. Three places, all north of Rockhampton, have been selected by the instructor as the most eligible—£18,000 for one, £20,000 for a second, and £12,000 for a third; but Mr. Hodgkinson, to whose judgment the business has been assigned by the Government, is in doubt whether, with low prices in sugar and untrustworthy labour, apt to strike at a critical time, success will follow the undertaking. He thinks one man and family might work 20 acres of cane, but this is doubtful in a moist and hot climate.

Sugar, like distilled spirits, is an artificial product. It was unknown in Europe in the present form in the fifteenth century, and about fifty years ago it was regarded as an article of luxury; now it is so abundant that even the poorest families are supplied with it. The vast increase in its consumption is principally owing to the simple and economic means of production.

The annual consumption in the United States has been stated to be 2,500,000,000 lb. This does not include molasses, made from corn starch and sorghum, nor the quantity of molasses and syrups that were imported. The total sugar product of the world is set down at over 7,000,000 tons, of which more than 2,000,000 are composed of maple and sorghum.

Sugar is now the leading export of Fiji, exceeding that of copra dried meat of the cocoa-nut, the former chief export of the country.

The organisation of companies for the manufacture of sugar should lead to the general introduction of American sugar making and refining machinery. Indeed so much attention has been directed to the superiority of American sugar-making machinery over that of the French or English, that it is slowly making its way into Queensland and other portions of Australasia. Messrs. Newell & Co., Melbourne, Victoria, succeeded in introducing into Queensland and New South Wales a considerable quantity of sugar-making machinery from the Colwell Iron Works, New York. Those who have examined carefully the American plant express a decided preference for it, but the habit of purchasing nearly all kinds of machinery in the United Kingdom seems to be difficult to overcome. The manufacturers of sugar machinery in the United States would find it to their interest, not only to establish agencies in Australasia, but to employ intelligent and practical men for the purpose of advertising their machinery in the leading journals of the Colonies, and to distribute drawings and catalogues, illustrating the special advantages of their manufacturing plant. For instance, it is not generally known that the American double and triple effects, clarifiers, beam vacuum pumping engines, centrifugal machines, cane-mills, char-kilns, and char-filters are the best and cheapest in the world, and that S. S. Hepworth & Co., at Yonkers, N. Y., have perfected a centrifugal machine for draining sugar and other substances, which is very much superior to anything of the kind ever made in Europe. These machines are largely used in Peru, Mexico, Sandwich Islands and Jamaica, Trinidad and Barbadoes, Cuba and Porto Rico. It has been pointed out in America that the "triple effect evaporating apparatus," made at the Colwell Iron Works, New York, uses less fuel and produces a better quality of sugar by boiling in vacuum at low heat than any similar apparatus of foreign manufacture. It is said that, with this apparatus, the actual quantity of steam for boiling any water for condensing is fully one-third less than required for the same work by an ordinary vacuum pan, and that beet-root sugar factories are compelled to use it from the nature of the juice. The sugar planters and manufacturers of the West India Islands are deeply sensible of the superiority of the American sugar machinery, and do not hesitate to avail themselves of it, and there is no just reason why the American manufacturers should not extend their trade to Australasia.

As yet none of the Australian refineries have found it profitable to manufacture cubes or block sugar; however, as this article is not only popular here, but is preferred to other kinds for table use, there should be little difficulty in inducing sugar companies to manufacture it. The cost of making these cubes is about the same as that of ordinary granulated or crystal sugar. Indeed, it is said that one-twentieth of a cent. a pound will more than cover the expense of converting sugar into cubes.

A refinery that does not make hard sugar could thus, by the employment of one of the American machines, and at a cost not to exceed £400 ($1,946) or £600 ($2,928), add largely to their profits during the year.

Some of these machines turn out easily four or five thousand pounds of sugar per hour. Only five men are required to run one of them, including the labour of putting the sugar in and taking it out from the stoves or drying rooms.

For many years small quantities of sugar have been shipped to this Colony both from the Atlantic and the Pacific coasts of the United States. This sugar is generally manufactured either in Saint Louis or San Francisco. It is of a very superior quality and designed for extra table use. The price is so low that it usually takes precedence over all other high grades of sugar, and besides, it is made of cane, and is readily distinguished from continental sugar, by the absence of the flavour of the beet. The American cubed sugar has also distanced all competitors, although unfortunately at present there is only a limited demand for this class of sugar except for table use, a lower grade being preferred, and especially in the country towns. The cubes made at the American Sugar Refinery, at San Francisco, are very white and glistening and contain far more saccharine matter than the English tablets of D. Martineau & Son, once so popular in this market. The latter also is of a much darker colour than the American cubes. The San Francisco sugar refineries also ship here small quantities of crushed sugar. Local dealers state that a fair profit is always made on American sugars, and that low freights and a more frequent steam service would push the trade to large proportions. The buyers also prefer the light American barrels and half barrels to the heavy cases in which the English sugar is shipped. The tare of the former is 11 lb. to 104 lb. and the latter 28 lb. tare to the 100 lb. of sugar.

The English manufacturers complain that the bounty system existing in Germany and Austria has closed up many of the refineries in the United Kingdom and glutted the market with an inferior quality of sugar. They also complain bitterly of the manner in which American granulated sugar is pushed in British markets.

The large and steady annual increase in the consumption of sugar in the Australasian Colonies has directed very general attention to the various methods for its production. So much interest was taken in the subject that the Government of New Zealand passed an Act for the encouragement of the manufacture of sugar from beet-root and sorghum.

Mr. W. A. Graham, of Hamilton, New Zealand, wrote an interesting pamphlet on the inducements offered for the manufacture of beet-root sugar, and Mr. Pond, the Government Analyst at Auckland, published the results of a series of experiments he had made with beet-roots, in which the average yield of sugar was 12·29 per cent., the highest being 15 and the lowest 9·82 per cent.

Mr. Pond's paper is so full of interesting and valuable material in the interests of beet-root cultivators, and contains the result of so many chemical experiments of a direct, practical character, that it is reproduced, although the opinion is expressed in various quarters that the production of sugar from cane will, in the end, prove more profitable than from the beet-root :

ON THE SUGAR VALUES OF BEET-ROOT GROWN IN THE WAIKATO, NEW ZEALAND.

(By I. A. Pond, Government Analyst.)

A PAPER was read before the New Zealand Institute, entitled "On the Growth of Sugar-beet in New Zealand," by Dr. S. M. Curl. In this paper the writer ably reviewed the subject and placed much valuable data before us, but when speaking of the values of sugar in the different varieties of beet-root examined by him, he claimed to have found as high as 17·5 per cent. This excessive amount, and the fact that parliamentary papers had been published giving analysis of New Zealand grown beets, showing much less favourable results, and the absence of any details of examination, led me to take up this subject with the view of practical operations should the experiments justify it. I had interested myself in the matter of sugar beet, owing to some superior seed having been brought from Hamburgh by Mr. G. S. Graham, and finding it had been distributed amongst some of the Waikato settlers for planting, I undertook the examination of the roots when they should be sufficiently grown. Mr. W. A. Graham, of Tamahere, who had taken a great interest in the matter, had papers printed according to a plan drawn out by himself, and forwarded to those settlers who had undertaken to grow the roots. These papers were designed to obtain data for the future guidance of a company, should one be formed through any satisfactory result of those experiments, and were divided into columns requesting information, as follows :—

Particulars of Waikato Beet-roots.

From whom forwarded, and name of estate.
Character of soil, and whether drained.
Whether manured or otherwise ; if manured, state character of manure.
Whether from imported seeds, or from where obtained.
Give approximate of weight to the acre, if possible.
Analytical results. Percentage of beet sugar and notes.

The first instalment I received was from Mr. L. O'Neill, Hamilton. There were three roots, grown from seed imported by Mr. Lavers, and resulted as follows :—No. 1, weight, 2 pounds 2 ounces ; percentage of cane sugar, 10·95. No. 2, weight, 1 pound 2 ounces; percentage of cane sugar, 10·17. No. 3, weight, 12 ounces ; percentage of cane sugar, 13·55.

A month later Mr. O'Neill forwarded a parcel of four roots from the same crop. Taking the largest of them, weighing 2 pounds 2 ounces, I found the percentage of sugar to be 14·25; the three others I aggregated with a like percentage of 14·25.

Finally I received a parcel of five roots from the same grower, which had been removed from the ground and stored. Two of these I have examined, with the following results :—No. 8, weight, 2 pounds 7 ounces ; percentage of sugar, 11·40. No. 9, weight, 2 pounds ; percentage of sugar, 14·25.

The further examination of these roots I will speak of again, in relation to the specific gravity of the juice.

I also received three roots from Mr. Ralph, Huntley, marked sugar beet. They were of a full red-coloured skin, but I have received no knowledge of the name of the seed or where procured. Result of analysis :—No. 1, weight, 5 pounds 5 ounces ; percentage of sugar, 4·31. No. 2, weight, 12 ounces ; percentage of sugar, 7·50. No. 3, weight, 9 ounces ; percentage of sugar, 11·87.

This root No. 1 was a well-shaped one, of large proportions, very watery, but with a very low percentage of sugar. This is the lowest result I have obtained, and far below any other. At the same time its excessive size would lead to the conclusion that its value in sugar was low.

One more parcel I received of unknown seed, from Raglan, through Mr. Will, comprising five small roots, badly formed, the largest of which, weighing 1 pound 12 ounces, yielded a percentage of sugar, 8·14.

I now proceed to note the results of the seed obtained by Mr. Graham from Hamburgh, and which had been distributed as already noted. There were three kinds in all.

No. 1.—Genuine white small Wanzlebenel imperial.
No. 2.—Deppe's pure white improved Silesian imperial.
No. 3.—Extra saccharine red-top imperial.

In the following notes I will simply call these varieties by their respective Nos. 1, 2, and 3.

I received three roots, one of each variety, from Mr. R. Watson, Pukerimu.

No. 1, weight, 13 ounces ; percentage of sugar, 13·57. No. 2, weight, 1 pound 1 ounce ; and No. 3 weight, 12 ounces, I treated in the aggregate, with the result of 15 per cent. of sugar, this being the highest value obtained.

I received a parcel of five roots from Mr. E. B. Walker, Cambridge, the weights of which were between 1 pound 1 ounce and 1 pound 15 ounces, and were of the three varieties, but without anything to distinguish them. These I treated in the aggregate, with the result of 13·57 per cent. of sugar. Taking the best proportioned root of the parcel, weight, 1 pound 10 ounces, I found it to contain 15 per cent. of sugar.

I received samples of the three kinds of root already named from Mr. T. Goodfellow, Alexandria, which gave the following results :—No. 1. Weight, 1¼ pound ; percentage of sugar, 12·66. No. 2. Weight, 1½ pound ; percentage of sugar, 11·40. No. 3. Weight, 2¾ pounds ; percentage of sugar, 9·82.

These roots arrived with the crowns removed. I had, therefore, no opportunity of observing whether there had been any late growth of leaves, but from the freshness of the roots and the results above quoted, I should think they had been left in the ground, and not dug up at maturity and stored.

I have now given the results of the examination of roots grown in the different parts of the Waikato, and will not unnecessarily multiply the details, but take as a last experiment the result of analysis of roots grown upon Mr. Graham's estate at Tamahere. It was my desire to examine these roots while they grew, and, if possible, to note the time at which they become matured, and on that account, the crop having been sown late, I received samples of the three varieties on the 8th February, resulting as follows :—No. 1. Weight, 1 pound 1 ounce ; percentage of sugar, 8·90. No. 2. Weight, 1 pound 6 ounces ; percentage of sugar, 7·50. No. 3. Weight, 9 ounces ; percentage of sugar, 8·38.

These roots were immature, and consequently the results were low. On the 26th March I received another parcel of the three kinds from the same estate, yielding as follows :—No. 1. Weight, 1 pound 2 ounces ; percentage of sugar, 10·55. No. 2. Weight, 2 pounds ; percentage of sugar, 11·87. No. 3. Weight, 1 pound 7 ounces ; percentage of sugar, 11·17.

On the 7th May I visited the ground and chose samples of the three varieties which were still in the ground, rather overgrown with weeds and certainly having been left too long in the earth, the leaves still growing vigorously, the result no doubt of the late rains which had then been falling. Still they were fine roots, averaging from 1 to 3 pounds. They had been planted too far apart, and much space had been lost and room given for weeds to accumulate in. Being rather pressed for time I was unable to make a separate examination of these roots, and therefore I treated them in the aggregate with a result of 12·79 per cent. of sugar.

Finally on the 29th August, I received samples of each variety fresh from the ground where they had still been allowed to remain, though fully four months had elapsed since they had reached maturity. These roots had been growing vigorously, a large crop of young leaves shooting up at the expense of the sugar stored up in the root. The result of the analyses, though low, has surprised me at the amount even yet left in the roots.

No. 1. Weight, 2 pounds 9 ounces ; percentage of sugar, 7·42. No. 2. Weight, 2 pounds 4 ounces ; percentage of sugar, 6·47. No. 3. Weight, 3 pounds 5 ounces ; percentage of sugar, 8·65.

Three of this parcel of roots were forwarded by Mr. Graham to Dr. Hector, Wellington, for analysis, with the result appended :—

Results of analysis.—Three roots of sugar beet for sugar. Received 13th September, reported on 23rd September, 1881 : No. 1. Weight, 1 pound 2 ounces ; sugar per cent., 8·42. No. 2. Weight, 1 pound 10 ounces ; sugar per cent., 8·01. No. 3. Weight, 2 pounds 10 ounces ; sugar per cent., 6·94.

These are fairly good yields.

In reference to the methods of analysis and the sampling of the roots, I may remark that in every case, to insure a true average, I have punctured the root from crown to apex, taking core for the purposes of analysis, as it is a well-known fact that the sugar is not found in equal proportions throughout, the root being richer in sugar in the lower than in the upper portion. Having thus obtained a fair average of the root, I have accurately weighed and then pulped the assay portion in a motar with distilled water, and inverted the sugar in the ordinary manner with dilute sulphuric acid, making my quantity up to a known amount, from which I have charged the burette in the ordinary way.

Fearful of the conversion of the woody fibre into glucose, and a consequent false increase of the results, I have frequently checked this process by filtering off the diffused juice from the pulp, well washing the latter, and then inverting the sugar contained, but in all these cases the pulp still retains a small amount of saccharine matter, but the difference between these two methods is so small as not to cause much disparity, and here I will give one experiment to show the difference. A root of the red-top imperial weighing 2¼ pounds was taken, and two cores from the puncture tube fairly chosen, to the weight of 2 grams each, pulped, and the one inverted with the pulp, the second filtered, the pulp washed and the filtrate inverted ; the percentages of sugar being 9·82 in the first portion and 9·50 in the second. The difference I attribute to the sugar still left in the pulp. The methods by which I have determined the percentages of sugar have been with Fehling's copper solution and Knapp's mercuric cyanide solution, both volumetric analyses, the former being in my opinion the most accurate. To ensure precision, I have frequently inverted pure anhydrous cane sugar, and estimated my standard solutions with it, and therefore feel justified in saying that the analyses given by me in this paper are reliable.

In addition to the chemical analysis we have the specific gravity, this being a very reliable guide to the value of sugar present, and this I have obtained after expression of the juice on several occasions by means of the balance. Before concluding this portion of my paper on the chemical manipulations, it will be interesting in a few cases to note the relative proportions between the chemical values and the specfic gravities.

The root already mentioned as having been received from Mr. Walker, Cambridge, and which I estimated to contain 15 per cent. of sugar, was grated until it had lost weight equal to 200 grams, the juice from which being expressed equalled 128 c. c., added water to the pulp and macerated, pressed to near dryness and made up the amount with water to 200 c. c. Found the specfic gravity of the pure juice before adding water to be 1·08087, and the percentage of cane sugar in the 200 c. c. to be 14·35, the difference being the amount of sugar still retained by the pulp. Again a root from Mr. O'Neill was grated, 1 pound of which yielded 14¼ ounces weight of juice, and 1¾ ounce pulp. The specific gravity equalled 1·0528, and the percentage of sugar in the juice was 11·4.

One more experiment I will give, that of a root weighing 2 pounds, of which 14 ounces was grated, yielding 12 ounces juice and 2 ounces pulp; the specific gravity of the juice being 1·0653, and the percentage of sugar present 14·25.

There is one point in connection with this subject which deserves more than a passing notice, and that is in reference to the presence of chlorides, and especially that of chloride of sodium—common salt—this being so detrimental as to result in a loss of 5 per cent. of sugar for every 1 per cent. of the salt. When making my examination for sugar I have also tested for the presence of chlorine, but only to find a trace in any of the Waikato beet-roots with one exception which, having been left in the ground at least four months too long, are heavily charged with chlorides. One interesting feature is in the absence, beyond a trace, of chlorides in the roots received from Raglan, already mentioned, and this though grown in the vicinity of the sea. I may state that I have not estimated the amount of chlorides, but simply as a qualitative test.

The distribution of the seed in the Waikato alone was in consequence of its distance from the sea and the very favourable situation and comparative absence of chloride of sodium from the pumice soil, but its cultivation in other portions of the Auckland district fairly deserves a trial.

The great objection to the presence of salt, either from the proximity to sea air, fertilization of the ground with it, or from an abnormal amount being naturally present, is owing to the impossibility of freeing the sugar from this substance, and in consequence the estimation of chlorides is only second in importance to that of the sugar present. So inimical is this salt that M. Baruchson says : "In some instances the undue proportion of this salt in sugar has nearly rendered the sugar unsaleable ; and so generally is this recognized abroad, especially in Germany, that the manufacturers in contracting with the growers of the root stipulate that it shall not be grown on certain soils, and often even name the manure which shall be used." It is owing to this substance, and the want of sufficient care in eliminating the molasses that beet sugar at one time was strongly objected to on account of the taste, and even here I have heard complaints of the same character. On this subject Grant, in his "Beet-root Sugar," remarks : "There was formerly a prejudice in the minds of many people against beet sugar ; but it is perfectly well ascertained that, if properly refined, it cannot be distinguished from the best sugar of sugar cane, either by taste, appearance, or chemical analysis ; the two are identical." Again, on page 24, he remarks : "The cost of producing from the beet a pure white sugar, entirely free from unpleasant smell or taste, is but a trifle more than is required to produce a lower grade. In Germany refined loaf sugar is produced directly from the beet. In France the brown is first produced, and then refined. Within the last two years, however, sugar has been produced of such purity and whiteness, that it has been sold directly for consumption without refining ; and there is no question that the peculiar odour of the beet may be entirely got rid of in the manufactory." I will quote one more authority to this subject, and that one of the highest we could have. I allude to Crookes, who says in his work "Manufacture of Beet-root Sugar": "Crystallized beet-root sugar is perfectly identical in composition with cane sugar, and is indistinguishable from it by the sight, the taste, or by chemical tests."

Proceeding from the foregoing facts to summarize my results, I find that the value of sugar obtained from the whole of the roots examined by me last season under 3½lb. in weight is a percentage of 11·66, but this average includes the immature ones from Tamahere, made when they were but half-grown, and also these roots now before us, which, having remained in the earth so many months after coming to maturity, have deteriorated considerably. If then we exclude these, the average result of the rest shows a percentage of 12·45 ; but as some of the roots examined were practically too small for manufacturing purposes, I propose to exclude all under 1lb. weight, and thus reduce the average to roots between 1 and 3lb. weight, this being a useful size for manufacturing purposes, large enough to pass safely through the washing machine without being lost or clogging the bars, and yet not too large to materially reduce the percentage of sugar. By this exclusion the average is 12·29, my highest being 15 and lowest 9·82.

In arriving at these results, I do so after a series of experiments extending over the past seven months, in which time I have made upwards of eighty analyses and examined more than sixty beet-roots grown in different parts of the Waikato, many of them raised under very unfavourable conditions ; some I found overrun with weeds, of others cattle had destroyed the leaves, while the majority were planted too far apart, and in almost all cases not sufficiently earthed-up, in consequence of which a portion of the sugar contained in the root, exposed to sun and air, becomes converted into other substances. . Yet, notwithstanding all these disadvantages, the average of all the analyses made by me, with the exception of one root weighing over 5lb., was 11·66, while the exclusion of those which would under no circumstances be permitted to enter a sugar factory brought up the total to 12·45, an average return so favourable that it would result in a very large profit were it achieved in the countries were beet sugar factories are established.

That these results are not exceptional is, I think, shown by the wide area over which I have obtained my supplies for examination; and that it will be fully equalled on the large scale is shown by the unskilled manner in which some of these roots were planted and tended, and also by the request, which in many instances was adhered to, that no manure should be used. So far from this, I feel convinced that with due attention, proper cultivation, and suitable manuring, a higher percentage will be obtained than from those which the past season's growth has furnished us with; and should a factory be established for the conversion of beet-sugar, I believe the true economy of procedure would be in the purchase of roots at a fixed rate per ton, with an additional schedule price for every degree of sugar above a minimum, a practice which works beneficially amongst some of the German factories; especially would this be the case in the Colonies, where the higher price of labour would naturally lead us to seek for the maximum of sugar from a minimum of root. It is not within the scope of this paper to dilate upon the value to this district should such an industry find a home amongst us, but the benefits would be so great and varied, while the returns which I have now brought before you give so large a promise of success, that I hope the early future may find such an establishment situated where it would be most profitably worked—in the centre of the Waikato district—where soil, temperature, and the absence of sea air proclaim its fitness for the growth of the beet.

The increase of the production of beet-root sugar in various parts of the world has led many to believe that it may supersede sugar made from cane.

Some idea of the growth and extent of the industry can be formed from the estimated production of beet-root in Europe.

The estimates of beet and cane sugar together give the following comparisons:—

	1886-7.	1885-6.	1884-5.	1883-4.
	tons.	tons.	tons.	tons.
Beet sugar	2,580,000	2,127,041	2,545,889	2,360,314
Cane sugar	2,368,000	2,197,000	2,210,000	2,150,000
	4,948,000	4,324,041	4,755,889	4,510,314

In 1878 the total production of all the countries in the world was 1,101,141 tons, which, as will be seen from the preceding table, is less than one-half of the amount of 1886-7.

In 1881 the output was 1,860,974 tons; in 1880 it was 1,403,929 tons; and in 1879 it was 1,574,153 tons. It will be seen from Mr. Pond's paper that he quotes from Grant's works on "Beet-root Sugar," to prove that the peculiar odour of the beet may be got rid of in the process of manufacture, and that there is no difference between sugar made from the beet-root and that made from the cane. Crooke's work is also cited to establish the fact that the two sugars are essentially the same. It should, nevertheless, be borne in mind that sugar cane is much richer in saccharine matter than the beet-root. Within the last few years the methods of manufacturing sugar from the beet have been greatly improved, but improvements of equal or greater value have been applied to the manufacture of sugar from the cane.

Much stress is laid on the fact that the improved systems of modern agriculture have very greatly raised the yield of beet-root crops, but it is none the less true that the same systems of agriculture have increased in quite as high a degree the yield of the crops of sugar cane. Mr. Steel, the analyst of the New Zealand Sugar Company, explains that, while crystallizable sugar is identical in all its properties, whether derived from the sugar-cane or beet-root, or from any other source, there are other circumstances which must be considered besides the mere identity of this substance when derived from different sources. For instance, associated with the crystallizable sugar, which is the sweetening element, there are naturally present in all sugar-producing plants other bodies which vary greatly in nature and amount in different plants, and which are more or less difficult to separate from the sugar according to their nature.

In the juice of the sugar cane the organic and inorganic impurities are exceedingly small in quantity and not of a nature to impart an objectionable flavour to the sugar; they are moreover comparatively easy of removal. In the beet-root the opposite is the case. Here we have to deal with organic and saline impurities, in very much greater proportion than is the case with the cane, and these impurities, all accounts agree, have a most tenaceous and objectionable flavour and smell. The amount of crop from an acre of land is much greater in the case of cane than of beet. In Germany the yield of cleaned beets per acre may be fairly stated at from 10 to 12 tons. In Queensland and New South Wales the yield of cleaned cane, ready for crushing, is about 25 tons per acre, at a low estimate for one-year-old cane, and for two-year-old it may be safely taken at from 40 to 50 tons. Here the cane has a decided advantage, even when we do not consider that it requires much less attention during its growth than the beet-root. Again, the amount of sugar contained in the cane is greater than that present in the beet. From 11 to 13 per cent. is a fair allowance as to amount of sugar in the best beet-root. In Australia the canes contain from 11 to 18 per. cent. (generally about 14 or 16), according to age and variety. Then, again, the beet crop has to be replanted after each harvest, while the sugar cane is "ratooned" twice at least; that is, a second and third crop are obtained in succeeding seasons from the same old roots without replanting.

The pulp resulting from the extraction of sugar from the beet can be utilized as fodder for cattle. The begasse, the residue from the crushing of the cane, is in all modern and well-regulated sugar mills utilized as fuel, being burnt along with coal or wood in specially constructed furnaces. Of late considerable attention has been directed to the subject of utilizing the begasse in paper-making. The chief impediment to its practical use is in the hard fibre from the joints of the canes, which is more difficult to pulp than that of the spaces between the joints. In refining the raw sugars produced from beet-root and from cane, the latter has important advantages over the former.

While there is no difficulty in the way of refining and disposing of the higher grades of raw beet-root sugar, when it comes to working up the lower products the matter assumes quite a different aspect. The impurities in beet sugar consist of saline and organic bodies, having a disagreeable taste and smell, and it is very generally admitted that these cannot be completely separated from the lower grades in the process of refining, and consequently the refined product contains more or less of them; besides, in working the lower grades of beet sugar, the accumulation of impurities renders it necessary to turn out the residual syrups, and this is done in the form of golden syrup. It is also admitted that the products of the cane can be worked to an infinitely further extent in the refining than those of the beet, without the necessity of turning out syrup. The golden syrup produced from the residues of the refining of beet sugar has an objectionable smell, and it is customary to mask this by the use of sulphuric acid, which gives a sharp, biting taste to the syrup. When cane sugar residues are worked up into golden syrup, the product is sightly and palatable, and of an entirely different flavour to that made from the beet sugar.

While it is difficult to distinguish between the higher grades of the refined products of the beet and cane, the lower grades are very palpably marked. The impurities in the two sugars, which differ so much in their properties, but which it is impracticable to remove, are, in the case of the beet-root, of a particularly persistent nature. Many contend that the sweetening power derived from the beet, and particularly in the lower grades, is inferior to that derived from the cane. It is not disputed that the sweetness is not there, for it is there, in exact proportion to the amount of cane, or crystallizable sugar present, but it is maintained that the sweetness is masked by the flavour of the impurities inherent to the beet sugar, and hence the inferior sweetening power. The impurities, even in the very lowest qualities of cane sugar, are of quite a different nature and do not tend to mask the intrinsic sweetening power of the sugar. If we taste a little of the lower grades of raw beet sugar, we find that it has little or none of the characteristic flavour or sweetness of sugar, but possesses a very disagreeable sickly, saline, oily taste. On the other hand, the lowest black "takas" or "concrete" sugars from the cane have always the strong, sweet taste. In a modified degree this is precisely the difference between the refined products of the two sugars. The advocates of the cane-sugar industry state that the wasteful methods of extraction which have always been applied to the sugar-cane have given the beet-root, with the fostering care bestowed upon it as an industry, a temporary advantage over its naturally more favoured rival, and they confidently believe that it is only a matter of time when the cane will reassume its old position as the principal source of sugar. There is, however, one point in favour of beet-root, and that is the possibility of cultivating it in climates too cold for the sugar-cane.

Mr. Steel has prepared the following valuable tables showing the analyses of various kinds of representative raw sugars, including beet-root sugars, Australian cane sugars, Fiji sugars, and sugars from Java, Formosa, and Takao, and the analyses of refined sugars, syrups, molasses. These tables were prepared by Mr. Steel while employed in various refineries in Europe, and have never hitherto been published.

Analyses of Raw and Refined Sugars, &c.

Beet-root Sugar.

Crystallizable sugar	96·00	95·00	94·00	94·00	93·60	91·20	90·50
Other organic matters	1·31	1·10	1·33	1·71	1·41	2·27	2·50
Ash (saline matters)	1·19	1·15	1·17	1·39	1·64	2·23	2·45
Water	1·50	2·75	3·50	2·90	3·35	4·30	4·55
	100·00	100·00	100·00	100·00	100·00	100·00	100·00
Net titre	90·05	89·25	88·15	87·05	85·40	80·05	78·25
Crystallizable sugar	92·00	91·00	88·40	88·50	86·00	86·00	86·60
Other organic matters	2·21	2·66	2·84	3·24	3·39	3·43	3·20
Ash (saline matters)	2·99	3·04	3·11	4·01	4·06	4·32	4·57
Water	2·80	3·30	5·65	4·25	6·55	6·25	5·45
	100·00	100·00	100·00	100·00	100·00	100·00	100·00
Net titre	77·05	75·80	72·35	68·45	65·70	64·40	62·85

Beet-root Sugars containing Fruit Sugar.

Crystallizable sugar	89·20	88·20	87·50
Fruit sugar	1·82	2·15	1·97
Other organic matters	2·20	2·45	3·29
Ash (saline matters)	2·43	2·60	2·74
Water	4·35	4·60	4·50

Cane Sugars.

Australian Sugars.

Crystallizable sugar	96·20	95·50	93·70	92·70	90·60	89·50	82·20
Fruit sugar	·96	1·00	1·17	2·08	3·81	4·12	5·88
Other organic matters	1·16	·75	2·22	2·00	1·48	1·74	4·53
Ash (saline matters)	·76	·66	1·18	1·69	1·29	1·53	2·75
Sand	....	....	....	....	....	....	....
Water	·92	1·19	1·73	2·14	2·82	3·11	4·64
	100·00	100·00	100·00	100·00	100·00	100·00	100·00
Net titre	91·44	90·30	86·13	81·47	80·29	77·73	62·57

Fiji Sugars. / Java Sugars.

	Fiji				Java		
Crystallizable sugar	95·00	92·40	89·70	87·30	97·20	95·10	94·50	92·30
Fruit sugar	1·12	2·63	3·29	3·69	·85	1·75	2·45	3·63
Other organic matters	1·01	1·43	1·90	2·80	·85	1·16	·97	1·15
Ash (saline matters)	·34	·67	1·14	1·28	·21	·33	·33	·40
Sand	·04	·03	·05	·05	·06	·07	·07	·13
Water	1·59	2·84	3·92	4·88	·83	1·59	1·68	2·39
	100·00	100·00	100·00	100·00	100·00	100·00	100·00	100·00
Net titre	93·08	86·42	80·71	77·21	95·30	91·70	90·40	86·67

China Sugars.

	Formosa Sugars.			Ho-Ilo.	Takao Sugars.		
Crystallizable sugar	80·00	80·00	76·70	82·10	80·60	78·50	76·30
Fruit sugar	7·13	7·38	8·56	6·29	7·02	5·69	8·26
Other organic matters	2·54	3·97	5·93	4·47	4·04	5·11	3·47
Ash (saline matters)	2·18	2·66	2·68	2·30	1·42	2·59	2·79
Sand	·30	·14	·20	·24	·09	·18	·20
Water	7·85	5·85	5·93	4·60	6·83	7·93	8·98
	100·00	100·00	100·00	100·00	100·00	100·00	100·00
Net titre	61·97	59·32	54·74	64·31	66·48	61·36	54·09

Refined Sugars.

	Loaf sugar.	First white.			First counters.			Yellow.		
Crystallizable sugar	99·50	99·30	98·20	97·70	96·20	94·10	93·30	87·70	86·60	85·40
Fruit sugar	·10	·16	·47	·57	1·05	2·57	3·10	6·34	8·10	7·85
Other organic matters	·14	·20	·12	·35	·49	·63	·53	1·38	1·45	1·67
Ash (saline matters)	·02	·02	·04	·05	·12	·31	·38	1·00	1·28	1·17
Water	·24	·32	1·17	1·33	2·14	2·19	2·69	3·58	3·57	3·91
	100·00	100·00	100·00	100·00	100·00	100·00	100·00	100·00	100·00	100·00

Syrup and Molasses.

	Golden syrup.		Raw beet molasses.	Raw cane molasses.	
Crystallizable sugar	39·50	27·82	48·80	51·14	46·02
Fruit sugar	28·57	35·71	·54	7·54	12·03
Other organic matters	9·61	13·55	23·22	14·88	10·34
Ash (saline matters)	5·27	5·47	10·94	9·79	11·36
Water	17·05	17·45	16·50	16·65	19·35
	100·00	100·00	100·00	100·00	100·00

It may be explained that crystallizable sugar is the body to which the sugar owes its sweetness. It is known by various other names, such as sucrose, cane sugar. Fruit sugar is glucose or uncrystallizable sugar. The net titre is the theoretical amount of pure loaf sugar which would be obtained were the sugar refined up entirely into loaf sugar and syrup. It is merely, however, an empirical figure, and its use is solely for comparative purposes, for which it is of great value. It is based on the assumption that each 1 part of ash prevents 5 parts of crystallizable sugar from crystallizing, holding it in solution as syrup ; and that each 1 part of fruit sugar has the crystallization of its own weight of cane sugar. Therefore, to find the net titre or theoretical available percentage of sugar in any sample, we multiply the ash by 5, add on the fruit sugar, and deduct the total from the crystallizable or cane sugar ; the result is the net titre.

On the examination of the table of analyses it will be seen that cane sugar is superior to the product of the beet in net titre. Thus, a cane sugar containing 90·60 per cent. of crystallizable sugar, has a net titre of 80·29 per cent. while a beet-root sugar has a net titre of 80·05 per cent. This holds good throughout the whole series. These analyses of beet-root sugar, Mr. Steel states, are fair representatives of the sugar of this class imported for the Greenock refineries. The analyses of cane sugars will give an idea of the composition of the sugar from the main sugar-producing districts, imported into Australia. The refined sugars are average products of a refinery working cane sugar. The golden syrup was made in a refinery in Greenock working a mixture of beet and cane sugars. The composition of the molasses from the beet and cane factories varies exceedingly according to the system of working. Beet-root sugar seldom contains any fruit sugar.

TOBACCO.

ALTHOUGH tobacco has been grown for many years in various parts of Australasia, the industry has not reached the proportions which people seem to have a reasonable right to expect. The quality of the leaf, thus far, produced is not good, and it has a strong rank taste and smell. At first these peculiarities were attributed to a want of knowledge as to the proper methods of growing the plant and curing the leaf, but it now appears that there are other difficulties to overcome. Mr. Augustus Morris, the New South Wales Executive Commissioner to the International Exhibition at Philadelphia, was instructed by his government, during his visit to the United States, to devote as much time as possible to the investigation of the various methods of cultivating tobacco and curing the leaf in that country. The results of Mr. Morris's investigations were embodied in an exhaustive report on the subject, the publication of which attracted much attention in tobacco growing countries. Mr. Morris states in his report that he paid particular attention to the growth of the plant in California, from the fact that the conditions in which it was grown there were similar to those in New South Wales and other portions of Australia. He argued that the difficulties which had been overcome in California could be overcome in the same way in Australia. He said that the most experienced planters found, after growing their crops, that they were unable to do anything with the leaf. The sources of failure lay, not in the properties of the leaf itself, but in the arid and dessicating atmosphere of a Californian autumn. The same trouble exists in many parts of New South Wales, where it is difficult to remove from the leaf all its moisture so gradually as to allow of sufficient time elapsing to provide for the decomposition of the green colouring matter, *chlorophyl*, that is, to ensure the partial conversion of the starch into gum and sugar, the changes, in short, which in a moister climate take place naturally in the plant after it is cut and before it is dried, the changes which constitute curing, as distinguished from drying. Mr. Morris said :—" The wide range over which the plant is grown in the United States ought to assure the most sceptical that there is nothing in its own nature to exclude it from the soils and climate of Australia. From Wisconsin with its intensely cold winters to Florida with its broiling summers, and from the rich lands of Missouri to the poor ones of Connecticut, it is a staple subject of husbandry."

The total tobacco product of the whole of the Australasian Colonies is about 5,000,000 lb. per annum, and very nearly one-half of that is grown in New South Wales, Victoria taking the second place on the list. In 1886 New South Wales had 1,603 acres under crop with a product of 2,570,064 lb. During the same period Victoria had 1,866 acres and a product of 1,538,208 lb. The agricultural returns for 1887 show a falling off in the production of tobacco in both colonies. In 1887 New South Wales had 1,203 acres and a product of 1,527,904 lb. Victoria 2,031 acres and a product of 1,344,876 lb.

The subjoined table shows the number of acres in tobacco in New South Wales and Victoria, and the quantity produced each year from 1880 to 1887 inclusive:—

New South Wales.			Victoria.		
Years ended 31 March.	Area.	Produce.	Years ended 31 March.	Area.	Produce.
	Acres.	lb.		Acres.	lb.
1880	592	696,752	1880	531	145,164
1881	1,791	2,190,528	1881	1,990	1,941,296
1882	1,625	2,050,832	1882	1,461	1,442,112
1883	1,815	1,964,480	1883	1,313	635,370
1884	1,786	2,240,672	1884	1,325	1,021,888
1885	1,046	1,110,368	1885	1,402	884,016
1886	1,603	2,570,064	1886	1,866	1,538,208
1887	1,203	1,527,904	1887	2,031	1,344,876

The bulk of New South Wales tobacco is grown between Tumut and Albury. Considerable quantities are also produced in the Western district, within a radius of about 50 miles of Bathurst. The plant was formerly extensively cultivated in the Valley of the Hunter in the North, but of late years little attention has been given to it there. The best tobacco produced in the Colony is at Tumut, along the banks of the river of that name, where the soil is composed of rich alluvial deposits, and the growth not affected by change of seasons. Tumut produced last year 739,500 lb. of the leaf. Several tobacco factories are located in the district. It is said, however, by agriculturists, that the plant will grow all over the Colony, especially on the river flats subject to inundations. The soil in the tobacco districts is seldom manured, and if there is no overflow, growing it soon becomes unproductive. The best tobacco in Victoria is grown in the King River country, a mountainous district. The land there is composed of rich loam, formed from the disintegration of slate and granite rocks. Mr. James Henly, a citizen of the United States, was the first to commence the cultivation of tobacco in that district, having obtained his seed from Kentucky and Virginia. Mr. Henly for a considerable period grew and manufactured his own tobacco; but the Colonial legislature having passed an Act requiring every manufacturer of tobacco to take out a license, at a cost of £150 to £250 ($730 to $1,217) per annum, according to the quantity manufactured, he was forced to abandon the manufacture and devote his time to the cultivation of the leaf. He found that his land yielded upon an average from 1,000 lb. to 1,500 lb. of tobacco per acre.

He noticed that the young plants were subject to blue mould, and that the leaf was not unfrequently injured by frost before matured. Its growth was also impaired by hail and rain storms. Mr. Henly says that, the crop may be regarded as precarious, not only in the King River district, but in other portions of Australia. He does not think that an average crop can be gathered in any portion of the great Island continent, more than once in every three or four years.

The season of 1887 being a good one, the tobacco crop amounted to about 250 tons in the King River district. The labour employed in tobacco culture in Australia is now almost exclusively Chinese, the Europeans fighting shy of the industry on account of the uncertainty of the crops, or not being sufficiently skilled in its cultivation and the preparation of the leaf.

Mr. Hugh Dixon, the senior partner in the Conqueror Tobacco Works, Sydney, who is a high authority with regard to the industry, is of opinion that tobacco culture at present cannot be made to pay with European labour in Australia. He says that whenever the leaf is grown by Europeans it is inferior to that grown by the Chinamen, from the fact that the former will not take the pains to cultivate it properly. Mr. Dixon says further, that there has been a great improvement in the quality of the Australian leaf during the last twenty years, but it is still far inferior to the American, and the latter is always preferred by those who can afford to use it.

The truth is, there is no bright-coloured tobacco grown in any part of Australia, and Mr. Dixon admits that his best brands of tobacco, such as the "Champion," are made wholly of the American leaf.

Mr. Angus Mackay, of the Technical College, Sydney, supplies interesting and valuable notes, hitherto unpublished, embodying his observations and experiences with the tobacco-plant in various parts of Australia.

Mr. Mackay expresses his obligations to Professors Johnston and Wilson, and the Orange, Judd, Tobacco Company, and other experts for information in regard to tobacco in the United States, which he said was especially valuable to him for comparative purposes. Mr. Mackay states that tobacco is an old crop in Australia, the seed having been brought by the first settlers. Tobacco was grown on land belonging to the Australian Agricultural Company, near Stroud, 124 miles north of Sydney, as far back as 1826, the year in which grant in fee simple of 464,640 acres of land was made to that Company. In those early days from 1,200 to 1,800 lb. of leaf per acre were obtained. Tobacco is still grown there, but in small quantities. The yield now seldom reaches 1,000 lb. per acre, except on new land or that which has had a long rest.

On new lands, near Mudgee, very fair returns are got, but in all cases, with scarcely an exception, the returns fall off after the third or fourth cropping. There is one notable exception, in the case of the very rich alluvial soils of volcanic origin at Tumut. There, tobacco has been grown for many years, and the yield keeps up in a manner that is surprising until explanation is afforded through the analysis of the soil. The crop is one of the most exhausting upon land. In that respect there is but little difference in what it takes from the soil here and what the American leaf is found to contain.

Mr. Mackay has made three analyses of leaf grown in New South Wales in the Tumut, the Hunter River, and Mudgee districts. The varieties are "Virginia" leaf from the Tumut and Hunter River, and the "Yarra" from Mudgee. He says:—"I find more difficulty in locating the exact varieties because Australian buyers do not, as a rule, put much store upon the variety. They buy the leaf for its qualities, that is about the gauge of the average purchaser. All the leaf mentioned was dry and in the form of hands when I got it, hence I cannot speak more definitely of the varieties."

Mr. Mackay found that the average proportion of ash from the dry eaf from Tumut was 26·25, Hunter River 28·40, and Mudgee 20·15, the latter had been touched by frost, and was materially deficient in "life" or "body," which gives toughness or quality to tobacco. The main object of the analysis was to get at the proportion of potash, lime, and silica, in comparison with the American Virginia leaf, which had also been tested. The proportions were:—*Potash*—Tumut, 25·20; Hunter River, 27·40; Mudgee, 9·00. *Lime*—Tumut, 30·00; Hunter River, 25·90; Mudgee, 10·18. *Silica*—Tumut, 13·20; Hunter River, 14·10; Mudgee, 13·05. The Virginia leaf received from Charlestown, South Carolina, yielded—Potash, 27·04; lime, 37·00; silica, 12·10. Mr. Mackay says:—" Possibly these figures will be of more concern to those who take a scientific interest in the subject than to others; but, in so far as my investigations and experiences in tobacco production here go, they present the key of the whole situation. The proportion of alkali and alkaline earth in the crop everywhere is excessive where the quality is good enough for manufacturers' purposes. Now, after taking over 100 analyses of soils from various parts of Australia, I can say that alkalies are a defective quality all over. If an exception to this conclusion could be found it would be in the Tumut soil, but potash is not abundant even there. Unless the tobacco land is refreshed by the sediment of floods or by a proper system of tobacco culture and use of the needed fertilizers, even the very rich plains about Tumut must give out."

The cultivation, as followed here, is much the same as in the United States and the West Indies. The main difference is in the harvesting. Here too much dependence is placed upon the climate. It has been a misfortune to the country, in a farming sense, that the climate is so good; for, relying upon that, very little effort is made to house and cure the leaf under proper cover. With a few exceptions, all the barns he had seen were unworthy of the name, and the result is that large proportions of every crop are wasted between the time of cutting and getting the leaf to market. Mr. Mackay concludes his notes with the statement that tobacco is not likely to become an article of export from these Colonies "until more attention is paid by growers to keeping up the fertile properties of the land and in housing and curing the leaf." The plants are set out in July, August, and September, and the crops are harvested in March and April.

The average price of the Colonial leaf is from 5d. (10 cents) to 6d. (12 cents) per lb. In 1887, on account of the short crops, it was about 7½d. (15 cents) to 8d. (16 cents) per lb. The duty on the imported leaf is 3s. (73 cents) per lb., except when imported for manufacturing purposes, then it is only 1s. (24 cents) per lb.

A much greater quantity of Colonial leaf is now used by the various tobacco factories than formerly. This change is not to be attributed to any special improvement in the quality of the leaf, but to the low price at which it can be purchased. Attention is directed to the fact that the Government have increased the excise tax on tobacco from 1s. (24 cents) to 1s. 3d. (30 cents) per lb. When the tax was first levied it was expected that manufacturers would use the Colonial and imported leaf in about equal proportions. The Colonial Treasurer stated that manufacturers instead of doing this used only 1 lb. of imported leaf to every 3 lb. of Colonial leaf, and the revenue had in consequence declined. Should the additional excise tax induce manufacturers to use more of the imported leaf, a decided improvement would soon be noticed in the quality of their products. Out of 2,147,418 lb. of tobacco manufactured in New South Wales during the year 1887 more than three-fourths consisted of Colonial leaf. The exact figures being 1,994,001 lb. Colonial leaf and 552,217 lb. of imported leaf.

There are 15 tobacco and 8 cigar and cigarette factories in New South Wales, employing 503 hands, 134 of whom are females. The estimated horse-power of the machinery in these establishments is 95, and the value of the plant is £69,860 ($309,974). These establishments manufactured, during 1887, 2,147,418 lb. of smoking tobacco valued at £342,289 ($1,665,749), cigars 6,057 lb. valued at £4,621 ($17,695), and cigarettes 10,269 lb., valued at £4,621 ($22,488).

The subjoined table shows the number of tobacco factories in the Colony of New South Wales during the years 1885, 1886, and 1887, together with the number of hands employed, value of plant, amount of horse-power, quantity of material used and manufactured for each year:—

Year.	No. of Tobacco Factories.	No. of Cigar and Cigarette Factories.	Hands employed. Male.	Hands employed. Female.	Value of Plant.	Horse-power of Machinery.	Tobacco leaf used. Colonial Leaf.	Tobacco leaf used. Imported Leaf.	Tobacco, Cigars, and Cigarettes Manufactured. Article.	Quantity.	Value.
							lb.	lb.		lb.	
1885	16	9	411	257	£62,980 / $306,492	120	1,825,854	672,485	Tobacco	2,133,163	£319,975 / $1,557,168
									Cigars	9,402	£5,641 / $27,452
									Cigarettes	6,901	£3,105 / $15,110
1886	17	9	559	144	£64,550 / $314,133	120	1,853,407	561,514	Tobacco	2,044,240	£306,632 / $1,492,244
									Cigars	7,125	£4,275 / $20,814
									Cigarettes	5,340	£2,403 / $11,594
1887	15	8	503	134	£69,860 / $309,974	95	1,994,001	552,217	Tobacco	2,147,418	£342,289 / $1,665,749
									Cigars	6,057	£3,634 / $17,685
									Cigarettes	10,269	£4,621 / $22,488

The Colonial leaf is valued at 5¾d. (12 cents) per lb.

Messrs. Cameron Brothers, Virginia Tobacco Works, Messrs. Dixon & Sons Conqueror Tobacco Works, the Saywell Tobacco Company (Limited), and Mr. M. Simmons, New York and Brooklyn Factory, are the four leading establishments in Australia. Messrs. Cameron Bros. have branch factories in Melbourne (Victoria), and in Adelaide (South Australia). Messrs. Dixon and Sons have a branch at Melbourne. Messrs. Dixon & Sons were probably the first to commence the industry in Australia, their connection with it dating as far back as 1839, the date of the arrival of the founder of the firm, the late Mr. Hugh Dixon, who came to Sydney especially for the purpose of manufacturing tobacco. Mr. Dixon died in 1880, and his son, the present head of the firm, succeeded to the business. Special mention should be made of the factory of Messrs. Wolfe, Gorrick, & Co., of West Maitland, also one of the oldest factories in the Colony. That establishment commenced operations in 1840, and Mr. Thomas, the present manager, has been connected with the firm since its foundation. The trade of Messrs. Wolfe, Gorrick, & Co., is principally with Newcastle and Sydney. They give employment to twenty-six hands, previous to the imposition of the excise tax they employed more than double that number. Mr. Thomas stated recently that the excise tax was doing the industry harm in every part of the Colony. When asked if protection would aid the matter, his answer was decidedly in the negative. He said, "More protection, that is, higher import duties on the foreign leaf, would place the trade in a far worse condition than at present. There are people so protection mad that they would put 5s. ($1·26) per cwt. on potatoes. What is wanted is the removal or modification of the excise duty."

The products of this factory have received as many as fifty prizes and certificates from various exhibitions, inclusive of one from the International Exhibition at Sydney. The following list comprises all the brands turned out of the factory :—

The " Prizetaker," eighteen-twist, dark.
The " Limerick," ten-twist dark.
The " O.K.," ten, six, and five-cake, dark.
American leaf, " The Rosebud," twist twenties, dark.
The " Homespun," twist tens, dark.
The " Bright Twist," tens, dark.
The " Meteor," ten-cake, light.
The " Star of Virginia," ten-cake, dark ; and
The " Snider Rifle," in cut tobacco.

The principal brands of Messrs. Cameron Bros. Virginia Factory, at Sydney, are the Raven, Negrohead, Twenty-twos, and the Raven Navy Twist twelves. The wholesale price of each of these is 3s. (73 cents) per lb. The Orion and Pathfinder are 2s. 6d. (61 cents) per lb. Dark Cavendish, such as the Signet, Lion, Conquest, Havelock, vary between 2s. (49 cents) and 2s. 9d. (67 cents). Their Nail Rods, Two Seas, bring 3s. (73 cents) and 1s. (24 cents) per lb. wholesale. Their Aromatics, Canary Bird Twist sixes, Bars twelves, Pocket pieces twelves, Twin Blocks four and sixes, sell wholesale in 25 lb. caddies at 3s. 5d (83 cents) per lb., to all of which must be added the excise tax, 1s. 3d. (30 cents) per lb. Their Cut Tobaccos, Emperor of Germany, ¼ lb. tins, Mixture Rough Cut Raven, 5 lb. parcels, sell 4s. (97 cents) per lb. Cameron's Cut Cavendish, Charmer Mixture, Loose Aromatic, Long Cut, and Rough Cut, sell wholesale at 3s. 6d. (85 cents) per lb. Messrs. Cameron Bros. experienced many difficulties in establishing the industry. A representative of their firm from America paid several visits to Australia before the construction of their factory in Sydney in 1873. This building, erected at a cost of £100,000 ($48,6650) was wholly destroyed by fire in September, 1886, but in a few months a larger and finer building was erected to take its place. The products of this new factory are becoming more and more popular. The present manager in Sydney is Mr. Alexander Cameron; he has infused a wonderful amount of energy into the business, and is quoted in Australia as an authority on tobacco. One secret of the success of this firm is the advantage it possesses in having all their American leaf selected and cured by their own firms in Richmond and Petersburg, Virginia. They seem determined that their Australian products shall be worthy of their world-wide reputation. They carried off the first prizes at the Sydney and Melbourne International Exhibitions, and their products at the latter exhibition were the only ones deemed worthy of a gold medal and of the Emperor of Germany's special prize of 1,000 guineas.

The leading brands of the Saywell Tobacco Co. (Limited), are Bright Aromatics, pocket pieces, Bright Flat Ruby, Twist Gold Bars, Dark Twists, Negrohead, Eagle Defiance, Dark Flat or Plug Eureka, I X L Navy, Cut Tobaccos—Rough Cut Ruby, Straight Cut, Gold Leaf Mixture, Barrett's Twist, Cavendish, Bird's Eye, &c. The Company also manufacture a number of popular brands of Cigars and Cigarettes.

The total quantity of all kinds of tobacco, cigars, and snuff, imported into the Colony of New South Wales during the year 1887, was 1,965,816 lb., valued at £193,577 ($941,441), against 2,253,497 lb., valued at £220,896 ($1,074,990) for 1886.

The subjoined table shows the quantity and value of all kinds of tobacco, cigars, cigarettes, and snuff imported into New South Wales for each year, from 1877 to 1887, inclusive:—

Imports from 1877 to 1887.

Kind.	Quantity.	Total.	Value.	Totals.	Total.
1877.	lb.	lb.	£	£	$.
Manufactured	653,751 }	2,264,740	{ 47,331 }	120,623	587,012
Unmanufactured	1,610,989 }		{ 73,292 }		
Cigars	114,253	....	38,950	....	189,560
Snuff	42	....	33	....	161
1878.					
Manufactured	1,030,063 }	3,478,167	{ 81,088 }	173,733	845,472
Unmanufactured	2,448,104 }		{ 92,645 }		
Cigars	184,149	....	52,501	....	255,496
Snuff	502	....	74	....	360
1879.					
Manufactured	755,049 }	957,638	{ 51,594 }	59,211	288,150
Unmanufactured	202,589 }		{ 7,617 }		
Cigars	122,859	....	33,408	....	162,580
Snuff	1,227	....	132	....	642
1880.					
Manufactured	525,539 }	1,003,149	{ 34,629 }	51,997	253,043
Unmanufactured	477,610 }		{ 17,368 }		
Cigars	107,105	....	31,450	....	153,051
Snuff	903	....	221	....	1,075

TOBACCO. 197

Kind.	Quantity.	Total.	Value.	Totals.	Total.
	lb.	lb.	£	£	$
1881.					
Manufactured	613,868 }	1,649,111	45,909 }	83,259	405,180
Unmanufactured	1,035,243 }		37,350 }		
Cigars	250,960	....	67,365	....	327,832
Snuff	299	....	64	....	311
1882.					
Manufactured	928,152 }	2,150,746	64,791 }	110,640	538,430
Unmanufactured	1,222,594 }		45,849 }		
Cigars	220,623	....	60,541	....	294,623
Snuff	744	....	100	....	487
1883.					
Manufactured	949,448 }	1,806,514	59,965 }	95,073	402,673
Unmanufactured	856,066 }		35,108 }		
Cigars	336,267	....	89,005	....	433,119
Snuff	744	....	174	....	847
1884.					
Manufactured	465,447 }	1,636,863	59,669 }	95,413	464,327
Unmanufactured	871,416 }		35,744 }		
Cigars	298,531	....	66,052	....	321,442
Cigarettes	10,411	....	6,256	....	30,445
Snuff	758	....	74	....	360
1885.					
Manufactured	955,059 }	1,472,010	69,117 }	93,425	454,653
Unmanufactured	516,951 }		24,308 }		
Cigars	317,995	....	76,359	....	371,601
Cigarettes	40,593	....	14,738	....	71,722
Snuff	770	....	120	....	584
1886.					
Manufactured	1,384,036 }	1,891,952	95,118 }	127,486	620,411
Unmanufactured	507,916 }		32,368 }		
Cigars	310,694	....	74,952	....	364,754
Cigarettes	49,923	....	18,265	....	88,887
Snuff	928	....	193	....	939
1887.					
Manufactured	1,197,416 }	1,656,880	87,984 }	106,108	516,374
Unmanufactured	459,364 }		18,124 }		
Cigars	257,312	....	68,022	....	331,029
Cigarettes	50,318	....	19,097	....	92,335
Snuff	1,406	....	350	....	1,703

The bulk of these imports consists of American tobacco, the unmanufactured being almost exclusively the product of that country. The actual quantity of American tobacco consumed in the Colony does not show in the returns, for no inconsiderable portion is shipped by way of London, and is entered as British produce. The direct shipments from the United States during the year 1886 amounted to 1,083,852 lb. valued at £69,339 ($337,438), against 821,639 lb., valued at £45,820 ($222,984) for 1887.

The subjoined table shows the quantity and value of the direct imports of all kinds of tobacco, cigars, cigarettes, and snuff into New South Wales for 1886 and 1887, together with the names of the countries whence imported :—

Country.	Kind.	1886.			1887.		
		Quantity.	Value.		Quantity.	Value.	
		lb.	£	$	lb.	£	$
Great Britain	Manufactured	563,371	43,206	210,262	498,621	35,816	174,299
	Unmanufactured	97,493	3,393	16,512	29,722	855	4,161
	Cigars	43,595	16,425	79,932	28,881	14,428	70,214
	Cigarettes	41,346	14,037	68,311	36,393	12,946	63,002
	Snuff	289	53	258	1,216	321	1,562
Victoria	Manufactured	78,108	6,572	31,983	145,487	11,552	56,218
	Unmanufactured	8,139	582	2,832	20,286	1,733	8,434
	Cigars	23,965	7,112	34,611	18,931	8,107	39,453
	Cigarettes	1,443	839	4,083	2,370	817	4,023
	Snuff	153	46	224	90	18	87
United States	Manufactured	678,933	38,165	185,730	427,693	28,527	138,827
	Unmanufactured	398,590	28,206	137,264	383,475	13,262	64,540
	Cigars	1,313	848	4,127	1,771	572	2,784
	Cigarettes	4,536	2,030	9,879	8,700	3,459	16,833
	Snuff	480	90	438	......	......	......
South Australia	Manufactured	46,467	5,774	28,099	86,493	9,191	44,728
	Cigars	4,683	1,196	5,820	5,234	2,441	11,879
	Cigarettes	418	268	1,304	572	447	2,175
	Snuff	6	4	19	......	......	......
Queensland	Manufactured	660	59	287	1,953	219	1,066
	Unmanufactured	827	62	302	370	15	73
	Cigars	2,540	779	3,791	147	86	419
	Cigarettes	813	379	1,844	850	621	3,022
Western Australia	Manufactured	......	......	......	2,500	306	1,489
Germany	Manufactured	405	68	331	25,159	1,472	7,163
	Unmanufactured	627	45	219	2,912	216	1,051
	Cigars	61,654	15,795	76,866	57,251	15,949	77,616
	Cigarettes	946	530	2,579	276	114	555
France	Unmanufactured	......	......	......	42	2	10
	Manufactured	200	27	131	......	......	......
	Cigars	28,515	8,210	39,954	4,774	1,408	7,164
	Cigarettes	281	126	613	180	300	1,460
New Zealand	Manufactured	275	17	83	1,440	64	311
	Cigars	1,050	426	2,073	512	137	667
	Cigarettes	125	48	234	410	176	857
Tasmania	Manufactured	1,568	100	487	......	......	......
Fiji	Manufactured	190	8	39	197	3	15
	Cigars	194	59	287	......	......	......
Hong Kong	Unmanufactured	......	......	......	6,518	441	2,146
	Manufactured	13,068	1,035	5,037	6,252	712	3,465
	Cigars	126,258	20,052	97,683	120,050	19,717	95,953
China	Unmanufactured	......	......	......	16,039	1,600	7,786
	Manufactured	791	87	423	200	9	44
	Cigars	7,703	1,463	7,120	9,417	1,654	8,049
Ceylon	Unmanufactured	2,240	80	389	......	......	......
India	Cigars	689	184	895	418	211	1,027
Singapore	,,	15	8	39	241	53	258
New Caledonia	,,	504	160	779	604	274	1,333
Belgium	Manufactured	......	......	......	7	1	5
	Cigars	8,016	2,235	10,877	8,938	2,938	14,298
Egypt	Cigarettes	15	8	39	514	198	959
South Sea Islands	Manufactured	......	......	......	1,354	112	545
Malta	Cigarettes	......	......	......	53	19	92
Italy	Cigars	......	......	......	44	7	37
Austria	,,	......	......	......	99	40	193

TOBACCO.

There is little or no demand for chewing tobacco in Australia. The small quantity used is manufactured by Messrs. Lorrilord & Co., of New Jersey, and Gail & Ox, of Maryland. The demand for American cigarettes is steadily increasing, and although cigarettes are manufactured in the Colony, the proportion is small compared with the imported. The demand is heaviest for the products of Messrs. Allen & Ginter, of Richmond, Virginia, and especially for their "Little Beauties," "Virginia Bright," "Richmond Gem," "Straight Cut." Messrs. Hyde, Todman, & Co. are the Sydney agents for the firm, and they distribute about 10,000,000 of these cigarettes annually. The cigarettes next in repute are those of Messrs. Emery & Co., of New York, sold under the brand of "Old judge," and "Gypsie Queen." The "Vanity Fair" cigarettes made by Messrs. Kembell & Co., are very popular. The bulk of cigars consumed in Australia are from Manilla, Germany, and Havana, amongst the latter those known as "La Fleur de Murias," Henry Clay's, are much liked. The sales of Messrs. Hyde, Todman, & Co. last year of Colonial tobacco, amounted to 690,000 lb., and of American, 1,200,000 lb. The American goods are usually shipped by steam from New York, *via* London, at £3 7s. 6d. ($16·41) to £3 15s. ($18·24) per ton freight.

It must not be supposed, however, that all the tobacco entered at the Customs is consumed in the Colony, for no inconsiderable portion is, re-exported. During the year 1886 the total quantity of all kinds of tobacco exported from the Colony amounted to 632,893 lb., against 810,906 lb., in 1885. In 1887 the total quantity was 682,768 lb.

Nearly all the leading American tobacco factories are represented in Australia. The popular brands of Messrs. Williamson & Co., of Richmond, Virginia, such as the "Imperial Ruby Twist," "Welcome Nugget," "Victory," "Golden Eagle," and "Nectar Leaf," are quite as well known as in the United States.

The sale of Messrs. Williamson & Co.'s tobaccos was at first limited on account of their light colour and mild flavour, as the Australians have for many years exhibited a decided preference for dark coloured, strongly flavoured tobacco, but now the taste is changing, and especially in the large cities and towns, where there is a steadily increasing demand for bright, mild tobaccos. In dark coloured imported tobaccos the products of Messrs. Cameron Bros. seem to be preferred to all others. The "Two Seas" and "Imperial" being the leading brands.

Messrs. Cameron Bros'. branch factory here manufacture the same brands out of the American leaf, which have become very popular on account of their low price. Amongst the various kinds of American tobaccos that have been successfully introduced into Australia mention should be made of Tennant's "Derby," Watson and M'Gill's "Navy," and Blackwell's "Durham."

FRUIT.

ALTHOUGH there are few countries in the world better adapted to the growth of all kinds of fruit than New South Wales, the Colony thus far has been unable to grow a sufficient quantity for home consumption, much less for export. One of the chief obstacles in the way is, that it is almost impossible to obtain land for fruit culture upon favourable terms. Another obstacle is the lack of cheap facilities for transportation; moreover, the farmers seem to take it for granted that the country is better suited to raising sheep than anything else, and even when engaged in other kinds of farming they persist in following the old beaten tracks with which they are familiar. Very few ever think of growing more than one or two kinds of crops, and it stands to reason and common-sense that when a farmer's dependence is placed entirely upon cereals or hay his returns must always be uncertain, on account of drought, rust, and other causes; and even if such were not the case, the local demands for cereals are usually more or less limited, and after they have been supplied, the surplus must find an outside market where the competition is keen. In order to grow fruit successfully in the interior districts of Australia it will be necessary to adopt a system of irrigation similar to that employed in the dry districts of California and in other States of the Union on the Pacific coast. On the distant plains of Australia, where the rainfall does not average more than 6 or 8 inches per annum, water would have to be obtained by some artificial means. In the north country, west of the mountain ranges, irrigation would not be needed, for in those districts apples, pears, peaches, grapes, passion-fruit, plums, guavas, strawberries, gooseberries, quinces, bananas, loquats, lemons, figs, and oranges grow to perfection.

The value of the various kinds of fruit imported into the Colony of New South Wales during the year 1886 was £316,166 ($1,538,622), against £317,080 ($1,543,070) for 1885, and £193,626 ($942,281) for 1877. Of the imports for 1886, £177,316 ($862,908) consisted of green or fresh fruit, £100,629 ($489,711) of dried fruit, £27,414 ($133,410) of canned or tinned fruit, preserves, £2,838 ($13,811) of bottled, and £7,969 ($38,781) of fruit dates.

The subjoined table shows the value of all kinds of fruit imported into New South Wales for each year, from 1877 to 1887 inclusive.

Year.	Value.		Year.	Value.	
	£	$		£	$
1877	193,626	942,281	1883	263,906	1,284,299
1878	150,212	731,007	1884	324,657	1,579,943
1879	133,207	648,252	1885	317,080	1,543,079
1880	149,525	727,663	1886	316,166	1,538,622
1881	230,664	1,122,526	1887	288,211	1,402,579
1882	249,570	1,214,532			

The annual value of the imports of fresh fruit has more than doubled during the last few years. The bulk of the supply is from Tasmania. The quantity imported from that Colony during the year 1886 was 238,972 cases, valued £93,722 ($456,098) against 187,216 cases, valued £68,742 ($334,533), for the year 1887.

The subjoined table shows the quantity and value of the imports of fresh or green fruit into the Colony of New South Wales for the years 1886 and 1887, with the names of the countries whence imported.

Country.	1886.			1887.		
	Quantity.	Value.		Quantity.	Value.	
	pkgs.	£	$	pkgs.	£	$
Great Britain	....	....	....	2	2	10
Victoria	72,451	27,265	132,685	39,572	14,914	72,573
South Australia......	4,780	2,485	12,088	12,215	4,178	20,339
Queensland	71,591	20,332	98,946	105,060	22,411	109,062
Tasmania	238,972	93,722	456,098	187,216	68,742	334,533
New Zealand.........	8,827	1,765	8,589	4,226	831	4,044
Fiji	173,010	28,234	137,406	260,964	37,288	181,462
United States	6,555	2,610	12,702	9,996	5,119	24,912
New Caledonia	672	278	1,353	2,240	546	2,657
Hong Kong	101	37	180	198	92	448
South Sea Islands...	4,472	462	2,248	32,263	4,099	19,948
Italy	130	117	569	....	....	....
India	60	9	44	....	....	....
China	....	....	....	10	1	5
Total.........	581,621	177,316	862,908	653,962	158,223	769,929

Tasmania and Victoria furnish the bulk of the apples and pears, Queensland and Fiji the tropical fruits, such as bananas and pineapples. The imports of apples from the United States declined from 40,024 cases, in 1885, to 9,996 cases, in 1887. The cause of the decline is attributed to the steadily increasing demand for Californian fruit in the Eastern market. Another reason is, that much of the Californian fruit of 1885 was affected with the codling moth, and prohibitory measures were adopted in the Australasian Colonies to prevent its introduction from California; yet, although the shipments which followed later in the season were wholly free from anything of the kind, dealers were somewhat shy of ordering further shipments. There is no reason why the fruit trade with the United States should not increase in the near future to very large proportions. Australia, being south of the Equator, the seasons are directly opposite from those of California, and when fruit is scarce in Australia it is most abundant there. The attention of the Oceanic Steamship Company has been recently directed to the value of this trade, and arrangements will shortly be perfected by which fruit can be carried between Sydney and San Francisco at lower rates and in better condition than formerly. The Steamship Company, it is also said, have determined to shorten the journey between San Francisco and Sydney, placing new vessels on the line, and accelerating the speed of their vessels.

The bulk of tinned or canned fruit imported into New South Wales is of American manufacture. The neighbouring colonies have not been able to supply the home demand. Fruit suitable for tinning is not cultivated in sufficient quantities to admit of the industry being profitable here for some time to come. All the principal American manufacturers are represented in Australia, and the various brands of the Cutting Packing Company, W. T. Coleman & Co., and many others, are quite as well known here as in the United States. Indeed, there are no other kinds of preserved fruits, except those imported in bottles from Great Britain, which enter into serious competition with the American.

The Australians have always been very partial to English bottled fruit, and there is no doubt the imports are of excellent quality, but they are much more expensive than the tinned fruits, and do not come within the reach of the classes who would be likely to increase the consumption; besides, the cost of packing fruit in bottles is more than in tins, and there is a further loss on account of breakage. A few American manufacturers have introduced into Australia various kinds of bottled fruit, but their products are not sufficiently known to come into competition with the English bottled fruit.

The imports of all kinds of tinned or preserved fruits into New South Wales during the year 1886, exclusive of jams and jellies, amounted to 1,298,644 lb., valued at £27,414 ($133,410), against 855,765 lb., valued at £18,132 ($88,239) for the year 1887.

The following table shows the quantity and value of tinned and preserved fruits, exclusive of jams and jellies, imported into New South Wales for each year, from 1880 to 1887 inclusive :—

Year.	Quantity.	Value.	
	lb.	£	$
1880	300,175	10,252	49,891
1881	614,145	19,487	94,833
1882	1,120,095	35,636	173,423
1883	882,975	26,547	129,191
1884	1,127,891	34,251	166,682
1885	1,281,901	36,313	176,717
1886	1,298,644	27,414	133,410
1887	855,765	18,132	88,239

Considerable quantities of American fruits, reach here by way of London and do not show in the returns, for, when shipped that way, they are entered as British produce.

The following table shows the direct imports of preserved or tinned fruits from the United States for each year from 1880 to 1887 inclusive :—

Year.	Quantity.	Value.	
	lb.	£	$
1880	40,244	1,226	5,967
1881	175,620	4,706	22,902
1882	647,633	19,461	94,607
1883	286,207	7,381	35,920
1884	423,750	11,960	54,797
1885	615,199	17,159	83,505
1886	483,696	9,675	47,083
1887	604,513	12,175	59,250

The imports of American tinned fruits would be much larger than at present if it were not for the Customs duty charged upon all such imports. There is, however, every prospect that these duties will be repealed during 1888.

A number of American firms have recently introduced several brands of Californian raisins that are highly appreciated. Mr. Charles Markell, of Boston, Mass., who has given much study to the condition of the fruit trade of this Colony, states that nothing stands in the way of the enlargement of the trade in American raisins except the method of packing them. They should be packed in air-tight cases similar to those in which dried fruit is brought from Spain.

The jams and jellies made in the Colonies are, with few exceptions, inferior to those imported from the United States and Europe. The principal supply for this market comes from Tasmania, but the Tasmanian product is much cheaper than the American. The Sydney market appears to be glutted with this kind of fruit, yet, notwithstanding its low price, it is a matter of surprise that people use it, as the greater part is indifferent in quality. The total value of the jams and jellies imported into New South Wales for the year 1887 was £63,352 ($308,303).

The subjoined table shows the quantity and value of jams and jellies imported into New South Wales for each year from 1877 to 1887 inclusive :—

Year.	Quantity.	Value.		Year.	Quantity.	Value.	
	lb.	£	$		lb.	£	$
1877	2,654,422	77,686	378,059	1883	4,310,945	106,647	518,998
1878	2,738,561	80,777	393,101	1884	4,121,944	101,702	494,933
1879	2,507,385	69,243	336,971	1885	3,795,774	85,321	415,215
1880	2,499,585	65,949	320,941	1886	3,878,060	73,101	356,746
1881	3,156,769	85,531	416,237	1887	3,501,669	63,352	308,303
1882	4,664,455	130,176	633,502				

In the southern portions of Australia there are few indigenous fruits, a small cherry with the seed outside, a diminutive wild grape in the mountains, and a few unimportant nuts form the list of the indigenous fruits. In the north, however, the case is altogether different, for there the pine-apple, banana, cocoanut, mangrove, and many other kinds of fruit and nuts are found to be indigenous. Mr. James Harold, of Sydney, is of opinion that Southern Australia was not originally destitute of fruit, and accounts for its disappearance through the neglect of the aboriginal inhabitants to cultivate fruit.

Almost all the European fruits that have been introduced here grow extremely well, and there is reason to believe that the cultivation of fruit will become one of the most important industries of Australia. With the exception of the grape, the orange is the most profitable fruit cultivated in New South Wales, and it is said on high authority that the orange groves of the Parramatta district, near Sydney, are equal to any in the world, and that the trees are unsurpassed. They appear to have been planted there soon after the foundation of the Colony. Some of the trees are known to be over sixty years of age, and they are still in their full vigour, and look as if they would last a century longer. They are certainly not less than 40 or 50 feet in height, and measure nearly 6 feet in circumference. Some idea of their productiveness can be formed from a recent statement that over 10,000 oranges were gathered from a single tree in one season. The principal variety of oranges grown in Australia is known as "The Parramatta," or "Poor Man's Orange." It is the common Rio orange, and came here from Brazil in the early days of the Colony. The variety known as the Navel does extremely well in various parts of the Colony, and sells for more than double the price of the Parramatta, but it is not extensively cultivated. It thrives best on the loamy soils, with water in easy reach of the tap-roots, so that they can spread out afar their network of lateral rootlets through a warm friable surface mould. The tree was brought here from Batavia, and was subsequently introduced into California as the Australian Navel, where it was rechristened Washington Navel. Nearly all the varieties of the Mandarin, or Chinese orange, thrive in New South Wales, and especially in the valley of the Hawkesbury River. Land suitable for orange groves can be obtained between Gosford and Newcastle at from £10 ($49) to £15 ($73) per acre, and between Parramatta and Windsor at from £20 ($97) to £30 ($146) per acre. Gordon is said to be the best orange district in the Colony. Land there costs between £40 ($195) and £50 ($243) per acre. The estimated cost for fencing, clearing, ploughing, and planting is £25 ($122) per acre. The trees begin to bear the fourth or fifth year. Mr. W. H. Keown, of Roseville, Gordon, states that he realised from his orange trees in the season of 1887 fully £50 per acre, and that he has great faith in the cultivation becoming profitable. The ground was trenched to a depth of about 2 feet. Grapes for wine appear to do better in the interior than along the coast. The peach does extremely well in Australia, especially in New South Wales and Victoria. The "Royal George" is one of the most valuable varieties. It has, however, a different name in almost every district. In New England it is called the "Murphy Seedling," and on the Manara Plains,

"Smith's Seedling." The apple, pear, quince, apricot, persimmon, plum, cherry, and many other fruits do quite as well here as the peach and grape. Passion-fruit, a fruit almost unknown in California, is found here in abundance. The cherries of the mountain districts are regarded as amongst the largest and finest in the world. Peanuts do not appear to do well.

The almond, walnut, and hickory nut are often met with; the two latter are not so common as the former. Melons of all kinds grow to great size, and are quite equal in flavour to those grown on the Pacific slope of the United States. Fruit of all kinds, however, is dear in Sydney, and the condition in which it is brought to market reflects very little credit upon those engaged in the trade.

Oranges and lemons are the only fruits cultivated for export in New South Wales. During the present year quite an impetus has been given to the orange trade by the exertions of several wealthy fruit-growers. Sir Henry Holland, Secretary of State for the Colonies, has addressed a circular letter to the Premier of this Colony, requesting certain information in regard to the development of the orange industry in Australia. The information collected by the Premier in response to the circular will be of value when published. The total quantity of fruit, the produce of the Colony, exported from New South Wales during the year 1886 amounted to 332,939 cases, valued at £112,169 ($545,870), against 450,837 cases, valued at £147,588 ($718,237), for the year 1887.

The following table shows the quantity and value of fruit, the produce of the Colony, principally oranges, exported from New South Wales for each year from 1877 to 1887 inclusive:—

Year.	Quantity.	Value.		Year.	Quantity.	Value.	
	packages.	£	$		packages.	£	$
1877	194,061	64,486	313,821	1883	377,925	117,224	570,471
1878	174,253	71,189	346,441	1884	245,859	98,339	478,567
1879	223,920	86,667	421,765	1885	290,250	114,501	557,219
1880	237,041	90,381	439,849	1886	332,939	112,169	545,870
1881	309,247	106,185	516,749	1887	450,837	147,588	718,237
1882	214,773	88,198	429,216				

Nearly all this fruit was shipped to the neighbouring Colonies, the bulk of it going to Victoria and Queensland. The former Colony in 1887 received 248,016 cases, valued at £73,763 ($358,968), and the latter 115,084 cases, valued at £44,039 ($214,316).

The subjoined table shows the quantity and value of fruit exports from New South Wales for 1886 and 1887, with the names of the countries whence exported:—

Country.	1886.			1887.		
	Quantity.	Value.		Quantity.	Value.	
	pkgs.	£	$	pkgs.	£	$
Great Britain.........	1,472	478	2,326	6,520	2,865	13,943
Victoria	184,636	55,681	270,971	248,016	73,763	358,968
South Australia ...	241	105	511	5,284	1,338	6,511
Tasmania	10,862	4,693	22,839	17,011	6,078	29,579
New Zealand	44,044	14,304	69,610	57,936	19,114	93,018
Queensland............	90,848	36,514	177,695	115,084	44,039	214,316
South Sea Islands...	10	7	34	3	2	10
New Caledonia	507	265	1,290	480	253	1,231
Fiji	188	96	467	75	23	112
Western Australia..	131	26	127	....	....	....
United States......	....	....	....	45	17	83
India	....	....	....	374	96	467

The successful shipment of a few small lots of fruit to the Colonial Exhibition in London paved the way for the establishment of an extensive trade in this article between Sydney and Great Britain. Mr. Alexander Wood, Agent-General for Canada to New South Wales, has recently pointed out the fact that Australian oranges occasionally find their way to the Canadian market by way of London, and he is very decided in the opinion that fruit can be profitably exported from Sydney to Central Canada and the north-western portions of the United States. The shipment of oranges direct to London, a distance of about 14,000 miles, is believed to have passed through an experimental stage. Already the Orient Steamship Company have expended large sums in fitting up chambers in their vessels for the shipment of fruit. The "Lusitania," on the 4th of November, 1887, carried with her 1,000 cases of oranges. Mr. Cairns, of Parramatta, is preparing to make, on the part of the orange growers, further shipments upon a more extensive scale. In the meantime the Orient Company have reduced the price of freights on fruit to about £4 ($19) per ton of 40 cubic feet.

Already the public press in Great Britain draw attention to the arrival of consignments of New South Wales fruit as an incident of no ordinary nature. The success of these experimental essays is sufficient to warrant the conclusion that with careful selection and packing Australian oranges and lemons will admit of regular transmission to Great Britain, in prime condition, at a period when the ordinary supply of the orange-producing countries of the Northern Hemisphere is usually suspended. The question of packing constitutes the chief difficulty which prevents Australia becoming the principle supplier of the fruit markets of Europe. The fruit referred to was packed in sawdust and paper dipped in a patent antiseptic preparation, the invention of Dr. John Storer of Sydney, which preserves the fruit and has the advantage of not necessitating any special stowage, but enables the fruit to be carried as ordinary cargo, notwithstanding a voyage of over fifty days.

The disparity of climate, and the facility of quick transit offered by the vessels of the great steam-shipping companies visiting the ports of Sydney and Newcastle, will enable good kinds of oranges to be laid down at a profit in the markets of North America and England, and will remove the orange-growers' chief complaint, that the demand for their produce in Australian Colonies is largely exceeded by the supply. It must, however, be noted that the average price of oranges in the Australian markets is excessive for the kinds which would obtain a sale in foreign markets. There are certainly immense numbers of oranges grown, but the general quality is defective. Orange-growers will now, doubtless, see the necessity of cultivating only the best varieties.

The following table shows the area of orangeries and the production of oranges for each year from 1879 to 1887:—

Year ending 31 March.	Area of Orangeries.	Production.	Average production per acre.
	Acres.	Dozen.	Dozen.
1879	4,287	3,398,445	793
1880	5,106	2,763,811	541
1881	5,939	3,810,356	642
1882	6,301	5,164,134	820
1883	6,717	4,978,820	741
1884	7,269	8,102,658	1,115
1885	6,912	4,097,666	593
1886	7,734	8,749,256	1,131
1887	7,920	6,376,868	805

WINE.

The quantity of wine imported into the Colony of New South Wales during the year 1887 was 195,894 gallons, valued at £100,578 ($489,463) against 185,022 gallons, valued at £109,680 ($533,855), for the year 1886.

Of the wine imported in 1887, 175,244 gallons consisted of still wine and 20,650 gallons of sparkling wine.

The following table shows the quantity and value of still and sparkling wine imported into the Colony of New South Wales for each year from 1880 to 1887, inclusive:—

Year.	Still Wine.			Sparkling Wine.		
	Quantity.	Value.		Quantity.	Value.	
	Gallons.	£	$	Gallons.	£	$
1880	167,961	56,881	276,811	10,442	17,792	86,585
1881	199,636	73,859	359,435	19,092	28,972	140,992
1882	235,499	85,141	414,338	10,803	18,080	87,986
1883	237,478	97,058	474,333	30,179	49,215	239,505
1884	181,015	77,963	379,407	27,226	47,286	230,117
1885	214,158	86,002	418,529	28,344	50,910	247,754
1886	159,956	64,036	311,631	25,066	45,644	222,224
1887	175,244	64,531	313,067	20,650	36,047	175,423

The fact that little or no California wine is used in New South Wales has been a subject of observation and inquiry. In the year 1882 only 6 gallons of American wine were entered at the Customs. In 1883 the amount was 63 gallons, but in 1884 not a single gallon was imported. The imports for 1883 consisted of a few choice varieties of Californian champagne. The wine was sampled by experts, who spoke highly of its flavour, but at the same time said that it was not of sufficient alcoholic strength to become popular in this market. The wine failing to meet with a ready sale, no further effort appears to have been made to introduce it again. It is hardly reasonable to suppose that the people here would continue the importation of the bad and adulterated wines of Europe if they were once made familiar with the very choice quality of the American product. It is said, however, that American manufacturers are perfectly indifferent about cultivating a foreign trade for their wines so long as they are enabled to find a brisk and profitable market at home.

The following table shows the exports of wines (still), the produce of New South Wales, in each year, from 1877 to 1887 inclusive:—

Year.	Quantity.	Value.	
	Gallons.	£	s
1877	10,591	4,502	21,909
1878	9,969	4,910	23,895
1879	17,519	6,965	33,895
1880	27,584	7,359	35,813
1881	22,377	7,233	35,199
1882	22,425	7,166	34,874
1883	43,288	14,430	70,224
1884	29,157	10,816	52,636
1885	28,499	8,156	39,691
1886	24,217	7,581	36,893
1887	17,718	6,654	32,382

TABLE showing the quantity and value of Wine, the produce of New South Wales, and the countries to which exported, during the years 1886 and 1887.

	Quantity.	Value.	
1886.	Gallons.	£	s
Great Britain	17,270	4,197	20,425
Victoria	897	269	1,309
Tasmania	107	53	258
New Zealand	2,737	1,649	8,025
Queensland	1,352	731	3,557
Other countries	1,854	682	3,319
Total	24,217	7,581	36,893
1887.			
Great Britain	7,447	2,457	11,957
Victoria	1,892	553	2,691
Tasmania	240	104	506
New Zealand	2,942	1,726	8,400
Queensland	2,205	1,076	5,237
Other countries	2,992	738	3,591
Total	17,718	6,654	32,382

New South Wales heretofore took the lead of all the other Colonies, not only in the production of wine but in the average quantity to the acre; but as far as production is concerned, Victoria, in the year 1886, became the first in the list, when she produced 1,003,827 gallons of wine and 3,875 gallons of brandy against 601,897 gallons of wine and 763 gallons of brandy for New South Wales; but the total product of the whole of Australasia is behind that of 1876, and probably does not amount to one-fifth of the average product of the State of California alone. A new impetus, however, has been given to the wine industry here on account of the prevailing opinion that the duties now charged in England on Colonial wines will shortly be abolished or reduced to a minimum.

o

The Agents-General of the Colonies at London, who have for some time been strongly pressing the reduction of the wine duties upon the British Government, are said to have at last succeeded in obtaining a promise that active steps shall be taken to secure the desired concession.

Sir S. Griffith, the Premier of Queensland, telegraphed to the Victorian Government that the Agent-General of his Government was instructed to co-operate with his colleagues in making representations with this object to the Imperial Government. The difficulty heretofore has been to secure united action on the part of the Agents-General; but now this having been accomplished, the only difficulty in the way seems to be the opposition of the British distillers and the London agents of the Continental wine-growers, who labor under the impression that the high alcoholic strength of Australian wines would lead to their substitution for spirits, and also for stronger kinds of European wines, such as port and sherry. The duties on the latter form an important item of imperial revenue, and all Chancellors of the Exchequer very naturally oppose any attempt to reduce them. Mr. Gladstone in 1860 reduced to a trifling figure the high duties on light wines, which for a century and a half shut out from England the produce of the French vineyards. Many thought that his object was to provide a cure for intemperance by placing mild wines within the reach of the people. To France it opened up a market for one of her most important products, and there was an immediate extension of vine planting in that country. It is often said that almost any kind of wine is good enough for the English market, but there is little truth in the statement. It stands to reason and common sense that there would be much better demand for Australian wine, not only in England but everywhere else, if more pains were taken in its manufacture. It is possible, that much of the wine sold in England as Australian may have been manufactured somewhere else. Complaint, however, has become so general against the so-called Colonial wine that a syndicate has been formed in London exclusively for the introduction of Australian wines, and Mr. Burgoyne, well-known in connection with the London wine trade, has leased the old Dowgate bonded vaults for the purpose of storing Australian wine. These vaults are capable of holding over 10,000 hogsheads. The offices and cellars of the firm are in Old Bond-street. The block of buildings are, as reconstructed, amongst the finest in London.

That the British Government is favourable to low duties on wines is shown by their admission of wines of 26° of alcoholic strength and under at 1s. (24 cents) per gallon. The duty on wine of 40° of spirit is 2s. 6d. (60 cents) per gallon. A tendency towards the reduction of duties was also shown by the favourable consideration given to the proposition submitted to the Anglo-Spanish convention to admit all Spanish wines up to 30° of alcoholic strength at 1s. (24 cents) per gallon. It is thought here that the reduction of the duties on Colonial wines would lead to extensive vine planting throughout Australasia. Mr. Henry Bonnard, the Executive Secretary of the New South Wales Commission at the Bordeaux International Exhibition, however, is opposed to the reduction of the duties. He says: "If the Colonies should succeed in bringing about a reduction of the duties on all Colonial wines imported into Great Britain, the result will in the end be very different from what they expect, for it will encourage them more than ever to produce wines of high alcoholic strength, a practice which has already done so much to injure the Colonial wine industry. There is, of course, in England a taste amongst the lower classes for strong drinks, such as brandy, whisky, and gin, but the climate there seems to create a preference for beer; therefore the consumption of wine will always be limited amongst the great mass of the English people. The higher classes prefer wine, but they want mild, soft wines, like those of France. Port and sherry are getting out of favor, owing principally to the spurious alcohol they contain."

Whether the duties are moderated or not, strong efforts will be made both here and in England to encourage the Australian wine industry. It is certain that the soil and climate of no inconsiderable portion of this great island continent are especially adapted to viticulture. The grape has been grown successfully in Queensland within three degrees of the tropics and as far south as the 38th parallel of south latitude in Victoria. There is an immense stretch of country in Australia from 1,200 to 2,000 feet above the sea where the climate resembles that of France and Italy.

The vineyards of New South Wales, and especially those in the valley of the Hunter River, appear to be in a much better condition than those of any other part of Australia. It is claimed, however, that Victoria possesses the largest vineyards, and that the grape for wine purposes is cultivated to a higher degree of perfection there than in any of the other Colonies. The vine-growers, however, of New South Wales are disposed to question the accuracy of the latter statement.

The St. Hubert vineyard is said to be the largest and finest in Victoria. It is situated in the valley of the Upper Yarra, and contains about 300 acres of vines. It is so highly cultivated that not a weed can be seen between the vines. One of the most interesting features connected with this vineyard is the many different varieties of grapes cultivated in it. M. de Charney, the well-known *vigneron*, visited the vineyard, and he was disposed to regard it as a magnificent experiment for the purpose of showing the best kinds of vines to be cultivated. He found the Sauvignon of Bordeaux, the Pineau of Burgundy, and the Chasselas of Fontainebleau, all growing with as much luxuriance as in Europe. The ground was divided into large blocks for each kind of grape vine. M. de Charney was surprised to learn that the wine made from these grapes preserved all the peculiar properties and flavour of the original stock, which, he said, was contrary to the law of assimilation and must sooner or later disappear, inasmuch as every species of vegetation, as well as every species of living beings, is modified by outward influences of soil, climate, habits, and food, and the transformation is more rapid as the organization of the individual is less perfect. He said: "It is evident that this vineyard, producing several wines, each of perfectly distinct character, will eventually produce only two types, the red and the white, which will bear uniform products and will no longer be similar to European wine, but will be Australian St. Hubert wines, but none the less delicious."

One of the largest vineyards in New South Wales belongs to Mr. J. T. Fallon, a gentleman who has had much experience in vine growing. His vineyard consists of 160 acres in the district of Albury, in the valley of the Murray, one of the finest rivers in Australia. The Murray Valley Vineyard produced, in one year, 63,315 gallons of wine. The quality of the wine is said to be very superior, and when it has aged a little more, it will be equal to the celebrated samples of Muscat, Burgundy, Tokay, and Cabernet that were sent to the International Exhibition at Bordeaux in 1882. The average alcoholic strength of the wines Mr. Fallon exhibited at Bordeaux was 26·84 per cent. Some of his brown Muscat averaged 33 per cent. The average strength of French wines exhibited was 17 per cent., the highest being 24 per cent. The cost of cultivating Mr. Fallon's vineyard was estimated at £25 ($121) per acre. His wine carried off the silver medal. The selling price of his red wine is about 30s. ($7) per dozen bottles.

Mr. Bonnard gives the following analysis of New South Wales wine :—

Table showing analyses of New South Wales wine.

Names of Exhibitors	Analysed Wines.	Alcohol in weight.	Density.	Saccharine matters.	Tannin.	Bitartrate of potassium.	Acidity.	Mineral salts.	Sulphate of potassium.	Coloring matter.	Unanalysed elements.	Total of solid elements in wine.
J. T. Fallon	Cabernet, 1869	121·00	0·992	5·18	·61	{ 2·52 / 0·28 }	3·86	3·10	0·62	0·84	12·0	20·0
Do.	Red, 1882				·74							
Hon. W. Macleay.	Malbec, 1873	117·60	0·990	0·82	·64	{ 4·32 / 0·48 }	5·42	3·40	·60	0·92	7·20	23·80
Dr. C. Mackay	La Bruscat, 1875	115·23	0·991	1·14	·48	{ 2·84 / 0·31 }	4·25	3·37	·64	0·50	10·37	23·90
W. Wyndham	Hermitage, 1876	143·	0·991	6·96	·88	{ 3·82 / 0·42 }	5·18	3·48	·52	0·76	14·48	36·50
J. Kelman	do	106·50	0·993	0·38	·63	{ 2·88 / 0·32 }	3·12	3·26	·55	0·86	12·25	24·25
Wyndeyer	Madeira, 1876	123·	0·991	2·40	·18	{ 3·08 / 0·33 }	3·75	3·20	·48	(*)	8·72	22·20
Wilkinson	Hermitage, 1876	115·	0·989	1·98	·10	{ 2·80 / 0·31 }	3·20	3·47	·44	(*)	8·00	20·30
G. Francis	Isabella, 1881	124·	1·004	29·45	·69	{ 2·25 / 0·25 }	5·20	3·02	·54	0·45	6·04	48·60
A. Munro	{ Hermitage, sweet, 1877 }	149·50	1·067	135·80	·68	{ 2·06 / 0·29 }	4·	3·90	·61	0·90	10·85	160·
J. Wyndham	{ Pineau noir, 1879 }	103·31	0·990	1·23	·43	{ 3·06 / 0·34 }	4·40	4·46	·96	0·48	10·89	26·25
Do	Red, 1882				·45							
A Murray	do				·78							

* White wine.

WINE.

Result of an analysis by late Mr. Chas. Watt, Government Analyst, on twelve samples of Colonial wine submitted for examination by the Chief Inspector of Distilleries:—

No.	Description.	Spec. grav. of wine.	Spec. grav. of alcohol yielded.	Percentage of absolute alcohol by weight.	Percentage of proof spirit.	Percentage of acid.	Grains of acid per gallon.	Total of extract.	Remarks.
1	Port Wine	1·0115	·9760	16·42	35·46	·48	326·0	9·70	⎫ Inferior articles; appear to have been made up.
2	do.	1·0084	·9780	14·75	31·99	·50	350·0	8·34	⎬
3	Sherry	1·0183	·9780	14·77	25·50	·52	364·0	7·08	⎭
4	do.	·9912	·9707	13·39	28·95	·67	409·0	3·10	Fairly good Colonial sherry.
5	Port Wine	1·0044	·9829	10·91	23·76	1·99	1,393·0	4·34	This article contained much acetic acid, and was more a vinegar than a wine.
6	do.	1·0102	·9784	14·42	31·22	·53	371·0	7·08	Inferior article; appears to have been made up.
7	Madeira	·9979	·9806	12·09	27·48	·45	336·0	5·02	⎫
8	Vin ordinaire	·9974	·9818	11·77	25·50	·75	525·0	4·48	⎬ These are all good sound wines.
9	Claret	1·0052	·9828	11·00	23·87	·61	427·0	4·60	⎭
10	Port Wine	1·0031	·9753	17·09	36·61	·62	423·0	7·50	
11	Muscat	1·0102	·9798	14·00	30·26	·65	455·0	4·30	⎫ Very good.
12	do.	·9945	·9770	15·58	33·78	·52	364·0	4·10	⎭

No foreign colouring matter or anything noxious was detected in any of these samples.

At the International Exhibition at Sydney, the light wines of Australia were preferred to all others. M. Jules Joubert, who reported for the judges, stated that the wines, spirits, and liquors submitted were, with few exceptions, creditable alike to the countries whence they came and to the producers. The Commission adjudicated upon some thousands of samples, which were classed as follows:—

1, Australian (light and full bodied); 2, French; 3, German; 4, Austrian and Hungarian; 5, Italian; 6, Spanish and Portuguese; 7, Sparkling Wines (all nations); 8, Brandies; 9, Whiskies; 10, Gin; 11, Rum; 12, Liquors. Judges were appointed for each group, the instructions from the Commission being to classify the wines and to append to them numbers ranging from 1 to 4 for each separate section. The wines, spirits, and liquors were brought into the Judges' room in wine glasses bearing a distinguishing number only. A list was prepared of wines to be judged on each day, containing, besides the distinguishing numbers above mentioned, the nationality, age, name of grape, strength, where obtainable, quantity for sale, and price. The Judges began their duties on the 22nd of January, and completed them on the 24th of March, after holding fifty-one meetings. The French Wines, with four exceptions, were said to be in bad condition; the red wines from the same country were superior to the white, but the majority were harsh, heavy, and deficient in bouquet.

The competing Colonial wines were from New South Wales, Victoria, South Australia, Queensland, Western Australia, and New Zealand. The wines were perfectly distinct in character. The climate and soil of Victoria and New South Wales, more particularly as regards the Upper Yarra in the former and the valley of the Hunter in the latter, were found to produce wines assimilating to those of Burgundy and Bordeaux, whereas those from the Murray and South Australia will become fair substitutes for Spanish, Portuguese, Madeira, and Cape wines. The exhibits from Queensland were few, and inferior to those of the other Colonies. Queensland rum, however, was declared to be of excellent quality. New Zealand excelled in wines, syrups, and liquors extracted from fruit other than the grape. The Commission, in concluding its report, recommended that some of the cheap wines of Australia be sent to France for blending purposes.

The wine industry of the Colony, notwithstanding the quality of the vintage, and the great interest taken in it, both here and in England, has not made a corresponding advance. The quantity produced during 1887 was only 601,897 gallons, against 602,000 gallons for 1881.

The following table shows the quantity of wine made in New South Wales for each year from 1881 to 1887 inclusive:—

Year.	Quantity.	Year.	Quantity.
	Gallons.		Gallons.
1881	602,000	1885	442,012
1882	513,600	1886	555,470
1883	543,600	1887	601,897
1884	589,604		

The vintage of 1888 will probably be smaller than that of 1887, although the grapes for table use are said to be of better quality and more abundant than usual.

The cultivation of the grapes of Australia, especially for the manufacture of wine, is an industry capable of expansion, but, strange to say, no successful attempt has ever been made here to manufacture raisins. The judges at Bordeaux expressed the opinion that the kind of grapes cultivated in Australia for wine-making purposes do not ripen fast enough, and the vintage being thus delayed, acquires a greater alcoholic strength than necessary. The grapes, moreover, do not gather, either from their skins or stalks, tannin enough to assist in making good wine. M. Bonnard does not think that Colonial wines improve after four or five years. He says, however, that the samples taken by him to Bordeaux and back were improved by the sea voyage. He thinks that they have more solid matter than California wines, but less acidity and colour, and that those at present engaged in wine making in the Colony continue to grow the wrong kind of vines, and refuse to profit by the experience of others. He deprecates their attempts at making champagne and white wine, for which he says they have neither the requisite knowledge nor skill. He admits that their white wine is popular, but says there is no great demand for any kind of white wine on the Continent, and that the colonists would find it much more advantageous to turn their attention to the manufacture of brandy, from the fact that it is almost impossible to obtain genuine spirits of wine in any part of Europe.

The disease known as the *Phylloxera vastatrix* has made its appearance in various parts of Australia, and M. Bonnard is apprehensive that unless some more effective means are adopted than at present the whole of the vineyards of this Colony will eventually be destroyed. At the request of the New South Wales Government in 1884, he visited about 300 vineyards, and found that the insect existed in one district only. Since that time, he says, the disease has been distributed by roots and cuttings in other directions.

The *Phylloxera* appeared in Victoria in 1875, and was for a considerable period confined to the Geelong district, and extended from the Leigh Road to Germantown, a distance of 16 miles. An Act of Parliament was passed in 1878 for the purpose of getting rid of the pest, but failing in its object, subsequent Acts were passed by which the Minister of Agriculture was authorized to order, whenever it should be deemed necessary, the destruction of all vines found growing in infected districts

BEER.

The quantity of beer and ale imported into New South Wales during the year 1886 was 2,330,476 gallons, valued at £419,454 ($2,041,273), against 2,334,228 gallons, valued at £382,843 ($1,863,105), for the year 1887. Of the bottled beer Great Britain furnished 1,189,199 gallons; Victoria, 38,039 gallons; South Australia, 36,254 gallons; Queensland, 2,570 gallons; New Zealand, 547 gallons; United States, 243,809 gallons; Belgium, 6,115 gallons; and Germany, 81,399 gallons.

The subjoined table shows the quantity and value of beer and ale in bottle imported into New South Wales from all countries for each year from 1879 to 1887 inclusive :—

Year.	Quantity.	Value.		Year.	Quantity.	Value.	
	gallons.	£	$		gallons.	£	$
1879	762,031	166,174	808,686	1883	1,072,783	232,875	1,133,286
1880	678,172	113,481	552,235	1884	1,139,925	262,697	1,278,415
1881	562,958	123,054	598,842	1885	1,444,911	319,690	1,555,772
1882	926,075	195,440	951,112	1886	1,598,760	346,006	1,683,838
				1887	1,442,697	291,305	1,417,636

The following table shows the quantity and value of bottled beer and ale imported into New South Wales from Great Britain for each year from 1879 to 1887 inclusive :—

Year.	Quantity.	Value.		Year.	Quantity.	Value.	
	gallons.	£	$		gallons.	£	$
1879	667,983	144,284	702,158	1883	951,892	203,833	991,954
1880	597,675	94,939	462,021	1884	899,809	205,197	998,591
1881	470,093	101,136	492,179	1885	1,193,725	265,913	1,293,966
1882	809,550	169,064	822,750	1886	1,189,199	255,203	1,241,846
				1887	1,108,433	227,106	1,105,211

The demand for malt liquors here continues brisk and steady, and especially for favourite brands.

The beer imported in casks or barrels and sold here on draught is not so much liked as that imported in bottles.

The following table shows the quantity and value of the ale and beer imported into New South Wales in casks from all countries from 1879 to 1887 inclusive :—

Year.	Quantity.	Value.		Year.	Quantity.	Value.	
	gallons.	£	$		gallons.	£	$
1879	631,225	79,491	386,843	1883	518,330	57,731	281,143
1880	585,655	68,433	332,024	1884	574,926	60,268	293,289
1881	510,384	62,447	303,698	1885	654,646	69,992	340,616
1882	397,275	44,508	216,598	1886	731,716	73,448	357,435
				1887	891,531	91,538	445,740

The method employed in bottling beer is different from that in the United States. The process is not only more expensive, but the bottles are much heavier, and are without the attractive labels of the American manufacturers. Although the terms "beer" and "ale" are used here as synonymous, there is of course a difference, especially in regard to the method of brewing. The two substances, however, are essentially the same until the yeast is added. English, or British, ale is the product of what is called upper fermentation. It is said that in the process of manufacturing English beer the wort, or malt, is started at a temperature of more than 50° Fahrenheit. The fermentation, or conversion of the saccharine matter, being pushed forward rapidly, the yeast and clearings rise to the surface, and a considerable quantity of soluble gluten is left in the liquor, which upon exposure to the air has a tendency to cause the alcohol to ferment into vinegar and sour the beer. Lager, or Bavarian beer, on the other hand, is manufactured by a slower process. Mr. G. Pomeroy Keese, a high authority on the subject, states that in the manufacture of this kind of beer the wort is started with free exposure to the air, at a temperature under 50° Fahrenheit, by a kind of yeast which produces oxidation by a slow combustion. Less alcohol is produced. The product of oxidation is carried with this under-yeast to the bottom, as a sediment, and there is little gluten left to start the conversion of alcohol into vinegar. This is the lager beer, or store beer, of Bavaria, as distinguished from the *schenk-bier*, for immediate sale in winter, and its brewing was confined by law to the cool weather between October and April. The same authority states that American brewers use the word "beer" as synonymous with the above, but refrigerating methods enable them to disregard the outside temperature. It is enough to mention that in the slower process of fermentation much more nourishment is left in the beer, and the fermentation which follows developes a certain amount of carbonic acid gas. This gas is retained and the beer is kept clear. Ale, on the contrary, unless allowed to ferment in bottles, contains little or no carbonic acid gas, and, if brought below a temperature of about 65°, becomes flat and cloudy, and must be brewed strong to enable it to stand transportation and storage. English ale contains fully 9 per cent. of alcohol, whereas American lager beer seldom contains more than 4 or 4½ per cent. of alcohol. Of imported ales Bass's pale ale is the most generally used in the Australasian Colonies. Next to that comes Tennant's, then Allsops', McEwan's, and others. Those who purchase Bass's ale do not inquire for it as such, but ask for the bottled. For instance, Foster's ale is Bass's ale bottled by Foster. There are other popular bottlers. Another method of distinguishing ale is by the brand; for instance, the Bull Dog, or the Bugle brand.

Very little stout is imported here in casks, the great bulk coming in bottles. It is not kept on draught in any of the hotels. The following are the names of the principal brands of bottled stout sold here: Hall's Boarshead brand, Edmunds' Pighead brand, Foster's Bugle brand, Fish brand, Dauke's, and McEwan's Globe.

The value of the imports of American lager beer into New South Wales has increased so rapidly during the last few years that the industry bids fair to swell to large proportions. The people are beginning to find out that American beers are much better adapted to the Australian climate than those of English make.

It has been noticed that American beer is not only more nourishing than English ale, but is of a finer flavour. It does not contain, as previously mentioned, so large a proportion of alcohol, as the English and other imported beers, and is also comparatively free from stupefying and deleterious effects; moreover, it has been found to stand export quite as well as the English article. Although a larger quantity of beer is manufactured in Great Britain than in the United States, the growth of the industry in the latter country has been greater than in the former. It has recently been pointed out by Mr. L. Sackville-West, the British Minister at Washington, that the consumption of beer in the United States has increased during the last forty years at the rate of 642 per cent. per head, while spirits had decreased during the same period at the rate of 40 per cent. per head. The extraordinary growth of the American industry is in great measure to be attributed to the quality of the beer, and to the low prices at which the manufacturers are enabled to supply it. The American breweries are admitted to be complete and as well equipped in every way as any others in the world. The refrigerating machines and other cooling appliances have never been excelled by anything of the kind in Europe. Besides, several of the American breweries are conducted on a larger scale than any of the European establishments.

Attention was directed to the quality of American beer during the Sydney International Exhibition in 1879. That made by George Bechtel, of New York, received the first degree of merit. It was praised for its rich amber colour, full flavour, and fine hop aroma. The commission also highly commended the beer of Wise & Co., of Chicago, Ill. The fact that American beer was used in preference to any other by the passengers on the Pacific Mail steamers running between San Francisco and Australia did much towards making it popular here. It soon became very generally advertised throughout the Colonies, and now the leading hotels are pushing the various brands of Anheuser-Busch & Co., Clausen & Co., Philip Best & Co., and others. Butcher, Fehon, & Co., are the Sydney agents for the original Budweiser beer of the Anheuser-Busch Brewing Association, and for the Saint Louis Standard lager beer; Barron, Moxham, & Co. sell "W. J. Lemp's Saint Louis beer"; Walker Lemon and Co., Clausen's New York beer; and S. Marks, the Chicago Star lager beer. The recent publication of a series of valuable papers in the *New York Australasian*, on the manufacture and export of American beer, has done much to give an impetus to the trade, for the papers referred to have been extensively copied in the colonial newspapers.

The following table shows the quantity and value of bottled beer imported into New South Wales from the United States for each year since 1880:—

Year.	Quantity.	Value.		Year.	Quantity.	Value.	
	Gallons.	£	$		Gallons.	£	$
1880	1,777	308	1,499	1884	43,055	10,689	52,018
1881	2,634	627	3,051	1885	70,727	15,537	75,611
1882	4,434	1,023	4,978	1886	243,809	56,131	273,162
1883	4,125	955	4,648	1887	109,837	22,793	110,854

There are many favourite brands of American beer which could be advantageously introduced into the colonial market. For instance, a brisk demand has been created in Melbourne for the brand called Liebotshaner, which ought to sell readily in Sydney. It is said to be made after the Bohemian process. Its colour is very pale, being brewed of the choicest quality of malt. It has a fine fruity flavor, and a wine-like taste. Then there is another brand of beer called "pale lager." It is of light amber colour, with a small percentage of alcohol, especially adapted for hot seasons and for the use of ladies. Then there is the Faust beer. This brand was brewed originally for the establishment of A. E. Faust, of St. Louis, but is now supplied to the general trade in America. It resembles the "Standard" beer, and is not drawn for bottling purposes until after a storage of four months.

Now that American lager beer has found a lodgment in the Colonies there is no reason why some of the stronger ales could not be introduced, especially as the Colonists are partial to what are called "heavy-headed beers;" but it must be remembered that the quantity of alcohol required to give additional strength to these beers materially lessens their health-giving properties. One of the stronger American beers which would find a ready market is the "Erlander" brand. This beer is of a dark rich color, and bears a close resemblance to English porter and stout, but is greatly superior to the latter, both in flavor and nourishing qualities. The prejudice existing against American liquors in the British Colonies is gradually being overcome. Some years ago when American whiskies were first introduced into British Columbia they met with such determined opposition that the importers despaired of making any headway whatever, but in time the prejudice was overcome by excellence of quality, and the result is that the people of that colony prefer American whiskey to other kinds. The prejudice against American beer will be overcome in the same way.

During the year 1884 the German imports consisted of 86,829 gallons, valued at £19,393 ($94,376), while in 1886 only 81,399 gallons, valued at £15,161 ($73,781), were imported; and in 1887 only 73,417 gallons, valued at £12,357 ($60,135). The low price at which German beer is sold is one of the reasons of its popularity, and at present the American importers are not able to compete in price with the German article. The charges on all business transactions with Europe, such as freight, commission, insurance, exchange, in spite of the greater distance and risk, are much less than with the United States. The fact that American importers have been enabled to find a market for their merchandise in these Colonies under such circumstances is itself an evidence of the superiority of American products. It may be mentioned that during 1887 Messrs. Butcher, Fehon, & Co., imported— including imports in bond—over 1,100,000 bottles of Anheuser-Busch, St. Louis lager beer.

There are 77 breweries in the Colony of New South Wales, employing 987 hands, and the quantity of beer made in 1887 was 9,720,000 gallons. All the breweries, with perhaps one or two exceptions, have proved to be great sources of wealth to their owners. The colonial beer is nothing like as good as the imported article. The water is not always suitable for beer-making purposes, as it is not rich enough in carbonates. Professor Liversidge gives the following analysis of the water used in the principal brewing establishments in New South Wales :—

Analysis of waters—Sydney and South Creek.

Constituents.	Sydney.	South Creek.
	Grains per gallon.	Grains per gallon.
Chloride of sodium (common salt)	2·863	27·72
Chloride of potassium	0·112	......
Chloride of magnesium	0·118	3·45
Chloride of magnesia	0·059	2·48
Sulphate of magnesia	0·128	......
Sulphate of lime	0·233	1·10
Silica	0·222	1·10
Peroxide of iron with trace of phosphate of lime	0·082	......
Carbonate of lime	......	2·00
Total inorganic matter	3·817	35·85

The subjoined tables of British waters are given for comparison.

Analysis of London waters.

Constituents.	Thames water.	Kent water.
	Grains.	Grains.
Carbonate of lime	10·90	7·02
Sulphate of lime	3·26	11·03
Calcium nitrate	Trace.	·07
Magnesium carbonate	1·17	3·42
Sodium chloride	1·40	3·50
Sodium sulphate	·18	......
Potassium chloride	......	·44
Potassium sulphate	·61	·70
Silica	·45	·76
Iron oxide, alumina, and phosphates	·67	Trace.
Organic matter	3·07	2·61
Grains per gallon	21·71	29·54

Analysis of water used by Bass & Co.

Calcium carbonate	9·93
Calcium sulphate	54·40
Calcium chloride	13·28
Magnesium sulphate	·83
	78·44

The water used at Burton is from wells, and not from the Trent, as commonly supposed.

Analysis of water used by Allsop & Sons in the manufacture of their beer.

	Grains per gallon.
Sodium chloride	10·12
Potassium sulphate	7·65
Calcium sulphate	18·96
Magnesium sulphate	9·95
Calcium carbonate	15·51
Magnesium carbonate	1·70
Iron carbonate	·60
Silica	·79
Total	65·28

The water used by Tetley & Son, Leeds, has the following constituents :—

	Grains per gallon.
Calcium carbonate magnesium	19·78
Iron carbonate	·93
Calcium sulphate	4·97
Sodium sulphate	13·09
Magnesium sulphate	9·73
Sodium chloride	7·11
Magnesium chloride	4·74
Loss	1·72
Total	62·07

The beer manufactured in Victoria and Tasmania is believed to be of better quality than that of New South Wales, but the industry in neither Colony is as remunerative as in New South Wales.

The estimate for Victoria for the year ended March, 1886, was given at 14,753,152 gallons, against 14,400,749 gallons for 1885.

Table prepared by Mr. Barney, the Chief Inspector of Distilleries at Sydney, estimating the quantity of beer or ale manufactured in the Colony of New South Wales for each year, from 1881 to 1887 inclusive :—

Year.	Quantity.	Year.	Quantity.
	Gallons.		Gallons.
1881	9,642,800	1885	*14,716,000
1882	*10,800,000	1886	*13,178,912
1883	*12,175,300	1887	9,720,000
1884	*13,068,920		

* Estimates probably too high.

The Customs duty charged on all kinds of beer imported into New South Wales in bottles is 9d. (18 cents) per gallon, and 6d. (12 cents) per gallon in wood or jar.

The total quantity of hops imported into New South Wales during the year 1887 was 961,129 lb., valued at £42,173 ($205,235). Of the imports for 1887 Great Britain furnished 300,364 lb. ; United States, 49,004 lb. ; Tasmania, 170,699 lb. ; Victoria, 284,495 lb. ; South Australia, 26,710 lb. ; Queensland, 21,279 lb. ; New Zealand, 56,139 lb. ; Germany, 49,449 lb. ; and Belgium, 2,990 lb.

Hops grow very well in New Zealand and Tasmania, and they can be exported to Great Britain at a cost not exceeding 1s. 6d. (36 cents) per 100 lb. (which is considerably less than the cost of freight on hops from Kent to London). The price of hops is fluctuating. It has been known to advance to as high as 4s. 11d. ($1·20) per lb., and then decline suddenly to 6d. (12 cents) per lb.

A reason for this is that hops are only used for one purpose, and as they deteriorate rapidly by age, a good season in Germany or England would cause the price to decline at once, not only in Europe, but in the United States and elsewhere.

The bulk of the malt imported into the Colony comes from Great Britain, and the remainder from New Zealand and the other Australasian Colonies. During the year 1887 the total imports of malt into New South Wales amounted to 314,218 bushels, valued at £105,422 ($513,037). Of the imports for 1887, Great Britain furnished 266,059 bushels; New Zealand, 23,455 bushels; Victoria, 11,992 bushels; South Australia, 12,300 bushels; Tasmania, 200 bushels; Germany, 212 bushels.

The barley imports have come hitherto from the neighbouring Colonies. The total imports of barley for the year 1887 amounted to 68,424 bushels, valued at £10,215 ($49,711). Of this amount Victoria furnished 16,387 bushels; South Australia, 3,226 bushels; Tasmania, 2,576 bushels; New Zealand, 10,339 bushels. In this year the United States sent 35,896 bushels.

The large profits made both by the wholesale and retail dealers in American beer, together with the high cost of freight and the absence of a direct medium of exchange between Australia and the United States, are the principal obstacles in the way of increasing the trade to very large proportions. The American beers bring the highest price on account of their superb quality. Messrs. Butcher, Fehon, & Co., the Sydney agents, sell the St. Louis "Budweiser" wholesale at 10s. 6d. ($2·55) per 1 dozen quart bottles, and pints at 7s. ($1·70) per dozen, duty paid.

The agents of Flensburg beer charge 9s. 6d. ($2·31) per dozen quarts. Some German brands sell as low as 8s. ($1·94) per dozen quarts, and 5s. 3d. ($1·27) per dozen pints. The various brands of St. Louis, New York, Milwaukee, and Chicago beer fluctuate between 10s. 6d. ($2·55) and 12s. ($2·92) per dozen quarts, duty paid.

The following are the Sydney prices of some of the principal brands of British beer:—Foster's ale, 10s. 6d. ($2·55) per dozen; stout, 9s. 6d. ($2·31); Reid's ale, 10s. 6d. ($2·55) per dozen; stout, 9s. 6d. ($2·31); Tennant's ale, 8s. 3d. ($2) per dozen; McEwan's, 8s. 3d ($2) per dozen; stout, 7s. 6d. ($1·82); Danks' ale, 10s. 2d. ($2·49); stout, 9s. 3d. ($2·25); Porter's ale, 10s. 6d. ($2·55) per dozen; stout, 10s. ($2·43); Hall's ale, 9s. 6d. ($2·31) per dozen; stout, 9s. 6d. ($2·31) per dozen. These beers, if bought in bond, would be 1s. 6d. (36 cents) per dozen less.

In 1886, a Royal Commission was appointed in Sydney to make full inquiry into the intoxicating drink question, and they caused the British and Colonial beers, as well as the American and German Lager beers, to be analysed by the Government Analyst, with results of a startling character.

The Commission reported that they were scarcely prepared to find fusel oil in liquors which had not undergone the process of distillation, but only of fermentation. They attributed the presence of fusel oil, in a measure, to the high temperature at which the beer was brewed. They reported as follows :—

But whether high temperature be the true cause or not, we regard the fact that fusel oil is present in Colonial beers to be as serious in one aspect as it is suggestive in another; and although the percentage of fusel oil found in the beer is not perhaps more than a fifth or sixth of the percentage in cheap whisky or brandy, yet the result on the beer drinker, who probably consumes more than six times the weight of beer than the whisky or brandy drinker does of spirits, is about the same.

The Commission recommended that steps should be taken by the Government to prevent such spirits, whether imported or manufactured in the Colony, from passing into consumption. They deemed it would also be advisable to adopt a similar course in regard to beer, for the reason that that most pernicious substance (amylic and its kindred alcohols), though present in very small quantities, is as widespread a bane as the fusel oil of the cheap whisky, and the sham brandy.

The Commission said that the manufacture of wholesome beer could be carried on as successfully in New South Wales as in any other country in the world.

Dr. W. M. Hamlet, F.C.S., the Government Analyst, obtained fourteen samples of beer from the undermentioned breweries :—

    Pyrmont Brewing Co., Pyrmont.
    Castlemaine Brewing Co.
    Vincent M'Donald, Edinboro' Brewery, Leichhardt.
    M. Marks' Brewery, Newtown.
    Burrows & Gleeson, Waverley Brewery.
    Tooth & Co., Kent Brewery.
    J. T. & J. Toohey, Standard Brewery.
    J. & J. S. Marshall, Paddington.
    Bladen & Burrows, Surrey Brewery, Waterloo.
    J. & S. Cornwall, Australian Brewery, Waterloo.
    W. J. Dirwin & Co., Red Heart Brewery, Ultimo.
    Stephenson & Co., Eagle Brewery, Marrickville.

Instead of taking the usual quantity, only half-pint samples, he obtained 2 gallons of each kind, making in all 28 gallons, so that the deleterious substances, if any, might be shown in sufficient quantities to be easily detected.

Dr. Hamlet stated that, as the ordinary analysis of beer includes the estimation of the amount of alcohol, extract acetic acid, ash, salts, dextrin, and maltose, together with the number of grains of salt per gallon, he determined to put the ordinary analysis aside, and direct his investigation towards the discovery of the deleterious ingredients mentioned in the New South Wales Licensing Act, 1883, and any other ingredients injurious to health.

Dr. Hamlet stated that in six samples analysed by him, no other bitter principle existed in the beer than what was derived from the hop plant (*Humulus capulus*). Each of the fourteen samples of beer was examined for the ingredients enumerated in the Licensing Act of 1883, with entirely negative results. He said :—

The nature and character of the alcohol in the beers have received my close attention. With this object in view the alcoholic distillate has been submitted to the process known as fractional distillation, that is to say, the volatile alcohols have been more or less separated from each other in the order of their boiling points. In this way iso-butylic and amylic alcohols were detected. These compounds are present in the complex liquid called fousel or fusel oil, and give a character to the beer different from that of malt liquors properly fermented at a low temperature [not above 70 degrees Fahrenheit.]

The following are the results of Dr. Hamlet's analyses :—

Samples collected in June, July, and August, 1887.
Average composition of Sydney beer. (The so-called colonial ale.)
Specific gravity (water = 1000) at 60° F., from 1008·5 to 1010.

	Per cent.
Total solids, or extract, a variety of substances giving both body and flavour to the beer	6·882
Ethylic alcohol	6·505
Other alcohols and acids	·072
Water (by difference)	86·541
	100·00

A more detailed analysis, showing the total composition :—

		Per cent.
Total solids, *i.e.* extract.	Dextrin, Albumenoids, Maltose, Colouring matter, Bitter principle, Common salt, Magnesia, Carbonates, Phosphates and sulphates of lime, Silica, Potash, Latic acid, Glycerine, Catechu (Catch), Carbolic acid, Salicylic acid	6·882
Ethylic alcohol		6·505
Higher alcohols, including fusel oil		·002
Acetic acid		·070
Carbonic acid		·028
Water (by difference)		86·513
		100·000

Salt in beer.—The quantity of common salt found in the beer throws some light upon the mode of manufacturing this article. Knowing the actual amount of common salt in the water supplied to the City of Sydney, and the maximum possible quantity of salt found in genuine malt and hops, as well as the amount of malt and hops required to produce one gallon of beer of the same original gravity as the average of Sydney beers, it is easy to calculate how much salt ought to be found in the beer. For instance, the water supplied to Sydney, as shown by the analysis of samples, taken from the engine pond, Botany, Crown-street servoir, and the Lachlan Swamp, averages 4 grains of salt to the gallon.

Therefore we have :— Grains per gallon.
Salt derived from the water .... 4·00
Total possible quantity of salt derived from enough malt to make a gallon of strong beer .... 2·65
Total possible quantity of salt from the hops required to flavour one gallon of beer..... .... 3·35
Salt derived from dust, dirt, or inserted by inadvertence, say ... ·50
                     10½

Dr. Hamlet, at a subsequent period, operated upon a number of samples of imported American and German Lager beer, also upon samples of English ales. The results are set forth in the following reports :—

Report of the Government Analyst on Lager beers, both German and American.

In consequence of its having been reported to the Commission on Intoxicating Drinks that the alcoholic strength of Lager beers, both German and American, had of late greatly increased, the following sixteen samples were procured, and an analysis made as follows :—

The alcoholic strength, or the percentage of absolute alcohol by weight, varied from 3·88 per cent. in the Flensburg Stock to 5·62 per cent. in the Vereins beer.

Percentage of Alcohol.

No. of samples.	Name of beer.	Absolute Alcohol by weight.	Proof Spirit.
1	Milwaukee, U.S.A.	5·00	10·94
2	St. Louis, Anthony & Kuhn, U.S.A. ...	4·94	10·81
3	St. Louis, Anheuser-Busch, U.S.A.	4·37	9·58
4	San Jose, California, U.S.A.	4·31	9·45
5	H. Clausen & Sons, U.S.A.	5·37	11·76
6	Vereins Brauerei	5·62	12·30
7	Pilsener	5·19	11·35
8	Drehers, Vienna	4·87	10·67
9	Ernest Barre	5·06	11·08
10	Dittman & Sauerländer	4·69	10·26
11	Bremen	5·25	11·40
12	Frydenlund	5·25	11·40
13	H. H. Grave & Co.	5·37	11·76
14	Flensburg Stock	3·88	8·51
15	German Castle	5·12	11·21
16	Pilsen (Malm & Ohlerich)	4·81	10·54

Extract.—The amount of extract derived from malt, or malt substitutes, and hops, varied from 6·55 per cent. to 8·14 per cent.

Ash. The quantity of ash which was left after burning off the above extracts, was in all of the beers about the same as may usually be found in good Lager beers, varying only beween the limits of 0·18 and 0·26 per cent.

Acidity.—The amount of acid calculated as acetic acid was in all of the samples less than that found in English beers, amounting on the average to 0·01 per cent.

Carbonic Acid.—All the beers were fully charged with carbonic acid gas, a special feature in export Lager beer, and one that gives the beer the pleasant pungent flavour peculiar to bottled beers.

Lactic Acid. The beers were free from lactic acid at the moment of uncorking, but when left to stand with the cork removed, the beer became flat with development of lactic acid and acetic acid.

Metalic Impurities, Additions, and Adulterations.—All the samples were remarkably free from such.

Microscopic examination. A microscopic examination was made of each beer to discover in the dregs of the bottle ferment organisms, starch cells (if any), artificial bitters, &c.

The result was, in almost every case, to show that the beers had been brewed with low yeast in the usual manner of Lager beer fermentation, in many cases fragments of hop flowers were found, indicating the origin of the bitter principle employed in their manufacture.

In each of the beers a secondary fermentation had taken place while in bottle, and thus had produced a fairly large amount of carbonic acid gas, which adds very much to the character of the beer.

One result of this is the increased percentage of alcohol.

All the Lager beers that have come under my notice in Australia have a somewhat higher percentage of alcohol than the Lager beer commonly consumed in Germany.

General Conclusions.

From the chemical analysis and microscopical examination of the residues of the beers, I am of opinion that all the sixteen samples submitted are genuine wholesome drinks, remarkably free from noxious additions and adulterations.

All the beers, however, do not appear to have been brewed wholly from malt and hops. The Pilsener and Frydenlund beers are made from other materials, probably rice.

The bitter principle varies very much. In the Vienna beer, Drehers, it is at its maximum, ranging in others to a mere trace or flavour.

In the extracts were found albuminous substances, glucose, and glycerine, but as these are normally present in all good beers, the fact calls for no further remark.

WILLIAM M. HAMLET, F.C.S.,
Government Analyst.

Sydney, 15th March, 1887.

Report of the Government Analyst on imported British Ales.

Amongst the numerous criticisms evoked by the publication of my report on the composition of Colonial ale, many of which were of the most extraordinary nature, it was suggested, that in fairness to the Sydney brewers a similar investigation ought to be made on the imported beers.

This being a perfectly reasonable demand, not only on behalf of the brewers themselves, but in the interest of the public generally, I have accordingly been furnished with samples of the following beers, which were taken through the agency of the Police and Customs Officers from consignments of beers recently arrived, the names or brands of the various beers being as follows:—

No. 1. Bass' draught pale ale, ex "Port Jackson," Dalgetty & Co. (Limited) Sydney agents.
No. 2. Truman, Hanbury & Co's. English ale, Allt & Co. Sydney agents.
No. 3. Robert Younger & Co's. ale, Farbury's Bond, Sydney.
No. 4. M'Ewen's English ale, 'Towns' Bond, Sydney, Peyton, Dowling & Orme, agents.
No. 5. Aitkins' English ale taken from Bond, Sydney.

The following table shows the composition of these British Ales:—

	Bass'.	Truman Hanbury & Co.	Robert Younger & Co.	M'Ewen's	Aitkins'.
Specific gravity of distillate	·9900	·9908	·9897	·9892	·9898
Percentage of absolute alcohol by weight	5·87	5·37	6·07	6·43	6·00
Percentage equivalent of proof spirit	12·81	11·76	13·27	14·04	13·11
Higher and less volatile alcohol in grains per gallon, (fusel oil.)	minute traces.	·086	minute traces.	·070	·090
Acetic acid, per cent.	·01	·02	·01	·01	·01
Total solid matter (extract) per cent.	5·19	5·35	4·95	4·82	4·62
Salt, grains per gallon	7·7	28·8	37·8	22·7	20·3
Percentage of ash	·30	·51	·28	·32	·36

The methods of chemical analysis were the same as those employed in my research on Colonial Ales, and each of the samples was found to be properly sealed and secured.

No bitter principle other than that derived from the hop plant was discovered in any one of the beers.

The quantity of fusel oil extracted and estimated as amylic alcohol was found to vary from the most minute traces to 9-100ths. of a grain per gallon. Traces were however found in all the beers examined.

The number of grains of salt per gallon ranged from 7 in the case of Bass' to nearly 38 grains in Robert Younger & Co.'s ale.

Each of the samples was examined for the noxious ingredients mentioned in Section 89 of the Licensing Act, but none were present.

WILLIAM M. HAMLET, F.C.S.,
Government Analyst.

Sydney, N.S.W.,
9 January, 1888.

DAIRY FARMING.

You may search Sydney through, and yet fail to find a single firkin of Cork butter. The days are past when the people depended for butter on supplies of rank salt stuff sent out to the Colony under the name of "Prime Cork Butter." The United States led the way in showing agricultural countries what could be done, when aided by science and attention to practical details, to build up a vast trade in dairy products. The introduction within the last few years of improved methods for making butter and cheese has given an impetus to dairy farming in the Australasian Colonies which will not die out.

Diseases among cattle, prevalent in other countries, are unknown in Australasia. Pleuro-pneumonia certainly was introduced by the import of cattle from Great Britain, and the dread of a visitation of foot and mouth disease and trichinosis influenced the authorities in the Australasian Colonies to prohibit the import of live stock, except under somewhat absurd quarantine regulations. These operated prejudiciously on the dairy farming interests, by preventing the introduction of fresh blood among the dairy herds; and the prohibition, so far as any cattle imported from Great Britain are concerned, has now been removed in Queensland, New South Wales, and South Australia, and will shortly be removed in the other Australasian Colonies.

An Intercolonial Live Stock Conference was held in Sydney during 1886. Delegates from all the Australasian Colonies attended. A resolution was passed to the effect that the time had arrived when the restrictions on the importation of cattle could be safely removed, under proper regulations, and earnestly requesting the various Governments of Australasia to give effect to the resolution. The absurdity of the prohibition was pointed out at the Conference, when attention was directed to the admission of cattle from the Colonies where diseases exist, and refusing admission from countries enjoying absolute immunity from such diseases. New Zealand was the last Colony to adopt the prohibition, and the result has been that she has had a great advantage over the other Colonies. New Zealand, by keeping her ports open, has been enabled to improve the condition of her herds by the introduction among them of high-bred animals from foreign countries.

Mr. Meredith, a delegate to the conference from Tasmania, read a paper, in which he attributed the great progress made by the United States in raising cattle to the uninterrupted importation of high-bred stock. He was very decided in the opinion that the condition of cattle in America was far better than in Australia, and he argued that what had been done in the United States could be done in Australasia. He said :—"We must be prepared in the future for a keen competition in the butter and cheese export trade. The United States is rapidly developing a variety of breeds of cattle most suitable to the different conditions of climate and requirements in the several States of the Union. For developing an extensive dairying industry in these Colonies, it will be absolutely necessary to build up herds of various kinds or grades, and at present we have not the material to begin with."

No inconsiderable extent of Australasia is well adapted for raising cattle. Here there are no heavy snows. The spring, autumn, and winter are all that the farmer can desire. The summers may be disagreeable on account of the heat, but for about nine months of the year no fault can be found with the Australian climate, except in seasons of drought. In the more elevated parts, such as the high tablelands of Glen Innes, sharp frosts appear in the winter, but are soon dispelled by the sunshine. Snow is not found in any depth, except in one part of New South Wales—around Mount Kosciusco. In the coast districts the winters pass with scarcely the appearance of snow. Grass grows all the year round, and usually there is an abundance of natural pasture.

Some of the finest dairy farms in New South Wales are located in the celebrated Illawarra district, one of the most romantic in the Colony. It consists of tracts of undulating hills and rolling grass pastures, lying between the mountain range and the coast line. It may be said to commence 20 miles from Sydney, southwards. The district is thickly peopled by a farming and coal-mining population, and contains the rising towns of Wollongong, Kiama, Clifton, and Shellharbour. The geological formation is generally carboniferous, with granite and basalt cropping out.

One of the chief attractions of the Illawarra district is the beautiful lake of that name, 9 miles in length and 3 in breadth, surrounded by hills 300 or 400 feet high. The southern part of this district is broken by the wild spurs of the mountain ranges, which, at Mount Dromedary, jut out to the sea; but beyond these again the country assumes an undulating character, especially about Bega and Bodalla on the one side, and extending more or less to the tablelands of Monaro. The Illawarra lands are everywhere fertile, and will bear out the title of "Garden of New South Wales," so often given to the country round Wollongong. The chief town in the district, Wollongong, is situated 64 miles south of Sydney. It has a population of about 10,000 souls. The harbour is the most important south of Sydney, and ranks third in the Colony as to tonnage and number of shipping. The coal trade is its chief industry, and next to that comes dairy produce. Indeed, a great part of the Sydney supply of butter is from Wollongong district. The average annual export of butter from there is 1,600,000 lb.

The ease with which the port is reached by small coasting steamers has made the place very popular with the Sydney market dealers, and it will be still more so as soon as the railway is completed, which is intended to open up communication between Sydney and the districts on the coast southward.

The Camden and Mittagong districts, on the Great Southern line of railway, have become, mainly owing to railway communication, valuable feeders to the Sydney market. The produce of the Macleay and Hunter districts, to the north of Sydney, is of equal quality and quite as valuable; now it goes principally to supply the demands of Newcastle. When, however, the great railway bridge over the Hawkesbury River is completed, there will be direct means of sending dairy produce to Sydney, and the industry will extend.

Strong efforts are being made to encourage dairy farming in the Northern districts. Formerly, corn (maize) and timber were the chief products of those parts; but the advance in the price of butter, and the decline in that of maize, are inducing agriculturists to turn their attention to butter and cheese making. The climate is hot; but this, it is hoped, will be overcome by the use of improved cooling appliances.

The total number of cattle in New South Wales, on 1st January, 1888, was 1,581,078, an increase of 213,234 over the preceding year. The long series of droughts made sad havoc among the herds, and the result is that the number of cattle has declined from 3,131,013, in 1876. (a decrease of 1,549,935.)

The subjoined table shows the number of cattle in New South Wales for each year from 1876 to 1887 inclusive.

Year.	Number.	Year.	Number.
1876	3,131,013	1882	1,859,985
1877	2,746,385	1883	1,640,753
1878	2,771,583	1884	1,425,130
1879	2,914,210	1885	1,317,315
1880	2,580,040	1886	1,367,844
1881	2,597,348	1887	1,581,078

For the sake of comparison, it may be stated that the number of milk cows in the United States, on 1st January, 1887, was 14,522,083, and the number of oxen and other cattle was 33,511,750.

During 1887 there were imported into New South Wales 135,508 cattle from the neighbouring Colonies, valued at £607,728 ($3,264,098) against 80,677 head, valued at £433,568 ($2,109,959), for the year 1886.

The following table shows the number and value of cattle imported into New South Wales for each year from 1877 to 1887 inclusive.

Year ended 31 Dec.	Number.	Value.		Year ended 31 Dec.	Number.	Value.	
		£	$			£	$
1877	3,563	15,419	75,037	1883	3,460	39,319	191,326
1878	5,453	57,279	280,719	1884	36,186	315,110	1,533,483
1879	7,203	48,684	236,921	1885	36,602	195,602	953,897
1880	3,253	14,535	70,735	1886	80,677	433,564	2,109,959
1881	9,602	63,539	309,212	1887	135,508	607,728	3,264,098
1882	5,530	49,979	243,223				

During the year 1887, 259 head of cattle were imported from New Zealand—principally stud cattle, while Victoria sent 21,752, South Australia 1,042, and Queensland 112,455. The cattle trade with Queensland and Victoria is considerable, consisting chiefly in store cattle, sent to New South Wales to fatten.

Of the cattle exported from New South Wales in 1887, Victoria received 98,406 head and South Australia 7,130 head.

The following return shows the number and value of cattle exported from New South Wales for each year, from 1877 to 1887 inclusive :—

Year ended 31 Dec.	Number.	Value.		Year ended 31 Dec.	Number.	Value.	
		£	$			£	$
1877	67,989	463,135	2,253,846	1883	42,260	245,362	1,194,054
1878	55,026	421,672	2,052,067	1884	45,486	244,278	1,188,779
1879	58,051	405,101	1,971,424	1885	62,852	367,605	1,788,950
1880	86,757	454,754	2,213,000	1886	59,898	365,085	1,776,686
1881	55,340	256,929	1,250,345	1887	107,185	660,644	3,215,024
1882	53,085	289,326	1,438,005				

The Chief Inspector of Stock is of opinion that the only prevailing diseases among the herds in the Colony are pleuro-pneumonia and tuberculosis. He reports that :—

"In twenty-eight districts, on 177 runs, the cattle are reported as affected slightly with pleuro-pneumonia; and in thirty-one districts the cattle are reported as being free from that disease. In twenty-five of the infected districts the disease was caused by contagion from infected travelling stock from Queensland, in two districts its cause could not be traced, and in one district the cause not known. From twenty-seven districts it is reported that inoculation was successfully performed on 117 out of 119 holdings or runs. On the two holdings where the inoculation was unsuccessful the failure is attributed to bad virus, for a second operation proved successful. In every case the result was satisfactory, the disease leaving the herds. The number of owners in favour of inoculation is given as 4,592, against 1,106; undecided, 2,215; and 6,610 opinions not known. The number of owners in favour of compulsory inoculation in the case of infected herds is given as 3,645; against it, 1,682; undecided, 2,066; and 6,628 opinions not known. The Inspectors' reports show that the practice of inoculation for pleuro-pneumonia is becoming more and more general, and with very favourable results."

Much reliable information was obtained by the Chief Inspector of Stock from cattle owners as to their experience with virus, and abundant evidence is furnished of the benefit to be derived from inoculation. Mr. M'Kenzie, one of the delegates to the Live Stock Conference from New

Zealand, said that in importing cattle from Australia pleuro-pneumonia was introduced into the Otago District of that Colony in 1863, and that it continued there two or three years, but that with careful regulations and careful inoculation the disease had been stamped out. The same result followed when the disease was again introduced into the Auckland district of New Zealand in 1882 among some store cattle which were brought there from Newcastle in New South Wales. In neither instance was the disease allowed to spread, and now not a single case of pleuro-pneumonia can be found in the whole Colony of New Zealand.

In regard to tuberculosis, the Chief Inspector of Stock says that the disease should not be confounded with pleuro-pneumonia, as the former is altogether of a more subtile character and incurable nature. He recommends that as tuberculosis is hereditary, it should be stamped out by slaughter of all infected animals, more especially since the disease may even be communicated to the human subject by inoculation as it is by contact from one animal to another.

All the well-known breeds of cattle are represented in the herds of Australasia. The Shorthorns are most numerous. The number of cattle of each breed in New South Wales in the year ended 31st March, 1887, was :—

Shorthorns.—The number of pure bread and stud Shorthorns is estimated at 34,819 ; and ordinary 526,099 ; total, 560,918.

Herefords.—Pure and stud, 15,430 ; ordinary, 151,801 ; total, 167,231.

Devon.—Pure and stud, 5,699 ; ordinary, 43,138 ; total, 48,837.

Black-polled.—Pure and stud, 368 ; ordinary, 719 ; total, 1,087.

Ayrshire.—Pure and stud, 942 ; ordinary, 2,595 ; total, 3,537.

Alderneys.—Pure and stud, 298 ; ordinary, 175 ; total, 473.

Crosses. - First crosses, 3,485 ; ordinary, 582,276 ; total, 585,761. The crosses are estimated as follows :—Shorthorn and Hereford, 220,463, ; Shorthorn and Devon, 75,618 ; Hereford and Devon, 34,533 ; Shorthorn and Black-polled, 2,560 ; Ayrshire and Shorthorn, 4,000 ; the balance, 248,247 being unrecognizable.

There is in New South Wales, as elsewhere, much difference of opinion in regard to the best breeds of cattle for dairy purposes. On the model farm of Mr. Alfred Bennett, near Camden, are to be seen a superb herd of "Jerseys." These cattle are usually described as Alderneys ; but as a matter of fact, the Jerseys represent, notwithstanding their resemblance to the Alderney, an altogether different and distinct breed. The difference between them lies in the fact that the Jerseys have been kept pure on the Channel Island of that name for centuries, and no foreign cattle have been allowed to intermix with them or to land on the island for a period of over one hundred years. This has not been the case in the Isle of Alderney. There foreign cattle have been allowed to land, and the result is that the Alderney breed has not been kept pure, and is mainly made up from a cross of the Jerseys and cattle from Guernsey on the original stock. The Alderneys are not, therefore, regarded as so good as either the Jerseys or the Guernseys, and have not so many fine points, being more uneven in their make-up. The term "Alderney" was applied by the English to all cattle from the Channel Islands collectively, when they commenced to introduce them into England, on account of their high class dairy value, but importers now give to each breed its distinctive name.

The Shorthorn and Ayrshire form a cross breed much favoured by dairy farmers on account of their value for the butcher, as well as the butter and cheese making qualities of their milk. On the great runs in the interior, beef alone is considered, and there the herds are composed of Shorthorns, Devons, and Herefords intermixed.

Australasian cattle are not housed or stall-fed. Their food consists, with few exceptions, of the natural grasses of the country. The dairy farms vary very much in size—from 10 to 600 acres. In an average year, when there is not a scarcity of water, 4 acres of pasture would be sufficient to graze one cow. In the Illawarra District, cows give as much as 418 lb. of milk per week, yielding 18½ lb. of butter. This was the largest yield for the year 1886. The average value of a cow per year, supposing butter to sell at from 9d. (18 cents) to 1s. 6d. (36 cents), is £12 ($58·40). The cow would give milk for eight out of the twelve months. Calves are hand-fed, and, if not required, find a ready market as veal. The boundless gifts of Nature to this charming Colony may perhaps render the outlay of much capital on buildings for the dairy industry unnecessary, desirable though they are towards ensuring the yield of first-class products. A boy or man is employed to drive the cows into a stockyard, where they go into bails. The milking shed is often a roughly put together structure, composed of a few uprights and split slabs, open in front, and roofed with shingles, bark, or iron, the floor being paved with stones or blocks of timber. The bails are formed by uprights, set firmly in the ground, something after the manner in which stalls are fixed in stables. Strong lateral doubled braces are mortised into these uprights, one set close to the ground and the other set about 5 feet above the ground. These beams are securely fastened opposite one another, about 3 inches apart. Swinging bars are placed in the grooves of the bars at sufficient distance from one of the uprights to hold the neck of the cow. The lower end of the bar is fastened loosely by a bolt to the beams. This forms a pivot by which the top of the bar may be drawn forward or backward as required. The cow to be milked goes into the stall and is taught to insert her head under the top beam and alongside one of the uprights. The swinging lever is closed and fastened and the cow is thus kept in her place. A small rope, called a "leg-rope," with a noose on one end of it, is then passed round her hind leg nearest to where the milker sits, and tightened round a post, so as to stretch the cow's leg out slightly behind her, and so prevent her from kicking or upsetting the milk bucket while she is being milked.

The milking is then proceeded with in the usual way. As yet no machine seems to have been invented which will successfully perform the operation of milking without inflicting injury upon the cow.

The machinery and many of the appliances for dairy purposes come from Sweden, America, and England. The cream separators come from Sweden, and the churns most generally in use, butter-workers, and milk-coolers from America. A butter-box has been invented and patented by Mr. J. A. Pond, of Auckland, New Zealand, and is extensively used by dairy factories; it will doubtless come into more general use. The boxes are in the form of a cube and are made to any size, usually to contain 50 lb. of butter. They are made of New Zealand Kauri timber, grooves are cut in the top, bottom, and two of the side pieces. To put the box together, the sides are fixed in the grooves in the bottom piece by screws and are kept in place by two iron clamps until the box is full, when the cover-piece is put on and screwed down. The box can be used repeatedly, and when empty can be taken to pieces and packed in small compass. The parts with which the butter comes in contact are coated over, by a chemical process, with an enamel which prevents the flavour of the butter from being injured by the wood and yet is in itself innocuous to the butter. English butter dealers highly commend this box, but owing to the rough usage to which packages are exposed in Australia, butter tubs are in more general use among the dairy farmers.

During the last three or four years increased attention has been given to the dairy industry in New South Wales, as well as in Victoria and New Zealand, and the results so far are highly encouraging. The introduction of the co-operative system is giving general satisfaction. It is much more profitable than the old individual-farmer methods, and among its many advantages it enables cream separators and labour-saving appliances—costly to the individual—to be brought into use.

Although the Danish cream separator was the first introduced into Australasia, yet the Laval is in more general use. This useful labour-saving appliance was first introduced into this Colony by the Commissioner to the Amsterdam Exhibition of 1883, Mr. D. L. Dymock, President of the Kiama Agricultural Association, who saw it in use in the United States and in Holland. The Laval Separator Company of Stockholm, Sweden, through their enterprising and practical Sydney agents, Messrs. Waugh and Josephson, Civil Engineers, have rapidly overcome the initial difficulties in introducing Swedish separators, and they have designed and carried out the arrangements for the majority of the factories and private dairies. Over 120 factories and private dairies in New South Wales use this machine. All sizes of the Laval separators are at work, and the hand separators are coming rapidly into favour. The motive power is generally a two-horse power engine and three-horse power boiler, but many employ single horse power and occasionally bullocks. The work of separating, except in the hottest months of summer, takes place between 7 and 8 o'clock in the mornings. The evening milk is stored at night, in the morning the new milk is added to it, this raises the temperature sufficiently; but during hot weather separation is done morning and afternoon. Some farmers separate for their neighbours on terms, and the motive power is utilized for various farm works, such as cutting wood and chaff or pumping water.

Co-operative factories are arranged on a dual basis, suppliers and non-suppliers, to both guarantee is given of 10 per cent. per annum on the amount of shares as a first charge on output; then after working expenses are paid, the surplus remaining is divided *pro rata* according to the quantity of milk supplied by each shareholder, and the payments are made monthly. Landowners and others can, by taking non-suppliers' shares, largely assist their neighbours who are perhaps not possessed of sufficient capital, and at the same time secure a good return for their investments. In one or two instances the factories are owned by large metropolitan milk and butter distributing companies. In all other cases the factories are purely co-operative. The latter pay *pro rata*. Generally one-third of the price the best hand-made butter brings per lb. at auction, is paid for milk per gallon of 10 lb. weight; thus if butter is 1s. (24 cents) a lb., then suppliers get 4d. (8 cents) a gallon for the milk.

Frame buildings are usually erected for the factory, with verandahs all round. The floors are of wood and concrete.

One of the largest factories is at present operating on 33,000 lb. (3,300 gallons) of milk per day. The skim milk is used for feeding pigs, in some instances sold at ¼d. (½ cent) a gallon to bacon curers who rent the styes and yards from the company.

As a rule no test is applied to the milk, unless suspicion of watering is entertained. The richness of milk varies very much. In spring, when grass is fresh and watery, 27 lb. are required to produce a lb. of butter; but in the best season of the year as low as 18½ lb. has been recorded, and in one private dairy for one month 18 lb. 23 lb. is about a fair average estimate in the best dairies. The separator butter realizes quite 3d. (6 cents) per lb. more in the Sydney market than hand-made butter.

Much of the butter supply comes to market in tubs, and is sold out of the tubs, or pressed into 1 lb. pieces by the butter dealer. Those engaged in the industry have still much to learn. It is said that nowhere in Australasia is butter placed on the market in a manner equal to that in which it is turned out of the dairy factories of the United States, Sweden, Denmark, or England. With regard to cheese, although large quantities are made, the quality would be said, by an American, to be inferior. On some properties, as for instance at Bodalla, the magnificent property of Messrs. T. and L. Mort, only cheese is made at present; but, although "Bodalla cheese" is excellent and much sought after, it is considered by many not to be equal in quality to American cheese, or to that made in many of the New Zealand cheese factories.

Probably no city of its age suffered so long as Sydney for want of what may be described as a genuine, certain, and ready emporium for dairy and farm produce; and the loss was twofold. First, the producer found, in a big city with an increasing population, a most uncertain and unremunerative market. Then, the consumer could never make sure of reliable source of supply, fresh and good.

The direct result was the retarding if not the crippling of inland development, the farmer receiving so little encouragement. Lengthy discussions took place in the public press, and while all sorts of impracticable schemes were proposed, a number of practical men in the business, especially among the largest centres of dairy farming in New South Wales, formed a company in June, 1881, under the style of "The South Coast and West Camden Co-operative Company," with a capital of £10,000 ($48,665), increased in November 1887 to £50,000 ($243,325), South Coast, being the name by which the coast to the south of Sydney is locally known.

Operations were commenced in rented premises by receiving consignments of every description of farm and dairy produce. The directors, all practical farmers, were men of considerable standing in various parts of the districts, and nine-tenths of the shareholders were producers. Hence the fact that the Company's business has been one of remarkable success. Each year has seen dividends of from 10 to 15 per cent. paid to shareholders.

In 1885 the directors decided to erect premises suitable for conducting the steadily increasing business. They secured a detached block of land having a frontage of 588 feet, and a ground space of 12,200 superficial feet in Sussex-street, Sydney, adjacent to the wharves and terminus of the railway lines, and at a cost of nearly £35,000 ($170,327) erected premises five stories high, with a storage capacity of 2,310,000 cubic feet, replete with every facility for the proper exposition of all kinds of produce. The cold storage chambers, six in number, are well built and roomy, with a storage capacity of 34,000 cubic feet. The machinery used is Haslem's latest improved dry air method. Two machines are in use, capable of distributing 70,000 feet of cold air per hour. The advantage of these cold chambers for the storage of butter, cheese, beef, mutton, poultry, fish, and game, besides keeping milk fresh, is fully recognised by the public.

The butter room is on the same floor as the sale room, and should occasion require, butter arriving in a soft state could, after the lapse of a few hours, be placed before buyers in a firm saleable condition. The chamber affords space for the storage of surplus butter during plentiful seasons, and ensures its export as a prime article. Thus, independently of yearly dividends, the benefits received by producers are enormous. Between September, 1887, when the export commenced, and the end of February, 1888, 374,080lb. of butter were despatched to the English market. This could not have been satisfactorily effected without the aid of cold storage.

The butter forwarded to this company is drawn chiefly from districts where the farmers have adopted the co-operative factory system. The factories in these districts have advanced the dairying interests wonderfully, weeding out, as they do, all the worst class of butter-makers and producing a prime article of uniform quality.

After six years of success, unparalleled in the Colonies, the company's output in 1887 was £180,000 ($875,970), and would have been probably much larger had the country entirely recovered from the severe droughts, as the output of the company in 1883–84 reached £203,953 ($992,537).

The Fresh Food and Ice Company, and the Country Milk Supply Company, are other highly useful enterprises, and ably minister to the hungry and thirsty wants of the people of Sydney and her suburbs.

The Kiama Agricultural Association pays great attention to the promotion of the dairy interests. Among other means it has, for years past, awarded a number of prizes for cows producing the largest quantity of milk. The Association admits to its herd-book any cow that can produce 350 lb. of milk, or 12 lb. of butter per week. A series of prizes were offered by the Association for cows giving the most milk. It was determined that the tests should take place in the same locality, the object being to place competing animals on an equal footing.

The following extract from the Kiama Agricultural Association's Dairy Herd-book gives the result of tests which were conducted on Mr. N. Craig's farm, Jarra Park, near Kiama :—

Name of Owner.	Date of Test.	Weight of Milk for week.	Weight of Butter made.		Nature of Pasture.	Weather.
		lb.	lb.	oz.		
H. Colley, jun.	12–19 Nov.	419	18	0	Rye, grass, and clover.	Strong westerly winds for some days, remainder of time hot and dry.
H. Colley, jun.	,,	392	15	0	,,	Same as above.
Cole Bros.	15–22 Nov.	343	13	4	,,	Windy and hot.
Cole Bros.	,,	293	12	0	,,	Windy and hot.
J. M'Caffrey	17–24 Dec.	289	14	4	,,	Excessively hot and windy for three days out of seven.
H. Dudgeon	2–9 Dec.	301	12	0	Grass pasture only.	Hot but moist.
Spinks Bros	,,	312	14	10	,,	Same as above.
H. Colley, jun.	24–31 Jan.	266	12	4	Broadcast corn.	Windy, hot, and dry.
W. Gray	1–8 Feb.	300	12	8	Grass (dry), supplemented with broadcast corn.	Close and dry.
J. T. & F. Cole.	1–7 June	256	12	12	Grass pasture only.	Cold.

Prizes are given for cows and heifers giving the largest quantity of milk in twenty-four hours, varying from £2 ($9·73) to £10 ($48·66). In both classes competing animals have to be milked three times within twenty-four hours, in the presence of two members of the Committee, the second and third milking only being weighed.

The Royal Agricultural Society of New South Wales held a show in Sydney during the Centennial celebrations, in January, 1888, when a new departure was made in the exhibition of a working dairy on the Show grounds. The advantages of this exhibition were appreciated by crowds of inquiring farmers.

The total quantity of butter imported into New South Wales during the year 1887 was 1,034,544 lb., valued at £39,481 ($192,134), against 3,129,392 lb., valued at £159,536 ($776,832) for 1886.

The following table shows the quantity and value of butter imported into New South Wales in each year, from 1877 to 1887 inclusive :—

Year ended 31st. Dec.	Quantity.	Value.		Year ended 31st. Dec.	Quantity.	Value.	
	lb.	£	$		lb.	£	$
1877	713,776	39,809	193,730	1883	1,813,504	88,860	432,437
1878	451,920	21,379	103,554	1884	2,791,936	147,148	716,096
1879	105,056	3,919	19,072	1885	3,624,992	188,195	915,851
1880	228,144	7,063	34,372	1886	3,129,392	159,536	776,832
1881	600,128	30,741	149,601	1887	1,034,544	39,481	192,134
1882	1,634,016	90,422	440,039				

The following table shows the quantity and value of butter imported into New South Wales during the years 1886 and 1887, and the countries from whence imported :—

Country.	Quantity.	Value.	
1886.	lb.	£	$
Great Britain	9,408	408	1,986
Victoria	723,184	35,331	171,939
South Australia	54,880	3,561	17,330
Queensland	14,784	752	3,660
Tasmania	106,400	5,881	28,620
New Zealand	2,169,776	110,046	535,539
Western Australia	360	12	58
Fiji	1,008	83	404
United States	2,800	139	676
France	7,504	550	2,677
Germany	896	60	292
Italy	35,952	2,633	12,813
India	2,240	80	389
Total	3,129,392	159,536	776,382
1887.			
Great Britain	6,022	203	988
Victoria	225,022	7,986	38,864
Queensland	7,937	299	1,455
South Australia	158,175	7,171	34,898
New Zealand	595,503	21,206	103,199
Tasmania	60	3	15
France	1,200	73	355
Germany	6,450	379	1,844
Italy	31,225	2,119	10,312
India	2,460	30	146
New Caledonia	490	12	58
Total	1,034,544	39,481	192,134

The export of butter, the produce of the Colony, during the year 1887, was 722,322 lb., valued at £20,758 ($101,019), against 58,047 lb., valued at £2,862 ($13,927), for 1886. The export has been confined almost exclusively to the neighbouring Colonies; however, several shipments of New South Wales butter have been made during the last few months to London, the mail steamship companies having fitted storage rooms on their vessels with suitable refrigerating appliances. The shipments are said to have realized very fair returns in a depressed market.

DAIRY FARMING.

The subjoined table shows the quantity and value of butter, the produce of the Colony, exported during the years 1886 and 1887, and the countries to which exported:—

Country.	Quantity.	Value.	
1886.	lb.	£	s
Victoria	9,006	401	1,951
South Australia	8,928	417	2,029
Queensland	34,234	1,684	8,193
South Sea Islands	1,210	75	365
New Caledonia	2,754	157	764
Fiji	153	10	49
Western Australia	1,438	98	477
New Guinea	324	20	97
Total	58,047	2,862	13,927
1887.			
Great Britain	483,657	12,411	60,398
Victoria	427	18	88
South Australia	823	32	156
Queensland	210,586	7,509	36,542
Western Australia	882	31	131
South Sea Islands	2,420	75	365
New Caledonia	6,209	233	1,134
Fiji	52	3	15
Sandwich Islands	17,166	440	2,141
Kaiser Wilhelm's Land	100	6	29
Total	722,322	20,758	101,019

The following table shows the quantity and value of butter exported from New South Wales, distinguishing the produce of the Colony, during each year from 1877 to 1887 inclusive:—

Year ended 31st Dec.		Quantity.	Value.	
		lb.	£	s
1877	Produce of the Colony	599,088	28,302	137,732
	Other produce	118,272	4,900	23,846
1878	Produce of the Colony	624,736	33,780	164,390
	Other produce	42,112	1,884	9,168
1879	Produce of the Colony	1,098,496	39,431	191,891
	Other produce	....	....	....
1880	Produce of the Colony	1,222,592	35,708	173,773
	Other produce	4,880	141	686
1881	Produce of the Colony	740,880	24,672	120,037
	Other produce	21,504	1,002	4,867
1882	Produce of the Colony	317,744	18,041	87,797
	Other produce	120,064	7,862	38,260
1883	Produce of the Colony	639,184	26,842	130,627
	Other produce	139,440	7,636	37,161
1884	Produce of the Colony	441,504	18,772	91,354
	Other produce	179,760	9,778	47,585
1885	Produce of the Colony	169,232	8,928	43,418
	Other produce	352,240	18,825	91,612
1886	Produce of the Colony	58,047	2,862	13,928
	Other produce	228,982	11,991	58,354
1887	Produce of the Colony	722,322	20,758	101,019
	Other produce	318,901	11,079	53,916

The total quantity of cheese imported into New South Wales during the year 1887 was 318,099 lb., valued at £10,801 ($52,563), against 1,229,334 lb., valued at £43,508 ($211,732) for 1886.

The following table shows the quantity and value of cheese imported into New South Wales in each year from 1877 to 1887 inclusive:—

Year ended 31st Dec.	Quantity.	Value.		Year ended 31st Dec.	Quantity.	Value.	
	lb.	£	$		lb.	£	$
1877	711,240	29,519	143,654	1883	161,753	8,012	39,136
1878	541,919	20,112	97,875	1884	725,177	22,088	103,404
1879	246,139	8,240	40,100	1885	769,148	29,163	141,922
1880	115,678	4,462	21,714	1886	1,229,334	43,508	211,732
1881	171,544	5,687	27,076	1887	318,099	10,801	52,563
1882	331,944	12,428	60,481				

The subjoined table shows the quantity and value of cheese imported into New South Wales during the years 1886 and 1887, with the countries from whence imported:—

Country.	Quantity.	Value.	
1886.	lb.	£	$
Great Britain	99,055	3,797	18,478
Victoria	198,073	6,304	30,678
South Australia	37,857	1,755	8,541
Queensland	1,823	66	321
Tasmania	32	1	5
New Zealand	859,824	30,350	147,698
Western Australia	106	2	10
Germany	11,007	395	1,922
New Caledonia	170	6	29
France	10,270	480	2,336
Belgium	7,105	235	1,144
United States	4,012	117	569
Total	1,229,334	43,508	211,731
1887.			
Great Britain	74,751	2,557	12,444
Victoria	39,345	1,285	6,253
Queensland	2,097	46	224
South Australia	52,455	1,971	9,592
New Zealand	124,650	3,638	17,704
Tasmania	35	1	5
France	16,913	990	4,818
Germany	4,372	176	857
Belgium	2,932	113	550
Italy	415	17	83
New Caledonia	134	7	34
Total	318,099	10,801	52,563

The quantity of cheese, the produce of the Colony, exported during 1887, was 163,648 lb., valued at £3,494 ($17,006), against 11,370 lb. valued at £417 ($2,029) for 1886.

DAIRY FARMING.

The following table shows the quantity and value of cheese, the produce of the Colony, exported during the years 1886 and 1887, with the countries to which exported:—

Country.	Quantity.	Value.	
1886.	lb.	£	s
Victoria	1,414	49	238
South Australia	130	5	24
New Zealand	150	5	24
Queensland	3,857	155	754
New Caledonia	5,915	184	896
Western Australia	624	19	93
Total	11,370	417	2,029
1887.			
Great Britain	18,418	322	1,567
Victoria	9,410	175	852
South Australia	2,507	70	341
Queensland	113,839	2,506	12,195
Western Australia	112	3	15
South Sea Islands	249	8	40
New Caledonia	14,396	310	1,509
Fiji	206	3	15
Sandwich Islands	1,407	18	88
Ceylon	776	19	92
India	2,328	60	292
Total	163,648	3,494	17,006

The following table shows the quantity and value of cheese exported from New South Wales, distinguishing the produce of the Colony, during each year from 1877 to 1887 inclusive :—

Year ended 31st Dec.		Quantity.	Value.	
		lb.	£	s
1877	Produce of the Colony	39,568	1,428	6,949
	Other produce	38,113	1,920	9,387
1878	Produce of the Colony	52,546	1,744	8,487
	Other produce	29,245	1,289	6,273
1879	Produce of the Colony	122,698	3,648	17,753
	Other produce	18,440	686	3,338
1880	Produce of the Colony	155,578	4,308	20,965
	Other produce	18,251	774	3,766
1881	Produce of the Colony	123,372	3,669	17,855
	Other produce	22,461	912	4,438
1882	Produce of the Colony	103,880	3,944	19,193
	Other produce	59,498	2,272	11,057
1883	Produce of the Colony	234,359	10,871	52,904
	Other produce	25,383	1,049	5,105
1884	Produce of the Colony	123,828	4,067	19,792
	Other produce	123,509	4,032	19,622
1885	Produce of the Colony	45,144	1,500	7,300
	Other produce	78,441	2,486	12,098
1886	Produce of the Colony	11,370	417	2,029
	Other produce	74,445	3,042	14,804
1887	Produce of the Colony	163,648	3,494	17,006
	Other produce	84,178	2,546	12,390

LEATHER.

At the beginning of the year 1887, the number of tanneries in operation in the Colony of New South Wales was ninety-seven, employing 627 hands. The number has probably increased since then, as the leather industry appears to be in a flourishing condition. The country is so well adapted to the raising of sheep and cattle that it would be a matter of suprise rather than otherwise if very general attention were not given to the leather trade.

Although tanneries were established here soon after the first settlement of the Colony, it has only been within the last few years that any great progress has been made in the art of tanning. The industry, however, has reached such a state that very favourable results may be expected from it in the near future. The bulk of the leather produce of the Colony is admitted by judges to be of very fair quality. There is, however, much complaint against the careless manner in which the skins are removed from the animals. They are often so cut and slashed about that it is almost impossible to make use of them. These cuts do not show in the green state, and it is only after they have been dressed that their defects become known. A large amount of local capital is employed in the leather trade. Sydney offers many advantages for the development of this trade. Besides being the great shipping port and depôt, it is connected by railways with all the important districts in the Colony in which the tanning industry is carried on. Amongst the towns where tanneries are located are Bathurst, Orange, Mudgee, Glen Innes, Wagga Wagga, Albury, Grafton, Penrith, Windsor, Braidwood, Ulladulla, Armidale, Tamworth, Bega, and Parramatta; but the principal works are situated in and around Sydney, and include those of Messrs. Alderson & Sons, Begg & Sons, Davenport & Sons, Farleigh & Nettheim, James Forsyth & Sons, and Walsh, Elliott, & Rennie, whose brands of leather are well known in the London market.

The tanneries in the neighbourhood of Sydney are mainly supplied from the public abattoirs at Glebe Island in Sydney Harbour, but every town of importance in the Colony has a tannery which serves as a depôt for the surrounding country. The hides are carefully looked after by the farmers, who regard so small a number as twenty hides a year worth sending to a tannery. On account of the great distance between stations, one tannery is often the deposit for hides from a large extent of country.

The system of fire-branding cattle is almost universally practised in the Colonies, and is of course injurious to the hides. The small value of cattle and the difficulty of shepherding them in thinly populated parts of this Continent are the principal reasons why this method of designating ownership is not discontinued.

The average price paid for hides at the Sydney tanneries is from 3d. (6 cents) to 4d. (8 cents) per pound. The tanneries, however, do not consume by any means all the hides produced in the Colony, for large numbers of them are exported to England. They are usually loaded in the wool ships, under the wool. The skins of sheep are also largely exported, but numbers are used at the local tanneries. A carefully cut sheep-skin, without any wool on it, will sell readily for 6d. (12 cents) in Sydney. The price of the skins containing wool depends, of course, on the quantity and quality of the wool.

Australian sheep-skins, properly prepared, are said to make the best imitation of morocco leather known to the trade. Buyers of these skins take the precaution to instruct the butchers to see that the animals are properly flayed and that no particles of fat are left on them, for otherwise decay is certain to set in and the leather will become spotted and discoloured.

The great bulk of the material used for tanning leather in Australia consists of wattle, or *mimosa*, bark, the produce of various species of the Acacia. This bark yields a higher percentage of tannin than any other vegetable material, with the single exception of the celebrated *taneka* bark of New Zealand, a product peculiar to that Colony.

An interesting feature connected with the *mimosa* bark is that its percentage of tannin increases for about two years, then decreases if kept in a dry place. The bark is usually gathered in the spring, which begins here in the month of September. The bark is so highly prized for tanning that considerable quantities are exported to England, the exports for 1886 being 2,705 tons. The demand for it has been so great that at one time it was thought the trees would disappear altogether. The Government, however, has taken very active measures to promote their growth, and has caused numbers of them to be planted in various parts of the Colony and especially on the railway reserves. Strong efforts are also being made to encourage planting these trees by private enterprise. Many varieties of the wattle are very beautiful, with graceful, wavy, feathery foliage, and a few of them have highly perfumed white or yellow coloured flowers.

Mr. J. H. Maiden, Curator of the Technological Museum of Sydney, who has given much study to the economic botany of Australia, states that wattle barks are usually found in commerce in four forms : First, in narrow strips about 3 feet long, pulled off the tree ; second, in small pieces, 1 inch in length and about the same in breadth ; third, ground bark, having the appearance of retted fibre ; fourth, powdered bark, forming a very fine powder. The wattle bark forms a hard and heavy tannage when used strong, but soft leathers may be tanned with it in weak liquors. Extracts are now made of this bark, and some English tanners prefer it sent to them in that form.

In the proceedings of the Royal Society of New South Wales for 1887 will be found four papers by Mr. Maiden, entitled " Some New South Wales Tan Substances," and analyses are given of seventy-eight of them. Mr. Maiden intends to continue his investigations, as there are hundreds of more or less astringent substances in this Colony alone, which it is desirable to examine.

Subjoined will be found a list of the barks analysed, with the results. Those marked with asterisk are articles of regular consumption by tanners, while several of the others are used locally, but to what extent it is impossible to say.

The three substances put under the heading " Miscellaneous " are interesting. *Rhus rhodanthema* is a fine handsome tree, with valued timber. The genus yields the sumach of commerce, and also the North American sumachs, of which a full account is given in a report of the Department of Agriculture, Washington. *R. rhodanthema* has never been used as a tan, so far as is known, but it would prove useful for that purpose, and it is quite possible the Department of Agriculture might deem it worthy of experimental cultivation in the United States.

The aboriginals of the interior use the bruised leaves of *Eremophila longifolia* and other species, for tanning the skins of the male wallaby for water-bottles. The bush is not used by the colonists.

Polygonum plebejum is a plant which will interest the people of the United States, from the fact that another species *P. amphibium*, which, like many others of the genus can be mown and stacked like hay, is used in the production of a superior leather in Chicago. Mr. Maiden has drawn comparisons between the various species of *Polygonum* in the papers above referred to.

His papers also contain some researches on a number of eucalyptus kinos, and also on the tanning power of various leaves, viz., wattle, acacia, and gum eucalyptus. The kinos are used almost exclusively in medicine on account of their powerfully astringent properties; the leaves are for the most part too weak in tanning power for use in the manufacture of leather, but there are some exceptions which may be brought into notice as astringent substances become more scarce.

BARKS found in New South Wales.

Botanical Name.	Vernacular Name.	Percentage of extract on substance dried at 100°C.	Percentage of tannic acid on substance dried at 100°C.
Acacia scutis, F. v. M.		18·02	6·32
,, *penninervis*, Lieb.	Hickory	22·88	16·24
		45·5	16·96
,, *melanoxylon*, R. Br.	Blackwood	20·63	11·12
,, *aneura*, F. v. M.	Mulga	10	4·78
		20·72	8·02
,, *decurrens*, Willd.	Black Wattle	42·16	32·08
,, *colletioides*, A. Cunn.	"Wait-a-while"	10·56	4·4
,, *rigens*, A. Cunn.	Nealie	19·05	6·26
,, *restita*, Ker.		50·82	27·96
,, *pendula var.*, A. Cunn.	Yarran	17·91	7·15
,, *binervata*, D. C.	Black Wattle	58·03	30·4
,, *longifolia*, Willd.	Golden Wattle	30·35	18·93
,, *glaucescens*, Willd.	Myall	14·29	8·10
,, *dealbata*, Link.	Silver Wattle	29·86	21·22
,, *homalophylla*, A. Cunn.	Narrow-leaved Yarran	21·51	9·06
,, *Oswaldi*, F. v. M.	Miljee	20·7	9·72
Eucalyptus stellulata, Lieber	Black Sally	27·64	12·86
,, *siderophloia*, Benth.	Ironbark	26·56	10·4
,, *Gunnii var.*, Hook.	Flooded Gum	19·4	9·45
,, ,,	Red Gum	20·84	11·35
,, *viminalis*, Labill	Manna Gum	18·65	7·5
,, *sheartiana*, F. v. M.	Apple-tree	15·39	5·25
,, *corymbosa*, Smith	Bloodwood	12·16	5·85
,, *maculata*, Hook	Spotted Gum	20·865	9·74
Everyphia Moorei, F. v. M.	Plum-tree	21·4	7·74
Fusanus acuminatus, R. Br.	Quandong	39·46	18·84

Botanical Name.	Vernacular Name.	Percentage of extract on substance dried at 100°C.	Percentage of tannic acid on substance dried at 100°C.
Elæocarpus grandis, F. v. M.	Blue Fig	21·566	10·28
Rhus rhodanthema, F. v. M.........	Deep yellow-wood ...	44·79	23·15
Eremophila longifolia, F. v. M......	Emu-bush	19·11	5·107
Grevillea striata, R. Br.	Beefwood	22·02	17·84
Hakea Clueoptera, R. Br.	Needle-bush............	14·95	10·99
Banksia intequifolia, Linn. f.	Coast Honeysuckle...	14·2	10·825
Banksia serrata, Linn. f.	Honeysuckle	27·38	23·25
Casuarina glauca, Lieb................	Belar	17·2	11·58
Exocarpus cupressiformis, Labill ...	Native Cherry	29·99	15·75
Miscellaneous.			
Rhus rhodanthema, F. v. M. (leaves —a N.S.W. sumach.)	Deep yellow-wood ...	32·2	16·91
Eremophila longifolia, F. v. M. (leaves used by the aboriginals for tanning wallaby skins for water-bottles.)	Emu-bush	42·92	9·7
Polygonum plebejum, R. Br.	....	28·11	11·19

The following are some of the principal wattle barks used in tanning :—

The black wattle, *A. decurrens* indigenous in New South Wales, Victoria, and South Australia. It is a small or middle-sized tree, attaining a height of about 40 feet with a diameter of 18 inches. It has slightly angulated branchlets. The leaves are reduced to phyllodia, usually 3 or 4 inches long, with two or three longitudinal nerves. It flowers at first on peduncles in an axillary raceme, which, after flowering, often grows into a leafy branch with the peduncles at the base, each bearing a globular head of about twenty flowers. The bark yields about 30 per cent. of tannin. A ton of this species is sufficient to tan twenty-five or thirty hides. It is best adapted to sole leather. Leather tanned with it is believed to be fully as durable as that tanned with oak. It improves in tanning powers from 10 to 15 per cent. if stowed carefully for a season. The cultivation of this wattle is extremely easy, it being done either by sowing broadcast or in rows. The cost of a package containing 40,000 seeds is about 5s. ($1·20). The seeds retain their vitality for several years, and should be soaked in hot water before sowing. A full-grown tree yields about 120 lb. of bark.

The *Acacia decurrens*, variety *dealbata*, known as the silver wattle, is another valuable variety. It is, however, thinner in size than the black wattle and not so rich in tannin. The silver wattle is easily distinguished by its pale or ashy foliage.

The golden or green wattle, *Acacia pycnantha*, Benth. This variety is indigenous in Victoria and South Australia, and is often cultivated here. The bark is thought by some Australians to be the best tan bark in the world. A sample in the Technological Museum yielded 33·5 per cent. of tannin according to an analysis by Mr. Thomas, of Adelaide. The growth of this tree is much slower than that of the black wattle, nor does it yield so large a proportion of bark, but it is sometimes richer in tannic acid than the black wattle.

Acacia inplexa, Benth., is another valuable variety, indigenous in Queensland and Victoria.

Acacia penninervis, Blackwood, is another valuable variety of wattle used for tanning. The tree reaches a height of 40 feet. It is found on the Blue Mountains and in various other parts of the Colony, and also in the southern part of Queensland.

The native willow, *Acacia salicina*, is also a favourite bark for tanning. It was formerly extensively employed by the aboriginal or native inhabitants for tanning skins for water-bottles. The tree is found in every part of the interior of Australia.

Large quantities of wattle bark are always forthcoming, and heavy shipments are imported from Tasmania and South Australia. The bark is sent in bags and bundles, and may be classified as follows:—

```
                                                        Per ton.
Ground, in bags, value in Sydney............... £7 to £10   ($34 to $49)
Chopped, in bags, value in Sydney ............ £5 to   9   ($24 to $44)
Bundled, in bundles, value in Sydney ... ..... £2 to   4   ($10 to $19)
```

Tallow and bees-wax are used to a considerable extent in dressing leather. Both of these articles are produced in the Colony in large quantities. The oils used here for dressing consist of whale-oil, blackfish, cod, and other fish oils, whale-oil heading the list, the Colonies drawing their supply from New Zealand and the South Pacific Islands, and occasionally from the United States.

In regard to the total quantity of leather manufactured in the Colony of New South Wales, considerable difficulty exists in arriving at anything like an approximate estimate, inasmuch as no returns bearing upon the subject are available. That the quantity reaches large figures there can be no possible room to doubt. It is estimated that in Sydney alone something like £100,000 ($486,650) worth of colonial-made leather is sold at auction in the course of a year, probably two-thirds of which goes into local consumption, the balance being bought for export, while two or three of the large tanneries have extensive boot factories of their own, in addition to which they supply the local trade with leather, so that the actual output must be a matter of conjecture.

The value of the various kinds of unmanufactured leather imported into New South Wales during the year 1887, was £62,832 ($305,772).

The subjoined table shows the quantity of unmanufactured leather imported into New South Wales for each year since 1877:—

Year.	Quantity.	Value.		Year.	Quantity.	Value.	
	packages.	£	$		packages.	£	$
1877	2,027	47,874	232,979	1883	2,611	72,754	354,057
1878	1,866	45,438	221,124	1884	2,298	74,543	361,376
1879	1,519	45,664	222,224	1885	2,654	78,451	381,782
1880	1,779	43,070	209,600	1886	2,378	67,710	329,511
1881	2,194	66,798	325,072	1887	3,206	62,832	305,772
1882	2,558	78,197	380,546				

The imports of leather are very small for a population of over 1,000,000 souls; if we put aside the leather imported from Victoria and other Australian Colonies, the number of packages would be only 1,271.

The bulk of the foreign leather imported into the Colonies is from Great Britain and the United States. The value of the leather imported from the United States during 1886 was £26,050 ($126,759). While the imports from the United States are increasing, those from Great Britain are declining. In this importation are included sole leather and leather for uppers. The leather imported for the use of carriage-makers consists of black enamelled hides of two weights—one for tops and the other for trimmings. Japanned split leather for dash-boards and various kinds of coloured imitation of morocco leather for trimmings are also imported. Enamelled ducks and drills and rubber drills find a ready market here, the American articles being considered the best. Competition, however, is keen, and the English goods are a shade lower in price.

There is no doubt whatever that the American sole and upper leather is by far the best introduced into this market. As yet its superiority is known to only a few dealers. At recent auction sales the American product commanded much higher prices than any other.

It is perhaps not generally known that the best and finest patent leather comes from America, and is made from the hides of cattle raised in the State of Kentucky. The cattle of the bluegrass region of that State produce the largest, thickest, and heaviest hides known to the trade. The greatest possible care is taken in tanning and preparing these skins. The tannage used is a mixture of hemlock and oak bark known to the trade as "union tannage." The "bate" is worked out very carefully by means of a hide-mill, through which passes a stream of water. The hides are then worked over with a "bate" stone.

Mr. C. T. Davis, a high authority on leather, in describing the preparation of these skins, says that after the bate-stone is used the hides are placed in a wash-wheel, and worked for about twenty minutes, after which they are in a condition to be properly swelled for the reception of the tanning liquors. The hides are not laid away in the ground bark like those intended for sole and upper leather, but are placed in vats having a circular bottom, and above which there is placed a revolving wheel, which agitates both the tanning liquor and the hides. The hides then have the buffing removed and are passed through the splitting-machine. The split portions are very carefully worked, and when thoroughly tanned are scoured by the most improved machinery. They are next put upon stretchers, and when perfectly dry are coated with enamel made of white lead, litharge, and linseed oil. They are then placed in an oven in which the heat is gradually increased from 80° to 250° Fahrenheit. The next process is to rub them with pumice-stone, and with linseed oil and ivory-black, and then varnish them with a mixture of turpentine, copal, asphaltum, and linseed oil.

Many of the boot-makers in Sydney prefer American sole leather to English or any other make. Messrs. Abbey & Co. state that Kron & Co., of Santa Cruz, Cal., ship to this market considerable quantities of extra heavy sole, from 24 pounds average, and that they prefer it to the best

English make. Twenty bales of Kron & Co.'s sole leather (each bale containing twenty sides) lately brought the sum of £534 ($2,600). The tannage of this leather is of chestnut oak and very light in colour.

During 1887, 762 packages of leather were imported from the United States, valued at £19,787 ($96,293).

Light-coloured leather appears to be preferred, very little light-coloured sole leather being made in New South Wales; indeed the art of giving it a light shade does not appear to be understood here. In Victoria, however, the tanners succeed in making light-coloured leather by passing the hides through a solution of valonia after they have been tanned with the wattle. Boot-makers believe that the light-coloured leather makes a better finish than that coloured with red or hemlock, and perhaps that is one of the reasons why California leather, which is always of a light colour, commands a better price than any other, even in the United States.

The American leather is wholly free from that sickening and disagreeable smell common to the colonial product.

American leathers for saddlery and harness have distanced all competitors in the Sydney market. The demand for these articles by saddle and harness makers is constantly increasing, and there is every reason to believe that the trade, if properly pushed, will increase to large proportions.

The best means to extend the trade in American leather is through intelligent travelling agents who thoroughly understand their business. The goods should be in the market before any attempt is made to advertise them. If samples are sent, they should fairly represent the goods.

The New Zealand Loan and Mercantile Company, Alderson & Sons, Harrison & Whiffen, I. E. Bigg, Davenport & Sons, Forsyth & Sons, F. L. Barker, Harrison, Jones, & Devlin, Mort & Co., Hill, Clark, & Co., are amongst the principal leather dealers in Sydney.

A factory has been established in Marrickville, one of the suburbs of Sydney, for the manufacture of compressed leather. The process was invented and patented several years ago by Mr. A. E. Arnold, and large results are expected from it. It consists in the utilization of scraps, cuttings, and every description of waste leather, by compressing them into bricks, blocks, and various designs, by means of hydraulic pressure. The scraps are placed in a chemical solution, and after becoming thoroughly saturated are put into a mould and subjected to a hydraulic machine, capable of pressing with a force of 450 tons into blocks 12 inches square. After undergoing the pressure the blocks can be turned or planed into various artistic shapes, such as statuary, brackets, wainscoting, and panels. All these articles are capable of receiving a most brilliant polish. One of the chief excellencies of the material is its durability. Specimens are shown at the factory which have been soaked in water for twelve hours, and when the surface is scraped off are found to be perfectly dry. The strength of a block, about 5 inches square, was tested by a rifle ball fired at a distance of 60 feet, and it was found to have penetrated the material only an inch and a half, and without making the slightest splintering.

Amongst the uses to which compressed leather is applied may be mentioned, brakes for wagons and carriages, railway blocks, stair-treads, in place of the much-used and unserviceable oilcloth or slippery coverings usually in vogue for covering stairs. Rooms floored with these blocks, in their polished form, would become not only luxurious in appearance, but perfectly cleanly. The blocks being entirely free from splintering, they might be used very advantageously as padding for war vessels.

Admiral Tryon, R.N., lately in command of H.M. ships on the Australian station, took great interest in this compressed leather. He spoke in eulogistic terms of the blocks being used for naval warfare. He said that compressed leather would be brought into general use for such purposes.

There is no duty charged either on manufactured or unmanufactured leather imported into the Colony of New South Wales. The admission of these articles, as well as boots and shoes, free of duty, forms a striking contrast to the course pursued by the other Colonies, and is the subject of much complaint amongst the leather manufacturers of Sydney. In Victoria there is a duty of 5 per cent. *ad valorem* on calf and kid leather imported, and $7\frac{1}{2}$ per cent. on patent, coloured, and fancy leathers, and $13\frac{1}{2}$ per cent. on all other leathers, except crust or rough-tanned hog-skin, calf, and goat, and sumach-tanned sheep, which are free.

The tax in Victoria on boots and shoes is as follows:—Men's No. 6 and upwards, 33s. ($7·02) per 1 dozen pairs; slippers, men's, women's, and children's, 9s. ($2·18) to 4s. (97 cents) per 1 dozen pairs.

The evidence taken before the Commission for the investigation of the operations of the tariff in Victoria was strongly in favour of admitting free of duty all leather known as wax-calf, calf, kid, glove and glove-kid, morocco, goat, and seal, and levant and patent calf. The Commission reported that the quality of colonial calf-skin was greatly inferior to the imported article, on account of the want of necessary skill in preparing and dressing the skins. Fault was also found with the reckless manner in which cattle were branded and flayed, and recommended that an Act of Parliament should be passed to prevent these abuses.

In regard to boots and shoes, the Commission was of opinion that the fiscal policy of the Colony gave a great impetus to the import trade, and at the same time aided materially in developing home manufactures. The manufacturers of the ordinary and common class of boots and shoes thought that the last increase of duties in the tariff had been detrimental to their business, inasmuch as it caused a number of competitors to commence manufacturing. The Commission recommended that efforts be made to increase the export trade to the adjacent Colonies, and at the same time admitted that Victoria laboured under some disadvantages in trying to compete with New South Wales free of duty. It further stated that the manufacturers were opposed to any system of drawback in their leather exports, from the fact that such systems were not only troublesome, but opened the door to fraud, in consequence of the impossibility of Custom-house experts being able to detect uppers made of colonial from those made of imported leather. As to saddlery and harness, the Commission thought that the manufacturers and journeymen were quite satisfied with the tariff, with the exception of the duty on patent leather. One of the largest manufacturers, who employed ninety-five hands, said that he would not object to the removal of the duty from saddles and harness if hog-skins, patent leather, saddle-trees, plated spurs, stirrups, bits, seal-skin, blue serges, twine, and tacks, were admitted free. The only dresser of hog-skins in Victoria stated, that on account of the difficulty experienced in obtaining tanned hog-skins from England, it was his intention to discontinue dressing them.

At the last International Exhibition New South Wales took the lead of the other Australasian Colonies in number, variety, and excellence of the different kinds of dressed hides. It was noticed, however, that the bags and portmanteaus exhibited by New South Wales manufacturers had little to commend them.

The strong and heavy boots made, sell at low prices, and are well adapted to the country trade and bush life. Much improvement has also been made during the last few years in the manufacture of women's and children's boots and shoes. It is estimated that the annual output of these articles is four or five times greater than in 1881, a fact said to be due to the introduction of skilled labour and to the application of machinery.

There appears to be a wide and profitable field in Australasia for the introduction of American leather-working machinery. The colonists are slow, however, to adopt improvements, and importers would at first have some difficulty in overcoming the prejudice against untried machines. The prejudice will in time be overcome, as has been the case with the American agricultural machines and implements. Muller & Co., of London, have succeeded in introducing a number of their machines here for working in leather. These machines consist—first, in a cylinder or barrel set with knives, which are arranged in a right and left spiral from the centre to the end (the knives are made of either brass or steel, and may be sharp, blunt, or wire-edged, according to the character of the operation required); second, a roller covered with india-rubber, revolving in a frame under the knife-roller and acting as a beam, this roller being brought up by the operator's foot on a treadle and its closeness being regulated by a set-screw ; third, a clip-frame sliding in front of the machine to and fro from the rollers, this clip holding the hides or skin in its grip while it is pulled back against the action of the knives. The whole working of the machine is as follows :—The skin held in the clip is thrown over the beam or roller, and on being raised into contact with the knife-cylinder, the spiral action right and left stretches it out and operates on its surface in the way desired, either in removing wool or flesh, in thickening, or in the various operations of setting out. These machines, however, will soon be superseded by American ones. Leather manufacturers are much pleased with the Lockwood automatic leather-scourer and setting machine. This machine will scour all kinds of leather, and will set calf skins, kip, buff, and wax. It can, however, only be used in large tanneries, as its cost is considerable, but everywhere it has been used it has given very general satisfaction. Mr. Davis states in his recent work on the manufacture of leather that he saw seven of these machines in Messrs. Bryan & King's tannery in Woburn, Mass., and was surprised at the ease with which they were worked and the excellence of their finished work. Among some of the improvements in this machine over the one patented by the inventor in 1876 is the method of driving the operative parts of the machine by means of shafting and gearing instead of belting, and the substitution of a single lever in lieu of the double hand-levers for controlling the truck on the ways and the so-called cross-head and carriage. Another improvement is the attachment of a large table on which to place the stock, so that one workman can be preparing a side at one end, while the other will be directing the machine in the automatic setting out of a side previously arranged on the other end. The working thus keeps two men constantly busy, but the physical labour required is light. The strokes made are either strong or light, as desired, being directly under the control of the operator, who, with his hand on the wheel, guides them; so, in going over the bellies and flanks, working out folds, and thoroughly setting out thick portions of a side, the work is not only done quickly and well, but the leather is made to measure more than enough on all stock sold by the foot to quickly pay for the machine in the gain thus made.

The value of various kinds of unmanufactured leather exported from the Colony of New South Wales during the year 1887, was £100,309 ($488,154) against £112,491 ($547,194) for the year 1886. The exports were heavier in 1882 than in any other year in the history of the Colony, having amounted to as many as 6,689 bales, valued at £154,971 ($709,039).

The following table shows the quantity and value of the total exports of leather from New South Wales for each year since 1877:—

Year.	Quantity.	Value.		Year.	Quantity.	Value.	
	packages.	£	$		packages.	£	$
1877	4,590	99,314	483,312	1883	5,343	111,460	542,420
1878	4,311	95,086	462,736	1884	6,115	130,771	636,397
1879	3,298	67,643	329,185	1885	5,382	116,735	568,091
1880	5,103	108,985	530,366	1886	5,282	112,491	547,194
1881	6,285	145,698	708,966	1887	4,644	100,309	488,154
1882	6,689	154,971	753,289				

The total exports of raw hides from New South Wales during the year 1887, amounted to 161,055 hides, £143,968 ($700,620). Of these Great Britain received 105,368; Victoria, 49,822; Queensland, 651; San Francisco, 215; South Australia, 2,477; Tasmania, 2,145; and New Zealand, 377. Of the hides of New South Wales it is difficult to estimate the quantity produced, but the return of cattle for the year 1887 amounted to 1,581,078 head, and as, in addition to the ordinary butchers' consumption, there are meat preserving works in operation, the number forthcoming must be very considerable.

With regard to the relative value of hides, those from New Zealand and Queensland are most in request, and usually realise top rates, on account of their superior substance and compactness rendering them specially suitable for the manufacture of the more expensive descriptions of sole leather and belting. The greater portion of the hides used in

ruminants, and occasionally chew the cud. When attacked by dogs, they not infrequently tear them open with their hind feet. Sometimes they have been known to clasp them in their forearms and drown them when attacked in the water, and they have been known to get rid of their human assailants in the same way. The skin from these animals makes very strong, smooth, and elastic leather. It bears some resemblance to kid, but is stronger and far more durable.

During the year 1887 New South Wales imported from Victoria, Queensland, South Australia, and Tasmania 690 packages of kangaroo-skins, valued at £10,484 ($51,020). The exports of kangaroo-skins from New South Wales during the same period were 1,083 packages, valued at £43,214 ($210,301). Of these, Victoria received 541 packages, Great Britain 335, and the United States 140 packages.

Next to the kangaroo, the skins of the wallaby and paddymelons are most in demand, the wallaby and paddymelon being a smaller species of the kangaroo. Then there are a number of different kinds of opossum skins used. In fact, the skins of nearly all the native animals are being used for leather, such as the koala (or native bear), the bandicoot (native pig), the dingo (native dog), and the platypus.

The platypus is one of the most extraordinary mammals known, and although its skin has long been a highly prized article of commerce, scientists have for the last fifty years been trying to settle the question whether it is born alive or hatched from an egg. A cablegram was sent to London by Professor Liversidge, of the University of Sydney, to the effect that Mr. W. H. Caldwell, who holds the Balfour travelling Fellowship of Cambridge, had at last settled this question. Mr. Caldwell was especially commissioned by the British Association for this purpose, and the results of his investigation have created no little commotion in scientific circles both in Europe and Australia. Many bushmen have positively declared the platypus to be oviparous, but no platypus egg had ever been found by any one previous to Mr. Caldwell's discovery. Mr. Gerard Krefft used at intervals to offer £50 for an egg. Although numbers of platypus have been caught during the pairing season and dissected, no trace of eggs had been found, and scientists accepted the theory that these curious creatures were viviparous; hence the sensation created by the cablegram above referred to. The apparatus and instruments which Mr. Caldwell brought to Australia to aid him in his investigation cost over £1,000 ($4,886). This amount, together with other expenses connected with his visit was borne by the British Association.

The body of the platypus resembles that of a mole, or small otter, and is covered with a close, short, grayish-brown fur. After a few stiff hairs are removed, the fur is very soft, and will stand very rough wear. It is made into caps, tippets, slippers, and rugs. Its tail is broad and flattened. The jaws are produced to form a beak like a duck's. The margins of the jaws are sheathed with horn, and are supplied with transverse horny plates, two in each jaw, but there are no true teeth. The toes are united by a membrane or a web, so that the animal is enabled to swim with great ease. It inhabits streams and ponds. Its food consists principally, if not wholly, of insects. It makes extensive burrows in the banks of rivers and creeks. Mr. Caldwell spent many months in Australia studying the habits of this curious creature. His studies have been rewarded with the discovery that it lays eggs, from which the young are hatched. The young are born quite blind and nearly naked. The method by which they obtain milk from the mother is still obscure, as there are no nipples, but simply a flat surface; nor is there any marsupial pouch. The beak of the young animal is different from what it is in the adult condition.

The platypus is extremely timid, and is very difficult to shoot or catch. It swims with its head partly above the water, but disappears under the surface upon hearing the slightest noise or on catching a glimpse of any moving object, even at a great distance.

The factory system is largely carried on in New South Wales in the manufacture of boots and shoes. Machinery is employed to a greater or less extent in all the factories in the Colonies. Elastic sides, Balmorals, and ordinary walking shoes are the prevailing styles of imported goods. A decided preference is expressed for narrow and pointed toes. It is said that the American shoes are too wide and broad, and look larger on the feet than other imported goods. The principal difficulty in the way of the introduction of American boots and shoes into this market is the strong prejudice in favour of the goods of English make. The people are accustomed to purchasing their goods and wares from Great Britain, with which country they have a direct exchange, and some time will elapse before the present system can be altered.

The following are some of the largest boot and shoe importers in Sydney : Enoch Taylor & Co.; McMurtrie, Kellerman & Co.; I. McEvoy; John Hunter; Callaghan & Son. The first named firm has an extensive establishment in Melbourne, Victoria. McMurtrie, Kellerman & Co. make a speciality of fine work, and it is said all their goods are guaranteed. They are also large dealers in leather.

The export of boots and shoes produced in the Colony does not appear to have increased within the last ten years, and the trade is confined to the other Colonies and the South Pacific Islands.

The following table shows the number of packages and the value of boots and shoes of colonial produce exported from New South Wales for each year since 1877 :—

Year.	Number of packages.	Value.		Year.	Number of packages.	Value.	
		£	s			£	s
1877	2,083	58,258	283,315	1883	2,270	52,610	256,027
1878	1,875	46,763	227,574	1884	2,761	55,378	269,497
1879	2,106	47,759	232,274	1885	2,054	45,710	222,448
1880	2,205	48,097	234,064	1886	921	23,164	112,728
1881	2,192	45,150	199,723	1887	1,300	35,774	174,094
1882	2,383	48,378	236,405				

Although there has been little increase in the quantity and value of the export of colonial boots and shoes since 1875, the home consumption of these articles is considerably greater than heretofore.

The Australians use a greater number of boots and shoes in proportion to population than the people of any other country. Indeed, anything like a correct statement of the actual number of boots and shoes purchased by the average Australian during the year would scarcely be credited in the United States.

HARDWARE.

Although there was a falling off in the value of the imports of hardware into the Colony of New South Wales during 1887, the trade began to rally again in the beginning of the present year, and has steadily increased since, especially with the United States. The direct American imports are, however, very small when compared with those from Great Britain; but it must be borne in mind that no inconsiderable quantity of American hardware is shipped to Sydney by way of London, and appears in the Customs returns as coming from Britain.

The total value of the imports of hardware into New South Wales from all countries during the year 1887 was £364,686 ($1,774,744) against £617,249 ($3,003,842) for 1886. These imports, however, do not include many articles sold by dealers in hardware, such as cutlery, iron and steel nails, brass and iron castings, steam-fittings, plain and galvanized wire fencing, iron pipes, iron and steel bars, tinware, tin plates, galvanized manufactures, surgical and scientific instruments, fire-arms, grindery, agricultural implements, machinery. If these articles were added, the total value of the imports would amount to a sum not less than $10,000,000.

The articles usually called hardware are edge-tools, axes, hatchets, planes, chisels, hammers, saws, monkey-wrenches, locks, door-knobs, latches, fastenings for shutters, iron buckets, wringers, mangles, stoves, pots, kettles, and other cooking utensils; meat-choppers, bells, roller-skates, &c.

Table showing the quantity and value of hardware imported into New South Wales for each year from 1877 to 1887, inclusive.

Year.	Quantity.	Value.		Year.	Quantity.	Value.	
	packages.	£	$		packages.	£	$
1877	64,982	357,634	1,740,426	1883	123,195	793,622	3,862,161
1878	93,488	462,198	2,249,287	1884	126,874	716,892	3,488,755
1879	81,728	475,399	2,532,522	1885	145,561	649,132	3,159,001
1880	62,011	372,761	1,814,041	1886	177,719	617,249	3,003,842
1881	96,948	542,969	2,642,359	1887	90,944	364,686	1,774,744
1882	134,068	737,840	3,590,698				

Quantity and value of hardware imported direct from the United States into New South Wales for each year since 1877.

Year.	Quantity.	Value.		Year.	Quantity.	Value.	
	packages.	£	$		packages.	£	$
1877	10,012	35,942	174,912	1883	20,170	102,001	501,254
1878	10,113	37,480	182,396	1884	29,146	90,597	440,890
1879	13,241	65,204	317,315	1885	21,452	90,670	441,246
1880	10,703	56,838	276,602	1886	22,048	79,427	386,531
1881	15,659	81,860	398,372	1887	15,821	54,941	267,370
1882	18,429	87,224	424,476				

The absence of a direct medium of exchange with the United States is one of the principal obstacles in the way of American trade with these Colonies. Another obstacle is the want of a more frequent steam service with the American ports; but, in spite of these and other disadvantages under which the American importer labours, a large number of American products, such as axes, hatchets, chisels, planes, and all kinds of edge-tools, castings, cutlery, locks, have taken such a hold on the market that they may be said to have distanced all competitors.

The British manufacturers are unwilling to acknowledge the superiority of American hardware, and while they have failed to keep it out of the market they are persistent in asserting their ability to produce articles quite as good as the American ones. Every effort, however, in that direction has thus far proved a failure. Some of their best houses have recently been complaining of a prejudice in favour of the American products, not only in New South Wales but throughout the Colonies. They state that if the Australian hardware dealers will furnish them with American patterns they will undertake to produce articles precisely like them, and at about the same price.

The firm of Messrs. John Yates & Co., one of the best known hardware manufacturers in Great Britain, in a recent letter to the London *Ironmonger*, took exception to the emphatic statement of Messrs. Ford Brothers, of South Africa, that the American axes are the only ones worth sending to the Colonies. Messrs. Yates & Co. said :—" It is useless for us to be continually stating that we can make axes equal to American ones, without having these statements put to the test. As your correspondent states, if these axes can be made, and packed, and the price be the same as the American, we should hear very little more of 'prejudice.' This is what we doubt. What we propose is this :—Let Ford Brothers send us an order for a case of wedge axes; we will send it out on these conditions, that if the axes do not turn out like the American ones, in shape, finish, &c., they shall return the axes to us, with the case of one dozen axes of American manufacture, which they say are superior. We will pay all expenses connected with this transaction. Our axes and the American axes shall be examined by an independent party, and a report shall be made, through your columns, of the result. As we wish to have the axes here so that the difference can be pointed out and shown to an independent party, let us have something before us which will definitely prove the argument. Our make of tools is very well known, and we don't think there should be any difficulty in selling our axes if it was not for the prejudice we complain of."

This has been tried over and over again by British manufacturers, and with such indifferent success that it is a matter of surprise that the attempt should be so often repeated. An English axe bears about as much resemblance to the American as the base counterfeit to the genuine golden coin.

The editor of the *Ironmonger* has been forced to admit that the American axes have the run, not only in South Africa but in all the British colonies. In a recent number of his paper he devotes considerable space to the subject of American hardware, and gives the opinion of a gentleman whom he describes as "a thoroughly practical Australian, of English birth and sympathies, now in London, but who has spent the greater part of his life in the antipodes." The article has attracted much attention in Australia :—

I can fully indorse (said the gentleman to the reporter of the *Ironmonger*), all that has been said about the marked superiority of American axes over those of English make, and I believe that every disinterested person would do the same. To talk about prejudice in the matter as being the cause of the preference for America is simply nonsense. When the Americans first came to Australia they had as stiff a job as ever they could have expected to have, but they stuck to it with a vigorous determination which was much to be admired, and as they presented the colonists with an axe which was practically a new revelation to them, it is not surprising that they begun to get a footing. The character of their axe was not so widely different from the English axe as might be supposed, but the chief points were a peculiar shape of the handle, which gave the man working with it a much greater purchase over it, and also in the shape and temper of the axe, which also gave a great advantage, notwithstanding that the points of difference were apparently so small and insignificant. To illustrate this I should require drawings, but as they are not at hand it will be sufficient if I say that a comparison between the English axe as originally made (and some makers still continue to make them) and the American axe would fully show what I mean. Yet, in spite of this, the English makers pooh-poohed the Americans, and prided themselves upon their long-established position in the market, with what result we all know. But, to come down from the general to the particular, I could quote several instances of how the English makers have lost trade simply and solely by their disregard for the minor points in making an article ; but one will answer the purpose. We have in Australia what we call a ' long-handled shovel ;' I believe it is not used in this country. Well, as the Americans make it, it is a very convenient tool to work with, but as the English make it—and they, assumedly, copy the American pattern—it would be necessary to sit down to work it as it should be used. The result of this I need hardly point out. Why it should be so I cannot understand, except that the English makers will not trouble themselves to depart from what they believe to be the proper course. They get a pattern to work from and follow it in its general details, but they say that this little point and that little bend are of no consequence, and, as to make them would perhaps be some trouble, they pass them by, and turn out a thing which is of no use to the colonists, and which they will not have at any price, for no other reason than the negligence of the makers to attend to those little details. And it is not merely so with regard to axes, shovels, and spades, but in other goods also.

It was the same thing in regard to scissors, both for the household and for tailors' use ; and when the foreigners, as they may be termed, came to the colonies with their wares they encountered much opposition, but that has now largely died out. The same applies to lath-axes, shingle-axes, carpenters' claw-hammers, saws, and and in such small things as hat and coat hooks, besides others which I have not mentioned. The fact of the matter is the colonists are better educated than they were, and they want something light and ornamental as well as useful ; and, without their having sought it from the Americans, they (the Americans) have brought it to them. This latter fact, and its why and wherefore, seem to be utterly forgotten or overlooked by the English makers. It may be a delicate point to touch upon, but I cannot help remarking that the Americans seem in many respects more suited to meet the requirements of the colonists than the English do, and I say this from my own knowledge of them, having lived amongst them two or three years. They are all more or less technically educated, and they take a deep interest in all things pertaining to them. I remember while living in Hong Kong, that the American Ambassador often set up a column or two of type for mere amusement, whilst one of the missionaries from the States was as good a practical carpenter as ever I met with.

Can the same sort of thing be said about the English manufacturers ? So far from educating themselves up to the necessities of the times, they seem most unwilling to advance, and they do not move except when they cannot help themselves, or at such times when they have nearly lost their markets. My impression is that if the Australian trade is to be kept by this country, a very different class of men to those now engaged in the task will have to steer the ship. What

English makers ought to do is to travel, and make themselves perfectly acquainted with colonial necessities, and then, having done that, to go back to their works and pay personal attention to the production of the articles that are required. I do not think I can advise them to do anything better than this.

A large number of other American articles could very well have been included in the list, such as door-knobs, keys, horseshoe-nails, and plated ware. It is perhaps not generally known that nearly all the recent improvements in what is called shelf hardware originated in the United States. Amongst the articles that have taken a strong hold on the market are all kinds of locks, with flat, slender keys. The keys made by the Yale Lock Company, of Stamford, Conn., are of rolled steel, nickel-plated. The Yale Company also make the "Standard locks," so popular here. These locks are provided with steel tumblers and the flat nickel-plated keys referred to. The private boxes at the General Post Office, and indeed nearly all the public buildings in Sydney, are furnished with American locks, many of which are supplied by the Yale Lock Company. The same company also supply the Australian market with screwless door-knobs and spindles. It is interesting to note that the invention of the screwless door-knob and spindle originated in California, where they were first used.

The various kinds of locks made by the Eagle Company have a large sale. The locks, however, of Russell & Erwin, of New York, are perhaps in greater demand than any of the others, partly on account of their low price and excellent quality, and from the fact that during the last eight years the agents of this firm have thoroughly canvassed the Colonies and made themselves familiar with the kind of locks best suited to the market.

The American pumps are preferred to other kinds; those made by Messrs. Douglas & Co., of Middletown, Conn., being very popular. This firm has also succeeded in introducing their hydraulic rams, garden engines, and street-washers in various parts of Australia. The American meat-choppers are fast superseding the English ones. Those of the Enterprise Manufacturing Company, of Philadelphia, seem to have the run at present. Unlike the English machines, the American choppers do not grind the meat, but chop it. These choppers are especially desired for making sausage-meat and mince-meat. The American metallic wash-boards, monkey-wrenches, and wind-mills are preferred to those of any other manufacture. The "North Star" wash-board, manufactured at Chicago, Ill., is also in very general use. This wash-board is of hard, durable wood, and is said to be the only double board made of a single sheet of zinc, both sides alike. The fluting is deep enough to hold a good supply of water, and the frame, instead of being fastened with nails, is held together with an iron bolt running through a tube formed on the lower edge of the zinc, binding the whole together in the firmest possible manner. The lever wrench made at Hamilton, Ohio, is said to be the best in use. It is certain that no English wrench will compare with it. The flour sifters, socket framing chisels, plane irons, wire cutters, are all from the United States, or else made after American patterns. There is a general demand in Australia for the combined "wire cutter and plier" for putting up iron fences. It would be impossible to include within the limits of this paper all the articles of American manufacture which have made their way into this market. Some mention, however, should be made of the various kinds of scales, weighing machines, and of iron safes, ice machines, rock drills, paper-cutters, emery wheels, waggon skein, writing machines, wood-working machines.

It is gratifying to note that the American locomotives which have recently been introduced into Australia have given very general satisfaction, and it is not unreasonable to expect that they will soon supersede all others. Until very recently the Australians seemed to think that the old-fashioned English locomotive built upon the lever motive principle was the perfection of mechanical ingenuity, and all the improvements made by the Americans during the last forty years in locomotives were wholly ignored. Now the people are beginning to understand that the English engine is too heavy and clumsy, and that it must give away to the American pattern.

It has been noticed that the English locomotive wears out too rapidly, and does great injury to the roadway.

A recent report of the Commissioner of Railways in New Zealand states that the American locomotives in that Colony have more than realized what was expected of them. The report says:—"The American engines have proved themselves to be both good and economical, and for attention to detail in design and general excellence in workmanship they stand out first in our catalogue of locomotives. American engines I thoroughly believe to be more suited to our lines than anything we can get in England."

The American engines in New South Wales are quite as well appreciated as in New Zealand, and Mr. Thomas Higinbotham, Engineer-in-Chief of the railways in Victoria, is a staunch advocate for their use in that Colony. In a recent report he says:—"I did not go to the States at all prepossessed in favour of American engines, but what I saw there satisfied me that for the light railroads of this country they are better adapted than any other kind."

American machinery and appliances for bridge building are also likely to supersede all others. The contract for the construction of the new railway bridge across the Hawkesbury River in New South Wales was awarded to the Union Bridge Company of New York. The construction of this bridge, on account of the great depth of foundation, involves some of the most difficult questions known to science, and the skill thus far displayed in its construction, and the rapidity with which it is being pushed forward, have attracted the attention and admiration of every one interested in the prosperity of the Colony.

The English engineers in building bridges still adhere to the practice of riveting the pieces, instead of fastening them together with pins as in America. The former takes about as many weeks as the latter does days, and does not give half the satisfaction. Another difference between the two methods of bridge building is that the Americans make bridges in workshops and spend little time in putting them up, whereas the English do most of their work on the banks of the stream where the bridge is wanted, but where they have not the steam riveters and other labour and time saving appliances to be found in the shops.

The United States labours under many disadvantages in competing with Great Britain for the Australasian trade. The chief obstacle, however, is the want of anything like reciprocity between the two countries. There is not one of the Colonies that is not anxious to trade with America, and this is especially the case with New South Wales. She has taken the lead in commercial matters, and is very likely to keep it. The total results of her export and import trade during the year 1886 amounted to £36,529,761 ($177,772,082) against £30,325,896 ($147,580,973) for Victoria. This vast trade, with the exception of a small portion enjoyed by the United States and a few other countries, is monopolized by Great Britain.

What is wanted is a more frequent and faster service than we have at present. A powerful steamer could easily make the voyage between San Francisco and Sydney in sixteen days; but whether we are to have a faster and more frequent service or not, it is certain that the American trade with Australia is increasing. There are now more sailing vessels loading both at New York and San Francisco for the Australian ports than at any other period in the history of the Colonies. This state of affairs, however, is not likely to be permanent, from the fact that these vessels, through the unwise legislation of the United States Government, are unable to obtain return cargoes. The duty on those classes of Australian wools especially adapted to the American market could very well be reduced or abolished altogether, for they cannot be grown in any of the States in the Union, and then we should have something like a reciprocity between the two countries. The cost of exchange and other expenses connected with the present banking system between the Colonies and the United States is 5 or 6 per cent. higher than with Great Britain. Indeed, the absence of a direct medium of exchange between New York and Australia has compelled many of the leading American manufacturers to open branch houses in London for the purpose of conducting their Australian trade. It often happens under the present banking system that the importer is compelled to pay for his goods before they arrive from the United States. It is difficult to find a banker in New York willing to cash the draft on the Australian merchant, and the result is it is sent out with the bill of lading by the first mail, and reaches here long before the goods, which sometimes occupy four months on the route. The London shipper labours under no such difficulty; the banker there advances the money as soon as the bill of lading is signed, and the draft is sent out with the goods. Only a moderate discount is charged, the cost of freight, insurance, exchange, and all other charges connected with the transaction being considerably less with London than New York.

CUSTOMS TARIFF.

The Government of New South Wales has returned to what is regarded as a free-trade policy. The present tariff was passed by a majority of 39 to 13, in the House of Representatives, on 23rd June, 1887. The Act provides that it shall be deemed to have come into effect on the 30th day of March, 1887, but that the repeal of the Customs Duties Act of 1886 shall not affect the past operations, and that the duties, both specific and *ad valorem*, heretofore levied, shall be collected until the 30th day of September, 1887. These duties also apply to goods in bond if taken out before 30th September.

It is very interesting to note, notwithstanding certain duties of a strictly protective character, and which have always been levied, that the policy of the Government has been, practically, one of free trade, since the year 1852. At various intervals, however, departures have been made and large numbers of specific duties added, but they have never remained long in force. It is stated that it would not be difficult to show that whenever the Government abandoned the policy of free trade, injury to the commercial interests of the Colony invariably resulted, and that wealth is most easily obtained when it is followed in natural channels, since people will take up industries in the order of their value if they are left alone. The fact that valuable industries receive no attention is generally a proof that others still more valuable employ all the available labour. Wool is the chief industry of New South Wales, and the rapid strides made in that industry is attributed to the free trade policy, inasmuch as the pastoralist has always been permitted to obtain his supplies of food and manufactured goods without having to pay prohibitive duties to producers and manufacturers. The Colony has, therefore, been enabled to carry on this vast industry upon the most favourable terms, and at the same time to receive the highest price for the raw product in the markets of the world. During the last decade New South Wales has increased the number of her sheep from 21,521,662 to 46,687,859, and this irrespective of a loss of over 6,000,000 in 1884-5, owing to unprecedented drought; while the number in her sister colony, Victoria, where the policy of protection prevails, declined during the same period. The woollen-mills of New South Wales, though not so numerous or valuable as those of Victoria, have been built up without artificial aid. The Victorian woollen-mills, on the other hand, have been assisted by an *ad valorem* duty of 15 per cent.; but even that has proved insufficient to make the industry pay. At the last Session of the Victorian Parliament an additional duty of 5 per cent. was added, and the manufacturers clamour for a still further increase. Mr. Munro, a member of the Victorian Parliament and a manufacturer, stated in the Assembly that the mill with which he was connected lost the whole of its capital, £18,000 ($87,597), of which £3,000 ($14,600) was contributed by himself, and that the woollen industry of the Colony was on the verge of ruin. The Ballarat mill, he said, which was regarded as the most substantial in Victoria, had not paid a profit for years; and that an *ad valorem* duty of only 20 per cent. might possibly enable the mills to struggle along for a few years ; then they would die an agonizing death. He did not think that a duty of even 50 per cent. *ad valorem* would make them profitable to the owners.

In 1876 the woollen-mills in Victoria gave employment to 611 hands, but in 1887 the number had increased to 780. Besides the *ad valorem* duty of 20 per cent., it is estimated that the natural protection of having the wool on the spot is equal to fully 10 per cent. more.

The woollen-mills of New South Wales do not employ more than 200 hands, but it can scarcely be said that these mills are worse off than those in Victoria. Improved machinery is wanted in both colonies, not protection. The high cost of labour is one of the principal obstacles with which the manufacturers have to contend in the colonies.

It is a mistake to suppose that Victoria has all the manufactories and New South Wales none. The statistics heretofore published have never done New South Wales justice. There are certainly some industries in Victoria, such as iron interests, flour mills, boot and shoe factories, and furniture factories, which are in advance of similar establishments in New South Wales. The statistics heretofore have represented the horse-power of the factories in New South Wales at 4,860, and 20,160 for Victoria, but for 1886 the Statistical Register shows the horse-power to be 25,199 instead of 4,860. The value of the plant in New South Wales is given as £5,801,757 ($28,234,250) against £3,660,723 ($17,814,908) for Victoria.

Both the imports and exports have for many years been much larger in New South Wales than in Victoria. Indeed, the average annual excess is nearly £6,000,000 ($29,199,000).

The comparison for the shipping trade between the two Colonies is even more favourable to New South Wales, as the average annual tonnage of the latter colony is about 1,000,000 tons in excess of that of Victoria.

The most sweeping change in the 1887 tariff of New South Wales was the abolition of the *ad valorem* duties ; next to that the reduction of the specific duties from a tariff on 175 articles to one on thirty-eight articles.

The following is the Schedule of Customs Duties levied on imports since 1st October, 1887 ; and for comparison the Customs Duties charged on the like articles in the United States of America are inserted opposite each article.

SCHEDULE.

		Rates under Tariff of	
		New South Wales	U. S. of America.
		s. d.	$ c.	$ c.
Beer, ale, porter, spruce or other beer, cider, and perry—			
In wood or jar	per gallon	0 6	·12	·20
In bottle	do	0 9	·18	·35*
For six reputed quarts or twelve reputed pints...	do	0 9	·18	·35
Biscuits—other than ship	per lb.	0 1	·02	20 per cent.
Butter	do	0 1	·02	·04

Also duty on bottles additional. Cider and Perry, 20 per cent.

CUSTOMS TARIFF.

		Rates under Tariff of		
		New South Wales.		U. S. of America.
		s. d.	$ c.	$ c.
Candles, per lb. or reputed package of that weight, and so in proportion for any such reputed weight and stearine	per lb.	0 1	·02	20 per cent.
Cement	per barrel	2 0	·49	20 per cent.
Cheese, bacon, and hams	per lb.	0 2	·04	·04*
Chicory, dandelion, and taraxicum—				
Raw or kiln-dried	do	0 3	·06	·02
Roasted, ground, or mixed with any other article	do	0 6	·12	·02
Chocolate—plain, or mixed with any other article, and chocolate creams	do	0 4	·08	·02
Cigars	do	6 0	1·46	2·50 and 25 per cent.
Cigarettes (including wrappers)	do	6 0	1·46	2·50 and 25 per cent.
Corn-flour and maizena	do	0 1	·02	20 per cent.
Cocoa—				
Raw, without allowance for husks or shells	do	0 3	·06	Free.
Prepared paste, or mixed with any other article	do	0 4	·08	·02
Coffee—				
Raw	do	0 3	·06	Free.
Roasted, ground, or mixed with any other article	do	0 6	·12	·02
Confectionery (including cakes, comfits, liquorice, liquorice paste, lozenges of all kinds, cocoanut in sugar, sugar-candy, succades, and sweetmeats)	do	0 2	·04	·10†
Essences, flavouring and fruit, containing not more than 25 per cent. of proof spirit	per gallon	4 0	·97	2·00 and 25 per cent.
Containing more than 25 per cent. of proof spirit	do	14 0	3·41	2·00 and 25 per cent.
Fish—dried, preserved, or salt	per lb.	0 1	·02	½ cent.
Fruits—dried and candied (exclusive of dates)	do	0 2	·04	35 per cent.
Glucose—				
Liquid and syrup	per cwt.	3 4	·81	20 per cent.
Solid	do	5 0	1·22	20 per cent.
Iron—				
Galvanized, in bars, sheets, or corrugated	per ton	40 0	9·73	44·80
Iron and steel wire	do	20 0	4·86	56·00
Galvanized manufactures (except anchors)	do	60 0	14·60	45 per cent.
Jams—per pound or reputed package of that weight, and so in proportion for any such reputed weight	per lb.	0 1	·02	35 per cent.
Milk, condensed or preserved	do	0 1	·02	20 per cent.
Naphtha and gasoline	per gallon	0 6	·12	20 per cent.

* Bacon and hams, 2 cents per lb.   † Cakes, lozenges, and sweetmeats, 50 per cent.   Comfits, 35 per cent.   Liquorice, 7½ cents. per lb.   Cocoanut in sugar, 2 cents. per lb.   Sugar candy, 5 cents. per lb.

		\multicolumn{4}{c}{Rates under Tariff of}
		\multicolumn{3}{c}{New South Wales.}	U.S. of America.
		s.	d.	$ c.	$ c.
Oils, except black cocoanut and sperm and palm	per gallon	0	6	·12	20 per cent.
In bottle—					
Reputed quarts	per dozen	1	6	·37	25 per cent.
Reputed pints	do	0	9	·18	25 per cent.
Reputed half-pints and smaller sizes	do	0	6	·12	25 per cent.
Opium, and any preparation or solution thereof not imported for use as a known medicine	per lb.	20	0	4·86	10·00
Paints and varnish—					
Paints and colours ground in oil	per cwt.	3	0	·73	25 per cent.
Varnish and lithographic varnishes	per gallon	2	0	·49	40 per cent.
Powder and shot—					
Sporting powder	per lb.	0	3	·06	·06 to ·10
Blasting powder	do	0	1	·02	·06 to ·10
Dynamite and lithofracteur	do	0	1	·02	·06 to ·10
Shot	per 112 lb.	5	0	1·22	3·36
Preserves, jellies, and fruits, boiled in pulp or partially preserved other than by sulphurous acid	per lb.	0	1	·02	35 per cent.
Rice	per ton	60	0	14·60	33·60
Sago, tapioca, and semolina	per lb.	0	1	·02	Free
Salt	per ton	20	0	4·86	2·69
Sarsaparilla and bitters—					
If containing not more than 25 per cent. of proof spirit	per gallon	4	0	·97	2·00
If containing more than 25 per cent. of proof spirit	do	14	0	3·41	2·00
Spirits—On all kinds of spirits imported into the Colony the strength of which can be ascertained by Sykes' Hydrometer	per pr. gal.	14	0	3·41	2·00
No allowance beyond 16·5 shall be made for the under proof of any spirits of a less hydrometer strength than 16·5 under proof.					
On all spirits and spirituous compounds imported into the Colony the strength of which cannot be ascertained by Sykes' Hydrometer	per liq. gal.	14	0	3·41	2·00
Case spirits—reputed contents of two, three, or four gallons shall be charged—					
Two gallons and under as two gallons					
Over two gallons and not exceeding three, as three gallons.					
Over three gallons and not exceeding four, as four gallons.					
Methylated	per gallon	4	0	·97	·50 per lb.
Perfumed spirits, perfumed water, Florida Water, and Bay Rum	per liq. gal.	15	0	3·65	2·00* and 50 per cent.

Perfumed and Florida Waters, 50 per cent. Bay Rum, $1·00 per gallon.

		Rates under Tariff of	
		New South Wales.	U. S. of America.
		s. d. $ c.	$ c.
Sugar—			
Refined	per cwt.	6 8 1·62	3·08
Raw	do	5 0 1·22	1·57
Molasses and treacle	do	3 4 ·81	·04 per gall.
Tea	per lb.	0 3 ·06	Free
Timber (other than laths, building shingles, dyewoods, palings, undressed sandalwood, staves, and casks in shooks)—			
Dressed	per 100 ft. superficial	3 0 ·73	·10
Rough and undressed	do	1 6 ·37	20 per cent.
Doors, sashes, and shutters	each	2 0 ·49	35 per cent.
Tobacco—delivered from ship's side, or from a Custom's bond, for home consumption—manufactured, unmanufactured, and snuff	per lb.	3 0 ·73	From ·15 to 1·00 and Inland Revenue Duty of ·08
Unmanufactured, entered to be manufactured in the Colony. At the time of removal from a Customs bond or from an importing ship to any licensed tobacco manufactory, for manufacturing purposes only, into tobacco, cigars, or cigarettes	do	1 0 ·24	
Sheepwash	do	0 3 ·06	
Wines—			
Sparkling—for six reputed quarts or twelve reputed pints		10 0 2·43	3·50
Other kinds	per gallon	5 0 1·22	·50
Other kinds, for six reputed quarts or twelve reputed pints		5 0 1·22	1·30

All other articles are free.

It is to be regretted that specific duties are retained upon a number of articles of import from the United States, which is the largest Foreign market of the colony.

Timber.—The duty on timber is 3s. (73 cents.) per 100 superficial feet on dressed, and 1s. 6d. (·37 cents.) on rough or undressed timber. The timber trade with the United States has been increasing for many years, and while the duties for a time check the imports, the colony will continue to draw on America for no inconsiderable portion of its timber supply, as the Australian hardwoods are not so suitable for building purposes. Doors and sashes are charged a duty of 2s. (49 cents.) each, but shingles, palings, and laths are admitted free. The Hon. J. F. Burns, Colonial Treasurer, has stated to Parliament, that he will propose the abolition of these duties during the Session of 1888.

Beer.—The duty on beer is 6d. (12 cents) per gallon in wood or jar; if in bottles it is 9d. (18 cents.) per gallon. Six reputed quarts or twelve reputed pint bottles are regarded as containing 1 gallon. The beer duty is charged on all kinds of beer, ale, porter, spruce, cider, and perry. The imports of bottled beer have increased largely during the last few years, especially from the United States.

The quantity of beer brewed in New South Wales during the year 1886 was 13,178,912 gallons against 9,720,000 gallons for 1887.

An excise duty of 3d. (6 cents.) per gallon has been imposed on beer brewed in the Colony. This tax met with much opposition on the part of the brewers, who urged that it was more than double the tax in Great Britain, and that it would not only fall heavily on the consumer, but tempt brewers to supply an inferior article. The tax however became law. It is the first time that it has been levied in this Colony.

Bacon and Hams.—The duty on bacon and hams is 2d. (4 cents.) per pound, and has been levied here since 1871. It has utterly failed to be of the slightest benefit to the produce of the Colony. In fact at no period in the history of the Colony has the curing of bacon been so much neglected. Moreover, since the duty has been charged the number of pigs in proportion to population has steadily declined. In 1861, the decade previous to the imposition of the duty, the number of pigs in the Colony was 162,556, and the population 421,924.

The subjoined table shows, in the form of five periods of three years each, the number of pigs to every 100,000 of population:—

1861-70	38,527 average supply.
1871-73	41,870 ,,
1874-76	33,279 ,,
1877-79	32,987 ,,
1880-82	29,035 ,,
1883-85	22,407 ,,

These figures show unmistakably that since the duty was imposed New South Wales farmers have been unable to supply the population. Only in two out of sixteen years have the actual numbers of pigs ever equalled the numbers in 1870, and even then they were far below the supply of that year on the basis of population. This duty will however, the Treasurer has stated, be abolished during the session of 1888.

Butter.—The duty on butter is 1d. (2 cents.) per pound. No duty was charged on this article until 1886, but prior to that period the exports from New South Wales of butter, the produce of the Colony, frequently exceeded the imports, more particularly in years not subject to droughts. There is no valid reason why the duty should have been imposed, or why it should be retained. Until the late disastrous droughts the number of cattle raised in the Colony was on the increase. In 1887 there were 1,000,000 less cattle in the Colony than in 1881, and consequently the production of butter and cheese in the Colony has declined and the imports have increased. The farmers have been slow to adopt labour-saving appliances and improved systems of conducting their dairies, and as a result consumers go to the best markets and the imports are increased. The Treasurer will propose the removal of this duty also during the session of 1888.

Cheese.—The duty on cheese is 2d. (4 cents.) per pound. There seems to be no more necessity for this duty than for that on butter, and similar remarks apply to both industries. The cheese, when made under the factory system, is excellent. This duty, the Treasurer stated, will cease to be levied during the session of 1888.

Candles.—1d. (2 cents.) per pound is the duty on candles. It is strictly of a protective character, and is for the benefit of the manufactories here. It falls heavily on people in the country districts.

Confectionery pays a duty of 2d. (4 cents) per pound, or £18 6s. 8d. ($89·21) per ton, while the duty on sugar is only £5 ($24·33) per ton. It is not to be expected that confectionery should be admitted free, when sugar is taxed, but there ought to be something like uniformity. The equivalent of the sugar duty would be about £7 ($34·06) per ton.

Jams are taxed at the rate of 1d. (2 cents) per pound, but the sugar duty in 1 pound of jam is covered by about ¼d. (½ cent), so that the remaining ¾d. (1½ cent) is a protective duty.

Sugar.—The tax upon refined sugar is 6s. 8d. ($1·62) per 112 pounds, and upon raw sugar, 5s. ($1·22) per 112 pounds. All the Colonies are much exercised by the question of the European bounties to sugar, and it has been suggested in various quarters that steps should be taken to place an extra tax on sugar made from beets. It must be recollected that, owing to the great improvements in sugar machinery, and in chemical knowledge of the subject, the beet is frequently made to yield 20 per cent. of sugar, a degree of sweetness which, Mr. E. W. Knox, of Sydney, observes, he had met with only rarely in his own records, which dealt with a very large quantity of cane each year, and further, that there is no reason to doubt that this degree of sweetness may be still further increased.

Tinned Fruits.—Preserves and fruits partially preserved pay a duty of 1d. (2 cents) per pound. This duty is also of a strictly protective character. Several local factories have recently improved the quality of their products through the introduction of machinery and skilled labour, and it is said that competition between the local and the American article is likely to be very keen, especially in pears, peaches, and pine apples. The kinds most suitable for canning purposes are not at present produced in the Colony, but are brought here from the adjacent Colonies.

Spirits.—The duty on spirits is 14s. ($3·41) per proof gallon. This is an enormous duty, being nearly twice as much as in the United States. The tax applies to all kinds of spirits imported into the Colony, the strength of which can be ascertained by Sykes' hydrometer.

Perfumed Spirits, Florida Water, and Bay Rum, pay a duty of 15s. ($3·65) per liquid gallon. It has been pointed out to the authorities that these articles cannot be imported and sold in Sydney at a profit under this tariff. It is expected that some concession will be granted, inasmuch as these spirits cannot be used for drinking purposes, but are used chiefly in the composition of the several flavours. Bay rum is made by steeping the leaves of the bay tree in spirits. It is manufactured in bulk at St. Thomas, West India Islands, and is bottled off at Boston, Mass. The duty in the United States is 4s. 1¼d. ($1) per gallon.

Tobacco, the greater bulk of which comes from the United States, is taxed at 3s. (73 cents) per pound. The unmanufactured leaf has also to pay the same duty, unless it is entered at the Customs to be manufactured in the Colony; then the duty is only 1s. (24 cents) per pound. However there is an excise duty of 1s. 3d. (30 cents) per pound to be paid on the manufactured article.

The imports of tobacco are very heavy from Great Britain, but much of the tobacco that reaches these Colonies from Britain is of American growth, having been sent to London for transhipment.

Cigars and cigarettes are taxed at 6s. (1·46 cents) per pound.

The bulk of cigars used is imported from France and Germany, where the low rate of wages lessens the cost of production. Several prominent Sydney cigar dealers express the opinion that the Pennsylvania manufacturers, who make a speciality of cheap, fair, common cigars, could find a market for their products in New South Wales. These cigars are of much better quality than the German ones, and besides, since the imposition of the excise tax, importers are enabled to obtain higher prices than heretofore. It would be of little use for American manufacturers to consign these goods to Sydney, for they would in all probability be left on the market until the consignor ordered a sale at auction, which would be almost certain to result in a sacrifice. The best plan would be to send out a suitable representative agent to remain with the goods until they were fairly introduced into the market. The tax on tobacco has not affected materially the sale of American cigarettes, which have distanced all competitors. The demand for American cigarettes is always greater than the supply, and the reason given for this is that either the manufacturers cannot fill the orders promptly or else the importers delay too long in sending for their goods. At all events it is well known that several favourite brands of American cigarettes cannot be found in the markets.

The duties imposed on *iron galvanized, iron and steel wire*, and *galvanized manufactures*, and on *paints and varnish* are very high, and only for protection interests.

Gasoline and kerosene pay a duty of 6d. (12 cents) per English gallon. Considering the cost of the article this duty is enormous, and can be for no other purpose than as a protection to the kerosene manufacturers in two parts of New South Wales where, owing to the expensive machinery erected by the companies for the extraction of the oil from the shale deposits, they are now enabled to produce an oil equal in most respects to the best imported. The trade in American kerosene, however, is steadily increasing.

In urging reduction of the duties upon American products, it should not be forgotten that it is to the interest of the Australasian Colonies as well as of America that the trade should be fostered. During 1886, a year of great depression in the Colonies, the United States was the only country in the world that increased her export trade with Australasia.

The repeal of the *ad valorem* duties is regarded as a great boon, not only to importers but to all classes of the community. It would be difficult to over estimate the benefits which will result therefrom when we consider the various interests that have been affected by Customs duties. The duties operated against several thousand different articles in the various trades and manufactures. The repeal of the duty on machinery will be sure to increase the imports from America. It is now very generally known in Australasia that American machinery is much more simple in construction and in many ways better adapted to the requirements of the people in a new country than that made in the old world.

Sir Julius Vogel, the late Colonial Treasurer in New Zealand, stated, in a speech at Auckland, that, from patriotic motives, the Government ordered from Great Britain a number of locomotives the same pattern as those made in the United States, but that when they were nearly ready for shipment to the colony, they were found to be so heavy that the engineer in charge of the New Zealand roads stated that some of the bridges would have to be strengthened before the locomotives could be put on the roads, and that they were much heavier than laid down in the plans and specifications. The English manufacturers replied that they could not make the engines of the limited weight prescribed. The New Zealand Government thereupon cabled to the United States for the required supply.

FISH.

The fisheries of New South Wales are becoming more and more important every year, and those interested look forward confidently to the time when they will prove a lasting source of wealth to the Colony. The list of food fishes is a lengthy one, and they exist in practically inexhaustible quantities; but, strange to say, no attempt has been made to utilize them as an article of export. A few individuals from time to time prepare and send abroad small lots of smoked and dried mullet, schnapper, and bream, but such shipments are looked upon more as experiments than as a serious effort to establish a permanent trade. In fact, there are only two fish-preserving establishments in New South Wales, and these are so small as to give employment to only about eleven hands. The value of the plant is stated in the " Colonial Statistical Register" for 1886 to be £210 ($1,022). The annual output is not given, but it would probably not exceed £200 ($973).

There are a large number of fish which could be prepared for export, but they appear at certain periods for a short time only, and no facilities are at hand for utilizing them.

The mullet, *Mugil grandis*, is the only variety which seems to offer any special inducement at present for tinning. They appear during the months of April and May in large shoals along the coast, never going far from land; they proceed in a southerly direction, entering every inlet and harbour. During those months the mullet is in the best condition, and is full of roe, being on its annual migration in search of spawning grounds. This fish is said to be too fat to be preserved with salt, and is apt to become rancid. The roe, when salted and smoked, is as delicious as anything of the kind can be. The Royal Commission on Fish specially recommends this fish for tinning purposes, and says that it has many of the properties of salmon. The form of the tins need not be like that used for preserving California salmon, but like the long slender tins used by the Hollanders. The flavour of the New South Wales mullet is certainly very fine, but it is not equal to the same kind of fish caught off the coasts of New Zealand.

The fish of Australasia differ very little from those of Europe and America. The Rev. J. E. Tenison-Woods, F.L.S., F.G.S., who has given much thought and labour to the fish fauna of Australia, points out the fact that the great mass of the fish belonging to the coasts and rivers of the great island continent have relations similar to those of neighbouring seas, or to those where the same condition of temperature and coastline prevails. The differences in species, where they exist, are minor ones. These differences are more marked on the southern than on the northern coasts. The more remote the Australian coast is from other lands the more peculiar and distinct are the forms of animal life. Thus, Mr. Woods remarks, " on the north, the north-west, and the north-east coasts the fauna is closely connected with that of the Indian and tropical seas, and is in very many species identical with it. The tribes of the colder regions are here wanting, and in places we have the fish of the equatorial zone in all their gorgeous liveries of red, blue, green, and gold, arrrayed in those fanciful patterns which awaken the enthusiasm of every naturalist. We find also that as we go southward on either coast there is a gradual disappearance of the tropical fauna, and a mingling with that of the temperate regions."

New South Wales occupying an intermediate position in Australia, the fish very naturally partake of an intermediate character. Scientists enumerate several varieties of Australian fish, such as the *Ceratodus* and the *Cestracion*, which have disappeared from every other part of the world. The *Cestracion*—Port Jackson shark—has teeth like those of the fossil *Acrodis*, found in the Mesozoic deposits. The *Ceratodus* is described as an existing ganoid fish, exclusively represented in the Trias formation, its anatomy showing a connecting link between a lizard and a fish.

Mr. Woods, in enumerating some of the exceptional fish of New South Wales, directs particular attention to several varieties of the frog fish or *Antennarius*, belonging to the order *Pediculati*, a name which expresses the foot-like office of the fins, more formed for walking on the ground than for swimming. These fish are found floating on the seaweed. They are all highly coloured, but their hues are associated with the surrounding medium, so it is often difficult to distinguish them in the water. Attention is also directed to some peculiar *gobies* or sea-gudgeon, one of which is called the hopping fish. The fins of this fish are developed into legs by means of which it leaps along the mud flats. The eyes are on the top of the head, and can be thrust far out of the sockets and moved independently of one another.

There are several varieties of sea-horses, *Hippocampus*, in New South Wales waters. These fish take their name from the resemblance of the head and the fore part of the body to those of the horse. One of the most striking peculiarities of the sea-horse is that the male carries the eggs in a sac at the base of the tail, opening near the vent.

The *Phillopteryx*, Mr. Woods thinks, is the most remarkable fish in Australian waters, if not in the world. He describes it as, "The ghost of a sea-horse, with its winding-sheet all in ribbons around it, and even as a ghost it seems to be in the last stage of emaciation, literally all skin and grief." The long ends of the ribs which poke through the skin and excite compassion are really protective resemblances, and serve to allure prey. It is therefore an impostor in spite of its rags and emaciation, and, like many a sturdy beggar, puts on the aspect of misery more effectually to ply its trade.

Amongst some of the curious and indeed wonderful fishes of Australasia should be mentioned the Dugong, *Halicore dugong*. This fish resembles the porpoise in shape and size, but is unlike it in having no dorsal fin. The skin is very thick, and is said to make excellent leather. The bones are as heavy as ivory, and are capable of taking a beautiful polish. When struck together they give out a metalliferous sound. The eyes are small and deep-set, like those of a fat pig. The tail is like that of the whale. The fins, which are its only propelling power, are very small for its size. Its habits are those of granivorous ruminants; its stomach is exactly like that of the ox. The Dugong not unfrequently weighs as much as 300 lb., and measures 14 ft. in length and 10 ft. in girth. Such a fish would yield 250 lb. of meat and 10 gallons of oil. It suckles its young, and has flippers with joints like human arms. It frequents the reedy mud flats and shallows along the shores of Queensland, and feeds upon the herbage growing thereon. Seldom to be found south of Moreton Bay, although it was formerly to be seen at the mouths of the Tweed and Richmond Rivers. The colour of the Dugong is a light olive brown. Its flesh is rich and nourishing, and meat can be cut from the same animal resembling beef, veal, and mutton. Messrs. Lionel Ching & Co., manufacturing chemists, of Dunheved Island, off Great Barrier Reef, Queensland, make an oil from the Dugong, which, it is said, has all the properties of cod-liver oil. It is recommended by leading physicians for consumption and general debility. The oil is devoid of any unpleasant taste, and may be used as a substitute for lard or butter for cooking purposes.

Fifty-nine different families or species of New South Wales fish have been described. The largest of these families, the *Percidæ*, perch, is represented by fifty species. The next largest family, the *Sparidæ*, has fourteen species. Fifteen have one species. Eight have two species. The different families of fish found in the New South Wales waters, together with the number of species belonging to each, are thus described by the Rev. J. E. Tenison-Woods :—Percidæ, 50 ; Squamipinnes, 4 ; Nandidæ, 2 ; Mullidæ, 3 ; Sparidæ, 14 ; Cirrhitidæ, 6 ; Scorpænidæ, 11 ; Teuthididæ, 2 ; Berycidæ, 3 ; Kurtidæ, 2 ; Polynemidæ, 2 ; Sciænidæ, 2 ; Xiphiidæ, 1 ; Trichiuridæ, 1 ; Acronuridæ, 1 ; Carangidæ, 15 ; Cyttidæ, 1 ; Coryphænidæ, 2 ; Scombridæ, 10 ; Trachinidæ, 5 ; Batrachidæ, 1 ; Pediculati, 4 ; Cottidæ, 7 ; Cataphracti, 1 ; Gobiidæ, 15 ; Blenniidæ, 17 ; Sphyrænidæ, 3 ; Atherinidæ, 4 ; Mugilidæ, 7 ; Fistularidæ, 1 ; Ophiocephalidæ, 1 ; Trachypteridæ, 1 ; Pomæcentridæ, 4 ; Labridæ, 18 ; Gadopsidæ, 1 ; Gadidæ, 4 ; Pleuronectidæ, 9 ; Siluridæ, 5 ; Scopelidæ, 6 ; Salmonidæ, 1 ; Galaxidæ, 7 ; Scombresocidæ, 6 ; Clupeidæ, 12 ; Chirocentridæ, 1 ; Symbrachidæ, 1 ; Murænidæ, 11 ; Syngnathidæ, 6 ; Sclerodermi, 21 ; Gymnodontes, 12 ; Carcharidæ, 8 ; Lamnidæ, 1 ; Scyllidæ, 3 ; Cestraciontidæ, 2 ; Spinacidæ, 1 ; Rhinidæ, 1 ; Pristiophoridæ, 1 ; Rhinobatidæ, 2 ; Trygonidæ, 3 ; Torpedinidæ, 1 ; Raiidæ, 1.

Mr. J. Douglas Ogilby, Assistant Zoologist, Australian Museum, Sydney, has described a number of fish not included in the above list.

The edible fish of New South Wales comprise 115 different species. Mr. Ogilby is of opinion that some of the best food fish of the Colony are never seen in the markets, although numerous along the coasts. He places *Gerres ovatus*, the silver or white bream, in the first rank of Australian fish. *Arripis salar*, the Australian salmon, comes next, but principally on account of the great numbers in which it is to be found; it is of a greenish lead colour, the upper part of the body of a deep black, with numerous black spots on other parts of the body.

Mr. J. Douglas Ogilby, F.L.S., has specially prepared the following list of the edible fish of New South Wales, arranged systematically:—

The local names are those which are used in Australia.

1. Percidæ (20 sp.)

1. *Lates colonorum* .... Perch.
2. *Enoplosus armatus* .... Old Wife.
3. *Caprodon schlegeli* .... Long Fin.
4. *Serranus dæmeli* .... Black Rock Cod.
5. *Plectropoma ocellatum* .... Wirrah.
6. *Lutianus fulviflamma* ....
7. *Lutianus macleayanus* .... Macleay Perch.
8. *Glaucosoma scapulare* .... Pearl Perch.
9. *Macquaria australasica* .... Silver Perch of the Murray.
10. *Ctenolates ambiguus* .... Golden Perch.
11. *Therapon curieri* .... Trumpeter.
12. *Therapon richardsonii* .... Silver Bream.
13. *Therapon macleayanus* ....
14. *Lobotes surinamensis* ....
15. *Histiopterus labiosus* .... Boar Fish.
16. *Gerres ovatus* .... Silver Billy.
17. *Oligorus macquariensis* .... Murray Cod.
18. *Arripis salar* .... Salmon. Adult and S. trout, young.
19. *Priacanthus macracanthus* .... Red Bull's Eye.
20. *Dinolestes muelleri* .... Sea Pike.

2. Squamipinnes (2 sp.)

21. *Scatophagus multifasciatus* ....
22. *Scorpis æquipinnis* .... Sweep.

3. Mullidæ (2 sp.)

23. *Hypeneichthys porosus* .... Red Mullet.
24. *Hypeneus signatus* .... Spotted Mullet.

4. Sparidæ (9 sp.)

25. *Girella tricuspidata* .... Black Fish.
26. *Girella simplex* .... Black Fish.
27. *Girella elevata* .... Rock Black Fish.
28. *Girella cyanea* .... Blue Fish.
29. *Haplodactylus lophodon* .... Butter Fish.
30. *Pagrus unicolor* .... Schnapper.
31. *Chrysophrys sarba* .... Tarwhine.
32. *Chrysophrys australis* .... Black Bream.
33. *Pimelepterus meridionalis* .... Drummer.

5. Cirrhitidæ (5 sp.)

34. *Chironemus marmoratus* ....
35. *Chilodactylus morwong* .... Morwong.
36. *Chilodactylus macropterus* .... Jackass Fish.
37. *Chilodactylus fuscus* .... Carp.
38. *Latris ramsayi* .... Trumpeter.

6. Scorpænidæ (2 sp.)

39. *Scorpæna cruenta* .... Red Rock Cod.
40. *Scorpæna cardinalis* .... Red Rock Cod.

7. Teuthididæ (1 sp.)

41. *Teuthis nebulosa* .... Black Trevally.

8. Berycidæ (1 sp.)

42. *Beryx affinis* .... Nannygai.

9. Sciænidæ (2 sp.)

43. *Sciæna neglecta* .... Jewfish.
44. *Otolithus atelodus* .... Teraglin.

10. Acanthuridæ (1 sp.)

45. *Prionurus microlepidotus* ....

11. Carangidæ (7 sp.)

46. *Caranx trachurus* .... Yellow-tail.
47. *Caranx georgianus* .... White Trevalley.
48. *Seriola lalandii* .... King-fish.
49. *Seriola hippos* .... Samson-fish.
50. *Temnodon saltator* .... Tailor—Blue-fish of New York.
51. *Trachynotus russellii* .... Dart.
52. *Psettus argenteus* .... Batfish.

12. Cyttidæ (1 sp.)

53. *Zeus australis* .... John Dory.

13. Scombridæ (5 sp.)

54. *Scomber pneumatophora* .... Mackerel.
55. *Pelamys australis* .... Bonito.
56. *Cybium commersonii* .... Great striped Mackerel.
57. *Cybium guttatum* .... Spotted Mackerel.
58. *Elacate nigra* .... King-fish, West Indies.

14. Trachinidæ (2 sp.)

59. *Sillago maculata* .... The Whiting.
60. *Sillago ciliata* .... Trumpeter Whiting.

15. Cottidæ (3 sp.)

61. *Platycephalus fuscus* .... Flathead.
62. *Trigla kumu* .... Red Gurnard.
63. *Trigla polyommata* .... Flying Gurnard.

16. Sphyrænidæ (2 sp.)

64. *Sphyræna obtusata* .... Pike.
65. *Sphyræna novæ-hollandiæ* .... Pike.

17. Atherinidæ (1 sp.)

66. *Atherina lacunosa* .... Hardy-head.

18. Mugilidæ (4 sp.)

67. *Mugil dobula* .... Sea Mullet.
68. *Mugil peronii* .... Flat-tail Mullet.
69. *Myxus elongatus* .... Tallygalane.
70. *Agonostoma lacustris* .... Lake Mullet.

19. Labridæ (5 sp.)

71. *Cossyphus unimaculatus* .... Pig-fish.
72. *Cossyphus gouldi* .... Blue Groper.
73. *Coris lineolata* .... Rainbow-fish.
74. *Odax semifasciatus* .... Rock Whiting.
75. *Olistherops brunneus* .... Herring Cale.

19a. Gadopsidæ (1 sp.)

76. *Gadopsis marmoratus* ....

20. Gadidæ (2 sp.)

77. *Lotella limbata* .... Ling, Beardy.
78. *Pseudophycis barbatus* ....

21. Pleuronectidæ (4 sp.)

79. *Pseudorhombus russellii* .... Flounder.
80. *Pseudorhombus multimaculatus* ...... Flounder.
81. *Ammotretis adspersus* .... Long-snouted Flounder.
82. *Synaptura nigra* .... Sole.

22. Siluridæ (3 sp.)

83. *Copidoglanis tandanus* .... River Catfish.
84. *Cnidoglanis megastoma* .... Sea Catfish.
85. *Arius thalassinus* ....

23. Scopelidæ (2 sp.)

86. *Saurus tumbil* .... Ranning.
87. *Aulopus purpurissatus* .... Sergeant Baker.

24. Scombresocidæ (5 sp.)

88. *Belone ferox* .... Long Tom.
89. *Belone gavialoides* .... Long Tom.
90. *Hemirhamphus intermedius* .... Sea Garfish.
91. *Hemirhamphus regularis* .... River Garfish.
92. *Arrhamphus sclerolepis* .... Short-billed Garfish.

25. Galaxiidæ (1 sp.)

93. *Galaxias coxii* ... . Mountain Trout.

26. Clupeidæ (5 sp.)

94. *Chatoïssus richardsonii* .... Bony Bream.
95. *Clupea sagax* .... Pilchard.
96. *Clupea sundaica* .... Maray.
97. *Clupea hypselosoma* .... Maray.
98. *Clupea novæ-hollandiæ* .... River Herring.

27. Muroenidæ (4 sp.)

99. *Anguilla reinhardtii* .... River Eel.
100. *Anguilla australis* .... River Eel.
101. *Murænesox cinereus* .... Silver Eel.
102. *Muræna afra* .... Green Eel.

28. Sclerodermi (3 sp.)

103. *Monacanthus hippocrepis* .... Leather Jacket.
104. *Monacanthus chinensis* .... Leather Jacket.
105. *Monacanthus ayraudi* .... Leather Jacket.

The following is a list of New South Wales edible fishes arranged in the order of their economic value, also prepared by Mr. J. Douglas Ogilby, F.L.S.:—

1. Represented in market every day.

Gerres ovatus .... Silver Billy.
Arripis salar—only from its great numbers Salmon.
Girella tricuspidata .... Black Fish.
Pagrus unicolor .... Schnapper.
Chrysophrys sarba .... Tarwhine.
Chrysophrys australis .... Black Bream.
Sciæna neglecta .... Jew-fish.

Caranx trachurus—chiefly valuable as bait Yellow-tail.
Caranx georgianus .... White Trevalley.
Seriola lalandii—comes in large shoals at King-fish.
   intervals.
Temnodon saltator.............................. Tailor.
Sillago maculata................................. Whiting.
Sillago ciliata...................................... Trumpeter Whiting.
Platycephalus fuscus .... Flathead.
Mugil dobula .... Sea Mullet.
Mugil peronii .... Flat-tail Mullet.
Hemirhamphus intermedius .... Sea Garfish.
Hemirhamphus regularis .... River Garfish.
Anguilla australis .... River Eel.

2. Common in markets.

Lates colonorum .... Perch.
Macquaria australasica) First-class fresh- Silver Perch.
Ctenolates ambiguus ... } water — never in Golden Perch.
Oligorus macquariensis) Sydney markets. Murray Cod.
Girella simplex .... Black Fish.
Chilodactylus fuscus .... Carp.
Sphyræna obtusata............................ Pike.
Myxus elongatus .... Talygalane.
Pseudorhombus russellii................... Flounder.
Pseudorhombus mulimaculatus........ Flounder.
Synaptura nigra................................. Sole.
Belone ferox .... Long Tom.
Belone gavialoides .... Long Tom.
Anguilla reinhardtii .... River Eel.

3. Appear irregularly, often in large numbers.

Plectropoma ocellatum .... Wirrah.
Priacanthus macracanthus................ Red Bull's Eye.
Scorpis æquipinnis .... Sweep.
Hypeneichthys porosus .... Red Mullet.
Pimelepterus meridionalis................. Drummer.
Scorpæna cruenta .... Red Rock Cod.
Scorpæna cardinalis .... Red Rock Cod.
Teuthis nebulosa .... Black Trevalley.
Beryx affinis .... Nannygai.
Otolithus atelodus .... Teraglin.
Seriola hippos .... Sampson Fish.
Psettus argenteus .... Batfish.
Zeus australis .... John Dory.
Scomber pneumatophorus .... Mackerel.
Trigla kumu .... Red Gurnard.
Sphyræna novæ-hollandiæ .... Pike.
Cossyphus unimaculatus .... Pig-fish.
Coris lineolata .... Rainbow-fish.
Odax semifasciatus............................ Rock Whiting.
Lotella limbata .... Ling, Beardy.
Saurus tumbil .... Ranning.
Aulopus purpurissatus .... Sergeant Baker.
Clupea sagax .... Pilchard.
Clupea sundaica .... Marny.
Clupea hypselosoma .... Maray.
Murænesox cinereus .... Silver Eel.
Muræna afra .... Green Eel.

4. Common in market, but of little commercial value.

Therapon cuvieri .... Trumpeter.
Atherina lacunosa .... Hardy-head.

5. Scarce in market.

Enoplosus armatus	Old Wife.
Serranus dæmeli	Black Rock Cod.
Hypeneus signatus	Spotted Mullet.
Girella elevata	Rock Black Fish.
Girella cyanea	Blue Fish.
Haplodactylus lophodon	Butter Fish.
Chilodactylus morwong	Morwong.
Chilodactylus macropterus	Jackass Fish.
Latris ramsayi	Trumpeter.
Trachynotus russellii	Dart.
Pelamys australis	Bonito.
Trigla polyommata	Flying Gurnard.
Agonostoma lacustris	Lake Mullet.
Cossyphus gouldi	Blue Groper.
Olistherops lrunneus	Herring Cale.
Ammotretis adspersus	Long-snouted Flounder.
Arrhamphus sclerolepis	Short-billed Garfish.
Monacanthus hippocrepis	Leather Jacket.
Monacanthus chinensis	Leather Jacket.
Monacanthus ayraudi	Leather Jacket.

6. Rare or accidental in market.

Caprodon schlegelii	Long Fin.
Lutianus macleayanus	Macleay Perch.
Glaucosoma scapulare	Pearl Perch.
Histiopterus labiosus	Boar Fish.
Dinolestes muelleri	Sea Pike.
Cybium commersonii	Great-striped Mackerel.
Cybium guttatum	Spotted Mackerel.
Elacate nigra	King-fish.

7. Fish which never appear in market.

Therapon richardsoni	Silver Bream.
Copidoglanis tandanus	River Catfish.
Cnidoglanis megastoma	Sea Catfish.
Galaxias coxii	Mountain Trout.
Clupea novæ-hollandiæ	River Herring.

Amongst the edible fishes especial mention should be made of the *Beryx affinis*, the Nannygai of the Sydney market. This fish is often 20 inches in length, and is not only a delicious food fish, but is interesting as being one of the oldest forms of bony fishes still remaining. The Schnapper, *Pagrus unicolor*, is one of the most abundant and favourite fish in the Colony.

Its flavour is not quite so fine as that of some others of the perch family, but it is unquestionably a superb table fish, wholesome and nutritious. It is found on all parts of the Australasian coasts, and is nowhere more abundant than in New South Wales. Being a deep-water fish, it is usually found on or near the rocky points or reefs. The report of the Fish Commission says that its food is principally the mollusca living on the rocks. The readiness with which it snaps up bait of the most varied description indicates its omnivorous taste. Like most fish, it has its periods of migration, and appears in schools in early summer. It is then believed to be about three years old, the previous stages of its existence being known as "Red Bream" at one year, and "Squire" at two years.

Another favourite fish is the Black Rock Cod, *Serranus daemeli*. It is found on all the rocky points of the coast, and in the harbours about bold headlands. It attains a great size, not unfrequently weighing 100 lb. In addition to the Black Rock Cod, there are two species of Red Rock Cod, four Flat-heads, and two Flying Gurnets, all of which are excellent table fish.

The Whiting.—There are four species of Whiting in Australia. The species known as the Sand Whiting, *Sillago maculata*, one of the best table fishes, is very abundant in New South Wales. It is in more general use than the Schnapper, and is in the best condition when it first comes in from the sea, about midsummer. It is caught both with the hook and seine. The Trumpeter Whiting, *Sillago ciliata*, is not so good as the Sand Whiting. It comes in from the sea a month or two later than the other.

The colour of the Sand Whiting is a white olive, marbled with large brown spots. There is a broad longitudinal band on each side of the body. The fins are transparent, and the rays spotted with orange. This fish is said to command a higher price than any other in the market. The other species are not so valuable for food. The variety known as the Rock Whiting, *Odax semifasciatus*, is soft and ill-flavoured. If cooked when perfectly fresh it tastes fairly well.

The Trumpeter, *Latris ramsayi*, is also highly prized as a table fish. It is wholesome and nourishing, and of delicious flavour.

The Jew-fish, *Sciæna neglecta*, is common in the Sydney markets. It is caught, sometimes 5 feet in length, at all seasons of the year, but is most abundant during the summer months. This fish occasionally appears in the market at Melbourne, Victoria, and is known there as the King-fish, but is said not to be abundant.

The Murray Cod is the name given to two species of fish, *Oligorus macquariensis* and *Oligorus mitchelli*. It is the largest fresh-water fish in Australia, and sometimes weighs as much as 150 lb. It is found in most of the larger western rivers. It is of voracious habits, and devours every fish or animal that comes within reach of its enormous mouth. The season for spawning is in midsummer. The largest fish of this genus are found in the Brisbane River. One described by Mr. Ramsay measured over 6 feet in length, and weighed 160 lb. The Groper is the name given to it in Queensland. The Murray Cod belongs to the perch family, and has an oblong body, covered with scales. The teeth are villiform. It has one long dorsal fin, eleven rays of which are spinous. The anal fin has three spines, and the tail is rounded.

The fresh-water fish of Australia, with the exception of the Murray Cod, and one or two species of Cat-fish found in the rivers west of the Great Dividing Range, are very small, and far from being abundant. The frequency of drought and the absence of large rivers are the principal causes for this fact. Beyond the Murray and its tributaries, the Darling, Murrumbidgee, Lachlan, and Macquarie, fish are seldom seen in New South Wales streams. The streams beyond this river system are so small as to be unworthy of the name, and are dried up during the greater part of the year. In the far western country, fish, on the authority of Mr. Tenison-Woods, are unknown.

The Golden Perch, *Ctenolates ambiguus*, is common in the streams and lagoons of the interior of New South Wales. It is a finely-flavoured fish, and sometimes weighs 6 or 7 lb. When fresh its colours are very bright and beautiful. The body is green and golden. The head is a mixture of green, purple, red, and gold.

The Black-fish, *Girella tricuspidata*, are frequently met with in New South Wales waters and along the Australian coasts. They are sometimes 16 to 18 and even 24 inches in length.

The Fresh-water Cat-fish, *Copidoglanis tandanus*, are also abundant, but there is a great prejudice against them. These fish are, when fully grown, 2 feet in length, very fat, and have an eel-like flavour.

Count Castlenau has described several species of Australian herring, *Clupeidae*, but he says they are not abundant.

The various species of trout, *Galaxiidæ*, that have been found are small and scarce.

There are two species of gar-fish, *Hemirhamphus intermedius*, found on the coast of Australia; the most common in New South Wales is *Hemirhamphus regularis*. This fish enters the rivers from the sea about the latter part of the summer to deposit its spawn. It is caught with the net, and moves in large shoals or schools.

Several species of bony bream and *Apogon* have been described, but they are not suitable for food.

Very little has been done in the way of acclimatisation of fish in New South Wales. The river trout, *Salmo furio*, has been successfully introduced into Victorian and Tasmanian waters. This fish is occasionally seen in New South Wales rivers, near the Victorian border. The Crucian carp, several varieties of gold-fish, and a few perch, from European rivers, are about the only fish that have been successfully acclimatised in the Colony. The Royal Commission on Fish have strongly recommended the introduction of Californian salmon, *Oncorhyncus quinnat*. These fish are said to be especially adapted to the mild latitudes of Australasia.

Three or four varieties of oysters are found in abundance on the Australasian coasts. The mud oyster, *O. angasi*, is of such good quality that it has been regarded as identical with that of European seas. The differences are that the valves are dentate at the margin, and the sculpture is finer in the Australasian variety.

The Rock Oyster, *O. glomerata*, is very abundant on all the coasts of Australia, especially in New South Wales. The flavour is very fine, and is free from the copperish taste common to the rock oyster in tropical latitudes. There is another kind, also abundant, known as the drift oyster. This variety is believed to be the same as the rock oyster, under different conditions. It gets the name of drift, it is said, from the fact that its beds are shifted by the influence of storms and tides. Its shell is oblong in shape, and rather heavy. It narrows towards the umbones and widens at the ventral margin; the lower valve is deep.

The Fish Commission in their report deplored the destruction of the natural oyster beds, and said that the process of exhaustion was going on even in the oyster beds that have been leased. The Fisheries Act of 1881, however, appears to have remedied the evil by making it to the interest of those leasing oyster beds to conserve, improve, and keep up the supply, instead of continuing the process of exhaustion. The Act forbids oysters from being removed from the beds until they have reached a certain size. License has to be obtained for dredging, and holders of such license were required to pay for every 3 bushels of oysters obtained a royalty of not less than 1s. 6d. (36 cents). An Act has, however, been passed by the present Parliament repealing this royalty from 1st January, 1888. The license must be taken out annually at a fee of £10 ($48·67), or quarterly at a fee of £3 ($14·59). The penalty for unlawful dredging for oysters is a fine not to exceed £20 ($97·33), and not less than £5 ($24·33), and the forfeiture of all oysters found in the offender's possession. Every one employed in dredging is required to produce his license on demand. The Act also provides for the registration of holders of dredging licenses, and for the marking of dredging boats.

There are few molluscs in New South Wales except the oyster of any importance. There is a mussel, *Mytilus hirsutus*, common in the harbours. It is eaten by some people, but it is not sold in the markets, and has no commercial value.

The crustacea are well represented in Australia. The sea crab, *Neptunus pelagicus*, cray-fish, *Palinurus hugelii*, and the prawns, *Penæus esculentus*, and *canaliculatus*, are especially fine. Some of the cray-fish weigh as much as 6 lb., and when in season are filled with meat of delicious quality. They are usually caught with circular hand-nets, and are in their best condition during the summer.

The prawn, *Penæus esculentus*, is abundant in all the shallow bays and harbours. The Fish Commission reported that there was little or no danger of this delicious food becoming exhausted. It recommended, however, that the same protection should be extended to it as to all other fish while young.

The supply of fish in Sydney is almost wholly from the home division of fisheries—that is, from Port Stephens in the north to Shoalhaven in the south. In 1886, 15,583 baskets of mixed fish were brought to the Fish Market, also 1,130½ dozen of schnapper, 1,060 dozen of mullet, 19½ dozen of jewfish, 173½ dozen of king-fish, 660 dozen of salmon, 117 dozen of crayfish. The sales of these fish realised £34,332 ($167,077).

The bulk of the tinned or canned fish imported into New South Wales comes from the Pacific Coast of America, and consists principally in Columbia and Fraser River salmon. The total imports were 3,836,905 lb., in 1887 of all kinds of fish, including dried, preserved, smoked, salted, and tinned fish. About one-half comes from the United States, 1,544,285 lb. of salmon, valued at £34,230 ($166,580), being imported, against 2,083,593 lb., valued at £40,488 ($196,034), for 1886.

Considerable quantities of dried and salt fish arrived from Great Britain. All the ling, kipper, and white herrings and anchovies are from Britain, but oysters, sardines, mackerel, and cod fish are from the United States.

American sardines are now more popular than any other kind, owing to their superior flavour. The lobsters imported are both from Great Britain and the United States, those from Boston being in special favour. The American lobsters usually sell here at from 7s. to 8s. ($1·70 to $1·95) per dozen 1-lb. tins; cod fish, salted, dry, and tinned, from 4½d. to 5d. (9 cents to 10 cents) per lb.; sardines, ¼-boxes, 7s. 6d. ($1·82), and ⅛-boxes, 3s. 9d. to 4s. (91 cents to 97 cents) per dozen; oysters, from 5s. 6d. to 6s. ($1·34 to $1·46) per dozen 1-lb. tins.

The Customs duty of 1d. (2 cents) per lb. on imported fish operates seriously against the trade, especially from the United States. When the cost of salmon in America is taken into consideration, it will be seen that 1d. (2 cents) per lb. is equal to a duty of about 25 per cent. *ad valorem*, a very heavy duty, which, together with the profit of dealers, renders the article expensive. This kind of fish is very suitable for this climate.

The subjoined table shows the quantity and value of all kinds of drieds preserved, and tinned fish imported into New South Wales for each year from 1877 to 1887 inclusive:—

Year.	Quantity.	Value.		Year.	Quantity.	Value.	
	lb.	£	$		lb.	£	$
1877	4,207,394	161,970	788,227	1883	6,083,168	181,660	884,048
1878	4,063,890	133,334	649,870	1884	6,253,642	184,442	897,587
1879	3,427,626	92,992	452,546	1885	4,692,580	117,909	573,804
1880	2,145,503	71,172	346,358	1886	4,413,441	102,991	501,206
1881	4,243,765	143,974	700,649	1887	3,836,905	97,858	476,129
1882	4,921,696	157,159	764,813				

The following table shows the quantity and value of fish, principally salmon, imported from the United States into New South Wales for each year from 1879 to 1887 inclusive:—

IMPORTS from United States.

Year.	Quantity.	Value.		Year.	Quantity.	Value.	
	lb.	£	$		lb.	£	$
1879	1,029,291	20,602	100,260	1884	3,338,225	80,499	391,748
1880	1,200,033	32,348	157,422	1885	2,340,979	49,596	241,359
1881	2,381,690	64,711	314,916	1886	2,083,593	40,488	196,034
1882	2,315,715	63,555	309,290	1887	1,544,285	34,230	166,580
1883	2,524,115	70,306	342,144				

The following table shows the quantity and value of fish imported into New South Wales during the years 1886 and 1887, together with the countries whence imported:—

Country.	Quantity.	Value.	
		£	s
1886.	lb.		
Great Britain	1,959,484	50,786	247,150
Victoria	167,199	4,697	22,858
South Australia	70,173	2,637	12,833
Queensland	10,411	240	1,168
Tasmania	54	5	24
New Zealand	31,245	632	3,076
Hong Kong	71,709	2,787	13,563
China	7,765	228	1,110
United States	2,083,593	40,488	197,035
New Caledonia	108	2	10
France	9,309	358	1,742
Germany	317	38	185
Norway	439	29	141
India	1,635	64	311
1887.			
Great Britain	1,890,705	50,931	247,856
Victoria	152,827	4,493	21,865
South Australia	105,248	3,571	17,378
Queensland	9,261	228	1,110
Tasmania	1,506	41	200
New Zealand	13,953	341	1,659
India	96	6	29
Hong Kong	84,351	2,998	14,590
China	627	37	180
United States	1,544,285	34,230	166,580
New Caledonia	888	17	83
France	5,008	251	1,221
Germany	24,776	648	3,153
Norway	406	54	263
Italy	250	4	19
W. Australia	1,818	8	40

The total export of fish from New South Wales during the year 1887 was 1,212,519 lb., valued at £31,603 ($153,796), but of this amount only 25,286 lb., valued at £330 ($1,606) consisted of the produce of the Colony. The remainder consisted of foreign produce, principally American salmon sent here for transhipment.

The subjoined table shows the quantity and value of the fish produce of the Colony exported for each year from 1877 to 1887 inclusive.

Year.	Quantity.	Value.		Year.	Quantity.	Value.	
	lb.	£	s		lb.	£	s
1877	40,691	567	2,759	1883	46,854	567	2,759
1878	20,249	383	1,864	1884	30,307	369	1,796
1879	47,222	513	2,497	1885	8,229	107	521
1880	39,644	884	4,302	1886	8,242	119	579
1881	35,929	1,381	6,721	1887	25,286	330	1,606
1882	9,414	112	545				

It will be seen from the preceding table that the export of fish has declined since 1877. This produce was sent to the neighbouring colonies, Victoria receiving the largest share.

The subjoined table shows the quantity and value of fish, the produce of New South Wales, exported during the years 1885, 1886, and 1887, and the colonies to which exported:—

Country.	Quantity.	Value.	
1885.	lb.	£	s
Victoria	568	7	34
New Zealand	5,357	67	326
Queensland	1,296	19	92
Fiji Islands	1,008	14	68
1886.			
Victoria	5,003	68	330
New Zealand	2,348	34	165
Queensland	891	17	83
1887.			
Victoria	11,536	186	905
New Zealand	3,438	56	273
Queensland	524	9	44
South Australia	1,680	15	73
Tasmania	6,372	50	243
Hongkong	1,736	14	68

The export of fish, other than the produce of the Colony, has also declined since 1877, but this is due chiefly to the fact that no inconsiderable portion is now sent direct to Victoria and other colonies, instead of to New South Wales, for transhipment, as formerly.

The following table shows the quantity and value of the export of fish, not the produce of New South Wales, principally American salmon, from 1877 to 1887 inclusive :—

Year.	Quantity.	Value.		Year.	Quantity.	Value.	
	lb.	£	s		lb.	£	s
1877	933,937	34,998	170,318	1883	1,196,713	35,984	157,305
1878	582,905	19,926	96,970	1884	1,333,732	36,635	178,284
1879	1,197,674	32,762	159,436	1885	1,338,493	32,324	157,305
1880	858,072	25,799	125,551	1886	1,126,831	28,576	139,065
1881	1,054,494	33,363	162,234	1887	1,187,233	31,273	152,190
1882	849,622	25,935	126,213				

PEARL-SHELL.

The pearl-shell fisheries of Torres Straits in the colony of Queensland, are situated 1,500 miles from Brisbane and more than 2,000 miles from Sydney.

Torres Straits are about 80 miles in width and separate Queensland from the island of New Guinea. They lie between the parallels 9° 20′ and 10° 40′ south latitude. The navigation of the Straits, although said to be safe and practicable, is in fact difficult, on account of the innumerable islands, reefs, and shoals scattered through them. The Prince of Wales Channel, which has recently been surveyed, is the route usually adopted by steamers. The chief places at which the fisheries are conducted are Wai Weer, Albany Island, Jervis Island, Endeavour Strait, Friday Island, Prince of Wales Island, Possession Island, and Thursday Island, the last named being the most important, as it is the headquarters of the fisheries. The name of the town is Port Kennedy. It has about 350 inhabitants, a bank, two hotels, a post-office, court-house, and gaol. The customs revenue for the district amounts to about £7,000 ($34,065) per annum. The mail steamers stop at Thursday Island for the purpose of transhipping cargo, and the London Missionary Society use the port as a way station for supplies.

The inhabitants of the islands are almost wholly dependent upon the provisions they secure from abroad, as very few things can be grown there. The grass is said to be poisonous to cattle, and little success has attended the efforts to cultivate fruit and vegetables.

The harbour of Port Kennedy is formed by four islands, Thursday, Hammond, Goode and Friday Islands. It is almost completely landlocked, and although apparently safe, is subject to rapid tidal currents and fluctuating eddies. Captain Withers, of the steamship "Quetta," of the British India Company's service, recently complained that he was obliged to keep up steam all the time his ship was in port. On a previous occasion he said that during a storm, while his vessel was moored to the Company's hulk, he was compelled to cut his four cables and get under way and steer through dangerous reefs and shoals into open water in order to save his ship. It is thought that a better harbour for the company's steamers can be found at Berlie Bay, 4 miles westward on the eastern coast of Goode Island, where a signal station has been established.

The vessels at present engaged in the pearl fisheries at Torres Straits, with the exception of the American schooner "Eudora," and one or two other vessels, belong to the port of Sydney, where they are fitted out with supplies and equipped for the voyage. Although the industry properly belongs to Queensland, it is almost wholly supported by Sydney capital. The vessels, however, pay a license to the Queensland government, for the privilege of engaging in the fisheries, and also a tax upon every portion of Crown land used by them in connection with the fisheries. The charge for a suitable piece of land is fixed at £5 ($24·33) per annum, but it is provided that in no case shall the whole of any one island be leased to one person or firm. The cost of the license to fish depends on the size of the vessel. Small boats pay £1 ($4·86). A boat is described as any vessel not exceeding 2 tons in burden which is usually hoisted to a ship's davit or carried on board of a ship or attached to a ship. A ship is every description of vessel used in navigation or in the fisheries, not being a boat. The charge for ships of 10 tons or under is £3 ($14·59) and for every ship above 10 tons burden 10s. ($2·43) for every ton or part of a ton up to 30 tons, and for every ship above 30 tons the sum of £20 ($97·33). The license to engage in the pearl fisheries may be granted by any principal officer of customs in Queensland. A failure to take out a license, or to have it renewed at the time of expiration, will make the master of the vessel liable to a penalty of three times the cost of the license. The number of vessels licensed during the year 1887 was 187 against 195 for the year previous, and 33 licenses were granted to occupy fishing stations. The number of men employed in the vessels at the end of 1886 was 1,202; new boats were added to the fleet during the year, but the amount of pearl-shell obtained was not as great as in 1885, owing principally to the bad weather and the increased depth of water in which the divers were obliged to work. The fleet received some important additions in 1886 and there was also, during that year, a considerable increase in the quantity and value of shell exported.

Some of the larger vessels average about 18 tons burden, but the greater part of the fleet is composed of small boats, varying from 3 to 8 tons. About 80 vessels are supplied with the diving dress, or apparatus, and the remainder consists of swimming boats and tenders. All the vessels are strong and well built, and usually have straight bows and elliptical sterns. They draw from 3 to 6 feet of water, and are rigged with two standing lug-sails and jib. The cost of each vessel at Sydney, with diving apparatus, is from £300 ($1,460) to £500 ($2,433). The diving dress or apparatus used is made by Handcock, of London, and the helmets and pumps are of the manufacture of Siebe & Gorman. All these articles are much heavier and more expensive than those made in the United States. The dress is composed of solid sheet rubber, covered on both sides with canvas.

The helmet is made of tinned copper, and is fitted with three glasses, one in front and one on each side, so as to give the diver as good a view as possible. The glasses are protected by small metal bars. The helmet has a double collar, the inner one coming up around the neck, and the other hermetically fastened to the dress. The breastplate is made of tinned copper and has a valve by which the driver can regulate at will the pressure of atmosphere. The air is supplied by a small hose which the diver, before going into the water, coils around his arm. A signal line is tied to his waist, and by it he is enabled to communicate with the men above. The cost of the complete dress is about £140 ($681).

A good diver can earn from £12 ($58) to £30 ($146) per month. He usually signs shipping articles for a period not exceeding three years, at a fixed sum per month, and an interest in the catch or lay. The divers and crew are composed of South Sea Islanders and Malays and a few Chinese and Lascars. The diver is the captain of the boat, and the men have to obey his orders. The duties of the tender consist in waiting on the diver, helping him to dress, and looking after him while in the water. The pay of the tender is £2 ($9·73) per month with a small interest in the catch ; generally one-sixtieth to one-eightieth part of the value of the shell. The vessels usually have one diver, one tender, and four other hands. The tenders are shipped on regular ships' articles and are paid off like any merchant seamen.

The method pursued in pearl-fishing is for a number of vessels to start out together and fish on the same ground. When the shelling ground is reached, if the tide is slack, the diver, clothed in his diving dress, will go overboard. His boots, heavily weighted down with lead, hasten his descent. He carries with him a bag to hold the shell, and as soon as it is filled it is lifted up, emptied out, and sent down to him again, he being able to remain under water several hours at a time. Some divers remain down from 9 o'clock in the morning until 5 o'clock in the afternoon. The shell lies open on the ground and great care is required in handling it, for if it is touched in the wrong way it will close up on the hand like a vice. The apparatus boats, except in very rough weather, are enabled to fish all the year round. They are, of course, more successful during calms or light winds, which sometimes occur, even in the most inclement seasons. The monsoons which blow in the Straits, last from May to the end of September, and are often so severe that the boats are compelled to lay up for a week or ten days at a time. The average catch for each boat is from 1 to 1½ tons of shell per month.

Unlike the fisheries at Ceylon and in the Persian Gulf, there is little difficulty in removing the shell, for it either lies loose on the ground or is only partially buried in the mud or sand.

The fisheries off the coast of West Australia, and especially at Sharks Bay, produce the true pearl oyster, the *Avicula margaritifera*. For a long time this shell was supposed to be valueless, on account of its thin and fragile structure, but now there is a great demand for it, both in Europe and America. It is especially prized by French and German artists for fine inlaid cabinet work. During the year 1886, 284 tons of pearl-shell were exported from West Australia, valued at £41,000 ($199,526), and the value of the pearls exported during the same period was £17,500 ($85,163). Several of these pearls were of extraordinary size and beauty, one weighing 234 grains.

The shell obtained on the North-west Coast is mostly shipped by P. and O. steamers from Albany, King George's Sound. The vessels of the Adelaide Steamship Company call at the fishing ground and receive the shell from the schooners, delivering it at Albany. A portion is also shipped from Port Darwin for London, by way of Singapore.

Pearl oysters are gregarious in their habits, and whenever one is met with it is almost certain that numbers of others will be found in the immediate neighbourhood.

Pearling or fishing for pearls and pearl shells, is now one of the chief industries of Western Australia, and the principal fishing ground is on the north-west coast of Australia.

In 1868 Captain Hastings, of Sydney, fitted out a brigantine, the crew being South Sea Islanders, and sailed for the north-west coast on a prospecting voyage. He found shell, and returned to Sydney with 25 tons as the result of that trip. The mode of fishing was primitive. The shell was gathered by the crew at low tide, when either left dry or in very shallow water. No diving was attempted. The following year Captain Hastings again visited the north-west coast, and found an extensive patch of shell in Exmouth Gulf. After collecting 20 tons the crew contracted small pox from the aboriginals—to whom it had been transmitted by the Malays who visited the coast for pearl-shell,—and Captain Hastings had to return to Sydney, losing nine men by that disease. After Captain Hastings left, 200 tons of shell were obtained from the patch he had discovered.

From that time till about two years ago, pearling was carried on by West Australians with success—the mode of fishing being by swimming divers—the men employed being natives of the locality. As there was a danger of overworking the natives, an act of the West Australian Parliament was passed regulating the labor traffic. No employer is allowed to employ aboriginals in diving operations, under heavy penalties, between the 15th April and the 15th October, it being considered that the temperature of the water during that time is too low. No employer can use natives for diving in water over seven fathoms. Diving for shells by swimmers is from dingies, accompanied by a cutter or schooner, which anchors on the banks, and stores the shell as well as provides shelter for the divers.

Diving apparatus was hardly known on that coast until 1885, when the schooner "Pearl" and 2 luggers, owned by Messrs. Findlay & Baynes, of Sydney, with a complete outfit of diving apparatus, pumps, &c., reached King's Sound and struck a large patch of shell. The captain and mate were murdered by the natives, consequently only 21 tons of shell were obtained.

The news of rich finds of shell at King's Sound reached Torres Straits, and the following season—March and April, 1886—was opened in that locality by a fleet from Torres Straits of about a dozen schooners and 100 luggers, all fully equipped with diving gear, and they soon worked out the shell patch there. Diving was carried on with some difficulty owing to the rapid currents—the rise and fall of the tide being 36 feet.

On leaving King's Sound the fleet proceeded to the Lacepedes, where shell in great abundance was found at a moderate depth. This shell was, however, old and wormy, unlike the King's Sound shell, which was almost free from faults. The fleet moved down the coast, making fresh finds of shell wherever they went, and in November, as the hurricane season was approaching, many of the schooners and luggers took shelter in Port Headland, about 80 miles east of Cossack.

A royalty of £4 ($19.46) per ton is charged upon all shell found in Western Australian waters, and customs duties are charged upon all stores used on the schooners; these were formerly exempt. The price of shell has fallen fully £30 ($146) per ton, owing to over-production. West Australian shell in 1887 only netted in London £100 ($486) per ton, at which price very little profit is left for the owners.

The mode of fishing on the north-west coast is somewhat different from that at Torres Straits. Instead of having land stations, the schooners act as floating stations, and follow the luggers from patch to patch. The schooners carry all supplies necessary for working the industry. One object aimed at by this change is that the owners have a better chance of obtaining the pearls. At Torres Straits the shells are opened on board the luggers and many are secreted by the divers and crew. On the north-west coast all shell must be placed by the divers on board the schooners unopened, under a penalty, and the shells are then opened in presence of the master and mate.

Very good pearls have been obtained, and it is found that the better the shell the fewer the pearls. The bulk of the pearls are of little value, as they are badly shaped and otherwise faulty. In 1885, in one shell a collection of pearls was found at Nickol Bay, joined together in the form of a cross. This cross was first sold for £80 ($389); it was resold for £250 ($1,216), and the purchaser sent it to the Indian and Colonial Exhibition, London, where it was much admired. In almost every shell there is a small crab about the size of a marble, which lives on the best of terms with the oyster.

One hundred (100) shells is a good day's work for a diver. When the Lacepedes shell was first found, the divers got as much as 250 shells a day, and on a patch further down the coast, one diver got 700 shells one day. The average weight of shells is 2 lb. In Exmouth Gulf the shells obtained are only half that size, while at the Montebello Islands they weigh as high as 15 lb."

The hurricane season on the north-west coast lasts from December to March, and the locality subject to the visitation extends from North-west Cape to Roebuck Bay. In 1887 the pearling fleet, which had taken shelter in Port Headland, left that harbour about the end of March and proceeded to the fishing ground, off the Ninety-mile Beach, about 100 miles N.E. of Cossack. While fishing in fancied security on an open coast, about the end of April, a hurricane from the east suddenly, and without warning, struck the fleet. The news of the disaster first reached Sydney by wire from Cossack, and, as is usual in such cases, was greatly exaggerated, the report stating that nearly the whole fleet and 500 lives had been lost. For about a month no reliable information could be obtained as to the loss of life and property, as many of the schooners and luggers had been driven out to sea. At last it was ascertained that one schooner and over twenty luggers had gone down with all hands, the loss of life being fifteen white and over 100 coloured hands. Of the surviving vessels all were more or less damaged. Had the wind come from the north the whole fleet would have been destroyed.

The boats that have no diving dress or apparatus are called swimming boats. They are dingies. These boats fish in the same way as the apparatus boats. As soon as they reach the lee side of the fishing ground, the men dive in about 4 or 5 fathoms of water, and when they get a shell they pitch it into the boat. The wages paid them is from 10s. ($2·43) to 12s. 6d. ($3·04) per month. They are all expert swimmers, and it is said that some of them can remain under water two minutes at a time, but the interval of time is perhaps exaggerated.

The occupation of the diver is a very unhealthy one, and produces deafness and diseases of the chest and lungs. Blood not infrequently flows from his mouth, ears, and nostrils after the usual dip of forty or fifty seconds, which is repeated fifty or sixty times a day. The men also run the risk of being attacked by sharks, although death from this cause is not apt to occur, as the noise of the divers is almost certain to drive the sharks away. The authorities of Queensland have often been unjustly censured for allowing the natives to follow the occupation of diving. The truth is the actual number of deaths from such causes is much smaller than is generally supposed. Mr. Henry M. Chester, the resident magistrate, says, in a report on the fisheries, that the natives are never overworked, and that they are always well fed and kindly treated. He further says that payment is usually made them in blankets, clothing, knives, hatchets, and beads, and that whenever they are dissatisfied with what they receive they seek other employment. The competition for their services is of such a character as to invariably secure for them fair treatment. The available adult population of the islands are employed as swimming divers, under "The Masters' and Servants' Act," and while their pay is small, it is made in the presence of the local authorities, and all the old men, women, and children receive food in seasons of scarcity.

Mr. Chester admits, however, that the occupation of a diver is dangerous, and not at all conducive to longevity, but adds that the loss of life amongst the natives is more than counterbalanced by the abundant supply of wholesome food given them, and by the decrease in savage practices to which they were formerly addicted.

All accounts received from the fisheries bear very strong evidence in support of Mr. Chester's statement. Lieutenant de Hoghton, who visited the fisheries while in command of Her Majesty's ship Beagle, states in one of his reports that the stations are uniformly well managed, and that the men are quite capable of taking care of themselves. He says:—"In point of fact the divers have almost entirely their own way; and will not bear any superintendence from the whites whilst fishing, so that the practical part of getting the shell, *i. e.*, the management of the boats, the locality of the fishing, the time of fishing, besides the actual gathering of the shell, is entirely left to the divers, the managers of the different stations looking out for the fortnightly provisioning of the boats, the collecting, cleaning, packing the shell, repairing the boats, pumps, dresses, and general management of the stations."

Lieutenant de Hoghton commends very highly the local authorities for providing for the families of those engaged in the fisheries, and says that the fact of a man being employed is a recognized claim for his wife and children to receive rations from the station, little or no work being required in return.

All the pearl-shell stations in Torres Straits bear a very close resemblance to one another, and consist of a residence for the manager, and one of less pretension for the men, a warehouse for storing provisions, and several sheds for drying the shell. Before the shell is brought to the station the men open the oysters, take out the pearls if any, and throw the fish overboard. The shell is then roughly cleaned

T

and stowed under the hatches. At the end of the voyage it is taken to the station, where it is counted and thoroughly cleaned. It is then assorted and dried, it is packed in cases, each weighing from 270 to 300 pounds, and is ready for shipment. It is important that the shell should be kept under cover, as exposure to the rays of the sun changes its colour and lustre.

No systematic effort has yet been made to collect pearls at the Torres Straits. Some very fine specimens of pearl, about the size of a hazel nut, and of remarkable beauty and clearness, have found their way to the Sydney market from Torres Straits. Other specimens of a much larger size have been found there, but they were imperfect in shape and colour.

There has always been a mystery connected with pearls, and especially as to the manner of their formation, and even at the present time very few know what pearls really are. Scientists tell us they are hard, white, smooth, shining substances found in a testaceous fish of the oyster kind. Poets refer to them as "the globe of light," "the moon of waters," "the hoar frost of heaven." The ancient Greeks and Romans esteemed pearls more highly than any other jewels, and with very good reason, for, unlike other gems, they require no aid from art to bring out their beauty and lustre. Frequent reference is made to them in the Bible, and they are associated with many superstitions. The Chinese believe that they possess extraordinary medicinal properties, and the Egyptians dissolve and drink them as a love potion. Cleopatra is said to have only followed the custom of her race when she drank the famous pearl draught to the health of Mark Antony. This custom, silly as it is, does not appear to be wholly confined to the Egyptians, for there is strong reason to believe that the story of Sir Thomas Gresham having drunk a dissolved pearl that cost £15,000 ($72,998) is not without some foundation in fact.

The Persians are said to be the best judges of pearls and pay the highest prices for them. The Hindoos are firm in the belief that pearl oysters descend from the clouds, and after a long immersion in the ocean rise to the surface and receive in their gaping mouths drops of rain water, which are congealed into pearls. This pleasing theory is shared by many Oriental races, but, it is almost needless to add, has been long since exploded by science.

The substance of which pearl is composed is simply the carbonate of lime interstratified with animal membrane. Some authorities contend that it is the result of a diseased secretion, but that theory admits of some doubt. Linnæus was the first to establish the fact that pearls can be produced by introducing small particles of sand or other foreign substance into the oyster, and he was knighted for the discovery, but it is now known that the Chinese practised the art for many centuries, only they used small shot and particles of shell instead of sand. Sometimes they cut or stamp out of iron images of Buddha and insert them into the oyster, and when sufficiently coated proclaim that they have been produced by supernatural means. Pearls formed by the introduction of foreign matter into the oyster are necessarily hollow and crude in shape, and have little more commercial value than the ordinary artificial pearls made out of glass beads and lined with wax and quicksilver or some kind of pearl-coloured varnish. It is more than probable that the introduction of foreign matter into the oyster injures the character of the secretion. The oyster reproduces itself by means of spat, which is sometimes found floating on the water. It moves about until it settles on a rock or some solid substance, and develops into an oyster. It attains the size of a shilling in six or seven months. The necessities of its existence appear to be clean-growing coral, free from sand grit, and a considerable influx and outflow of the sea at the rise and fall of the tide. Oysters are not in all cases confined to lagoons, but exist in vast quantities under the breakers that beat upon the outer reefs, and possibly at greater depths in the sea beyond them. They are said by some instinct of their nature to make their way into calm water. The oysters which are spawned in the lagoons are formed in congeries attached to the parent shells or clustered in numbers, fastened one to another, attached to the rocks. It has been generally believed that the pearl oyster is a fixture, and the appearance of the cord or byssus by which it is fastened to solid substances would show some reason for the opinion. This cord has the appearance of a tassel, and is composed of an infinite number of slender filaments. It often requires very great force to dislodge it, and has all the appearance of being permanent, but, nevertheless, it does move, and from one coral shelf to another when at no great distance.

The best pearls are found when the oyster is about four years old, the age being determined by the weight and appearance of the shell. The shell, like the pearl, is formed by the secretion of the animal and becomes hardened by the deposits of lime. The iridescent hues on the inside of the shell are occasioned by the edges of the thin, wavy concentric layers overlapping one another and reflecting the light. The minute furrows, containing translucent carbonate of lime, shed a series of more or less brilliant colours, according to the angle at which the light falls upon them. The external surface of the shell is of a dark brownish color, but does not penetrate to any great depth and is easily removed. Occasionally some of the finest pearls are found loose in the shell. As many as one hundred pearls have been found in one oyster, but they are generally of little or no value. The pearls of a young oyster are of a yellow color, and those of the older ones have a pinkish hue; sometimes they are found of all shades, such as white, brown, steel, and silver color, and even a deep black.

The largest pearl ever found was presented to Phillip II, of Spain. It was about the size of a pigeon egg, and cost 80,000 ducats. The value of pearls in most cases is a fictitious one. The famous pearl necklace of the Empress Eugenie, which originally cost £20,000 ($97,330), was sold not long since for the sum of £6,000 ($29,199).

Although pearl-shell has been known to exist for many years in the Torres Straits, it was not until recently that any systematic effort was made to collect it. In 1874 only 2 lb. of shell were entered for export at Thursday Island. In 1875 5 tons and 12 cwt. were exported. In 1878 the quantity increased to 476 tons. In 1882 the quantity was 840 tons. In 1883 the quantity declined to 621 tons; but rose again in 1884 to 701 tons.

The following table shows the quantity and value of pearl-shell exported from the Colony of Queensland for each year from 1874 to 1886 inclusive:—

Year.	Quantity.			Value.	
	Tons	cwt.	lb.	£	s
1874	0	0	2	12	58
1875	5	12	0	799	3,888
1876	144	6	0	15,655	76,234
1877	338	8	0	48,723	237,110
1878	476	10	0	54,149	263,516
1879	439	0	0	57,509	279,868
1880	425	0	0	55,475	269,969
1881	397	14	0	48,963	238,460
1882	840	9	0	105,869	515,211
1883	621	11	0	80,714	392,795
1884	701	18	0	94,021	457,553
1885	659	9	0	87,110	423,921
1886	585	0	0	67,991	330,848

The price of pearl-shell at the Straits is regulated by the European and American markets. At one time it was controlled by a London syndicate, but now competition for the trade is so general that no serious attempt is made to monopolize it. The prices, according to the invoices entered at the customs of Queensland, during the last few years have varied from £125 ($608) to £150 ($730) per ton. There is no export duty charged on pearl-shell either at Sydney or Queensland. West Australia is the only one of the colonies where such a duty is charged. The price of shell in Europe is at present so low that only a small margin of profit is left after paying the cost of the freight and insurance. The shipments to the United States this year are larger than usual, although the bulk of the supply is sent by way of London instead of direct to America.

A small shipment of Thursday Island pearl-shell was sold at public auction in New York in January, 1885, for £200 ($973) per ton. Another lot, described as "small, of good substance and thin medium," brought £144 ($700) per ton. A third lot, described as "medium, bold, fair substance, and good colour," brought £280 ($1,363) per ton. A fourth lot, described as "wormy and blistered," brought £105 ($511) per ton.

The pearl-shell shipped from Australia to the United States and Europe is used principally for the manufacture of knife-handles, shirt-buttons, studs. Considerable quantities of the shell are also used in *papier maché* and other ornamental work. The pearl buttons and shirt studs now made in the United States are said to be the best and cheapest in the world, a fact due in a great measure to the care used in selecting the material and to the improved method of cutting it.

The young or chicken shell is the best and commands the highest price. When the pearl is five or six years old it becomes blistered and wormy, the oyster ceasing to live after a period of seven years. The divers in fishing make no effort to select any particular kind of shell, but take everyone that they can get, even the dead shell, which is the least value of any on account of its blemishes, rottenness, lack of lustre. Pure white silver-edged shell is the most desired; some varieties of pink and golden edged are also highly prized as ornaments, but of course are not so valuable as the white. The pearl oyster of commerce is in fact not an oyster at all, but a mussel known to science as the *Meleagrina margaritifera*. Its shell is nearly circular in shape, and will average 8 or 10 inches in diameter. Its average weight is about 1½ lb., exclusive of the fish, although some specimens in the Torres Straits weigh as much as even 15 pounds. It is distinguished from the oyster by squareness and length of hinge.

The pearl oyster beds are very extensive in the waters of Australia and New Guinea. In the latter the beds extend along the coast to the Tawai Tawai Islands, and thence to Sulu and Baselan. The pearls of the Sulu oysters are said to be superior to those of Ceylon or of the Persian Gulf. The value of the shell, however, is considerably lessened by a peculiar yellowish tinge on the back and border, by which it can always be distinguished.

The entire pearl-shell product collected at Thursday Island was formerly shipped to Europe and America by way of Sydney, but now the greater part of it goes direct from Torres Straits to London in the steamers of the British India Company's service.

The cost of freight to Europe by the direct route is about the same as from Sydney to London, viz., £3 10s. ($17·03) per ton. A considerable quantity, however, of shell still finds its way to Sydney, and it is improbable that Sydney will altogether cease to be a market for this important article of commerce.

The value of the export of pearl-shell from Sydney during 1887 was £13,547 ($65,926) against £31,614 ($153,850) for the year previous.

The cost of freight on pearl-shell to San Francisco by the Pacific Mail Steamship Company is £3 ($14·60) per ton, and to New York or Boston by sailing vessel £1 12s. 10d. ($8) per ton; but it is seldom that American vessels engaged in trading with this port return direct to the United States, on account of their inability to obtain cargo, except coal, and the result is they usually go to China, Japan, or the Phillipine Islands, and thence to New York. Occasionally, during certain wool seasons, return cargo may be obtained, but seldom otherwise. Therefore, the bulk of Australasian products intended for the American market is shipped by way of London, and the total charges on same is from £3 15s. ($18·25) to £4 ($19·47) per ton.

The pearl-shell shipped from Thursday Island to Sydney is generally sent, by way of Cooktown, in the vessels of the China Navigation Company, and the Eastern and Australia Steamship Company, at a cost of about £1 10s. ($7·29) per ton, exclusive of insurance. Although navigation by that route is comparatively safe, accidents seldom occurring, nevertheless, insurance companies refuse to grant insurance on such freight except at high rates.

www.ingramcontent.com/pod-product-compliance
Lightning Source LLC
Chambersburg PA
CBHW030818230426
43667CB00008B/1267